STUDIES IN EARLY MODERN CULTURAL, POLITICAL AND SOCIAL HISTORY

Volume 15

COMMON LAW AND ENLIGHTENMENT IN ENGLAND, 1689–1750

AF706655

Studies in Early Modern Cultural, Political and Social History

ISSN: 1476–9107

Series editors

Tim Harris – Brown University
Stephen Taylor – Durham University
Andy Wood – Durham University

Previously published titles in the series
are listed at the back of this volume

COMMON LAW AND ENLIGHTENMENT IN ENGLAND, 1689–1750

Julia Rudolph

THE BOYDELL PRESS

© Julia Rudolph 2013

All Rights Reserved. Except as permitted under current legislation no part of this work may be photocopied, stored in a retrieval system, published, performed in public, adapted, broadcast, transmitted, recorded or reproduced in any form or by any means, without the prior permission of the copyright owner

The right of Julia Rudolph to be identified as the author of this work has been asserted in accordance with sections 77 and 78 of the Copyright, Designs and Patents Act 1988

First published 2013
The Boydell Press, Woodbridge

ISBN 978-1-84383-804-3

The Boydell Press is an imprint of Boydell & Brewer Ltd
PO Box 9, Woodbridge, Suffolk IP12 3DF, UK
and of Boydell & Brewer Inc.
668 Mt Hope Avenue, Rochester, NY 14620-2731, USA
website: www.boydellandbrewer.com

A catalogue record for this book is available from the British Library

The publisher has no responsibility for the continued existence or accuracy of URLs for external or third-party internet websites referred to in this book, and does not guarantee that any content on such websites is, or will remain, accurate or appropriate.

Papers used by Boydell & Brewer Ltd are natural, recyclable products made from wood grown in sustainable forests

MIX
Paper from responsible sources
FSC® C013604

Printed and bound in Great Britain by
CPI Group (UK) Ltd, Croydon, CR0 4YY

For Matthew

Contents

Contents

Acknowledgements

I have learned a great deal in the course of researching and writing this book, and I have benefited from the assistance of many individuals, groups and institutions. Among the most crucial support was that provided by the National Endowment for the Humanities and the Folger Shakespeare Library: the year I spent as an NEH fellow at the Folger Library was vital to the development and expansion of this project. I wish to thank the staff of the Folger Library and of the Folger Institute, especially Carol Brobeck, Kathleen Lynch, Betsy Walsh, Owen Williams, Heather Wolfe and Georgianna Ziegler for all their help. I also want to acknowledge the influence of other fellows, including Katherine Eggert, Hannibal Hamlin, Wolfram Schmidgen and Linda Peck, whose questions and comments improved this work. Linda continues to be an especially valued colleague, and I am grateful for her advice and friendship.

The Folger Library was also the place where, as a graduate student years ago, I first met John Pocock. The importance of his scholarship to my own work will be evident in the pages that follow, just as it was in my first book. What may be less obvious is his professional and personal influence. John Pocock is, of course, a formidable intellect and an imposing figure, but he is also an individual of real humanity and generosity. His interest and encouragement have meant a great deal to me.

Several other scholars have also offered invaluable advice. Kathy Brown, D'Maris Coffman, Janelle Greenberg, David Ibbetson, Alan Kors, Dana Rabin, Peter Stallybrass and Margo Todd read and commented on various papers, portions and drafts of my work. Discussions with John Cairns, Ann Carlos, Tim Harris, Cynthia Herrup, Tim Hitchcock, John Marshall, Leslie Patrick, Richard Ross, Bob Shoemaker, Stephen Taylor and Richard Waller helped me to expand my research and sharpen my analysis. Stephen Taylor also kindly shared some manuscript materials relating to the trial of the Earl of Macclesfield with me. Catherine Styer and Phelim Dolan provided important research assistance, and I was helped enormously by staff at the various archives and libraries listed in the bibliography to this work; I wish particularly to thank archivists at the Free Library of Philadelphia, and the Harvard Law School Library. I have also benefited from the questions and comments of participants in seminars, workshops and conferences where I have presented my research, at Cambridge University, the Folger Institute, Johns Hopkins University, North Carolina State University, Temple University, University of Hertfordshire, University of North Carolina at Chapel Hill,

University of Pennsylvania, Vanderbilt University, Yale University, American Society for Eighteenth-Century Studies, American Society of Legal History, Delaware Valley British Studies Seminar, Mid-Atlantic Conference on British Studies, and the North American Conference on British Studies. I owe many thanks to Jonathan Ocko of North Carolina State University and David Levi of Duke University for their encouragement of my work at a crucial moment.

My friends and family have given me unwavering love and support, and I am glad to express my gratitude to all of them here. In addition, special thanks are due to Anne Stetson and Mark Dibble for providing me with a splendid home during research trips, and to Kathleen Kaslow for talking, and walking, things through. Extra-special thanks go to my sons, Jonathan and Spencer, who inspire me and challenge me.

Finally, this book is dedicated to my husband Matthew Adler, not only because he truly believes in equity, in every sense of the word, but also because he believes in me. That has made all the difference.

Abbreviations

BL	British Library
CUL	Cambridge University Library
DLL	Arthur W. Diamond Law Library, Columbia University
English Reports	*The English Reports*, Full Reprint (1220–1865), Hein Online, Buffalo, NY, 2002
FLP	Free Library of Philadelphia
FSL	Folger Shakespeare Library
HALS	Hertfordshire Archives and Local Studies
HLS	Harvard Law School
IT	Inner Temple
NA	National Archives
NLW	National Library of Wales
ODNB	Colin Matthew, Brian Harrison and Lawrence Goldman eds, *Oxford Dictionary of National Biography*, Online edn, Oxford 2004-
State Trials	W. Cobbett and T.B. Howell, *Cobbett's Complete Collection of State Trials, and Proceedings for High Treason and Other Crimes and Misdemeanors from the Earliest Period to the Present Time*, 34 vols, London, 1809–28

1

Against Decline

The history of eighteenth-century English common law jurisprudence – and common law culture more generally – has often been narrated as a story of decline and fall. The first half of the century, a period delineated between the Bill of Rights of 1689 and the labours of Blackstone in the 1760s, has particularly been characterised as a time when the common law stood apart from the progressive and enlightened impulses of the era; a time when common law struggled, and largely failed, to maintain its former intellectual and cultural significance. Since this is a narrative that adheres to the pattern of Polybius' cycles – wherein decay invariably succeeds a period of strength and perfection – it relies on the convention of a reversal of fortune, and depicts the century preceding 1689 as a peak in the development of key common law principles.[1] The seventeenth century, an age of Coke, Selden and Hale, is regarded as a triumphal period for the common law, when a language of ancient custom, and a theory of historicised legal authority, flourished and expanded in important ways.[2] By the eighteenth

[1] Polybius, *The Rise of the Roman Empire*, trans. Ian Scott-Kilvert, F.W. Walbank ed., see bk 6, sects. 9, 43–44, 51. For the general historiographical tradition of decline and fall, from ancient to enlightened histories, see J.G.A. Pocock, *Barbarism and Religion, Volume 3: The First Decline and Fall* (Cambridge, 2003), and Joseph M. Levine, *Humanism and History: Origins of Modern English Historiography* (Ithaca, 1987).

[2] J.G.A. Pocock, *The Ancient Constitution and the Feudal Law: A Study of English Historical Thought in the Seventeenth Century* (Cambridge, 1957; reissued with a retrospect 1987); Glenn Burgess, *The Politics of the Ancient Constitution: An Introduction to English Political Thought 1603–1642* (University Park, PA, 1992); Alan Cromartie, *The Constitutionalist Revolution: An Essay on the History of England, 1450–1642* (Cambridge, 2006); James S. Hart Jr., *The Rule of Law 1603–1660: Crowns, Courts and Judges* (New York, 2003), Allen D. Boyer ed., *Law, Liberty and Parliament: Selected Essays on the Writing of Sir Edward Coke* (Indianapolis, 2004); Michael Lobban, *A History of the Philosophy of Law in the Common Law World, 1600–1900*, vol 8. of Enrico Pattaro ed., *A Treatise of Legal Philosophy and General Jurisprudence* (Dordrecht, 2007); Gerald Postema, 'Classical Common Law Jurisprudence (Part I)', *Oxford University Commonwealth Law Journal*, 2, 2 (Winter 2002): 155–80, Postema, 'Classical Common Law Jurisprudence (Part II)', *Oxford University Commonwealth Law Journal*, 3, 1 (Summer 2003): 1–28. For some challenges to this story of the hegemony of common law in the seventeenth century see, for example, Jeffrey D. Goldsworthy, *The Sovereignty of Parliament: History and Philosophy* (Oxford, 1999); J.W. Tubbs, *The Common Law Mind: Medieval and Early Modern Conceptions* (Baltimore,

century, however, scholarly convention holds that English common law jurisprudence and common law culture went into a period of defensiveness, irrelevance and ultimate decline. Its practitioners were no longer at the centre of English cultural life; its arguments for custom and precedent were ultimately and fatally outstripped by new discourses and practices of rational contract, legislative change and commercial interest.

This book challenges these conventions and recovers the history of English common law thought and culture during the seminal period 1689–1750. Here is a history of common law in the early eighteenth century that sets aside the focus on decline and takes seriously the question of jurisprudence. This period was, in fact, an enormously important and interesting time for the development of common law jurisprudence, with its understanding of law's authority founded in ancient custom, in a system of pleading and precedent, and enshrined in judicial decisions. Eighteenth-century English lawyers and theorists did not simply overlook questions about the authority and validity of common law, and the answers they gave must be investigated if we are to analyse the enduring importance of precedent in the development of modern jurisprudence.[3] This work sets out to understand how eighteenth-century defenders of the common law thought about the justice of those rules, remedies and precedents. Equally important, it explores the ways in which legal ideas, practices and publications related to other eighteenth-century trends, like the flourishing print culture and new practices in the dissemination of knowledge, or the growing interest in science, experimentation and collection, or the expansion of commerce and colonisation. These are some of the issues that must be addressed if we are to rethink that unexamined assumption that a 'conservative' and 'complacent' English common law was the antithesis of eighteenth-century Enlightenment.

In this way the project also contributes to work by scholars like Knud Haakonssen, Sankar Muthu or John Pocock, which has continually sought to destabilise our conception of 'The Enlightenment'.[4] The accepted image

2000); J.P. Sommerville, 'The Ancient Constitution Reassessed: The Common Law, The Court and the Languages of Politics in Early Modern England', in R. Malcolm Smuts ed., *The Stuart Court and Europe: Essays in Politics and Political Culture* (Cambridge, 1996), 39–64.

3 It should be clear from the outset that my focus is on *English* common law jurisprudence; for discussion of the ways in which my work is situated in relation to scholarship on a colonial American ancient constitutionalism see below pp. 16–17.

4 Knud Haakonssen, 'The Idea of Early Modern Philosophy', in J.B. Schneewind ed., *Teaching New Histories of Philosophy* (Princeton, University Center for Human Values, 2004), 101; Haakonssen, 'The History of Eighteenth-Century Philosophy: History or Philosophy?', in Knud Haakonssen ed., *The Cambridge History of Eighteenth-Century Philosophy*, vol. 1 (Cambridge, 2006), 3–25; Haakonssen, ed., *Enlightenment and Religion: Rational Dissent in Eighteenth-Century Britain* (Cambridge, 1996); Sankar Muthu, *Enlightenment against Empire* (Princeton, 2003); J.G.A. Pocock, *Barbarism and Religion*, 5

of eighteenth-century common law as traditional, irrational, and particularist, relies upon a contrasting depiction of eighteenth-century Enlightenment thought as rationalist, empiricist, universal and, eventually, utilitarian. But this is a narrow definition of Enlightenment, one that is restricted essentially to a French incarnation and one that excludes other modes of Enlightenment – moderate, Protestant, critical, provincial – as these Enlightenments developed elsewhere in Europe. Modern scholarship on national and regional Enlightenments has provided a useful corrective to that narrow interpretation, famously championed by Peter Gay, of a singular, Gallocentric and secular Enlightenment.[5] Moreover, within contemporary debates about the significance of these national and regional Enlightenments investigation of the nature of a British Enlightenment has been particularly important, especially for our understanding of the roles of commerce, manners and religion in Enlightenment.

The matter of Scotland's centrality has been at issue here, first in the assessment of its sceptical and moderate Enlightenment as a period of intellectual fervour which produced influential moral-philosophical, sociological, and economic ideas.[6] Also relevant to the analysis of Scottish influence has been wider scholarly debate over the interpretation of Enlightenment as a social and cultural practice as well as a movement in the history of ideas. The concerns of the new British history and of the history of the book

vols (Cambridge, 1999–2011); Pocock, 'Historiography and Enlightenment: A View of their History', *Modern Intellectual History*, 5, 1 (2008): 83–96.

5 Peter Gay, *The Enlightenment: An Interpretation*, 2 vols (New York, 1966, 1970). As Richard Sher (among other scholars) notes, Gay's interpretation was largely directed against the argument of Carl Becker's *The Heavenly City of the Eighteenth-Century Philosophers* (New Haven, 1959). Richard B. Sher, *The Enlightenment and the Book: Scottish Authors and their Publishers in Eighteenth-Century Britain, Ireland and America* (Chicago, 2006), 12. The work that served as the harbinger of 'national Enlightenments' was Roy Porter and Mikulas Teich eds, *The Enlightenment in National Context* (Cambridge, 1981).

6 The literature on Scottish Enlightenment is vast. Some influential, and representative, articles, monographs and collections include: Nicholas Phillipson, 'Culture and Society in the Eighteenth-Century Province: The Case of Edinburgh and the Scottish Enlightenment', in Lawrence Stone ed., *The University in Society*, vol. 2 (London, 1975), 407–48; Duncan Forbes, *Hume's Philosophical Politics* (Cambridge, 1975); Jane Rendall, *The Origins of the Scottish Enlightenment* (New York, 1978); R.H. Campbell and A.S. Skinner eds, *The Origins and Nature of the Scottish Enlightenment* (Edinburgh, 1982); Istvan Hont and Michael Ignatieff eds, *Wealth and Virtue: The Shaping of Political Economy in the Scottish Enlightenment* (Cambridge, 1983); Richard B. Sher, *Church and University in the Scottish Enlightenment: The Moderate Literati of Edinburgh* (Edinburgh, 1985); Fania Oz-Salzberger, *Translating the Enlightenment: Scottish Civic Discourse in Eighteenth-Century Germany* (Oxford, 1995); Knud Haakonssen, *Natural Law and Moral Philosophy: From Grotius to the Scottish Enlightenment* (Cambridge, 1996); John Robertson, 'The Scottish Contribution to the Enlightenment', in Paul Wood ed., *The Scottish Enlightenment: Essays in Reinterpretation* (Rochester, 2000), 37–62; Robertson, *The Case for the Enlightenment: Scotland and Naples, 1680–1760* (Cambridge, 2005).

have further encouraged this interest in the sociocultural and sociopolitical dimensions of Scotland's Enlightenment.[7] Finally, the focus on Scottish Enlightenment and the matter of Britain has prompted some historians to question the direction of influence. Roy Porter, for example, forcefully argued that the origins of Enlightenment are to be found in the scientific and political revolutions of seventeenth-century England, which were only later developed by mid-eighteenth-century Scots. These English origins and Scottish contributions mean, Porter insisted, that such developments are better characterised as a *British* Enlightenment.[8]

This idea of a British Enlightenment not only called into question the narrative of Scottish exceptionalism but it has also helped to foster an argument for a distinctive English Enlightenment among the plurality of Enlightenments. And here sustained scholarly attention to the role of religion in English Enlightenment has been especially important because it has resulted in significant revision of the conventional understanding of anticlericalism and secularism as essential to Enlightenment.[9] A number of historians have

7 For the emphasis on a sociocultural interpretation of Enlightenment see, for example, Roger Chartier, *The Cultural Origins of the French Revolution*, trans. Lydia G. Cochrane (Durham, 1991), and Robert Darnton, 'In Search of the Enlightenment: Recent Attempts to Create a Social History of Ideas', *Journal of Modern History*, 43, 1 (March, 1971), 113–32. The concerns of the new British history, and of the history of the book, relevant to the focus on Scotland's Enlightenment found expression in works like John Robertson ed., *A Union for Empire: Political Thought and the Union of 1707* (Cambridge, 1995), Glenn Burgess ed., *The New British History: Founding a Modern State 1603–1715* (London, 1999), Colin Kidd, 'Gaelic Antiquity and National Identity in Enlightenment Ireland and Scotland', *The English Historical Review*, 109, 434 (November, 1994), 1197–1214, and Sher, *Enlightenment and the Book*.

8 Roy Porter, *The Creation of the Modern World: The Untold Story of the British Enlightenment* (New York, 2000); see also Gertrude Himmelfarb, *The Roads to Modernity: the British, French and American Enlightenments* (New York, 2004). And cf the debates over the role of Newtonianism in Enlightenment in Margaret C. Jacob, 'Newtonianism and the Origins of Enlightenment: A Reassessment', *Eighteenth-Century Studies*, 11, 1 (Autumn, 1977), 1–25; Larry R. Stewart, *The Rise of Public Science: Rhetoric, Technology and Natural Philosophy in Newtonian Britain, 1660–1750* (Cambridge, 1992); Jonathan Israel, *Radical Enlightenment: Philosophy and the Making of Modernity* (Oxford, 2001), ch. 27; Israel, *Enlightenment Contested: Philosophy, Modernity and the Emancipation of Man 1670–1752* (Oxford, 2006), ch. 8; and Brian Young, 'Newtonianism and the Enthusiasm of Enlightenment', *Studies in History and Philosophy of Science*, 35, 3 (September, 2004), 645–63.

9 It is helpful to recall that the subtitle of Gay's first volume in 1966 was *The Rise of Modern Paganism*. For surveys of this revisionist scholarship see the following review essays collected in the *American Historical Review*: Dror Wahrman, 'Introduction, God and the Enlightenment', Jonathan Sheehan, 'Enlightenment, Religion and the Enigma of Secularization: A Review Essay', Dale van Kley, 'Christianity as Casualty and Chrysalis of Modernity: The Problem of Dechristianization in the French Revolution', *American Historical Review*, 108, 4 (October, 2003), 1057–1104. See also B.W. Young, 'Religious History and the Eighteenth-Century Historian', *The Historical Journal*, 43, 3

demonstrated the importance of a clerical and Anglican Enlightenment, thus countering the more usual tendency to study Dissenting confessions, and freethinking criticisms of Christianity in eighteenth-century England.[10] This focus on an Anglican Enlightenment has provided new insight into what John Pocock long ago termed a 'conservative English Enlightenment' – an Enlightenment that aimed to conserve the constitutional principles, religious toleration and civil peace newly, and precariously, achieved in 1689. This was 'a broadly Whiggish Enlightenment' as Karen O'Brien notes, and it was also a broadly Protestant, polite and erudite Enlightenment which involved 'academics, churchmen and politically involved intellectuals such as Gibbon and Edmund Burke'.[11]

The study of religion and of an Anglican, clerical Enlightenment, is clearly pertinent, and especially exciting for the analysis of common law and Enlightenment. First, it has opened up that possibility of multiple Enlightenments, allowing for a range of interpretation within which a common law Enlightenment can be included. Like many other scholars who have heeded Pocock's suggestion that we 'think of a family of Enlightenments, displaying both family resemblances and family quarrels', I am persuaded that this

(September, 2000): 849–68, Robert Sullivan, 'Rethinking Christianity in Enlightened Europe', *Eighteenth-Century Studies*, 34, 2 (Winter 2001): 298–309, and Charly Coleman, 'Resacralizing the World: the Fate of Secularization in Enlightenment Historiography', *The Journal of Modern History*, 82, 2 (June, 2010): 368–95. A recent synthetic account can be found in David Sorkin, *The Religious Enlightenment: Protestants, Jews and Catholics from London to Vienna* (Princeton, 2008).

10 B.W. Young, *Religion and Enlightenment in Eighteenth-Century England: Theological Debate from Locke to Burke* (Oxford, 1998); Isabel Rivers, *Reason, Grace and Sentiment: A Study of the Language of Religion and Ethics in England, 1660–1780*, 2 vols (Cambridge, 1991, 2000). Young, *Religion and Enlightenment*, 3, n. 9, deliberately positions his work in response to the literature on freethinkers including, for example, J.A.I. Champion, *The Pillars of Priestcraft Shaken: The Church of England and its Enemies, 1660–1730* (Cambridge, 1992) and E.J. Hundert, *The Enlightenment's Fable: Bernard Mandeville and the Discovery of Society* (Cambridge, 1994).

11 Karen O'Brien, *Women and Enlightenment in Eighteenth-Century Britain* (Cambridge, 2009), 4. J.G.A. Pocock, 'Clergy and Commerce: The Conservative Enlightenment in England', in R. Ajello ed., *L'Eta dei Lumi: Studi Storici sul Settecento Europeo in Onore de Franco Venturi*, vol. 1 (Naples, 1985), 524–62; Pocock, 'Conservative Enlightenment and Democratic Revolutions: The American and French Cases in British Perspective', *Government and Opposition*, 24, 1 (January, 1989): 81–105; Pocock, *Barbarism and Religion, Volume 3*, 307, and compare Pocock, *Barbarism and Religion, Volume 1: The Enlightenments of Edward Gibbon, 1737–1764* (Cambridge, 1999), 5–9. One of the hallmarks of the work of scholars like O'Brien, Pocock, Haakonssen or Young, who explore the evidence for 'conservative Enlightenment', has been a willingness to trace a range of ideas and commitments within this Anglican, clerical thought and culture, allowing for an appreciation of more complex combinations of political affiliations, ideologies, theologies and philosophies than has been usual within the conventional narratives. See, for example, O'Brien, *Women and Enlightenment*, ch. 1, 'Anglican Whig Feminism in England, 1690–1760: Self-Love, Reason and Social Benevolence'.

recognition of diversity not only expands the programme for research but, more importantly, brings us closer to historical understanding.[12] Yet the pluralism within which a common law Enlightenment might be explored should not rely upon the notion of conflict between Enlightenments evoked by Pocock and pursued for example, and for very different ends, in the contested Enlightenments of Jonathan Israel. That kind of emphasis on contest or competition too often returns to a claim about winners and losers as part of the reconstruction of a singular, or in Israel's terms 'linear', definition of Enlightenment.[13] Rather more promising, and relevant for legal thought and culture, is a 'media-driven concept of the Enlightenment' in which, as Jonathan Sheehan explains, Enlightenment is defined as

> a new constellation of formal and technical practices and institutions....[that] might include philosophical argument, but would encompass such diverse elements as salons, reading circles, erudition, scholarship and scholarly techniques, translations, book reviews, academies, new communication tools including journals and newspapers, new or revised techniques of data organization and storage (dictionaries, encyclopedias, taxonomies), and so on.

These and other practices and institutions provide an indication, Sheehan concludes, of 'those places where the social, cultural, and intellectual horizons of religion' – and it should be added, law – 'and the Enlightenment fused'.[14]

Equally important, attention to the role of religion in Enlightenment has raised crucial doubts about the accepted narrative of secularisation and modernity and these doubts, in turn, have real implications for the analysis of common law. The 'powerful' and 'surprising' insight that has arisen out of the scholarship on Enlightenment and religion, Dror Wahrman avers, is the 'identification of religion at the heart of the project of modernity itself, a constitutive element of its very shaping'.[15] If Enlightenment is no longer easily equated with the attack on religion and church, then we must also

[12] Pocock, *Barbarism and Religion, Volume 1*, 9; Sheehan, 'Enlightenment, Religion, Secularization', 1068.

[13] Israel, *Enlightenment Contested*, 7, 11–12, 57. Compare also Ian Hunter, *Rival Enlightenments: Civil and Metaphysical Philosophy in Early Modern Germany* (Cambridge, 2001), and Darrin McMahon, *Enemies of the Enlightenment: The French Counter-Enlightenment and the Making of Modernity* (Oxford, 2002). Note that Jonathan Israel also laments the tendency towards pluralism, and calls for a return to a 'Europeanizing' focus against the chauvinism of Anglo-American historians and philosophers, Israel *Enlightenment Contested*, 59–60. Other scholars similarly advocate recognition of 'a larger pattern of unity' within a pan-European, progressive Enlightenment, despite multiple variations: see for example Sher, *Enlightenment and the Book*, Robertson, *The Case for the Enlightenment*.

[14] Sheehan, 'Enlightenment, Religion, Secularization', 1075–6.

[15] Wahrman, 'God and Enlightenment', 1058.

question the simplistic (and propagandistic) related claim that Enlightenment stood at the threshold of modernity because it posited 'freedom from the shackles of the past'.[16] Once it is possible to accept that the rejection of church and establishment, of tradition and inherited authorities, was not inevitable and everywhere at the heart of enlightened thought, then certainly we must recognise and investigate the ways in which common law jurisprudence – those evolving ideas about the authority of the past – also played a part in the emergence of an enlightened philosophy and culture.

This is simply to claim, of course, that English legal thought and legal culture should be understood, in the first instance, as part of what is termed a conservative or moderate Enlightenment. It is uncontroversial to say that English legal institutions, and the English legal theory of the ancient constitution, were marshalled as part of the defence of a Whiggish Enlightenment, but we must also recall that this meant a newly commercial, polite, clerical and erudite Enlightenment. Scholars continue to debate the nature of the Revolution that ushered in so many of these changes, and to debate the content of the project of modernity and enlightenment that ensued.[17] But they have failed to ask whether this modernity also entailed an appeal to custom, prescription and precedent. In what ways did these principles of common law jurisprudence contribute to Enlightenment? In what ways did these common law principles participate, with other strands of thought and practice, in what scholars have taught us to think of as a pluralised Enlightenment? It is perhaps more controversial, but even more important, to ask these questions because they invite a new kind of reflection on the role of common law jurisprudence as much as natural jurisprudence in the emergence of political ideologies and cultures – liberal, democratic, egalitarian, rational – usually designated as modern.[18] In the end, we must abandon the usual dichotomies between progressive and traditional, philosophical and practical, radical and conservative, and between Enlightenment and common law, in order to arrive at a better understanding of the development of such familiar, and revered, political and legal concepts and practices.

16 Sheehan, 'Enlightenment, Religion, Secularization', 1066.

17 Two important recent works that address such issues are Tim Harris, *Revolution: The Great Crisis of the British Monarchy 1685–1720* (London, 2006), and Steve Pincus, *1688: The First Modern Revolution* (New Haven, 2009).

18 See, for example, Israel, *Enlightenment Contested*, 60, as one among many places he characterises his work as a defence of the French, European and radical as the 'real' 'origins' of 'the accepted values and democratic principles of the egalitarian western world today'. Some historians of American law, like John Philip Reid or James Q. Whitman, have written about the role of common law jurisprudence in the development of a 'modern' 'liberal' 'democratic' political culture, but they have relied on many of the conventional chronologies and categories being questioned here.

This new investigation of the relationship between common law and Enlightenment will not only contribute to the ongoing revision of intellectual history, but it will also challenge an accepted narrative in legal history that depends upon a stark contrast between these two terms. Indeed, a primary concern of this book is to forge stronger connections between intellectual and legal historians, and at the same time to rework the connections that already exist between their narratives of eighteenth-century common law. It is no small irony that John Pocock, the scholar who has had such a formative impact upon our understanding of plural Enlightenments, conservative Enlightenment, and religion and Enlightenment, has also significantly influenced historians' narrative of common law's decline and fall, thus contributing to the exclusion of common law from Enlightenment. That story of the demise of eighteenth-century common law was, of course, powerfully articulated in Pocock's *The Ancient Constitution and the Feudal Law* more than fifty years ago and it has had a dramatic and enduring impact since then. Although this intellectual history was focused on 'historical thought' and in the seventeenth, not eighteenth century, Pocock's depiction of both stasis and decline at the end of the seventeenth century has been most important for historians of law.

In *The Ancient Constitution and the Feudal Law* a narrative of rise and hegemony preceded one of stasis and decline. Pocock elucidated the centrality of an early modern language of common law and ancient custom, but he also demonstrated the ways in which defenders of common law as custom, continuity and artificial reason confronted multiple intellectual challenges in the later seventeenth century. Pocock and others have argued that important developments in historiography, and the greater understanding of the nature of feudalism in England, gradually undermined the hegemony of the common law. The widening and deepening discourse of natural law, reason and social contract is also said to have posed a devastating challenge to the prestige and legitimacy of the common law.[19] Pocock concluded that these challenges resulted in a discursive shift away from common law and ancient constitutionalism towards rational contract, and in a shift away from a seventeenth-century 'law-centered paradigm' towards a new

19 Pocock, *Ancient Constitution and the Feudal Law*, 251; and cf also 233, 235, 239, 241, 245; Burgess, *Politics of Ancient Constitution*, 221–31. Even those like Sommerville who reject the 'common law mind' still adhere to this narrative of the rise of reason and contract; see his 'Ancient Constitution Reassessed', and his *Royalists and Patriots: Politics and Ideology in England 1603–40* (London,1999). Sommerville and others like Whitman, Sharpe and Brooks have sought to emphasise the significance of reason and natural law – and the influence of continental law – in the earlier 'common-law mind' period, and persisting thereafter. James Q. Whitman, 'Why Did the Revolutionary Lawyers Confuse Custom and Reason?', *University of Chicago Law Review*, 58, 4 (Autumn, 1991): 1321–68; Christopher Brooks and Kevin Sharpe, 'Debate: History, English Law and the Renaissance', *Past & Present*, 72 (1976): 133–42.

eighteenth-century civic and commercial paradigm, concerned with virtue and corruption. To be sure, there was a certain 'Janus-faced' quality to this analysis: at the same time as he pointed to this paradigm shift and decline, Pocock also noted that the historian Robert Brady's feudal researches failed to become the new orthodoxy, and he argued for the continuity or stasis of ancient constitutionalism into the eighteenth century.[20] In a 'Retrospect' to the text, added thirty years after its original publication, Pocock described this understanding of the 'inanition of the "common-law mind"' and the simultaneous attempt to explain its 'survival or revival in the prescriptivism of Edmund Burke' as the 'apparent paradox' of the original conclusion to his *Ancient Constitution and the Feudal Law*.[21]

The idea of decline has had a notable impact on the broader narrative of the history of English common law. There is a good deal of scholarly consensus among contemporary legal historians that the Revolution of 1688 ushered in an era of the decline of common law and the concurrent rise of legislative sovereignty; the eighteenth century is often depicted simply as a prelude to the period of positivism and law reform movements of the nineteenth century. Legal historians' general interest in tracing the evolution of nineteenth-century law reform may well have been spurred on by Pocock's remark, in his Retrospect of 1987, that '[t]here is room for a full-scale study of the ideological significance of Blackstone's *Commentaries on the Laws of England* and of Jeremy Bentham's lifelong campaign to discredit them'.[22] Yet such a statement fits with a long-standing preoccupation among historians of law, traceable to Holdsworth at least, with the changes of the late eighteenth and early nineteenth centuries.[23] Indeed, the tendency to ignore or denigrate the intervening period 'between Hale and Blackstone' may be traced even farther back, and tied to the influence of late eighteenth and nineteenth-century critics like Thomas Paine and William Godwin who railed against the traditionalist 'manuscript assumed authority of the

20 See, for example, Pocock, *Ancient Constitution and the Feudal Law*, 231–2, 242, 367. Pocock describes the idea of immemoriality in 'ancient constitutionalism' and the more 'sophisticated' notion of transmission of tradition, as both distinct and as closely connected, in his *Virtue, Commerce, and History: Essays on Political Thought and History Chiefly in the Eighteenth Century* (Cambridge, 1985), 94–5.

21 Pocock, *Ancient Constitution and the Feudal Law*, 363.

22 Ibid., 379. See also David Lieberman, *The Province of Legislation Determined: Legal Theory in Eighteenth-Century Britain* (Cambridge, 1989), 9, where Lieberman cites Pocock's influential remarks on this question of the origins of, and context for, Bentham's project made in some of his other works, such as Pocock, *Virtue, Commerce, and History*, and Pocock, *The Machiavellian Moment: Florentine Political Thought and the Atlantic Republican Tradition* (Princeton, 1975).

23 W.S. Holdsworth, *A History of English Law*, vol. 6 (London, 1924), 574; J.H. Baker, *An Introduction to English Legal History* (London, 2002), 190–1; A.W.B. Simpson, 'The Rise and Fall of the Legal Treatise: Legal Principles and the Forms of Legal Literature', *University of Chicago Law Review*, 48, 3 (Summer, 1981): 632–79.

dead' and the 'mountains of parchment' with which the common law was said to oppose truth and reason.[24] The most vigorous and well-known attack came, of course, from Jeremy Bentham, who disdained the 'general vein of obscure and crooked reasoning' in Blackstone's *Commentaries*, and depicted the majority of the English legal profession as

> A passive and enervate race, ready to swallow any thing, and to acquiesce in any thing: with intellects incapable of distinguishing right from wrong, and with affections alike indifferent to either: insensible, short-sighted, obstinate, lethargic, yet liable to be driven into convulsions by false terrors: deaf to the voice of reason and public utility: obsequious only to the whisper of interest, and to the beck of power.[25]

Bentham repeated some of the attacks against the pedantry of lawyers and the absurdity of common law procedures and judgments that would have been familiar to earlier critics. Such attacks and complaints were commonplace in the eighteenth century; 'it would be difficult to show that legal targets were being disproportionately singled out for heavier (let alone more effective) bombardment in the public prints than clerical/religious or medical ones', Wilfred Prest concurs, 'or indeed that such attacks amounted to something other than the recycling of well-worn stereotypes'.[26] However the radical and influential criticism of common law offered by men like Paine, Godwin or Bentham is more significant, and ultimately different, because it is a formative part of an enlightened narrative of common law's decline and fall.

Uncovering the roots of this critique of common law in philosophical radicalism can provide some important insights into the ways in which the conventional history of the common law, with its contrast between common law and Enlightenment, has developed. It will also help us to appreciate how and why that historiography of Enlightenment, with its early emphasis on a singular, secular, philosophical and French experience, was first articulated by participants in the eighteenth and nineteenth centuries. The key lies in an intertwined and progressive narrative in both law and philosophy that took shape in the later eighteenth century. Crucial, first, to the philosophical side of the narrative was a reliance upon what Knud Haakonssen

24 Thomas Paine and William Godwin quoted in James Epstein, 'Our Real Constitution: Trial Defence and Radical Memory in the Age of Revolution', in James Vernon ed., *Re-reading the Constitution: New Narratives in the Political History of England's Long Nineteenth Century* (Cambridge, 1996), 25, 28.

25 Jeremy Bentham, *A Fragment on Government*, J.H. Burns and H.L.A. Hart eds, (Cambridge, 1988), 12–13.

26 Wilfrid Prest, 'The Experience of Litigation in Eighteenth-Century England', in David Lemmings ed., *The British and their Laws in the Eighteenth Century* (Woodbridge, 2005), 147.

has termed an 'epistemological paradigm': an assumption that a theory of knowledge is at the centre of all true or 'sound' philosophy and, thus, that those men identifiable as early modern philosophers were either rationalists or empiricists. The focus on epistemology was the product of a philosophical historiography which Haakonssen traces from its first articulation by both Kantians and proponents of the Scottish Commonsense School at the end of the eighteenth century to its present-day influence among historians of philosophy. This narrative began by privileging the idea of a vital struggle against scepticism in order to allow for the culminating triumphs and novel breakthroughs of the philosophies offered by Thomas Reid, Dugald Stewart and Immanuel Kant.[27]

The identification of philosophy with epistemology, and then the delineation of its history, clearly excluded those modes of thought – moral, political, aesthetic and legal – that were not primarily concerned with the justification of beliefs and judgments.[28] A kind of critical, rejectionist stance towards those outside the paradigm, as well as those 'inferior predecessors' in early modern epistemology, has remained influential in the writing of histories of both law and philosophy, developing in complicated and interconnected ways. In legal history, and legal theory, the adoption of that nineteenth-century reformist and Benthamite definition of true jurisprudence as rationalist, positivist, and utilitarian has served to perpetuate the depiction of eighteenth-century common law as the antithesis or simple absence of jurisprudence. William Blackstone was once included in this depiction: harshly judged as unsystematic and illogical, he was described in the late nineteenth century as 'the somewhat indiscriminate eulogist of every peculiarity and anomaly in our system of laws'.[29] But Blackstone has, since the mid-twentieth century, been assimilated into the triumphal portion of the progressive narrative. He is now regarded as the author of an important synthetic and substantive account of English law, the *Commentaries*, that, according to one scholar, had a 'rare elegance and lucidity' and 'pursued a far more abstract and analytical classificatory scheme' than was seen in

[27] Haakonssen, 'History of Eighteenth-Century Philosophy', 6–12.

[28] Ibid., 7; Haakonssen, 'Idea of Early Modern Philosophy'. Cf also Stephen Darwall's argument against the simple division of early modern British thinkers into rationalists and empiricists, in Stephen Darwall, *The British Moralists and the Internal 'Ought': 1640–1740* (Cambridge, 1995), 20–1.

[29] Sir William James in *Re Goodman's Trusts* (1881) quoted in John W. Cairns, 'Blackstone an English Institutist: Legal Literature and the Rise of the Nation State', *Oxford Journal of Legal Studies*, 4, 3 (Winter, 1984): 318. Interesting complications regarding the differences between English and American assessments of Blackstone – and further variations in these histories of common law – are discussed by Cairns, 320, n.15. And see Wilfrid Prest, *William Blackstone: Law and Letters in the Eighteenth Century* (Oxford, 2008), 4–10, for a helpful discussion of the development of Blackstone scholarship.

his contemporaries' work.[30] For these and other reasons, Blackstone is said to have paved the way towards 'a new "science of English law"' and, some scholars add, his work specifically led towards the late nineteenth-century analytical jurisprudence of John Austin.[31] Wilfrid Prest, Blackstone's most recent biographer, not only emphasises the 'momentous consequences of his achievement' in the *Commentaries*, but also 'the distinctly radical nature of Blackstone's activities and attitudes outside the *Commentaries*', pointing especially to Blackstone's interest in science, improvement, and legislative reform.[32] Prest offers an important account of the institutional, social and cultural contexts within which Blackstone's work developed. And yet Blackstone's rehabilitation in Prest's and others' work is still conducted in the terms of rationalism and empiricism as part of the 'epistemological paradigm', and often still relies on a contrasting depiction of pre-Blackstonian common law thought as haphazard, technical and arcane.[33]

Similarly, the history of eighteenth-century philosophy has been dominated not only by an exclusive focus on epistemology, but also by a negative identification of that philosophy with something termed 'the Enlightenment'. Here the narrative, and narrowing, of eighteenth-century philosophy to mean Enlightenment philosophy – identified variously as French, rationalist, individualist, revolutionary – was effected by its critics; by late eighteenth-century counter-revolutionaries, nineteenth-century historicists and idealists, and by late twentieth-century post-modern critics of individualism, rationalism and universalism whose attacks were much more capacious in

30 David Lieberman, 'Mapping Criminal Law: Blackstone and the Categories of English Jurisprudence', in Norma Landau ed., *Law, Crime and English Society,1660–1830* (Cambridge, 2002), 146.

31 Michael Lobban, 'Blackstone and the Science of Law', *The Historical Journal*, 30, 2 (June, 1987): 334–5; Lieberman, 'Mapping Criminal Law', 161. Lobban's most recent assessment emphasises Blackstone's positivism, as well as areas of his incoherence and failure: Lobban, *History of Philosophy of Law in Common Law World*, 95–110. Cf also Randall McGowen, 'Law and Enlightenment', in Martin Fitzpatrick, Peter Jones, Christa Knellwolf and Iain McCalman eds, *The Enlightenment World* (Routledge, 2004), 513.

32 Prest, *William Blackstone*, 308. Prest discusses, for example, Blackstone's work towards city and university reforms, as well as broader legislative reforms for the relief of creditors, 228–31. Prest's intention is to demonstrate that Blackstone was not just a conservative defender of the status quo (a 'complacent, dyed-in-the-wool reactionary') but that he was also radical and enlightened.

33 Michael Lobban, *The Common Law and English Jurisprudence 1760–1850* (Oxford, 1991), 19; Lobban, 'Blackstone and the Science of Law', 318; David Lieberman, 'Law/Custom/Tradition: Perspectives from the Common Law', in Mark Salber Phillips and Gordon Schochet eds, *Questions of Tradition* (Toronto, 2004), 233; Lieberman, 'Mapping Criminal Law', 146–7, 150–2; Prest, *William Blackstone*, 310 and cf 142–4 for Prest's depiction of Blackstone's *An Analysis of the Laws of England* (1756) as 'coherent', 'organized', 'comprehensive'.

their scope.[34] The fact that the history of philosophy was promoted by critics of Enlightenment is of course related to the fact that a critical history of law was promoted by figures of 'French' and 'Enlightenment' ideals like Bentham. The intertwining of these histories of eighteenth-century law and of philosophy is an important and overlooked part of the historiography of Enlightenment outlined above. Most crucially, these histories have been mutually reinforcing because they produce binary opposites: philosophy as rationalist, empiricist, individualist and universal versus law as irrational, traditional, communal, and particularist. This opposition is another factor contributing to the remarkable stability in the idea of eighteenth-century philosophy as 'Enlightenment' philosophy. Even more, this opposition and, more broadly, the ways in which these histories of philosophy and law have developed, powerfully shape our conception of eighteenth-century common law jurisprudence. Not only is the common law defined as hide-bound, obscurantist, irrational and backward (the opposite of philosophical reason and science) by the heirs of the philosophes, but it is also defined *out* of philosophy altogether (incapable of jurisprudence) by critics of the rationalist and revolutionary aspects of eighteenth-century thought.

Clearly modern legal scholars' preoccupation with the positivist jurisprudence and practical reforms of the nineteenth century reflects the influence of these historical narratives. Michael Lobban, for example, presented his first work on common law jurisprudence and practice in the later eighteenth and nineteenth centuries as an attempt to contextualise 'Blackstonian and Benthamic views of law', while his subsequent examination of seventeenth and eighteenth-century views of law was envisioned as a search for 'the roots of English legal positivism'.[35] Lobban's latest survey of the history of common law jurisprudence also emphasises a shift to a 'positivist conception of law' in the seventeenth-century work of Selden and Hale, and largely ignores the contributions of jurists who worked between the eras of Hale and Blackstone. David Lieberman similarly conceived of his influential study of eighteenth-century English legal theory as a way to recover 'the historical background to Bentham', and to explain 'the emergence of Benthamic legis-

[34] Haakonssen, 'History of Eighteenth-Century Philosophy', 4–5; Karen O'Brien, *Narratives of Enlightenment: Cosmopolitan History from Voltaire to Gibbon* (Cambridge, 1997), 10. See also, for example, Keith Michael Baker and Peter Hanns Reill eds, *What's Left of Enlightenment: A Postmodern Question* (Stanford, 2001) especially the essays by David A Hollinger and Richard Rorty; James Schmidt ed., *What is Enlightenment: Eighteenth-Century Answers and Twentieth-Century Questions* (Berkeley, 1996); and cf Sher, *Enlightenment and Book*, 11–13.

[35] Lobban, *Common Law and English Jurisprudence*, 13; Lobban, 'Custom, Nature and Authority: the Roots of English Legal Positivism', in David Lemmings ed., *The British and their Laws in the Eighteenth Century*; and Lobban's earlier 'Blackstone and the Science of Law'. Cf also David Lemmings, 'Law' in Iain McCalman ed., *Oxford Companion to the Romantic Age* (Oxford, 1999), 75.

lative science' with its interconnected positivist and utilitarian approach.[36] In a recent essay on the 'jurisprudence of custom' Lieberman has focused, by contrast, on 'the ways in which the idea of tradition has been understood and valued in the arena of jurisprudence', and he offers a particularly nuanced account of modern as well as early modern analyses of the connection between custom as social or community practice, and custom as institutional and juridical practice. At the same time, however, Lieberman maintains those assumptions about a fundamental shift from a common law to a legislative regime, and about the contradiction between common law heterogeneity and Enlightenment 'rationalization' and 'reform'.[37]

The influence of enduring narratives of reform and Enlightenment is apparent in Lieberman, Lobban, and other historians' general attention to the rise of parliamentary sovereignty, legislative intervention, and the correlative theory and practice of positivism. In this view what is of most interest is the expansion of parliamentary law-making in the eighteenth century, and the development of a jurisprudence which ascribed authority to law because it was derived from the power of parliament as a sovereign and deliberative governing body.[38] One problem with this perspective is that it leads historians to accelerate the rate of change occurring in this era since they look at a later jurisprudence and then emphasise the factors leading up to it. Moreover, because these historians are less interested in continuities over time they lessen our appreciation of the complexity of change, and minimise the fact that positivism and parliamentary sovereignty did not emerge in a vacuum.

This emphasis on parliament and positivism has been further entrenched because it has been tied to another avenue of legal-historical research investigating the decline of the central courts in the eighteenth century.[39] David Lemmings, for example, has been particularly interested in connecting the conventional history of English jurisprudence to a narrative of an eighteenth-century decline in litigation, legal education and profession. He also linked what other historians have termed a 'crisis of litigation' to a concurrent crisis of confidence in the law among ordinary Englishmen, and even among legal practitioners themselves.[40] Although Lemmings' own acknowl-

36 Lieberman, *Province of Legislation Determined*, 9, 222–4, 287–8.

37 Lieberman, 'Law/Custom/Tradition', 233, 245, 249–50.

38 Lieberman, *Province of Legislation Determined*, ch.1; James Oldham, 'From Blackstone to Bentham: Common Law versus Legislation in Eighteenth-Century Britain', *Michigan Law Review*, 89, 6 (May, 1991): 1637–60; Oldham, *The Mansfield Manuscripts and the Growth of English Law in the Eighteenth Century*, 2 vols (Chapel Hill, 1992).

39 The thesis of decline in the courts is usually attributed to Christopher Brooks: C.W. Brooks, 'Interpersonal Conflict and Social Tension: Civil Litigation in England 1640–1830', in A.L Beier, David Cannadine and James Rosenheim eds, *The First Modern Society: Essays in English History in Honour of Lawrence Stone* (Cambridge, 1989), 357–99.

40 Prest, 'Experience of Litigation', 134. David Lemmings' two major works are *Gentlemen and Barristers: The Inns of Court and the English Bar 1680–1730* (Oxford, 1990)

edgement of the resilience and political prowess of the English bar, along with other historians' insights into demographic change and jurisdictional complexity, have modified this general image of the decline of the work and prestige of the courts, the eighteenth century is still widely depicted as an age of crisis for the common law.[41] Lemmings and others ultimately maintain the view that there was a significant marginalisation or decline of common law culture in England beginning in 1689 and worsening over the course of the century. And a key component of their analysis is that enduring contrast between common law and Enlightenment. Lemmings, for example, frequently points to the difference between 'conservative', 'backward' and 'obfuscatory' common law practices and 'rationalist', 'progressive' Enlightenment ideals as part of his insistence that the decline in litigation, and the associated decline in reputation of the common law among litigants, was related to the pressure of Enlightenment ideas.[42]

Lemming's broad narrative of 'the decline of common law itself' rehearses key elements of that enduring radical and philosophical critique when he concludes:

> Indeed from the perspective of the *longue duree* it may be suggested that the eighteenth century was a watershed in the history of law in English society; a critical moment when the culture of the common law began to move to the margins of national life....Of course, such a profound change had deep and complex roots which were hardly susceptible to individual influence: legislative activism was a natural corollary of the decisions made in 1689; the impact of revolutions in America and France seems to have undermined ideas about the fundamental status of the common law by associating Englishmen's birthrights with the Rights of Man; and in hindsight the development of positivist central administration appears inevitable when one considers the massive growth of British society and the British Empire during the century after 1750.[43]

and *Professors of the Law: Barristers and English Legal Culture in the Eighteenth Century* (Oxford, 2000).

41 W.A. Champion, 'Recourse to Law and the Meaning of the Great Litigation Decline, 1650–1750', in Christopher Brooks and Michael Lobban eds, *Communities and Courts in Britain 1150–1900* (London, 1997), 179–98; Henry Horwitz and Patrick Polden, 'Continuity or Change in the Court of Chancery in the Seventeenth and Eighteenth Centuries?', *Journal of British Studies*, 35, 1 (January, 1996): 24–57; Horwitz, 'Changes in the Law and Reform of the Legal Order: England (and Wales) 1689–1760', *Parliamentary History*, 21, 3 (October, 2002): 306–11, 323–4; David Lemmings, 'The Independence of the Judiciary in Eighteenth-Century England', in Peter Birks ed., *The Life of the Law: Proceedings of the Tenth British Legal History Conference* (Oxford, 1993), 137. And see Lemmings' more recent discussion of 'the Great Litigation Decline' in his introduction to *The British and their Laws in the Eighteenth Century*.

42 Lemmings, *Professors of the Law*, 8, 20–2, 108, 319–28. Note that Lemmings, like Prest, associates Blackstone with Enlightenment rationality and politeness.

43 Ibid., 328; cf 319 for his use of the phrase 'decline of the common law itself'.

In the last analysis legislation, positivism and revolutionary ideals are said to surpass and supplant old common law; reason and natural rights are shown to triumph over custom and privilege; and modernity is said to take the place of traditionalism. Lemmings follows the accepted historical narrative and openly cites John Pocock's work for evidence of the demise of a 'law-centered paradigm'.[44] This conventional chronology contrasts the highpoint of English ancient constitutionalism in the seventeenth century with its nadir in the eighteenth, and marks 1689 as the moment of the 'fall'. Lemmings does, however, also acknowledge that this chronology looks slightly different with the incorporation of colonial American history. Noting that the highpoint of ancient constitutionalism (defined here as the emphasis on 'the origins of rights under common law') in America came in the 'pre-revolutionary' years of the eighteenth century, Lemmings confirms the findings of a number of constitutional historians of colonial America who argue that a common law jurisprudence of immemorial law and custom continued to thrive as an essential component of the colonial argument against imperial government in the eighteenth century.[45]

This charting of 'the strain of common law constitutionalism in the American founding' or, in John Phillip Reid's terms, the 'Americanization of the ancient constitution', has been pursued by scholars like Reid and Jack Greene, again building upon but also revising John Pocock's claims about the legacies of the British political and legal traditions in eighteenth-century America. It is an interest, too, of some scholars currently exploring the flexibility and ambiguities of a transatlantic and an imperial constitution.[46] Reid's

44 Ibid., 325–6 citing Pocock's *Ancient Constitution and the Feudal Law*, and *Virtue, Commerce, and History*.

45 Lemmings, *Professors of the Law*, 325, and note his inclusion, 294, of a statement by Thomas Jefferson promoting this idea of the translation of common law and liberty (enshrined in Coke) from England to America. For a review of this literature of American constitutional history see for example Whitman, 'Why Did the Revolutionary Lawyers Confuse Custom and Reason?', 1321–29; Stephen A. Conrad, 'James Wilson's "Assimilation of the Common-Law Mind"', *Northwestern University Law Review*, 84 (Fall, 1989): 186–219; and Michael W. McConnell, 'David C. Baum Memorial Lecture: Tradition and Constitutionalism Before the Constitution', *University of Illinois Law Review* (1998), 173.

46 John Phillip Reid, 'The Jurisprudence of Liberty: The Ancient Constitution in the Legal Historiography of the Seventeenth and Eighteenth Centuries', in Ellis Sandoz ed., *The Roots of Liberty: Magna Carta, Ancient Constitution, and the Anglo-American Tradition of Rule of Law* (Columbia, MO, 1993), 148. See also Reid, *The Concept of Liberty in the Age of the American Revolution* (Chicago, 1988), *The Concept of Representation in the Age of the American Revolution* (Chicago, 1989), *Rule of Law: The Jurisprudence of Liberty in the Seventeenth and Eighteenth Centuries* (Dekalb, 2004), *The Ancient Constitution and the Origins of Anglo-American Liberty* (Dekalb, 2005) and *Constitutional History of the American Revolution*, 4 vols (Madison, 1986–93). Greene has also been prolific: two characteristic works are Jack P. Greene, *Peripheries and Centers: Constitutional Developments in the Extended Polities of the British Empire and the United States 1607–1788* (Athens, GA,

is perhaps the most detailed and influential account of a prolonged period in which common law thought retains its significance. Reid, and most of his successors, incorporate 1776 into a Whiggish and gothic history – that is, a history of the rise of the rule of law from Magna Carta to the Bill of Rights of 1789 (extended from that of 1689). Yet even if 1776 here marks a highpoint beyond 1689, it remains a highpoint within a more general narrative of decline shaped by that radical and philosophical critique – a Whiggish history conjoined with an Enlightened history. This is still, one reviewer of Reid's work concurs, 'a story of British constitutional declension', and it is a story that still privileges the significance of a shift taking place towards 'the emerging constitution of the nineteenth century – of sovereign command and of arbitrary parliamentary supremacy.'[47]

More respect is paid to the significance of eighteenth-century English common law, especially its doctrines and procedures, by historians of English criminal and commercial law. They have demonstrated the vitality of common law in the development of adversarial trial, alternative methods of punishment, and new strategies of policing,[48] as well as in the creative

1996), and Greene, 'From the Perspective of Law: Context and Legitimacy in the Origins of the American Revolution', *Southern Atlantic Quarterly*, 85 (1987): 56–77. Other contributions to this line of inquiry by scholars like Stanley Katz or Hendrik Hartog will be found catalogued in the review essays cited above. Among those interested in a 'transatlantic' and 'imperial' constitutionalism are Mary Sarah Bilder, *The Transatlantic Constitution: Colonial Legal Culture and the Empire* (Cambridge, Mass., 2004) and Daniel Hulsebosch, *Constituting Empire: New York and the Transformation of Constitutionalism in the Atlantic World, 1664–1830* (Chapel Hill, 2005), Hulsebosch, 'The Ancient Constitution and the Expanding Empire: Sir Edward Coke's British Jurisprudence', *Law and History Review*, 21, 3 (Fall, 2003): 439–82. While Bilder suggestively points to the persistence of this legal culture even after 1776, Hulsebosch sees increasing structure and constraint in the American/federal constitutional settlement; the account of a shift to legislative sovereignty in Britain is matched in Hulsebosch's narrative by an account of a shift to constitutional law and judicial review in America. Cf also Philip Hamburger, *Law and Judicial Duty* (Cambridge, Mass., 2008) for a similar focus on continuities, and ancient constitutionalism in America, but a different account of the origins of judicial review.

47 Eldon Eisenach, 'Review of John Philip Reid *The Ancient Constitution and the Origins of Anglo-American Liberty*', *Journal of American History*, 93, 1 (June, 2006): 194–5. Cf also Reid's claim that 'We must go back to the basics of an abandoned jurisprudence' in Reid, *Ancient Constitution and the Origins of Anglo-American Liberty*, 28. For other versions of this story of British decline and jurisprudential shift see, for example, Hulsebosch, *Constituting Empire*, 36–41; Bernadette Meyler, 'Towards a Common Law Originalism', *Stanford Law Review*, 59, 3 (December, 2002), especially 562, 581.

48 The emphasis on the elite status and savagery of English legal authorities has been modified by the many historians who have been a part of the 'crime wave' in the scholarship of the past few decades. See for example J.M. Beattie, *Crime and the Courts in England 1660–1800* (Oxford, 1986); Beattie, *Policing and Punishment in London 1660–1750: Urban Crime and the Limits of Terror* (Oxford, 2001); John H. Langbein, 'Shaping the Eighteenth-Century Criminal Trial: A View from the Ryder Sources', *University of*

intersections between common law and equity in the formation of trusts, bills of exchange, and other features of modern commercial society.[49] There has been some revision of the 'textbook view' of eighteenth-century English law trapped in an 'era of complacent stability' or clinging stubbornly to an 'old bloody-minded, irrational criminal justice system'.[50] Yet while English common law may not be caricatured as rigid, it is still generally characterised as unreformed, pre-positivist, and unenlightened – other key elements of the conventional decline narrative. Indeed even John Beattie, who clearly recognises the distorting influence of nineteenth-century reform discourse, and whose work has illuminated the process of legal change within the specific contexts of eighteenth-century urbanisation, war and demobilisation – even he resorts to that assumed contrast between common law and Enlightenment. For Beattie, English common law changed and developed apart from broader eighteenth-century intellectual and cultural contexts of Enlightenment which he, following the singular and narrow view, defines as a rationalist outlook concerned with core concepts of natural rights and equality.[51]

Chicago Law Review, 50, 1 (Winter, 1983): 1–136; Langbein, *The Origins of Adversary Criminal Trial* (Oxford, 2005); Peter King, *Crime, Justice and Discretion in England* (Oxford, 2000). Periodic review essays have catalogued other important contributions to this literature: Joanna Innes and John Styles, 'The Crime Wave: Recent Writing on Crime and Criminal Justice in Eighteenth-Century England', *Journal of British Studies*, 25, 4 (October, 1986): 380–435; Robert B. Shoemaker, 'The "Crime Wave" Revisited: Crime, Law Enforcement and Punishment in Britain, 1650–1900', *The Historical Journal*, 34, 3 (September, 1991): 763–8; John Stevenson, 'An Unbroken Wave?', *The Historical Journal*, 37, 3 (September, 1994): 683–95.

49 A.W.B. Simpson, *A History of the Common Law of Contract: The Rise of the Action of Assumpsit* (Oxford, 1975); David J. Ibbetson, *A Historical Introduction to the Law of Obligations* (Oxford, 1999); James Gordley, *The Philosophical Origins of Modern Contract Doctrine* (Oxford, 1991); Michael Macnair, 'The Conceptual Basis of Trusts in the Later 17th and Early 18th Centuries', in Richard Helmholz and Reinhard Zimmerman eds, *Itinera Fiduciae: Trust and Treuhand in Historical Perspective* (Berlin, 1998), 207–36; Macnair, *The Law of Proof in Early Modern Equity* (Berlin, 1999); Macnair, 'Common Law and Statutory Imitations of Equitable Relief under the Later Stuarts', in Christopher Brooks and Michael Lobban eds, *Communities and Courts in Britain 1150–1900* (London, 1997), 115–31; James Steven Rogers, *The Early History of the Law of Bills and Notes: A Study of the Origins of Anglo-American Commercial Law* (Cambridge, 1995). See also Lieberman, *Province of Legislation Determined*, chs 5–6, for discussion of Mansfield's jurisprudence and unrealised reform.

50 Wilfrid Prest, 'Law Reform in Eighteenth-Century England', in Peter Birks ed., *The Life of the Law: Proceedings of the Tenth British Legal History Conference* (London, 1993), 113; J.M. Beattie, 'London Crime and the Making of the "Bloody Code" 1689–1718', in Lee Davison et al. eds, *Stilling the Grumbling Hive: The Response to Social and Economic Problems in England 1689–1750* (New York, 1992), 70. Cf also Horwitz, 'Changes in Law and Reform', 311–23.

51 Beattie, 'London Crime and "Bloody Code"', 50; Beattie, *Crime and the Courts*, 421, and cf 621, 631, 632; and see also Innes and Styles, 'Crime Wave', 204. Like John

It is clear that we need to abandon the anachronisms and distortions of the conventional narrative if we are to understand the history of English common law thought and culture. In seeking to take the earlier period on its own terms, this study will train its focus deliberately on the last decades of the seventeenth and the first few decades of the eighteenth century. And towards that end of placing eighteenth-century legal thinking back into its immediate contexts, it will consider practice as well as ideas, the history of legal theory and professional legal culture. Here Michael Lobban's early methodological statement is relevant: 'in order to understand developments in th[e] conception [of law], and the impact of legal ideas', he convincingly argued, 'it is necessary to understand how the law worked in practice'. Legal thought, in the view expressed by Lobban and others, and adopted here, is essentially tied to a broader legal culture in which a legal theory is created, in large part by practitioners, 'out of a view of how the law in fact worked'.[52]

In this way, my study of Enlightenment and common law also aims to bridge some of the divide between what legal historians characterise as external and internal histories: law understood in its external or broader social, cultural, intellectual and economic contexts must be founded upon a deeper understanding of professional, procedural, doctrinal and other types of internal development.[53] Indeed this book is envisioned, in part, as advocacy not only for closer connections between intellectual historians and legal historians, but also for awareness among historians more generally of the development of legal doctrines and practices. The distinction between an internal and an external focus has long been an important part of legal historical methodology, but it has taken on a particular salience with the growth of sociolegal studies in the last several decades. The contemporary distinction, as Robert Gordon notes, drew upon Thomas Kuhn's influential critique of the historiography of science.[54] It also built upon debates in jurisprudence, famously instigated by H.L.A. Hart, concerning the nature

Langbein, Beattie rejects the claim that Enlightenment ideals changed eighteenth-century criminal law and penal practice. See J.H. Langbein, *Torture and the Law of Proof: Europe and England in the Ancien Regime* (Chicago, 1977; rev. edn, 2004), 10–12, 45–69.

52 Lobban, *Common Law and English Jurisprudence*, 13–14. Cf also Postema, 'Classical Common Law Jurisprudence (Part I)', 155–156; and Paul D. Halliday, *Habeas Corpus: From England to Empire* (Cambridge, Mass., 2010), 4.

53 David J. Ibbetson, 'What is Legal History a History Of?', in Andrew Lewis and Michael Lobban eds, *Law and History* (Oxford, 2004), 33–34; Robert W. Gordon, 'J. Willard Hurst and the Common Law Tradition in American Legal Historiography', *Law and Society Review*, 10, 1 (Autumn, 1975): 11.

54 Gordon, 'Hurst and Common Law Tradition', 17 (citing F.W. Maitland's essay *Why the History of Law is not Written*) and nn. 5, 22. And see, for example, Lawrence M. Friedman, *Law and Society: An Introduction* (Englewood Cliffs, NJ, 1977); Austin Sarat et al. eds, *Crossing Boundaries: Traditions and Transformations in Law and Society Research* (Evanston, Ill., 1998); Philippe Nonet and Philip Selznick, *Law and Society in Transition: Toward Responsive Law* (New York, 2001).

of social rules. When Hart insisted that social rules have an 'internal aspect', questions were raised concerning the nature of legal authority, and concerning the possibility of descriptive jurisprudence. Ensuing debates over how to negotiate the benefits and dangers of subjectivity, whether one took the perspective of a participant (internal) or an observer (external), were understood to be broadly relevant for thinking about the methodology of the social sciences.[55] The methodological issues raised by these debates regarding the problem of anachronism (or the imposition of a modern observer perspective into a past society) have been especially important for legal historians. Moreover, the basic conception of an internal story of law that exists in some relation to a broader, external story, obviously raised questions about contextualisation and causation that have preoccupied legal scholars.[56]

Many legal historians who follow a law and society approach address these questions by analysing law as a reflection of, or a response to, social and economic conditions.[57] While this is an important line of analysis the approach outlined by Barbara Shapiro and others, of 'integrat[ing] legal concepts and traditions into the general fabric of intellectual and cultural history', is even more relevant to the concerns of this book.[58] Equally relevant is the concept of legal culture, defined by Lawrence Friedman as 'the values and attitudes which bind the [legal] system together, and which deter-

55 Brian Z. Tamanaha, 'The Internal/External Distinction and the Notion of a "Practice" in Legal Theory and Sociolegal Studies', *Law and Society Review*, 90, 1 (1996): 163–204; Ibbetson, 'What is Legal History?', 34.

56 Michael Lobban, 'Introduction: The Tools and Tasks of the Legal Historian', in Andrew Lewis and Michael Lobban eds, *Law and History* (Oxford, 2004), 1–32; Ibbetson, 'What is Legal History?'; Bill Maurer, 'The Cultural Power of Law? Conjunctive Readings', *Law and Society Review*, 38, 4 (December, 2004): 843–50; Tamanaha, 'Internal/External Distinction'; Tamanaha, *A General Jurisprudence of Law and Society* (Oxford, 2001); Kenneth Einar Himma, 'Do Philosophy and Sociology Mix? A Non-Essentialist Socio-Legal Positivist Analysis of the Concept of Law', *Oxford Journal of Legal Studies*, 24, 4 (2004): 717–38; Ron Harris, 'The Encounters of Economic History and Legal History', *Law and History Review*, 21, 2 (Summer, 2003): 297–346.

57 For legal historians, like legal sociologists, the first impulse was to see law as a 'reflection' or 'mirror' of society, and to explain legal change as a product especially of social and economic change. Himma, 'Do Philosophy and Sociology Mix?', 719; Barbara J. Shapiro, *A Culture of Fact: England 1550–1720* (Ithaca, 2000), 2; Bruce H. Mann, 'Afterword: The Death and Transfiguration of Early American Legal History', in Christopher L. Tomlins and Bruce H. Mann eds, *The Many Legalities of Early America* (Chapel Hill, 2001), 442; for a recent admission of the lack of scholarly consensus regarding method see Lawrence M. Friedman, 'Coming of Age: Law and Society Enters an Exclusive Club', *Annual Review of Law and Social Science*, 1 (December, 2005): 1–16.

58 Shapiro, *Culture of Fact*, 2. Cf William W. Fisher III, 'Texts and Contexts: The Application to American Legal History of the Methodologies of Intellectual History', *Stanford Law Review*, 49, 5 (May, 1997): 1072–3

mine the place of the legal system in the culture of the society as a whole.'[59] And yet it has been notoriously difficult to define the nature of this relationship between legal culture, society, and culture more broadly conceived – a difficulty that also has implications for Shapiro's project of integration. The most prevalent idea employed by scholars is that of 'reciprocal influence' or 'mutual constitution' between law and culture, and between legal culture and society and culture – an interpretive position that threatens to devolve into an endless and ultimately uninformative recursion which never adequately grapples with the meaning of 'influence', 'intersection' and 'interaction'. Such reliance on circularity hinders us from adequately understanding a given society's general conception, and acceptance, of the authority of law.[60]

These methodological challenges will be faced here first by returning to a focus on the internal, that is, on the specificities and technicalities of doctrine and procedure in English legal development. In seeking to explain these internal operations of English law it is necessary not only to identify past rules and procedures, but it is also crucial to attend to the multiple, often subtle and always changeable conceptual frameworks within which they were articulated, employed and understood.[61] This is, of course, to return to the methods of intellectual history, especially those insights into the operation of language and discourse associated with the contextualist methods of proponents of the Cambridge School. Those questions about the relationship among expression, ideas, intention and action that have long been at the heart of methodological debates about intellectual (and, more recently, sociocultural) history are also implicated in the doubts that have plagued law and society scholarship.[62] The history of law then, like the

59 Lawrence M. Friedman, 'Legal Culture and Social Development', *Law and Society Review*, 4 (1969): 34, cited in Richard J. Ross, 'The Legal Past of Early New England: Notes for the Study of Law, Legal Culture and Intellectual History', *The William and Mary Quarterly*, Third Series, 50, 1 (January, 1993): 32.

60 Ross, 'Legal Past of New England', 33; Maurer, 'Cultural Power of Law?', 844, 847–8; Israel, *Enlightenment Contested*, 20–21, on the similar problem of circularity faced by historians of ideas and culture who seek to explain the direction of causation. For a useful articulation of this difficulty, and elaboration on the idea of legal culture, see the definition of 'legal vision' in P.S. Atiyah and R.S. Summers, *Form and Substance in Anglo-American Law: A Comparative Study of Legal Reasoning, Legal Theory and Legal Institutions* (Oxford, 1987), 411.

61 Ibbetson, 'What is Legal History?', 34–5.

62 Lobban, 'Tools and Tasks', 3–4; Fisher, 'Texts and Contexts', 1067–8. Quentin Skinner, John Pocock, and John Dunn are usually recognised as the major proponents of the Cambridge contextualist approach. For debates about this methodology see, for example, Israel, *Enlightenment Contested*, 15–26; James Tully ed., *Meaning and Context: Quentin Skinner and his Critics* (Princeton, 1988); Dominic LaCapra and Steven Kaplan eds, *Modern European Intellectual History: Reappraisals and New Perspectives* (Ithaca, 1982); Kari Palonen, *Quentin Skinner: History, Politics, Rhetoric* (Cambridge, 2003);

history of political thought with which it has long been associated, should be understood as a history of discourse and should be studied, similarly, as an excavation of past languages. What were the languages – that is, the vocabularies, idioms, rhetoric, paradigms – employed in eighteenth-century legal records? What could be said, and thought, and what was the nature of discursive change?[63]

The complexity of meaning described by scholars of political discourse is equally applicable to this legal discourse. For example, although it may easily be recognised that legal records were largely the expression of a specific professional community these records are nonetheless made up of multiple languages because that community was 'polyglot'.[64] This was a professional community that was multi-institutional and therefore multilingual, employing languages of common law, civil law, natural law, canon law, manorial law and so on. Moreover, these professionals also spoke in other 'non-legal' kinds of languages – of biblical exegesis, say, or of sociability and civility – that are also part of the history of legal discourse and law.

Members of this professional community are clearly the main actors in an intellectual internal history of law, and they are also crucial to understanding legal culture in its relationship with a broader, general culture. A second key aspect of the methodological approach employed here is to focus on lawyers, legal theorists and especially judges as a way to bring together discourse analysis with some important insights of cultural history. In addition to evidence left by average and anonymous eighteenth-century lawyers, this book will examine the writings and experiences of central legal figures such as Lord Chancellors Somers, Cowper, Macclesfield and Hardwicke, Chief Barons Atkyns and Gilbert, and Chief Justice Holt. These judges were not only makers of law but also important representatives of a learned legal community. These several men were deliberately chosen because of their prominence as officials in the Westminster courts, and as commentators on English common law. These men were also chosen because of their

Robert Darnton, *The Forbidden Best-Sellers of Pre-Revolutionary France* (New York, 1995), ch. 6; Mark Bevir, *The Logic of the History of Ideas* (Cambridge, 1999).

63 For the relevance of linguistic theory – especially the work of Searle, Austin, Wittgenstein, Quine and Saussure – to the development of this contextualist approach see, for example, Bevir, *Logic of History of Ideas*, ch. 2, and Annabel Brett, 'What is Intellectual History Now?' in David Cannadine ed., *What is History Now?* (Basingstoke, 2002), 116–17.

64 J.G.A. Pocock, 'The Concept of a Language, and the *Métier d'Historien*: Some Considerations on Practice', in Anthony Pagden ed., *The Languages of Political Theory in Early Modern Europe* (Cambridge, 1987), 21. See also Peter Goodrich, *Languages of Law: From Logics of Memory to Nomadic Masks* (London, 1990); Goodrich, 'Ars Bablativa: Ramism, Rhetoric, and the Genealogy of English Jurisprudence', in Gregory Leyh ed., *Legal Hermeneutics: History, Theory and Practice* (Berkeley, 1992), 43–82; Goodrich, 'Lex Laetans: Three Theses on the Unbearable Lightness of Legal Critique', *Law & Literature*, 17, 3 (2006): 293–319.

well-recorded personal involvement in everyday matters of legal process and principle. While some legal historians have studied the official actions, decisions and publications of these judges, my intention is also to consider their unofficial actions as plaintiffs and defendants in important cases having to do with murder and property, impeachment and jurisdiction. Thus, four out of seven chapters are presented as case studies. Integrating the method of case study into the established approaches of internal legal history and contextualist intellectual history will allow me to take another critical step towards the recovery of eighteenth-century legal culture. In trial records, in these judges' notes, in surviving indications of their reading practices, and in their actions we can find evidence of that 'common opinion' that is as important to the development of common law, John Baker reminds us, as the evidence of their judicial opinions.[65]

Lord Chancellor Cowper and Chief Baron Atkyns, for example, are the focus of chapters that investigate their contributions to legal theory and public politics as well as their intimate practical involvement in litigation. Cowper's role in his brother's 1699 trial for murder opens a window on to developments in evidentiary practices in law, philosophy and science in the early eighteenth century. Atkyns' personal frustrations with a 1694 suit at Chancery, and his assertion of the validity of common law in the face of doctrinal developments in trusts and contract, shed new light on his theoretical tracts on common law jurisdiction – tracts that were reprinted in 1734 and 1741 and continued to be influential well into the eighteenth century. The assessment of these and other legal actors' ideas will also attend to questions of reception and publication, combining a diffusionist approach with discourse analysis.[66] Here the analysis of such texts and cases will reflect upon those enlightened practices and institutions – like salons and clubs, banks and stock markets, newspapers and journals – that are essential for understanding the cultural and intellectual contexts of eighteenth-century common law.

A first chapter on law and print introduces this approach, foregrounding the commitment to cultural as well as intellectual history, and implementing from the outset that 'media-driven' conception of enlightenment with a special interest in new tools of communication and approaches to data organisation. The focus of this chapter is on the collections of cases, pleadings and statutes that were published as abridgments and manuals of

[65] J. H. Baker, *The Law's Two Bodies: Some Evidential Problems in English Legal History* (Oxford, 2001), 86–9.

[66] Darnton, *Forbidden Best-Sellers*, 170; Israel, *Enlightenment Contested*, 18–19; Roger Chartier, 'Intellectual History or Sociocultural History?', trans. Jane P. Kaplan, in Dominic LaCapra and Steven L. Kaplan eds, *Modern European Intellectual History: Reappraisals and New Perspectives* (Ithaca, 1982), 13–46; and note Pocock's discussion of the relevance of *l'histoire du livre* to the interpretation of meaning, Pocock, 'Concept of a Language', 20, 36–7.

the law in this period. These texts have often been taken to represent an unreflective adherence to narrow technicalities and derivative rules said to be characteristic of that 'irrational traditionalism' of a 'declining' common law.[67] But this burgeoning early eighteenth-century practical literature of law looks different when we consider the ways in which these texts articulate prevalent ideas about the role of print in an information age. The common law abridgments and manuals took part in enduring humanist scholarly traditions of commonplacing and can be better understood when read within the contexts of eighteenth-century legal education and note-taking practices. The practical legal literature took part, equally, in those large-scale eighteenth-century projects of compilation, like the Enlightenment encyclopedias and dictionaries. This early eighteenth-century proliferation of legal literature, both professional and more broadly popular, must be recognised as part of a pervasive interest in information management, data collection and knowledge production in a period of the profusion and commercialisation of print. Moreover, these law books reveal a deep belief in particularity, compilation, and in the relevance of accepted past practice to the authority of law, providing evidence that a common law jurisprudence may be found in places other than works of constitutional theory or formal treatises of law. Common law values, and legal culture more broadly, are here fully implicated in the development of a commercial and print-based Enlightenment.

In addition to these printed abridgments and manuals of the law, and the manuscript notebooks left by eighteenth-century law students and practitioners, published and manuscript records of select cases, such as those involving Cowper and Atkyns, Macclesfield and Gilbert, are an essential source for this project especially because these cases entailed debate over the jurisdiction of common law. Participants in the criminal trial involving William Cowper, for example – the focus of my second chapter on law and science – addressed questions about the scope of legal process and the proper role of science in the common law courtroom. Lawyers like Cowper, and prominent scientists like Hans Sloane and Samuel Garth, took part here, and elsewhere, in contemporary discussion about witnessing, integrity and fact. Analysis of such debates in this case sheds new light on the early development of the adversarial trial in the eighteenth century, and allows us to see the ways in which these debates contributed to contemporary conceptions of authority and justice.

Another significant aspect of this Cowper case was ongoing conflict over the use of the appeal of felony after acquittal. The appeal of felony was originally a legal method for initiating a criminal prosecution, but by the later seventeenth century it was evolving into a means of appellate review.

67 Holdsworth, *History of English Law*, vol. 6, 574; Baker, *Introduction to English Legal History*, 190–1; Simpson, 'Rise and Fall of Treatise', 632–79.

In this murder trial prosecution and defence articulated competing views of this common law procedure, and in so doing they raised troubling questions about the integrity of trial process, and the nature of common law justice. Furthermore, gendered definitions of integrity informed both the assize and appeal proceedings, and these contemporary ideas about male honour and female chastity only intensified doubts about the fairness of legal process. Arguments presented by prosecution and defence, and Chief Justice Holt's verdict on this case, represent a range of ideas about just adherence to common law procedure and precedent. These arguments demonstrate the complex and contested ways in which such ideas affected the development of eighteenth-century common law jurisprudence.

A series of chapters on law and equity follows that takes up this question of appellate review, and the issue of jurisdictional controversy, specifically regarding the scope of Chancery's power. Such disputes about the proper relationship between the common law courts and a separate equity court like Chancery had, of course, endured for centuries; most famous (and idealised) is the early seventeenth century rift between King James I and Sir Edward Coke over the power of the King's chancellor to override common law. Equally important and vigorous debates took place in the early eighteenth century, evident not only in case law but also in a published controversial literature on law reform, and in a treatise literature on natural law, civil law and equity. Chapter five examines this legal literature, and explores the ways in which eighteenth-century natural law jurisprudence emerged within the jurisdictional contest between common law and equity. This conflict encouraged the articulation of a classical conception of equity as expressive of principles of natural justice that underlie common law. But this conflict also facilitated the expression of equally important concepts of justice based on custom and adaptation, conflict and mixture. Custom, prescription, immemoriality and continuity were core values that were not simply discredited, nor seen as static, nor subordinated to reason and nature. Moreover, as natural law and common law jurisprudence were forged together through this contest and dialogue, both were shaped by wider philosophical and cultural trends – in the production and circulation of print, for example, or in the lively polemics regarding the growth of commercial society. Attention to these broader external contexts, as well as to the particular legal context of jurisdictional tension, allows us to see that the expression of legal principles in these eighteenth-century texts was not just the product of external influence, as some scholars have claimed.[68] This

[68] Ibbetson, *Historical Introduction to Law of Obligations*, ch. 11; Ibbetson, 'Natural Law and Common Law', *Edinburgh Law Review*, 5 (2001): 4–20; Gordley, *Philosophical Origins of Modern Contract Doctrine*; Gordley, 'Enforcing Promises', *California Law Review*, 83, 2 (March, 1995): 547–614; Gordley, 'The Moral Foundations of Private Law', *American Journal of Jurisprudence*, 47 (2002): 1–24.

realisation leads to the further conclusion that English jurisprudence should not simply be seen as part of a determined progress toward rationalisation.

The vitality of this jurisdictional struggle between law and equity, and the relevance of contemporary philosophical and cultural trends, can also be seen in the litigation involving prominent officials like Chief Baron Atkyns and Lord Chancellor Macclesfield. The disputes that occupied Atkyns in several Chancery and Exchequer suits revolved around problems of credit, and the potential for fraud in mortgage and trust agreements. Macclesfield faced legal action when he was accused of corruption in judicial office, stemming from suspect investment and failed trusteeship. These accusations culminated in his conviction during the impeachment trial of 1725. These cases, the focus of chapters four and six, clearly demonstrate the centrality of eighteenth-century economic change to the persistence of conflict between the courts. Indeed it is telling that both the Atkyns and Macclesfield controversies engaged with changes in commercial practices – with new forms of investment, new credit relationships and changing contractual expectations. Commercial and financial innovation went hand-in-hand with important developments in mortgage, trust and contract law, and these changes presented new challenges to common law instruments, forms of action, and to the jurisdiction of the common law courts. Early eighteenth-century judges and lawyers wrestled with the consequences of these new market practices. Many of them defended common law tradition and stability as a necessary counterweight to the expansion of commercial law being facilitated by Chancery. New conceptions of the justice of common law emerged, shaped by the experience of jurisdictional conflict, and stimulated by a contemporaneous and wide-ranging public examination of the social consequences of economic change.

These socio-economic and jurisprudential debates were, again, part of broader enlightened philosophical trends. The litigation engaging Sir Robert Atkyns, for example, and the legal treatises he produced in response, were firmly rooted in an enlightened discourse about credit and credibility. Similarly, evidence from the impeachment trial of Lord Chancellor Macclesfield indicates that participants conceived of the chancellor's jurisdiction, and Chancery's authority, in the terms of enlightened moral-philosophical debate about self-love, economic competition, and social welfare. Macclesfield's trial and other associated legal records are suffused with the languages of moral sense, moral reform and civic humanism. In this instance of jurisdictional controversy critics of Chancery reinforced, and also attached new meanings to, an enlightened discourse about virtue and corruption, tying it to arguments about the value of common law. Both critics and supporters of the Chancellor appealed to tradition and prescription as the basis of their claims to justice against wrongdoing. They attributed significance to these common law principles as part of thinking through the new challenges of a commercial and polite culture.

Finally, these new challenges were again, and significantly, understood in gendered terms. Both the Macclesfield and Atkyns cases provide key evidence of the kinds of gendered values and gendered discourse that were employed in public debate about the consequences of economic change. Like so many eighteenth-century disputes in Chancery, these suits had to do with the development of equitable protections for women that afforded women agency not recognised at common law. Disputes over trusts, jointure and separate maintenance reveal a range of contradictory attitudes towards women's subordination and male rights and responsibilities. The suits involving the lord chancellor and the chief baron are particularly expressive of contemporary ambivalence about female property ownership and, perhaps even more, about female participation in commercial society as investors, and as parties to new kinds of contracts. Since this gendered ambivalence was part of those wider enlightened discussions regarding integrity and credibility, sentiment and sociability, it is not surprising that this led in both cases to a heightened debate about the comparative justice of common law and equity. The defence of English common law was again part of Enlightenment here. As new economic practices and new cultural attitudes developed, English legal culture never simply rejected the value attributed to custom, stability and past practice in the law.

These common law principles, this book will argue, played a critical part in the emergence of an enlightened society, philosophy and culture in eighteenth-century England. One important implication of this argument is a new appreciation for the ways in which eighteenth-century Enlightenments involved working out a more complex relationship to tradition and the past. A final chapter on law and history elaborates on this insight through a conjoined analysis of eighteenth-century legal historical writing and Enlightenment historiography. While scholars have frequently noted the mutual influences between natural law jurisprudence and the development of Enlightenment philosophical and conjectural histories, the genre of legal history has been treated separately (if at all) from these and other enlightened historiographical trends.[69] Yet there are important connections. First, historians of English law and legal institutions were, like other eighteenth-century historians, interested in chronicling the course of socioeconomic change in England. Histories of legal institutions directed attention to the slow evolution of common law process and jurisdiction, but in so doing also outlined the scope of historical change in forms of property ownership, for example, or investigated the motivations of political and ecclesiastical authorities. Legal histories were also important in furthering

69 H.M. Hopfl, 'From Savage to Scotsman: Conjectural History in the Scottish Enlightenment', *Journal of British Studies*, 17, 2 (Spring, 1978): 19–40; Knud Haakonssen, *The Science of a Legislator: The Natural Jurisprudence of David Hume and Adam Smith* (Cambridge, 1981); Mark Salber Philips, *Society and Sentiment: Genres of Historical Writing in Britain 1740–1820* (Princeton, 2000); Frank Palmeri, 'Conjectural History and the Origins of Sociology', *Studies in Eighteenth-Century Culture*, 37 (2008): 1–21.

the contemporary analysis of feudalism, and conceptualising its impact on the emergence of commercial society in the West.

Second, these histories of law were rooted in Enlightenment print culture. They employed techniques of collection, compilation and abridgment familiar to other eighteenth-century law books and history books, and contributed to those new attitudes towards the organisation of knowledge that helped to validate the authority of prescriptive example. This recourse to collection as well as narrative and analysis is pronounced in the work of Geoffrey Gilbert, the author of numerous and influential histories of the English courts, legal procedure and doctrine. Gilbert is a central figure in this final chapter because his approach is characteristic of that eighteenth-century culture of 'information overload' within which both common law and historical thinking developed. Moreover, since Gilbert's texts circulated in manuscript for decades, and were published in different forms and editions by others after his death, they also allow for a return to the study of reception, and the ways in which scribal and print cultures played a role in legal and historiographical development.

Most important, however, Gilbert is a key figure for the analysis of eighteenth-century legal history and common law jurisprudence because he was engaged as a judge, as well as an historian, in the creation of both constitutional and institutional histories of law. During his tenure as chief baron of the Irish Exchequer Gilbert's most important verdict was in the case of *Annesley v Sherlock* (1719), a major jurisdictional dispute over the matter of appeals from the Irish courts to the British House of Lords. Fierce debate surrounded this case and led to the expression of varied ideas about the sources of law, the legitimacy of established authorities, and the nature of justice. These contests about the origins and authority of law were also tied to contemporary questions about the constitution of empire – especially questions about the prerogatives of kingship, and about the negotiation of commercial opportunities in the British Isles. Gilbert's involvement in this episode obviously shaped his subsequent judicial career but it also influenced his engagement with historical writing, and encouraged him to reflect on social and economic as well as legal and political trends. Authors of legal histories like Geoffrey Gilbert contributed to newly-emerging vocabularies and insights of an eighteenth-century historical culture. An appreciation of Gilbert's work, and of other eighteenth-century legal histories, is essential for a fuller understanding of Enlightenment historiography and its relationship to eighteenth-century common law jurisprudence. Common law thought and common law culture were, after all, a form of historical thought and culture: common law spoke in the language of custom, precedent and prescription, and valued tradition as it evolved through human and social experience.

The defence of the value and authority of the past was, these chapters will demonstrate, a dynamic part of Enlightenment in its multiple guises. As John Pocock once observed in making a case for his 'conservative Enlightenment', '[i]nnovations are sometimes made in the attempt to defend ruling structures as well as in that to overthrow them.'[70] The defence of common law in the eighteenth century entailed such innovation, not least because reflection on the nature of law and of justice was implicated in so many facets of enlightened discourse and practice. This guaranteed that common law took part not only in 'conservative' but also in 'philosophical', 'progressive' and other forms of Enlightenment – thus underlining the inadequacy or irrelevance of these terms. For all these reasons it is time to recognise that the eighteenth century was not a period of decline but was, rather, a critical period for the development of common law jurisprudence.

70 Pocock, 'Clergy and Commerce', 531 n. 12.

2

Law Books, Legal Knowledge, and Enlightened Encyclopedism

> ... but though I recommend to him to have a large Common Place-Book, I do not in the least insinuate that the Person who has the largest is the greatest Lawyer, any more than I do that he is, who hath the greatest Head: Things must be clear and well digested in both Cases, to make a man compleat.
>
> Giles Jacob, *The Student's Companion: Or, The Reason of the Laws of England* [1]

Giles Jacob's joking aside to his reader is rich with double meanings. His humorous, because absurd, denial that he is equating large notebooks or large body parts with legal prowess is a rhetorical flourish, a characteristic eighteenth-century satirical jibe. It is also, possibly, a ribald pun (and this from the purported author of the obscene *Tractatus de hermaphroditis*) on the manly anatomy of the 'greatest Lawyer', and a winking reference to the so-called temptations for the law student among the prostitutes, the 'pleasure grounds and fleshpots', which were in close proximity to the early modern Inns of Court.[2] Jacob's imagery may also have traded upon familiarity with the language of body politic, of head and members in proportion and not subject to the outsized, absolutist pretensions of an overweening head. Most clearly, however, Jacob is punning on the identity between the lawyer's, or law student's, head and the commonplace heading – the alphabetical heads or titles that provide the structure for the student's notebook and for Jacob's ensuing text. These heads or titles, he warns, are not enough; legal knowledge is not simply an assortment of practices, technicalities, cases and writs but must be informed by a more complete and clear understanding of the content and principles of law. To make 'things clear and well digested' legal thinking, like other types of thought, must be reasoned and deliberative.

Jacob's preface here defends common law learning as expressed in the abridgments, students' books and practical handbooks, those forms of legal

1 Giles Jacob, introduction to *The Student's Companion: Or the Reason of the Laws of England* (2nd edn, London, 1734), vii.

2 David Lemmings, 'Blackstone and Law Reform by Education: Preparation for the Bar and Lawyerly Culture in Eighteenth-Century England', *Law and History Review*, 16, 2 (Summer, 1998): 236; Lemmings, *Professors of the Law*, 131–2.

literature that proliferated in the early eighteenth century. This common law learning and literature was the target of some criticism in the eighteenth century, and it has been denigrated or dismissed by modern scholars. Indeed the whole period between Hale and Blackstone has generally been characterised as a wasteland for legal literature. W.S. Holdsworth's early assertion that the law books of the late seventeenth and early eighteenth centuries 'can be described as considerable in quantity but very ordinary in quality' is reiterated in J.H. Baker's current claim that 'the generality of law books in the first half of the eighteenth century were slight in character, and the period was more distinguished by abridgments than textbooks.'[3] Even A.W.B. Simpson, who has charted important continuities between the abridgments and more 'substantive' legal treatises, regards this practical legal literature as inferior in comparison to the work of a Hale or a Blackstone.[4] The abridgments and other practical texts suffer, by necessity, from the comparison with earlier 'classics' by Fortescue, Coke or Hale or the later 'reformist' jurisprudence of Blackstone and Bentham. Yet this comparison is limiting, and the underlying questions about periodisation and change are ill-posed. In attempting to get to a deeper and more sustained analysis of this literature we should not only orient ourselves around the relationship between the formal and informal, theoretical and practical literatures, but we should also consider other contexts within which this literature flourished.

What if we consider legal writing within the broader contexts of humanist education, and enlightened composition and publication? How do early eighteenth-century law texts stand in relation to evolving traditions of scholarship and commonplacing, and the intersections between print and manuscript cultures? Rather than contrasting the legal logic of the abridgments with examples of 'Enlightenment rationalism' we may more usefully compare it to other eighteenth-century projects (literary, scientific, philosophical) invested in the descriptive and classificatory. Relevant too, are eighteenth-century ideas about knowledge not only 'in terms of the activity (or passivity) of the individual person's mind' but also as something interpersonal and reliant on collective testimony.[5] Why should we see the encyclopedic projects of the early eighteenth century, for example, as epitomes

[3] Holdsworth, *History of English Law*, vol. 6, 574; Baker, *Introduction to English Legal History*, 190–1.

[4] Simpson, 'Rise and Fall of Treatise', 632–79.

[5] Haakonssen, 'Idea of Early Modern Philosophy', 114. See also Dario Perinetti, 'Philosophical Reflection on History', in Knud Haakonssen ed., *The Cambridge History of Eighteenth-Century Philosophy*, vol. 2 (Cambridge, 2006), 1107–40; Robert Wokler, 'Anthropology and Conjectural History in the Enlightenment', in Christopher Fox and Roy Porter eds, *Inventing Human Science: Eighteenth-Century Domains* (Berkeley, 1995), 31–52; Larry Wolff and Marco Cipolloni eds, *The Anthropology of the Enlightenment* (Stanford, 2007).

of Enlightenment text, but regard the abridgments and dictionaries of law as unenlightened and backwards? Increasingly available, portable and cheap, this legal literature can be seen as part of an early modern culture of 'information overload' and information management, a product of a burgeoning, data-collecting English society.[6] The characteristic logic of early modern English common law, which pursued argument through citation and compilation, and emphasised detail, specific remedies and formal rules, developed in important ways with the expansion of this legal literature within these enlightened contexts.

The practical legal literature was composed of many different kinds of texts, and different schemes of categorising these texts have been proposed by the authors themselves, by their publishers, by lawyers, bibliographers and historians. Simpson's interest in charting the 'rise and fall' of legal treatises, for example, led him to pose the dichotomous categories of treatise and non-treatise. And he identified non-treatises as collections of cases and statutes, abridgments of cases and statutes, indices, formularies, glosses on texts, and texts on terms and procedures. In charting the evolution from the dominant abridgment tradition to the legal treatise, Simpson also noted the appearance of books of legal maxims as a separate and intermediate category of texts.[7] A similar dichotomy between a practical, inductive, descriptive literature and a rational, analytic literature was proposed by Michael Lobban. According to Lobban the English practical or descriptive literature took a few characteristic forms: books of writs and pleading, abridgments, studies of the complex rules of a single branch of law, and law dictionaries. However, Lobban has also acknowledged the publication of treatises that were both 'systematic' and 'compendious' in the early eighteenth century. [8] Finally, significant flexibility and potential for overlap between types of texts appears in the long list of categories proposed by Holdsworth. He divided

6 Ann Blair, 'Reading Strategies for Coping with Information Overload ca. 1550–1700', *Journal of the History of Ideas*, 64, 1 (January, 2003): 11–28; Richard Yeo, *Encyclopaedic Visions: Scientific Dictionaries and Enlightenment Culture* (Cambridge, 2001); John Brewer, *The Sinews of Power: War, Money and the English State 1688–1783* (New York, 1988), 227–8; Roger Chartier, *The Order of Books: Readers, Authors and Libraries in Europe Between the Fourteenth and the Eighteenth Centuries*, trans. Lydia G. Cochrane (Stanford, 1992), 67–8.

7 Simpson, 'Rise and Fall of Treatise', 636–7, 642–51. David J. Ibbetson, 'Legal Printing and Legal Doctrine', *The Irish Jurist*, 35 (New Series 2000): 345–54, posits a similar development from abridgment to treatise (although without the negative evaluation of the earlier texts).

8 Lobban, 'Blackstone and Science of Law', 313. Cf Lobban, 'The English Legal Treatise and English Law in the Eighteenth Century', in Serge Dauchy, Jos Monballyu and Alain Wijffels eds, *Auctoritates: Law Making and its Authors, Iuris Scripta Historica*, 13 (Brussels, 1997), 74; and Wilfred Prest, 'Law Books', in Michael F. Suarez S.J. and Michael Turner eds, *The Cambridge History of the Book in Britain, Volume 5, 1696–1830* (Cambridge, 2009), 796–7.

early modern legal literature into: case reports, reprints of the Register of Writs and the Year Books, abridgments of the statutes, books on law and equity, students' books, books on pleading and practice, on conveyancing and land law, on criminal law, commercial law and ecclesiastical law, books on special branches of the common law (such as baron and feme, contracts, torts, insanity), books on local government, on central government, on legal history, on politics and finally a 'general' category of books which included law dictionaries, works of military, naval, maritime and colonial law, and a few works of legal theory.[9] Although Holdsworth's list encourages an appreciation of variety more than coherent categorisation, it does also convey a good sense for the profusion of these texts and the ways in which they were part of a more general demand for 'useful knowledge', part of a broader attempt at viewing and ordering the world.[10]

Specialised catalogues of law books published in the late seventeenth and early eighteenth centuries provided slightly different categories for these texts. One key example is the bookseller Thomas Bassett's *Catalogue of the Common and Statute Law-Books of this Realm*. Like other compliers of information, Bassett organised his contents alphabetically under the following heads, or titles: abridgments, arguments, constables, courts, crown, customs, interpreters of law terms, justice of peace, maxims and grounds of the law, parliament, precedents, readings, reports, sheriffs, statutes, tables, tithes &c, trials, wills and testaments, writs, and miscellanies.[11] Produced at the behest

9 Holdsworth, *History of English Law*, vol. 6, 551, 597–613. It should be noted, however, that Holdsworth excepts the work of Hale (and secondarily, Dugdale) from these categories and so still in some ways perpetuates the unfavourable comparison between the practical literature and the 'classic' legal texts. Holdsworth explains that his categories were drawn from the lists in the Term catalogues of 1668–1709; these were the quarterly catalogues issued by London booksellers, and edited by Edward Arber in the early twentieth century. Finally, Holdsworth proposes similar categories in describing the literature of the eighteenth century in particular: public law, civil procedure and pleading, criminal law and procedure, evidence, land law and conveyancing, commercial law, tort and contract, special branches of the law, legal history, students' books, Roman law and legal theory. Holdsworth, *A History of English Law*, vol. 12 (London, 1938), 332.

10 Brewer, *Sinews of Power*, 228; Yeo, *Encyclopaedic Visions*; cf Tore Frangsmyr, J.L. Heilbron, and Robin E. Rider eds, *The Quantifying Spirit in the Eighteenth Century* (Berkeley, 1990) and David N. Livingstone and Charles W.J. Withers eds, *Geography and Enlightenment* (Chicago, 1999).

11 Thomas Bassett produced London editions of *A Catalogue of the Common and Statute Law-Books of this Realm, with Some Others Relating Thereunto, Alphabetically Digested under Proper Heads* in 1671, 1680 (although dated 1682 on the titlepage, the Wing catalogue dates this as 1680) and 1694; further editions were produced by John Walthoe in 1714, 1715, 1722, 1725, 1731. Bassett's first edition did not include the heading 'trial' but after the addition of this topic in 1680 the headings remain constant through all subsequent editions. Bassett also produced a broadside of *An Exact Catalogue of the Common and Statute Law Books of this Realm, and Some Others Relating Thereunto* in 1673 and 1684; in the broadside the titles were simply listed alphabetically, with indications of whether

of customers, Bassett claimed, who 'hath demanded of me [an account] of all the Law-Books Extant,' he also advertised that this catalogue would be useful to those who '... living remote from London, are by Specious Titles trepann'd into the buying of some Law-Books, before they are assured whether (in truth) the Discourse tends, which how frequently it happens Experience sufficiently convinces'.[12] Bassett's claims provide some insight into reader expectations and practices, and some evidence that this legal literature circulated widely at a time when there were growing divisions between legal practitioners in London and in the provinces.[13] Although he acknowledged that his methods and titles might displease some customers, the fact that these titles persisted for decades is an indication that Bassett's categorisation of the legal literature was comprehensible and broadly acceptable. But just how was it comprehensible? What kinds of judgments about these texts, and uses for this knowledge, were conveyed by these lists? What kinds of books did the reader of law (if not 'trepann'd') think he was getting? Here an ongoing tradition of advice literature for law students provided assistance, enabling students and also practitioners to discern which books would, in fact, be most helpful.

Introductions to the practical literature, such as Jacob's introduction to his *Student's Companion*, or Matthew Hale's preface to Henry Rolle's *Un Abridgment des Plusiers Cases et Resolutions del Common Ley* (1668), was one form this advice took; published discourses and letters on legal study written by eminent lawyers and judges such as Roger North and Thomas Reeve was another.[14] These were short guides on what, when, and how to read the law

they were written in law French, Latin or English. It is interesting to compare the categories offered by the nineteenth-century American legal publisher, John Livingston, in his *Catalogue of Law Books, Comprising a Catalogue of a Select Law Library* discussed in Michael H. Hoeflich, 'Legal History and the History of the Book: Variations on a Theme', *Kansas Law Review*, 46, 3 (April, 1998), 428.

12 Bassett, *Catalogue* (London, 1694), A3v, A4v. And cf Ibbetson, 'Legal Printing and Doctrine', 346 on the importance of this growing legal literature for provincial lawyers, and for the standardisation of law.

13 C.W. Brooks, 'The Decline and Rise of the Legal Profession', in C.W. Brooks ed., *Lawyers, Litigation and English Society since 1450* (London, 1998), 133.

14 'Lord Chief Justice Reeve to his Nephew', in Francis Hargrave ed., *Collecteana Juridica: Consisting of Tracts Relative to the Law and Constitution of England*, vol. 1 (London, 1791; reprint Littleton, CO, 1980), 79–81; Roger North, *A Discourse on the Study of the Laws* (London, 1824). Reeve wrote in the 1730s, North probably composed his text in the late seventeenth or early years of the eighteenth century but it was not published until the nineteenth century. Other advice literature I have consulted includes William Phillips, *Studii Legalis Ratio, Or Directions for the Study of the Law Under these Heads* (London, 1662; 3rd edn, 1675); William Fulbecke, *Direction or Preparative to the Study of the Law* (London, 1600); John Dodderidge, *The Lawyers Light: Or Due Direction for the Study of the Law* (1629); Thomas Wood, *Some Thoughts Concerning the Study of Law, Particularly in the Two Universities*, 2nd edn (London, 1727); Nathaniel Cole, 'Prescription for Educating a Barrister', 14 August, 1736 (copy), reprinted in Lemmings, *Professors of the Law*, 341–5.

for students whose training, by the eighteenth century, consisted of individual apprenticeship rather than institutionalised and communal study at the Inns of Court.[15] Most of these guides distinguished between broad categories of texts. The Year Books and Reports, and 'classics' such as the works of Bracton, Fleta, Britton and Glanville, formed two distinct categories. Most authors also distinguished between introductory and more advanced texts, and some also divided the texts by subject matter or approach. So, for example, both Reeve and Jacob insisted that the student should begin with some texts that will provide 'a tolerable Knowledge of the Grounds of the Law',[16] and both pointed to dictionaries such as William Rastell's *Terms de la Ley*, as well as topically-organised texts such as Thomas Wood's *Institute of the Laws of England* or discursive texts like Christopher St German's *Doctor and Student*.[17] Both men organised books into distinct categories such as conveyancing and criminal law to aid understanding.

Overall, a number of essential texts were repeatedly recommended by this advice literature, with some variations and additions over time, but these same texts were not always categorised in the same way. Certainly texts were paired as complementary and, quite often, cycles of reading were proposed to guide the student from broader to more specialised law books, and then back again.[18] But texts could be seen as fitting more than one category and, even more, as having multiple uses.[19] The broad usefulness of common law texts was particularly emphasised by Thomas Wood, author of *Some Thoughts Concerning the Study of the Laws of England* (1708) and *A New Institute of the Imperial or Civil Law* (1704) as well as *An Institute of the Laws of England* (1720). Wood advocated greater intercourse between civil and common law learning, and advised young clerics of the special value of studying common law texts on estates, inheritance and conveyancing – two of these areas of overlapping jurisdiction, and potential conflict, between the ecclesiastical and common law courts.[20]

15 On self-education and reading practices see Lemmings, *Gentlemen and Barristers*, 98–109; Lemmings, 'Blackstone and Law Reform', 240–3; Lemmings, *Professors of the Law*, 107–48; Holdsworth, *History of English Law*, vol. 6, 493–9; C.W. Brooks, 'Apprenticeship and Legal Training in England, 1700–1850', in Brooks, *Lawyers, Litigation and English Society since 1450*, 149–78.

16 Giles Jacob, *Student's Companion*, iv. The first edition of 1725 did not include an introduction.

17 'Reeve to his Nephew', 79–80. Note both Reeve and Jacob remark that Wood's advice is flawed because of his omission of references to recent reports; and compare Cole who has the law student begin with Hale, Fortescue, St German and Terms de la Ley.

18 'Reeve to his Nephew', 80–1; Jacob, 'Introduction' to *Student's Companion*, iv–vii.

19 On categorisation see Lemmings, *Professors of the Law*, 136–7; Lemmings, 'Blackstone and Law Reform', 241; cf Lemmings, *Gentlemen and Barristers*, 101–2.

20 Wood, *Some Thoughts Concerning Study of Laws*, 14–15. Note that Wood recommends the abridgments of Brooke, Fitzherbert, Hughes and Sheppard. Compare also the preface to his *New Institute of Imperial or Civil Law* and see my discussion below, chapter 5.

Finally, much of the advice literature insisted that the student must read the original texts written by important authors like Coke, but abridgments of these texts as well as of writs, pleading, cases, statutes and many other areas of the law, were also acknowledged and recommended. Roger North, an exception here, sternly advised 'that a student must have a care of dealing in abridgments, indexes and common places, all of which are his enemies'.[21] But most agreed with Hale's sage judgment that such books were 'published for the help and benefit of students, not to abate their industry',[22] and that a book like Rolle's *Abridgment* was a current necessity: 'Whereas at this day the books of the law are grown very many and very large, so that many will not have the patience to read them all, the student will in this book [abridgment] have a considerable abstract and collection of most that is material in them.'[23] Hale's advocacy of the abridgment as a solution to the problem of 'information overload' was fairly typical. As Ann Blair has pointed out, a 'perception of an overabundance of books fueled the production of many more books, often especially large ones, designed to remedy the problem', and the recognition of the usefulness of these compilations and reference books was increasingly widespread in the early modern period.[24]

The publication of law books had, indeed expanded in the mid-seventeenth century, growing 'very many and very large' as an unsurprising consequence of the disruptions suffered by the Inns of Court, and of the movements toward law reform, in the 1640s and 1650s.[25] Moreover, this expansion built upon an already significant increase in the publication of law books which coincided with the advent of printing and accelerated from the 1590s on.[26] There are many examples of abridgments, tables, dictionaries,

21 North, *Discourse on Study of Laws*, 19, here referring by name to abridgments of Fitzherbert and Brooke; repetition of caution, with other texts named, 23.

22 Matthew Hale, 'Lord Hale's Preface to Rolle's Abridgment', in Hargrave ed., *Collecteana Juridica*, vol. 1, 280.

23 Hale, 'Preface to Rolle', 279.

24 Blair, 'Reading Strategies for Information Overload', 12, 22–3.

25 J.H. Baker, 'Readings in Gray's Inn, their Decline and Disappearance', in J.H. Baker, *The Legal Profession and the Common Law, Historical Essays*, (London, 1986), 35–7; Alan Cromartie, 'The Rule of Law', in John Morrill ed., *Revolution and Restoration* (London, 1992), 55–69; Wilfred Prest, *The Inns of Court under Elizabeth I and the Early Stuarts, 1590–1640* (Totowa, NJ, 1972); Prest, 'Law Reform and Legal Education in Interregnum England', *Bulletin of the Institute of Historical Research*, 75, 187 (February, 2002): 112–22; N.L. Matthews, *William Sheppard: Cromwell's Law Reformer* (Cambridge, 1984).

26 Simpson, 'Rise and Fall of Treatise', 636, 639; Ibbetson, 'Legal Printing', 345–6; Richard J. Ross, 'The Commoning of the Common Law: The Renaissance Debate over Printing English Law, 1520–1640', *University of Pennsylvania Law Review*, 146, 2 (January, 1998): 323–461. John Baker especially emphasises the importance of this advent of printing in marking a shift toward citation of authority in legal understanding: Baker, *Law's Two Bodies*, 10–11. One of the more influential of the new printed texts was William West's *Symboleography, Which May be Termed the Art, Description or Image of Instruments...Or the Paterne of Praesidents* (London, 1592). A similar proliferation of

collections of cases and statutes, works on conveyancing, or on pleading and practice that were first published in the seventeenth century and used and valued well into the eighteenth century. The authors and compilers of the eighteenth-century practical legal literature self-consciously relied upon and continued the work of earlier abridgments; they continued the tradition initiated by the fifteenth and sixteenth-century compilers Nicholas Statham and Anthony Fitzherbert, and perpetuated by later contributors like William West, Edmund Wingate, and William Style.[27]

The volume of law publications showed no sign of diminishing but rather continued, and showed further dramatic growth especially towards the end of the eighteenth century. These long-term trends in legal publishing were in keeping with wider advances in production, and the expansion in the number of presses operating in this period.[28] Such growth was also in keeping with changes in legal training, and the final demise of the Inns as educational institutions, as well as with continued efforts at law reform in the early eighteenth century. Proposals were debated and legislation enacted, for example, requiring the professional registration of attorneys and solicitors, regulating the expense of litigation, and ensuring that courtroom proceedings were conducted in English rather than law French and Latin. [29] These

medical literature took place in this period. See Mary Fissell and Roger Cooter, 'Exploring Natural Knowledge: Science and the Popular', in Roy Porter ed., *The Cambridge History of Science, Volume 4: Eighteenth-Century Science* (Cambridge, 2003), 129–58; Mary Fissell, *Vernacular Bodies: The Politics of Reproduction in Early Modern England* (Oxford, 2005); Adrian Johns, 'Science and the Book', in John Barnard, D.F. McKenzie and Maureen Bell eds, *The Cambridge History of the Book in Britain, Volume 4, 1557–1695* (Cambridge, 2002), 274–303; Johns, 'Print and Public Science', in Roy Porter ed., *The Cambridge History of Science, Volume 4: Eighteenth-Century Science* (Cambridge, 2003), 536–60.

27 Anthony Fitzherbert, *La Graunde Abridgment*, 3 vols (London, 1514–16?); Nicholas Statham, *Abridgment* (Rouen, 1488?); William Style, *Regestum Practicale: Or the Practical Register, Consisting of Rules, Orders and Obligations Concerning the Common Laws and the Practice thereof* (London, 1657); Edmund Wingate, *An Exact Abridgment of all the Statutes* (London, 1642). John D. Cowley, *A Bibliography of Abridgments, Digests, Dictionaries and Indexes of English Law to the Year 1800* (London, 1932), xxxv–lxix.

28 Lobban, 'English Legal Treatise and English Law'. On timing, and growth more generally, see James Raven, 'The Book Trades', in Isabel Rivers ed., *Books and their Readers in Eighteenth-Century England: New Essays* (London, 2001), 1–34; Sher, *Enlightenment and the Book*; M.F. Suarez, 'The Business of Literature: The Book Trade in England from Milton to Blake', in David Womersley ed., *A Companion to Literature from Milton to Blake* (Cambridge, 2000), 131–50; John Brewer *The Pleasures of the Imagination: English Culture in the Eighteenth Century* (New York, 1997), chs 3–4; Adrian Johns *The Nature of the Book: Print and Knowledge in the Making* (Chicago, 1998), 72–3; Philip Hamburger, 'The Development of the Law of Seditious Libel and the Control of the Press', *Stanford Law Review*, 37, 3 (February, 1985): 661–765.

29 On the law reform literature and commissions see Barbara Shapiro, 'Law Reform in Seventeenth-Century England', *The American Journal of Legal History*, 19, 4 (October, 1975): 289–311; Prest, 'Law Reform in Eighteenth-Century England', 113–23; Horwitz, 'Changes in Law and Reform', 301–24.

changes, too, contributed to the expansion, and influenced the content, of legal publishing in the period.

Yet many scholars have interpreted such expansion as a simple sign of trouble in legal education and in the legal profession. This literature is said to indicate the prevalent incoherence and confusion about the common law, even among practitioners. Or the literature is itself pinpointed as one of the *causes* of the decline of the Inns and formal legal education, contributing, in turn, to a general decline of the legal profession, a decline in reputation and in litigation of the late seventeenth and early eighteenth centuries.[30] Clearly the long-running debate about the 'backwardness' of the common law has shaped the questions scholars pose. Moreover, when scholars assume that the expansion in legal writing and publishing is somehow indicative of decline, they tend to endorse contemporary critiques of this literature without an appreciation for the professional and politico-economic agendas informing those critiques. Citing a 1734 text on bankruptcy law, for example, David Lemmings perpetuates the focus on crisis and decline, and the denigration of this literature. 'Educated laymen who were touched by the spirit of Enlightenment rationalism,' Lemmings claims, 'rejected the traditional legal learning of "*Ridiculous Common-Places*, or rather *Cobler Method*"' for its emphasis on precedents and procedure to the exclusion of principle and social utility; a failing which rendered legal culture backward and ungentlemanly in an age of politeness and progress.'[31] Here Lemmings reproduces a single part of an eighteenth-century debate over changes in commercial law, and replicates that definition of Enlightenment which privileges the rationalist and utilitarian, excluding other modes of Enlightenment that are more relevant to the analysis of this legal literature.[32]

If we want to understand the development of common law thinking and learning, and how that relates to the attribution of authority to the common law – and thus the complex *process* of eighteenth-century law reform – we must take this practical literature more seriously and with less emphasis on failure. Through a discussion of legal education and commonplace practices, followed by analysis of the legal literature and its uses, this chapter will elucidate the ways in which English lawyers engaged with the growth in print. It will further consider the kinds of common assumptions, or common

30 Lemmings, *Gentlemen and Barristers*, 98; Prest, 'Law Reform and Legal Education', 117.

31 Lemmings, *Professors of the Law*, 108.

32 Contemporary debate about bankruptcy was also bound up with discussions about the power of Chancery and comparisons between the common law and equitable jurisdictions. See, for example, W.J. Jones, 'The Foundations of English Bankruptcy: Statutes and Commissions in the Early Modern Period', *Transactions of the American Philosophical Society*, 69, 3 (1979): 1–63; Ann Carlos, 'Bankruptcy and Creditors' Rights in Early Modern England', Working Paper, September 2009, http://www.econ.yale.edu/seminars/echist/eh09/carlos-091026.pdf.

learning, generated in the course of this engagement.[33] Texts like *The Young Lawyers Recreation*, *The Impartial Lawyer*, William Nelson's *Abridgment of the Common Law*, Knightley D'Anvers' *General Abridgment of the Common Law*, Matthew Bacon's *New Abridgment of the Common Law*, Robert Gardiner's *Instructor Clericalis* and Giles Jacob's *Law Dictionary* have been chosen to represent the broad categories of abridgment, pleading and process, and dictionary from among the wide number of printed law books of the period. Texts from other categories, like crown or criminal law, special branches of the law like contract or baron and feme, and works of legal history are discussed in other chapters. Works on ecclesiastical law have generally been regarded as outside of the scope of this study.[34] Throughout, attention will be paid to ideas about custom, pleading and precedent in the texts under consideration, and the ways in which commonplace and rhetorical traditions, book culture and commerce, and new attitudes towards the organisation of knowledge all influenced the development of these ideas.

Among the texts and authors included, a particular emphasis will be given to the work of Giles Jacob, author of the enormously influential eighteenth-century *Law Dictionary* and 'the most prolific author of self-help legal manuals'.[35] Jacob makes for an interesting and important example because of his impressive output of legal texts, and because both law and literature form the obvious contexts for understanding his work. The number and types of texts that Jacob produced – within varied genres and formats, often reproducing and collecting other texts – encourage us to think about what scholars have termed 'author function', and the intentions and constraints on an author and text.[36] The range of Jacob's commitments also encourages an openness in defining multiple Enlightenments, as well as an awareness of the place of legal literature in relation to some other genres of English writing.

Legal writing was Jacob's primary occupation and contribution, but poetry, satire and literary biography were also a large part of his published work, and he became embroiled in literary controversy concerning the reputations of

33 Here I am building upon Baker's important insights into the persistence of 'a world of law outside the books', and his suggestions about new approaches to sources outside of the case reports. Baker, *Law's Two Bodies*, 87.

34 I have also decided, mostly in the interest of space, not to include discussion of texts on local administration (manuals for sheriffs, JPs, coroners etc.).

35 Lemmings, *Professors of the Law*, 67 n.18; Gary L McDowell, 'The Politics of Meaning: Law Dictionaries and the Liberal Tradition of Interpretation', *The American Journal of Legal History*, 44, 3 (July, 2000): 257–83; Matthew Kilburn, 'Jacob, Giles', *ODNB*. Note that Reeve's advice letter recommends two of Jacob's texts, the *Attorney's Companion* and the *Law Dictionary* (although Reeve cautions that 'the authority of this latter must not be too implicitly relied upon') 'Reeve to his Nephew', 79.

36 Chartier, *Order of Books*, 28–9.

John Gay and Alexander Pope.[37] Pope attacked Jacob for his authorship of the *Poetical Register*, and immortalised Jacob in *The Dunciad* as 'the Scourge of Grammar' and the 'Blunderbuss of Law' – thus ensuring Jacob's place as the symbol of the incivility of the eighteenth-century common law. Recognising this literary aspect of the debate over the inaccessibility and pedantry of the common law will allow us to reassess Giles Jacob's contributions to legal literature, and will also help to heighten our awareness of the diverse enlightened contexts within which this legal literature developed.

Legal education and commonplace traditions

With the decline of the Inns of Court in the late seventeenth and early eighteenth centuries, self-education and apprenticeship became increasingly important. The challenges of this kind of autonomous legal training were often acknowledged. One of the most difficult, and important, tasks was said to be the compilation of a legal commonplace book. The frustrations and missteps, and the high stakes involved, were frequently noted by contemporaries. The eminent judge and jurist Matthew Hale, for example, not only offered students recommendations of what to read, but also advice on *how* to read, outlining reliable methods of note-taking:

> What he reads in the course of his reading, let him enter the abstract or substance thereof, especially of cases or points resolved, into his common-place book, under their proper titles; and if one case falls aptly under several titles, and it can be conveniently broken, let him enter each part under its proper title: if it cannot be well broken, let him enter the abstract of the entire case under the title most proper for it, and make references from the other titles unto it.[38]

Hale acknowledged that, given the student's inexperience, this method was flawed and the 'student will waste much paper this way, and possibly in two or three years will see many errors and impertinences in what he hath formerly done, and much irregularity and disorder in the disposing of his matter under improper heads'. Yet Hale insisted that if such a method of reading and commonplacing was not followed, the student would likely forget almost all of what he read and studied. Indeed the mistakes and irregularities produced by the student could be of benefit to him, Hale added optimistically; the very necessity of frequently returning to and puzzling out

37 J. McLaverty, 'Pope and Giles Jacob's *Lives of the Poets*: The *Dunciad* as Alternative Literary History', *Modern Philology*, 83, 1 (August, 1985): 22–32; Pat Rogers, *Grub Street: Studies in a Subculture* (London, 1972), 288–9; 'Jacob', *ODNB*. The couplet in Pope's *Dunciad* is: 'Jacob, the Scourge of Grammar, mark with awe,/ Nor less revere him, Blunderbuss of Law.'

38 Hale, 'Preface to Rolle', 277.

'those first imperfect and disordered essays' would help to refresh and refine the memory of what he has read.[39]

Roger North, a noted scholar and member of a prominent legal family, offered even more practical advice to the law student. He too discussed the mechanics of reading and note-taking, and gave similar reassurance that initial failure is necessary in order to achieve ultimate success. One can only learn to commonplace by doing it, North says encouragingly, and there are aids one can use. While Hale recommended that the student might copy the alphabetical headings employed in books like Brooke's or Rolle's abridgments, North pointed out that printed sets of titles for commonplacing were readily available; or, if the student was fortunate enough, he could follow the titles used and passed down by a trusted friend or an experienced practitioner.[40] Thus armed with titles, and a 'good large paper book, as big (with some) as a church bible', the student should write in columns, using 'a small but legible and distinct hand, which in a common place book must be affected, for room will be required, and a fair French hand will eat upon it too fast'.[41] Each entry, North added, should conclude with a reference to the text, including title and folio number, from which it is derived.

This emphasis on detail and diligence is also notable in Giles Jacob's instructions for compiling that large commonplace book introduced at the beginning of this chapter. Jacob exhorted the student to employ both reflection and immediacy in reading and recording notes for his commonplace book:

> After a Treatise is fully read over, ask your self the Question, *What Knowledge you have gained thereby?* Do this immediately, and the Answer conceived in your Mind, instantly pen down under Heads, just as the subject Matter presents it self to you, and afterwards more methodically, on comparing the same with the Book, and referring to the Pages where it is to be found, in the Way of Alphabet; (and if the Treatise be large, and your Memory treacherous, it will be necessary to make Remarks as you proceed, or at the End of every Chapter). Then peruse these heads often, and when you have gone through all the Books, reduce the several Alphabets in a general *Common Place-Book*, without which no Man can be a thorough Lawyer.[42]

Jacob here also, obliquely, acknowledged the likely mistakes the student will make, and proposed this two-step method of note-taking as a remedy. The

39 Ibid., 277–8.

40 Hale, 'Preface to Rolle', 277; North, *Discourse on Study of Laws*, 26. And recall, of course, that Roger North benefited from the advice and help of his older brother Lord Keeper Francis North. Roger North, *Notes of Me: The Autobiography of Roger North*, Peter Millard ed. (Toronto, 2000), 160–1.

41 North, *Discourse on Study of Laws*, 27.

42 Jacob, introduction to *Student's Companion*, vi-vii.

study of law is not for the weak or faint of heart, Jacob has already warned, and in undertaking this course of reading and note-taking 'it is necessary that [the student] should pursue his Study with as great Diligence as his Strength of Constitution will permit.' Introducing the theme of manliness and potency, Jacob claimed that some men (including himself) could 'read through a thin Folio in a Day', but for most men this is too taxing – 'too Violent for Body and Mind' – and it would lead to confusion rather than education. The best course to follow is rather one of steady application, careful reading and copious note-taking. Each of these advisors emphasised the material context of reading, and recognised the impact of the page and its labours on the meaning derived from the text.

These authors' insistence upon rigorous work and persistence echoed a common earlier humanist refrain about the labours of scholarship.[43] They self-consciously took part in a longer tradition of advice about commonplacing and scholarly techniques which informed the evolution of legal commonplace books. The commonplace book first fully emerged in Renaissance Europe, developing from earlier ancient and medieval precedents. And since it flourished in conjunction with the advent of printing it is not surprising that the commonplace book significantly influenced the early modern student's 'receptivity as a reader of texts'. 'The invention of printing may not have fundamentally altered the technology of the commonplace book in terms of its storage, cross-referencing, and retrieval mechanisms,' Ann Moss has argued, 'but it did mean that texts of the approved authors were much more easily available....the Renaissance schoolboy was constantly using his common-place book as an interpretive grid for texts he was reading himself.'[44] This kind of 'interpretive grid' was most vital to the student of law whose commonplace book was meant to function as a mode of reading and remembering as well as a repository of arguments and precedents.

There was also that ongoing tradition of advice and instruction on commonplacing which clearly influenced the advice to law students offered by Hale and his predecessors and successors. Scholars and reformers like Erasmus, Vives and Melanchthon provided detailed guidance as to the

43 Blair, 'Reading Strategies for Information Overload', 16.

44 Ann Moss, *Printed Commonplace Books and the Structuring of Renaissance Thought* (Oxford, 1996), 136; and see chs 1–3 on ancient and medieval 'prehistory' and 'progenitors'. Cf Ian Williams on the significance of legal manuscript circulation even given the 'emerging preference for print' that he describes: Ian Williams, '"He Credited More the Printed Booke": Common Lawyers' Receptivity to Print, 1550–1640', *Law and History Review*, 28, 1 (February, 2010), 45. David Allan's *Commonplace Books and Reading in Georgian England* (Cambridge, 2010) is a valuable new work on the commonplace tradition in England. While I encountered Allan's book after completing the research and writing of this chapter, much of his work confirms my own findings.

organisation and content of these notebooks.[45] Erasmian *copia* were taught and extended in printed commonplace books throughout the sixteenth century, and these humanist educational reforms influenced English and Continental lawyers as much as they affected theologians and students of the arts.[46] Methods of commonplacing were also articulated in the seventeenth century by major figures, such as Charles Sorel and John Locke, who contributed to debates over commonplace techniques and the authority of quotation. The emphasis on the function of the commonplace book as a repository or home-made reference book, even more than its function as an aid to memorisation, was clear in Locke's *New Method of Making Common-Place Books*. Locke's elaborate advice provided technical solutions to the problems of ordering and space noted by Hale and North. A system of alphabetical indexing in folded columns by letter and succeeding vowel was proposed by Locke as the most precise way to organise headings and entries; and he too insisted that each entry must conclude with complete references to author, title and page number, as well as to size, total number of pages, place and date of the edition of the text used.[47]

Did English lawyers follow all this advice in creating their commonplace books? Not surprisingly, they are inconsistent: while some legal commonplace books are rigorously alphabetical and indexed at beginning and end, others proceed non-alphabetically, sometimes with multiple headings on a single page, and provide no index or table to guide the user.[48] Poorly used, or blank and unused examples of commonplace books are not unique to

45 Moss, *Printed Commonplace Books*, chs 5–7; Ann Blair, 'Humanist Methods in Natural Philosophy: The Commonplace Book', *Journal of the History of Ideas*, 53, 4 (October–December, 1992): 541–2.

46 Moss, *Printed Commonplace Books*, 186–91; Richard Ross, 'The Memorial Culture of Early Modern English Lawyers: Memory as Keyword, Shelter and Identity, 1560–1640', *Yale Journal Of Law and the Humanities*, 10 (Summer, 1998): 270–80.

47 John Locke, *A New Method of A Common-Place Book*, in *The Posthumous Works of John Locke* (London, 1706), 316–24; published first in French as 'Nouvelle methode de dresser des recueils' in Le Clerc's *Bibliotheque Universelle et Historique* (Amsterdam, 1686). Michael H. Hoeflich, 'The Lawyer as Pragmatic Reader: The History of Legal Common-Placing', *Arkansas Law Review*, 55 (2002): 97; Moss, *Printed Commonplace Books*, 278–9; Blair, 'Reading Strategies for Information Overload', 21; G.G. Meynell, 'John Locke's Method of Common-placing, as Seen in his Drafts and his Medical Notebooks, Bodleian MSS Locke D.9, f.21 and f.23', *Seventeenth Century*, 8 (1993): 245–67.

48 Two examples of non-alphabetical commonplace books are FLP, Carson LC 14.65 and LC 14.98. Other related examples include John Strange's commonplace book and collection of Chancery cases, FLP, Carson LC 14.86. According to a note on the front boards, Strange or a later owner prepared a 'Table of Matter Containd in this book in a Quarto book Intitled Table to Manuscripts' but this has been lost. Finally, like many others, Sydenham Fowke's commonplace book, DLL, Singleton 37, does include an index but its indication of page numbers does not match up with the body of the commonplace. An example of a relentlessly alphabetical and organised commonplace is Roger North's Law Commonplace, BL, Hargrave 319.

law and may have been becoming increasingly common in the later seventeenth century, an indication for Ann Moss of their declining usefulness and centrality. Moss adheres to the traditional story of the rise of science and empirical reasoning, and her history of the commonplace book is one of decline, in which the commonplace book was 'doomed to atrophy' when it was superseded by new rational and scientific modes of thought and learning.[49] Yet other scholars, like Ann Blair, have demonstrated that the commonplace method was instrumental not only to the survival of natural philosophy but also to the development of modern science, evident, for example in Francis Bacon's arguments for the collection and systematic sorting of material in his new scientific method. This kind of 'sophisticated' commonplacing could function as an important tool of critical reasoning, bringing 'material together in new ways, highlighting contradictions and interconnections and potentially yielding new insights'.[50] Bacon's arguments, Locke's commonplace practices, the publication of Locke's *New Method* in the early eighteenth century as well as an improved version of his method later in the century,[51] and the persistence of legal commonplace books, would all seem to indicate that the commonplace book was, as Moss admits, still deeply ingrained in European scholarly practices. Even more, these are indications that the commonplace book continued to be an important learning tool and an influential method for dealing with the profusion of print and knowledge. Indeed, like the encyclopedia, the commonplace book was increasingly viewed as a reference work and part of a system of information retrieval.[52]

Legal commonplace books are, then, a key to understanding that proliferation of legal texts for three essential reasons. First, printed law books and manuscript law commonplace books demonstrate reciprocal influences in their layout, methods, and content. The development of early modern commonplace techniques and, more broadly, humanist educational reforms, helped to shape the abridgment tradition. In turn, the growth of this tradition, coupled with the dramatic growth of print, influenced the ways in which commonplace practices endured into the eighteenth and nineteenth centuries. Second, considering the intersections here between manuscript

49 Moss, *Printed Commonplace Books*, 275–6.

50 Ann Blair, 'Annotating and Indexing Natural Philosophy', in Marina Frasca-Spada and Nick Jardine eds, *Books and the Sciences in History* (Cambridge, 2000), 73. See also Blair on 'cognitive dissonance' of natural philosophy, and compare this to what is called the 'incoherence' of common law, Blair, 'Humanist Methods in Natural Philosophy', 547–8, 550–1; and cf also Blair, *The Theater of Nature: Jean Bodin and Renaissance Science* (Princeton, 1997).

51 *A New Commonplace Book being an Improvement on that Recommended by Mr Locke*, 2nd edn (London, 1799). One example of the use of the first edition (undated) of this pre-printed commonplace book is FSL, M.a. 184.

52 Moss, *Printed Commonplace Books*, 277; Hoeflich, 'Lawyer Pragmatic Reader', 108; Blair, 'Reading Strategies for Information Overload', 28.

and print is vital to understanding the men who participated in the creation of all these books. Communities of readers, of law students and legal practitioners, become visible in their handwritten notes and in their silent impact on authors and publishers. Uses of these printed and manuscript texts over time also provide evidence of the lawyer's life span, from novice to advocate, and the common ground shared by ordinary attorneys, established solicitors and eminent barristers and judges. These texts further reveal the formation of intergenerational legal communities, appearing to us as traces of multiple owners in the margins and multiple hands of these printed and manuscript books.

Finally, recognition of a commonplace context can shed light on the persistence and peculiarities of legal thinking. If, as Michael Hoeflich has argued, there is a particular style of 'legal reading' which is purposive and 'rule-seeking', it is also true that the abridgments and commonplace books played a part in the evolution of methods of 'textual accessibility' that made this style of reading possible.[53] Moreover, because of the impact they had on the ways in which lawyers defined and accessed information, the abridgments and commonplace books helped to shape early modern conceptions of legal authority as precedential and prescriptive.

A survey of legal commonplace books composed between the mid-sixteenth and early nineteenth centuries provides evidence of these legal reading practices and of this legal thinking. Texts consulted include the manuscripts of prominent legal figures, like John Strange (d.1754), solicitor general under Walpole and member of the Privy Council and master of the rolls under Lord Chancellor Hardwicke[54]; Roger North (d.1734), author not only of educational advice but also noted biographer and scholar of music, architecture and mathematics, a prominent Tory and nonjuror and younger brother of Lord Keeper Francis North[55]; William Style (d.1679) author of two seminal publications, the *Modern Reports*, and *Style's Practical Register*, which was an abridgment of common law practice 'alphabetically digested under several titles' frequently reprinted in the seventeenth and eighteenth centuries[56]; and William Jones (d.1794), Welsh barrister, scholar of Arabic and Persian languages and of comparative law, and judge on the Bengal

[53] Hoeflich, 'Lawyer Pragmatic Reader', 88–92. Ian Williams, 'Common Lawyers' Receptivity to Print', following Baker, *Law's Two Bodies*, makes a convincing case for the increasing 'credit' attached to print beginning in the sixteenth century. My interest here is in the ways in which manuscript and encyclopedic practices shaped the recourse to print, and the growth of books as common learning.

[54] FLP, Carson LC 14.86. J.H. Baker, *English Legal Manuscripts in the USA Part II: 1558–1902* (London, 1990), 320; A.A. Hanham, 'Strange, John', *ODNB*.

[55] BL, Hargrave 319. Mary Chan, 'North, Roger', *ODNB*; F.J.M. Korsten, *Roger North (1651–1734): Virtuoso and Essayist* (Amsterdam, 1981); North, *Notes of Me*.

[56] HLS, 1144. Baker, *English Legal Manuscripts*, 147; Baker, 'Style, William' *ODNB*; Baker, 'Style, William', in A.W.B. Simpson ed., *Biographical Dictionary of the Common Law* (London, 1984), 495.

supreme court.[57] Some of the most interesting examples come from the later seventeenth and eighteenth centuries and include not only these notes written by exceptional men but also the manuscripts of ordinary and sometimes anonymous students and counsellors, conveyed in carefully transcribed presentation copies as well as in hastily scrawled and incomplete notebooks. Many of these commonplace books were produced while the compiler was a student, but there is evidence that the books continued to be used, and that further composition took place, over the course of a lawyer's career. These books were also passed down as prized possessions to multiple generations of lawyers, and stand as another testament to the importance of continuity and tradition in English legal learning.[58]

Each individual example bears its own character since, as the eighteenth-century compiler Matthew Bacon reminds us, 'Men having such different Modes of Thinking, … in Strictness, hardly any Two can be said to Common-place alike.'[59] And yet there are important similarities among these texts. First, the way in which information is laid out on the page tends to be broadly recognisable. Citation of the source for the material entered usually appears in the margins, or at the end of the sentence or paragraph. Although these citations are nowhere near as complete as Roger North and John Locke recommend, they do almost always include author and page number. Information is presented in short paragraphs or, sometimes, in enumerated points under heads or titles.[60] These heads often appear at the top or in the left margin of the page. However, for as many examples of commonplace books with distinct and beautiful titles written carefully across the top of the page, there are an equal number with simply a letter of the alphabet noted somewhere on the page or with headings that are

[57] FLP, Carson LC 14.79. Baker, *English Legal Manuscripts*, 318; see also C. W. Brooks, 'Jones, William', *ODNB*. Note also some other prominent examples I have consulted, such as the Sydenham Fowke manuscripts at DLL, or the manuscripts owned by Thomas Parker, chief baron of the Exchequer, at HLS. Since M.H. Hoeflich has focused on nineteenth-century examples, and Richard Ross on sixteenth and seventeenth-century examples, all of these manuscripts have been overlooked.

[58] The Inner Temple barrister Herbert Jacob (d.1725), for example, had his clerks transcribe his student notebook of case reports so that he could pass it on to his nephew. And Jacob conveyed his sense of a wider potential audience for his manuscript in a telling aside: 'I hope the candid reader will pardon any mistake he meets with and will consider that I was but of two years standing at the Temple when I began to write these reports for my own private use;' Jacob explained, 'wch I would have burnt but for the sake of my nephew to whom I thought they might possibly be of some use, there being many things in them wch seem to give some light into the Reason of the Law.' FLP, Carson LC 14.66, fol. 22.

[59] Matthew Bacon, A *General Abridgment of Cases in Equity, Argued and Adjudged in the High Court of Chancery*, 2nd edn (London, 1734), preface.

[60] Two good examples of commonplace books with numbered points: FLP, Carson LC 14.86 (numbered within each topic), and IT, Barrington 68 (continuous numbering from one entry to the next).

indistinguishable from the notes themselves, and hard to find. Frequently there are cross-references made from one entry to another related topic within the manuscript.[61] These cross-references appear within the body of the manuscript and in the indices to these commonplace books that are often included at the front or back of the volume.[62] Such indices or tables of heads may have been prepared by the initial compiler of the commonplace book, or added by later owners of these books (just as readers sometimes added their own indices to printed books).[63] In most commonplace books the handwriting of an initial or main compiler can be distinguished from the handwriting of other users who added headings, entries, citations or indices over time.

Headings appear alphabetically in the indices but the manuscripts themselves could be organised either alphabetically or thematically, with related topics clustered together. Among those that are alphabetical the title parameters typically range from an initial topic of 'acceptance' or 'annuitie' to a final entry on 'warrantie', or from 'abjuration' to 'woode', or from 'administration' to 'will'. Among the 1730s examples many commonplacers begin with 'abatement' and end variously with 'writs', 'wreck' or 'words'. This tendency may be due to the increasing influence of printed abridgments, when law students became more reliant on the work of D'Anvers and Nelson, or even the earlier abridgments of Hughes and Sheppard, which opened with abatement as their first term. Thematic or topical organisation was also an established commonplace practice, used not just by lawyers but broadly recommended to allow the compiler to pursue a particular concern.[64] So, for example, the entries in one early eighteenth-century legal commonplace book undertook typical questions about inheritance of property by proceeding from 'wills' to 'executors' to 'probate' to 'waste' to 'women' to 'infant'.[65] Other legal commonplace books are broadly alphabetical but deviate at times to a clustering of related topics before returning to the alphabet. Or they are alphabetical but additions are made non-alphabetically,

61 Two examples of lawyers' commonplace books with a good deal of cross-referencing are held in the Singleton Collection at Columbia University Law School: DLL, Singleton 36 and 37.

62 An example of an enormous legal commonplace book – more than 1140 folio pages – at the Folger Shakespeare Library includes a lengthy index that incorporates much cross-referencing between topics; many of the cross-references are added by a later hand. FSL, W.b. 269.

63 For an example of a manuscript that has indices provided by both compiler and later owner see FLP, Carson LC 14.80. Note also the examples of IT, Barrington 60, which includes a table/index to William Scroggs *The Practice of Courts-Leet and Courts-Baron* (1701); IT, Barrington 68, which includes an alphabetical table of abbreviations for works cited within the manuscript; and CUL, Dd. 14.19, which includes a table of books cited in the manuscript. See also Hoeflich, 'Lawyer as Pragmatic Reader', 100.

64 Blair, 'Humanist Methods', 546.

65 FLP, Carson LC 14.98.

and over time, in multiple hands, in the front and back of the commonplace book.[66] Still others are alphabetical or topical but are interrupted at times by the insertion of a case report, legal or financial memoranda, or records of marriages or indenture – indications that these notebooks were used for multiple purposes by men who also attended courtroom arguments and served as law-office apprentices as part of their legal training. For example, William Longueville's commonplace entries are frequently interspersed with other material such as family memoranda, or notes for speeches and cases. John Strange reused his commonplace notebook by reversing and inverting the volume to record Chancery cases and opinions.[67]

These examples provide some evidence for Hoeflich's claim that systems of alphabetical organisation, like Locke's, were not useful for the lawyer since lawyers, both past and present, 'tend to think and reason topically. If a lawyer were presented with a problem involving a sale of a horse,' Hoeflich explains, 'the key concept – or at least the first concept to be researched – is the topic of sale, not of horses.'[68] And yet it is important to remember that many lawyers and law students did regard alphabetical organisation as a method of learning and reasoning, and as a surer means of retrieval for future reasoning. One conceptual solution they proposed was further subdivision, to include topics such as 'horses'. The exemplary Roger North, who followed his own advice carefully and produced a copious and rigorously alphabetical commonplace book, included multiple headings such as 'hawk', 'horse' and 'kyne'.[69] Even more specific and atypical headings, such

66 Examples include: DLL, Singleton 37; DLL, M 73 and C 73; HLS, 1262; FLP, Carson LC 14 .73; CUL, Dd. 14.19.

67 BL, Add MS 50117. Similarly IT, Barrington 63 includes non-alphabetical entries interspersed with some reports of cases in multiple hands; IT, Barrington 68 sees commonplace entries begin only after an index, and initial pages of miscellaneous notes and cases; and IT, Barrington 60 includes a marriage agreement, an indenture and a grant, as well as a commonplace and the index to Scroggs. John Strange's notebook, FLP, Carson LC.14.86, was first used as a commonplace book during Strange's studies at Middle Temple; archivist's notes confirm that the notebook was reversed and used by Strange to record 'opinions of contemporary advocates and judges, and with reports of cases observed by himself in the courts, as well as some immediately before his time, during the years 1704–1724.' John Strange's case notes circulated in manuscript among his contemporaries; a version he prepared for publication was printed posthumously as his *Reports of Adjudged Cases in the Courts of Chancery, Kings Bench, Common Pleas and Exchequer* in 1755, and appeared in subsequent editions in 1782 and 1795. Another example of a compiler who reversed and reused his notebook in order to record both case reports and commonplace notes is FSL, V.a. 426. Finally, all these examples can be compared to another kind of dual text in DLL, Singleton, MS 69, which is a copy of Judge Geoffrey Gilbert's treatise on remainders, followed by a commonplace book. It remains unclear whether this commonplace was made by the person who transcribed the treatise or by a later owner.

68 Hoeflich, 'Lawyer Pragmatic Reader', 99.

69 BL, Hargrave 319. A few examples of other subdivisions here include: 'alehouses',

as 'hermaphrodite', 'form & substance', 'Jew', 'conies and cony burrows', are to be found in the commonplace book of John Strange.[70]

These types of headings tend to be quite variable and manuscript-specific. There are, however, many more conventional law commonplace titles, and it is possible to identify continuity over time in terms of the kinds of topics lawyers addressed. Most lawyers' commonplace books included entries on characteristic property issues (devise, jointenants, lease, executor), trade issues (consideration, merchant, debt, bankruptcy), criminal law (felony, murder, burglary), and legal process (action, barr, demurrer). The persistence of these typical headings reflects the fact that these commonplace books were a principal means of legal education, meant to provide a general foundation for legal study and practice. The persistence of typical headings further indicates the use, by students, of those standardised and printed lists of legal headings for commonplace books, and is another interesting example of the reciprocal relationship between manuscript and print. These 'canonical' lists were vital, Hoeflich avers, in the formation of an 'interpretive community' of legal professionals.[71]

If there were canonical heads, or topics, was there also some standardisation of content achieved by this interpretive community? Here it is even more difficult to generalise, and even more important not to impose a false coherence on these unwieldy volumes written by multiple authors over many years. Current scholarly interest in eighteenth-century criminal law, or long-standing interest in questions about 'common-law reason', might excite speculation about the significance of certain types of entries on theft or treason, for example. But typical property issues regarding inheritance and conveyancing were equally, if not more, characteristic and important; most frequently the lengthiest entries in a commonplace book appeared under the heading 'devise'.[72] Such entries are certainly telling about the general

'badgers', 'bakers', 'beere', 'eggs', 'fish', 'longbow', 'netts', 'tymber'. Compare FSL, W.b. 269, entries on 'dog', 'pigeon', 'conny'.

70 FLP, Carson LC 14.86. Cf also the entry on 'Mahometan' in DLL, Singleton 36. Varied entries in HLS, 4091, include: 'tenures', 'socage', 'homage', 'chivalry', 'burgebote' and 'theftbote', 'bribery', 'brothel house', 'felony by conjuration witchcraft sorcery & enchantment', 'hunting in the night'.

71 Hoeflich, 'Lawyer Pragmatic Reader', 103 relying, as he notes, on Stanley Fish's phrase; cf Ross 'Memorial Culture', 281–2. Holdsworth, *History of English Law*, vol. 6, 601 points to the first such list of titles published by Samuel Brewster of Lincoln's Inn, *An Alphabetical Disposition of all the Heads Necessary for a Perfect Commonplace* (London, 1680, 1681). Another example from the early eighteenth century is *A Collection of Heads and Titles proper for a Common Place-Book in Law and Equity, Interspers'd with many useful Words for the Benefit of References to the Titles, which renders the Whole a Copious Index to the Law* (London, 1733).

72 See, for example, FLP, Carson LC 14.86, LC 14.73; DLL, Singleton 37. On 'profusion' of surviving evidence regarding conveyancing more generally, see Baker, *Law's Two Bodies*, 71–3.

concerns and professional interests of the privileged group of men who formed the community of law students and their prospective clients.[73] One interesting example here is the commonplace book belonging to Thomas Parker, chief baron of the Exchequer and nephew of the disgraced lord chancellor, which combines a detailed attention to criminal law matters with a focus on matters of property law in terms of the development of land tenures.[74]

The most consistent content appearing in these commonplace books is material relating to the administration of property and adjudication of property disputes. Such entries covered both landed and commercial wealth, reflecting developments during this period in the law regarding contracts, mortgage and trusts, for example. Another broad area of common content that may be discerned is a general interest in issues of agency, or capacity, and questions of admissibility. This focus persists across topics in private and criminal law – in entries such as 'deeds', 'baron and feme', 'attorney', 'witness', and 'appeal'. Who can be legally recognised as a responsible and informed agent, and under what circumstances? Such questions underlie the content of many commonplace entries on the rights and responsibilities of attorneys and of wives. Authorities are adduced and cases cited to elucidate the extent of the force of coverture, and the nature of dower. There is also attention to instances of female liability to prosecution, or women's responsibility for fines, debts or joint property. This provides an important indication of lawyers' recognition of contestable areas of 'women's law', and their awareness of the changing nature of forms of ownership and contract in this developing commercial society.[75] The bond between attorney and client is also analysed through examples of liability for costs or instances of malpractice.[76] Finally, an interest in capacity, or the ability to perform as a responsible agent, is also evident in entries on deeds, guardianship and on witnesses and jurors; there is frequent discussion, under various headings, of the impact of a former conviction for crime on the capacity to serve in a responsible position.[77]

73 Horwitz, 'Changes in Law and Reform', 310–11.

74 HLS, 4091. This manuscript, and two others at Harvard Law, HLS, 4011, 1007, are bound in the same yellow vellum and each has the same bookplate, which reads 'Thomas Parker of the Inner Temple Esqr', in the front cover. The main handwriting of each manuscript differs from the others, and it is not wholly clear that Parker compiled this commonplace.

75 See content under 'baron and feme' in FSL,W.b. 269; DLL, Singleton 36, 37, 69; HLS, 1262.

76 FLP, Carson LC 14.86; DLL, Singleton 36; HLS,1262.

77 These headings included 'outlawry', 'transportation', 'piracy'. See also the entries on 'witness' in FLP, Carson LC 14.98 and 'jury & witness', FLP, Carson, LC 14.86; entry on 'deeds' regarding whether an 'unlettered' (i.e. illiterate) person can be bound to deliver a deed, in DLL, Singleton 37; and entries on aliens' capacity to purchase or lease in FLP, Carson LC 14.86 and HLS, 4091.

Attention to the problem of bias, corruption or conflict of interest is a related common concern. The recognition of limits to attorneys' or wives' agency because of the possibility of undue influence echoes discussion about witnesses' and jurors' capacity to serve. So, the caution against an attorney being privileged in his own action, and the examples of attorneys fined for their attempts to influence juries, are similar to discussions about the exclusion of witnesses who might benefit from a particular verdict. Compilers explore case law and custom to derive principles that would determine under what circumstances a servant, wife, child or client might serve on a jury or bear witness regarding their master, husband, father or patron.[78] This habit of recognising the potential for bias is also a common thread running through entries on the admissibility of evidence, another indication of common premises and modes of analysis shared by the legal community.[79] It is also an indication of commonalities between legal reasoning and scientific reasoning, here signalling the ways in which an emphasis on impartiality and credibility was an essential part of developing conceptions of scientific and legal expertise and truth.[80] Finally, this attention to the question of bias is also likely evidence of a contemporary concern with corruption, and an awareness of broader moral and political debates regarding, for example, the impact of luxury, the nature of human sentiment, or the value of sociability. Some early eighteenth-century law reform literature similarly addressed these issues of self-interest and corruption, as did legislation proposed – and passed – to regulate fees and other aspects of professional practice.[81]

While many other areas of common content might be discussed, only two more especially significant ones will be noted here. These are the entries concerning jurisdiction and language. Jurisdictional questions about when and where the law has authority, and about who is empowered to enforce that authority, are often tied to an evident concern about the potential for a conflict of laws – between local custom and common law, between temporal and spiritual jurisdictions, and between civil, canon and common laws. There are the expected entries about the interpretation of statutes, the superiority of common to statute law, the proper relations among the West-

78 Entries on 'evidence' in DLL, Singleton 36; HLS, 1273, 1262. Entries on 'evidence' and 'jury & witness' in FLP, Carson LC 14.86.

79 Entries on 'evidence' in FLP, Carson LC 14.86, LC 14.98; entry on 'trial new how granted' in DLL, Singleton 69. Cf Hoeflich, 'Lawyer Pragmatic Reader', 101–2.

80 See the discussion of the role of expert witnesses, and evolution of the adversarial trial, in chapter 3 below.

81 See for example Walter Williams, *Proposals Humbly Offered to the Consideration of the King's most Excellent Majesty, and of the Lords and Commons in Parliament...in Order to Regulate Proceedings in Courts of Equity* (London, 1701); *Reasons Humbly Offered to both Houses of Parliament, for Passing a Bill for Preventing Delays and Expences in Suits in Law and Equity* (London, 1707); *Proposals Humbly offer'd to the Parliament for Remedying the Great Charge and Delay of Suits at Law and Equity* (London, 1707, and see also additions to 4th edn, London, 1724).

minster courts and between Westminster and the inferior courts.[82] But there are also related jurisdictional, and imperial or commercial, topics having to do with extradition and relations between England and Ireland, or with the general applicability of English laws to her settlements and plantations. More than one commonplace includes entries distinguishing between colonies or plantations settled by Englishmen and those established by conquest; again, a focus of discussion is on a potential conflict of laws, and the persistence of customary or common law. Two commonplace books cite the same 1722 memorandum from the Master of the Rolls, Joseph Jekyll, on an 'appeal from the foreign plantations':

> If Englishmen settle in an uninhabited Country they are to be governed by the English Laws; but not by any enacted afterwards unless nam'd. But in conquer'd country is to be subject to such Laws as the conqueror shall impose, & till new ones are given 'em by their own, unless mal in se &c.[83]

Here these compilers relied upon William Peere Williams' popular collection of reports that circulated widely in England and North America. The distinction they noted, and copied, between settled and conquered territories was part of a lengthy legal, philosophical and historical debate about sovereignty, property and the extent of the king's law. These matters were addressed most famously in Calvin's Case at the beginning of the seventeenth century, and remained an important focus of debate regarding Britain's imperial constitution throughout the eighteenth century.[84] These questions were also part of a more general concern with matters of jurisdiction, which encouraged lawyers to reflect on jurisprudential questions having to do with the nature and sources of legal authority.

Finally, an interest in the interpretation of words is noticeable in many of these commonplace books. In entries entitled 'exposition', definitions are produced for mundane, yet at times legally significant, terms such as 'household goods' or 'wedding apparel'. In entries dealing with slander and libel

82 Entries on 'Courts Temporal Superior' and 'Courts Temporal Inferior' in DLL, Singleton 37; 'courts' in DLL, Singleton 36; 'law' in HLS, 1262.

83 Entry on 'law' in HLS, 1262, on 'statutes' HLS, 1273; cf entry on 'alien' in FLP, Carson LC 14.98. These compilers derived Jekyll's memorandum from a case reported in William Peere Williams' *Reports of Cases Argued and Determined in the High Court of Chancery, and of Some Special Cases Adjudged in the Court of King's Bench*, 3 vols (London, 1740–49) that concerned devising land and purchasing office in Jamaica and Barbados. See 2 P. Wms 75, 24 *English Reports* 646.

84 On the debates regarding imperial constitution and conflict of laws see, for example: Hulsebosch, 'Ancient Constitution and Expanding Empire', 469–75; Bilder, *Transatlantic Constitution*; Polly J. Price, 'Natural Law and Birthright Citizenship in Calvin's Case', *Yale Journal of Law and the Humanities*, 9, 1 (1997): 73–145; James Farr, 'Locke, Natural Law and New World Slavery,' *Political Theory*, 36, 4 (August, 2008): 495–522; and the articles by George van Cleve, Daniel Hulsebosch and Ruth Paley in 'Forum: Somerset's Case Revisited', *Law and History Review*, 24, 3 (Fall, 2006): 601–71.

there is discussion of proper methods for the interpretation of statutes, and salient examples of the interpretation of certain phrases.[85] Occasionally an entry will begin with the definition or etymology of the heading itself. For example, the French roots of escheat and of estrepment are discussed, and a basic definition of these terms offered, in that commonplace belonging to Chief Baron Thomas Parker.[86] Many commonplace books mingle English, law French and sometimes Latin interchangeably. The continued use of these commonplace books by multiple generations of lawyers provides some indication that the learning of law French persisted even after the legislation of 1731 ended the use of law French and Latin in all legal proceedings. This intermingling of languages was related to an enduring belief in the importance of learning the language of the law in order to grasp its meaning. 'A man may be a wrangler, but never a lawyer,' Roger North cautioned law students, 'without a knowledge of the authentic books of the law in their genuine language.'[87] Despite the continued comprehension of the archaic languages, however, it is true that most of the commonplace books composed in the eighteenth century were written in English, with very infrequent use of law French and Latin. Roger North himself composed his commonplace book in English.[88]

An appreciation for these changes in language, but also for the continuities in the headings, format and content of these legal commonplace books, can help us to assess the impact that these manuscripts came to have on the practical printed legal literature. The increasingly common printed abridgment texts were attractive and accessible because they conformed to the commonplace style and content. Further, the new printed books were meant to supplement, and even to replace, those home-made law books. It is fairly well accepted that the abridgments originally developed out of student commonplace books, but it has been less well understood why greater numbers of these practical texts were published in the eighteenth century and what kinds of impact they had on the commonplace tradition,

85 Entries on 'words, exposition of' and 'words actionable or not' in DLL, Singleton 36; on 'exposition of words and statutes' in DLL, Singleton 37; on 'exposition', 'words', in HLS, 1262; on 'words' in HLS, 1273.

86 HLS, 4091. Cf BL, Hargrave 319, which also offers definitions, for example in the entry on 'misprision'; or IT, Mitford MS 28 which provides the etymology of the term 'assets'.

87 North, *Discourse on Study of Laws*, 14.

88 J.H. Baker, *Manual of Law French* (Amersham, 1979), 13. Examples of eighteenth-century commonplace books composed in English (with insertions sometimes more frequently in Latin than law French) include: FLP, Carson LC 14.79, LC 14.86, LC 14.98, LC 14.100; HLS, 1007, 1262, 1273, 4011, 4091, 6019; DLL, Singleton 36, 37, 69; IT, Barrington 60, 68; IT, Mitford 27, 28, 29. Compare to examples of commonplace books composed earlier in law French and Latin, such as: FLP, Carson LC 14.34, LC 14.65, LC 14.73, LC 14.80; HLS, 1144; DLL, M 73, BL, Add MS 50117.

and on legal education more generally.[89] These printed abridgments should, in fact, be seen as the precursors to modern 'Gilberts' or 'Nutshells' – cram books useful for avoiding the more rigorous training involved in following a course of legal study and compiling a legal commonplace book for oneself.[90] Eighteenth-century abridgments were also regarded as useful reference books or textbooks that one could annotate or use as a template for one's own notebook. In these intersections with the commonplace tradition, the abridgments played an important role in the development of the modern casebook, and provide an indication that there were continuities underlying the so-called Langdellian revolution in legal education.[91] In these intersections with the commonplace tradition, the abridgments also played an important role in the evolution of legal thought, and help to explain the persistent value and authority attributed to prescription and precedent.

Abridgments and other useful texts

Like the student who set out to create a law commonplace book, authors of printed legal texts grappled with questions about organisation and inclusion. And like the advice literature for students, the prefaces to the practical legal literature are couched in a similar defensive tone, sounding similar themes about the purpose and function of these volumes. Compilers of abridgments often began by defending their projects, choosing to respond to those broad criticisms of the common law as haphazard and incomprehensible. These defences may be indications of perceived problems in the law, but we must take care not to read these prefatory comments simply as another indication that the common law was in danger and decline. These authors were also taking part in a long rhetorical tradition, and in a broader encyclopedic tradition. Compared to the excuses made by the authors of other ostensibly useful texts, like Ephraim Chambers in his preface to the *Cyclopedia* (1728), or the compilers of works such as the *Bibliotheca Anatomica, Medica, Chirugica* (1711), the defensiveness of the legal writer is unremarkable and even sometimes particularly sophisticated and adept.[92]

89 Cowley, *Bibliography of Abridgments*, xxxix; Richard Yeo, 'A Solution to the Multitude of Books: Ephraim Chambers's *Cyclopaedia* (1728) as "the Best Book in the Universe"', *Journal of the History of Ideas*, 64, 1 (January, 2003): 63–5.

90 Brian Simpson asserts that 'To this day the case class system only works in the American law schools because students make use of various commercially produced summaries of the law, "nutshells", "Gilbert", and the like, which serve to redress the disorderly confusion of the case book from which it is pretended that they learn the law.' A.W.B. Simpson, *Leading Cases in the Common Law* (Oxford, 1995), 7.

91 Hoeflich, 'Lawyer Pragmatic Reader', 121–2.

92 Ephraim Chambers explained: 'Such are the Sources from whence the Materials of the present Work were derived; which it must be allowed, were rich enough not only to afford Plenty but even Profusion: So that the chief difficulty lay in the Form; in

William Nelson, for example, introduces his three-volume *Abridgment of the Common Law* (1725–6) with a politic combination of humour and pretension. He cleverly contrasts his own prefatory arguments for the usefulness of the abridgment with the useless 'servile flattery' to great men that most books offer by way of introduction. Nelson then debates the merits of abridgment by marshalling, in flattering terms, the authority of two great law men, 'the most learned Lord Verulam', Francis Bacon, and Edward Coke, 'our Oracle in the Law'. Aligning himself with the measured and often repeated judgment of Bacon, Nelson agrees that despite the usual shortcomings 'an Abridgment might be useful, if it was a good one.' But Nelson is also careful to phrase his rejection of the authority of Coke in the language of humour and human frailty:

> 'Tis true, my Lord Coke, who is our Oracle in the Law, was of another Opinion, for he tells us, that *Compendia sunt dispendia*; one would wonder so great a Lawyer should affect a Jingle; but 'tis no wonder that he did not approve an Abridgment, since he himself was so *Voluminious a Commentator*.[93]

Coke could be satirised here as long-winded but he was also recognised as a fellow author who struggled with the demands of his material and his audience. William Nelson dealt with such demands by following the guiding principles of 'clearness' and 'perspicuity'. Nelson claimed that he selected information for inclusion guided by a concern not to be 'too Voluminous', and not to replicate the work done by others. The care taken here to explicate and defend his methods was also a care to defend his professional reputation. Nelson was a barrister, with a successful practice in the court of Chancery, and he was the author of many other law books on topics including evidence, wills, clerical rights, and the responsibilities of JPs.[94]

the Order, and Oeconomy of the Work: To dispose such a Variety of Materials in such a manner, as not to make a confused Heap of incongruous parts, but one consistent Whole.' Ephraim Chambers, *Cyclopedia: or an Universal Dictionary of Arts and Sciences*, vol. 1 (London, 1728), i. Cf the similar statements appearing in the preface to *Bibliotheca Anatomica, Medica, Chirugica, &c. Containing a Description of the Several Parts of the Body*, 3 vols (London, 1711–14).

93 William Nelson, *An Abridgment of the Common Law: Being a Collection of the Principal Cases Argued and Adjudged in the Several Courts of Westminster Hall*, vol. 1 (London, 1725), preface 1st page. See Blair, 'Reading Strategies for Information Overload', 13–15, on the influence and reprinting of Francis Bacon's 'Of Studies'.

94 William Nelson, *The Office and Authority of a Justice of Peace: Collected Out of all the Books that have been Written on That Subject* (London, 1704); Nelson, *The Rights of the Clergy of Great Britain, As Established by the Canons, the Common Law, and the Statutes of the Realm*; Nelson, *The Law of Evidence* (London, 1717); Nelson, *Lex Testamentaria, Or a Compendious System of all the Laws of England, as well Before the Statute of Henry VIII as Since, Concerning Last Wills and Testaments*, 2nd edn (London, 1724), as well as other texts on the poor laws, manorial law, game law, and on 'English Liberties'. Nelson

Many of Nelson's texts were reprinted in multiple editions, but his work was also criticised by later legal writers, notably by Charles Viner who justified his own work, in part, by accusing Nelson of plagiarism and inaccuracy.[95]

The three volumes of Nelson's text openly situate themselves within the abridgment tradition, and claim to be composed of 'Cases published in the several Volumes of Reports, (except those of Keble) ever since the Year-Books were abridged by those two great Lawyers, Fitzherbert and Brook'.[96] These cases are gathered under alphabetical headings and explanatory sub-headings. Each volume opens with a table of contents, or heads, and the last volume includes an index of cases. Volume one covers the topics from abatement to entry, volume two from error to profits, and volume three from prohibition to writs. Within each entry the cases are adduced as points concerning the topic at hand. So, for example, the very first entry on abatement is addressed under the following sub-headings: Abatement '(A) By Misnomer and not (B) By the Act of the Party (C) By the Demise of the King (D) By the Death of either Party (E) Pleas in Abatement and Bar'.[97] These sub-topics are often extended in the body of the text and cross-references to other relevant or related entries in the whole abridgment are noted. The subtopic is then illustrated by cases taken from the named reports (such as Croke, Moor and Leonard) which are listed as enumerated points. Nelson offered no definitions or descriptions of the topics under consideration, and cases were simply noted in a digest form with their source and authority clearly indicated.

This form was recognisable, it 'bore a structural similarity to the commonplace', Richard Ross agrees, and was also used by earlier legal authors such as Wingate, Staunford, Style and Bacon.[98] This structure was an outgrowth of one aspect of legal reasoning, the practice of deducing principles of law from such examples. We can see here the way in which the abridgments and commonplace books confirmed a conception of legal authority based on accepted past practice and exemplary tradition. But the structure of a legal

was educated at the Middle Temple, and called to bar in 1684. N.G. Jones, 'Nelson, William', *ODNB*; Lobban, 'English Legal Treatise and English Law', 80–1.

95 'Nelson', *ODNB*; Cowley, *Bibliography*, lvii; Holdsworth, *History of English Law*, vol. 12, 162 n.4. Charles Viner, author of the multi-volume *General Abridgment of Law and Equity, Alphabetically Digested Under Proper Titles* (Aldershot 1742, and many subsequent editions) accused Nelson of copying – and that inaccurately – the abridgment of William Hughes. Despite Viner's complaint, there doesn't appear to be an unusual amount of overlap between Nelson's and Hughes' works.

96 Nelson, *Abridgment of Common Law*, preface 1st page. See also the subtitle to Nelson's *Abridgment*: 'Being a Collection of the Principal Cases Argued and Adjudged in the several Courts of Westminster Hall. The Whole being digested in a clear and Alphabetical Method, under Proper Heads, with several Divisions and Numbers under each Title, for the more ready finding any Judgment or Resolution of the Law Cases.'

97 Nelson, *Abridgment of Common Law*, vol. 1, 1.

98 Ross, 'Memorial Culture', n. 184.

abridgment, like Nelson's, was also part of that more general confrontation with the problem of organising and conveying information, and another example of the sophisticated format that generated insights through comparison and juxtaposition. These headings, sub-headings and cross-references employed by Nelson and other law book authors were among the means also used by compilers of Enlightenment dictionaries of arts and sciences, and compilers of Enlightenment encyclopedias, in order to convey the unity of their work, combining the ease of alphabetical organisation with the coherence of thematic or systematic exposition.[99]

The legal abridgments, like these other early eighteenth-century texts, drew upon older continental commonplace traditions and participated in an equally long-standing global encyclopedic tradition. Like other examples of 'encyclopaedism' studied by scholars like Richard Yeo or Ann Blair, these law books shared a 'passion for systematic classification of knowledge' expressed in 'large-scale collection projects' and attempted 'comprehensive coverage of particular disciplines'.[100] Moreover, these law books were produced during an eighteenth-century 'age of encyclopaedias', along with John Harris's *Lexicon Technicum* (2 volumes, 1704, 1710) or Ephraim Chambers' *Cyclopaedia*, and they shared the goals of dissemination, and techniques of data organisation, of a genre that was at the heart of that media-driven concept of Enlightenment. All of these books were commercial enterprises, the law books as much as the encyclopedias, 'a stunning example of how the trade in knowledge was judged to be worth large capital investment.'[101] Written in the vernacular, and organised alphabetically, these books aimed to educate and communicate with an audience that was broader than the one for the older Latin encyclopedias. As Bassett's catalogue indicated, the law books could circulate widely to a community that formed a growing 'republic of lawyers' comparable, perhaps, to that expanding republic of letters. Alphabetical organisation afforded help in the process of selection, and simplicity in the categorisation of material. But the use of cross-reference, and the advocacy of systematic reading in the law books, like the new encyclopedias, indicated that these texts were also envisioned as systematic and coherent classifications of knowledge.[102]

99 Yeo, *Encyclopaedic Visions*, xiii, xv, 12, 16–27, 110–15; Yeo, 'Encyclopaedic Knowledge' in Marina Frasca-Spada and Nick Jardine eds, *Books and the Sciences in History* (Cambridge, 2000), 207–24; Blair 'Annotating and Indexing Natural Philosophy', 69–89.

100 Richard Yeo, 'Encyclopaedism and Enlightenment', in Martin Fitzpatrick, Peter Jones, Christa Knellwolf and Iain McCalman eds, *The Enlightenment World* (Routledge, 2004), 350.

101 Ibid., 354; Sheehan, 'Enlightenment, Religion, Secularization', 1075–6; Robert Darnton, *The Business of Enlightenment: A Publishing History of the* Encyclopedie *1775–1800* (Cambridge, Mass., 1979).

102 Yeo, 'Encyclopaedism and Enlightenment', 357–9; Yeo, 'Encyclopaedic Knowledge'; Chartier *Order of Books*, 67–8: Carey McIntosh, 'Eighteenth-Century English Dictionaries and the Enlightenment', *The Yearbook of English Studies*, 28 (1998): 8.

The three large folio volumes of Nelson's *Abridgment*, for example, likely served as law reference texts or bench books. Their alphabetical organisation and exposition were typical and, like the commonplace books and encyclopedias, aimed to produce a useful collection for students and 'common readers', as well as a repository for lawyers who could find within a way to locate precedents or 'parallel Cases' for arguments to be made in practice.[103] An important difference between these abridgments and the encyclopedias was that the entries in the law books tended to be much lengthier and to record the source of the information presented.[104] Moreover, the abridgments were not aimed at a widely popular audience in the same way as the new encyclopedias. Yet an abridgment like Nelson's was still similar to the encyclopedia in that it intended to record new information and to make accessible a broad sweep of knowledge. Two other influential abridgments compiled in the early decades of the eighteenth century, by Knightley D'Anvers and Matthew Bacon, also aimed to be comprehensive and accessible. These and other abridgments that followed varied in their level of detail and subdivision of information but they all played a role in the formation of a legal 'encyclopedic vision' – offering, like the Enlightenment encyclopedia, a text 'containing the collective knowledge of a community which might be put together again if all other books were lost'.[105]

Knightley D'Anvers' *General Abridgment of the Common Law* (1705–27) was an updated edition and translation of one of those other books, the abridgment produced by Henry Rolle (and praised and prefaced by Matthew Hale) in the later seventeenth century. The first and second volumes of D'Anvers' *General Abridgment* appeared in 1705 and 1713, before Nelson's volumes. A 'continuation' of the second volume was published in 1727 and further editions of all three volumes, concluding only with the term 'Extinguishment', were published between 1725 and 1737.[106] The compiler D'Anvers was a well-placed if not prominent legal figure. Admitted barrister at the Inner Temple in 1696, and engaged as deputy recorder of Northampton in 1705, D'Anvers was married to a fellow writer, the satirical poet Alicia D'Anvers.[107] Unlike Nelson, Knightley D'Anvers openly sought 'Patronage and Protection' for his abridgment, and in his first volume offered the requisite flattery in a dedication to John Holt, chief justice of the Kings Bench. The title page also carefully noted that his text had secured the approbation

103 Nelson, *Abridgment of Common Law*, vol. 1, preface 2nd page.

104 In Harris' and Chambers' works the typical entry is one or two paragraphs long, but there are exceptions, such as the multi-page entry on 'barometer' in Harris' *Lexicon*; or the lengthy entry on 'law' in Chambers' *Cyclopedia*.

105 Yeo, *Encyclopaedic Visions*, 3.

106 Cowley, *Bibliography*, lvi–lvii, 97–8, 109–10.

107 Alicia's father, who died when she was a small child, was the renowned biblical and 'orientalist' scholar Samuel Clarke. Alastair Hamilton, 'Clarke, Samuel', and Holly Faith Nelson, 'D'Anvers, [nee Clarke], Alicia', *ODNB*.

of 'the Lord Keeper, and the rest of the Judges', and so could be trusted to convey the accepted learning of the law.[108]

Like Nelson, D'Anvers relied on the authority of past abridgments. Indeed, D'Anvers did not simply indicate predecessors such as Fitzherbert or Brooke, but rather reproduced Rolle's highly esteemed abridgment in an expanded and more accessible form. By the early eighteenth century Rolle's text was recommended as a guide for commonplacing and as an authority for citation, and it was widely used and annotated by lawyers and law students. When it had first been published in 1668, however, it had been dismissed by some as 'a mere student's commonplace book' and as a confused mass of contradictory opinions.[109] In producing his text, then, D'Anvers was both invoking the authority of past abridgments and making a claim to improve upon Rolle's initial, flawed, attempts at collection and analysis.

D'Anvers' abridgment follows Rolle's alphabetical organisation, with topical headings and subheadings introducing the content of enumerated cases, statutes and other records. There is again a good deal of cross-referencing within the text, and a greater number of marginal citations and additions to the cases recorded. These additions are often indications of D'Anvers' own amendments to Rolle's text. D'Anvers quite self-consciously made a connection between his own methods of note-taking and commonplacing and the publication of his abridgment. 'Having made my Lord Chief Justice *Roll's Abridgment* the Basis of my Common Place-Book,' D'Anvers confessed to his reader, 'and collected great Part of the Law in a Method much like the following; I was perswaded to Review what I had done, and to make such Alterations and Additions as might render the whole Useful, as one intire Abridgment of the Law.'[110] These alterations and additions are made visible to the reader by the use of different typefaces, noted by D'Anvers, so that the reader can distinguish between the two authors. D'Anvers also explained that Rolle's text has been translated because D'Anvers, like other contemporary lawyers and law students, 'for a long Time had used to Common-Place in *English*' making translation of Rolle's text into English, rather than his own additions into law French, 'the more Easie and Pleasant Task'.[111] Here D'Anvers underscored the goal of wider communication, indicated by the fact that by the early eighteenth century the abridgments, like the growing numbers of encyclopedias, were no longer

108 In making this prefatory claim to authorisation and reliability D'Anvers was also reproducing the practices of the authors of early printed reports and abridgments. Williams, 'Common Lawyers' Receptivity to Print', 60–4.

109 Baker, *Introduction to English Legal History*, 186, quoting Chief Justice Vaughn.

110 Knightley D'Anvers, 'To the Reader', *A General Abridgment of the Common Law, Alphabetically Digested Under Proper Titles, With Notes and References to the Whole*, vol. 1, 2nd edn (London, 1725).

111 Ibid.

produced in Latin or law French but appeared in the vernacular.[112] D'Anvers offered these explanations as a defence of the accuracy of his abridgment, and as a persuasive to the reader to adopt these expanded resources as a supplement, or even substitute, for the reader's own commonplace book.

Matthew Bacon's five-volume *A New Abridgment of the Law* (1736–66) was an even more structured abridgment, one that attempted to define legal terms and offered more connected sub-headings and readable prose. Bacon's interest in definition and etymology is especially notable; this feature of his work is comparable to a similar focus in many eighteenth-century encyclopedias, and is another indication of the blurring of Enlightenment genres like encyclopedia, dictionary and abridgment that we now consider distinct.[113] The main topic of an entry in Bacon's work, such as 'abatement', was defined and then divided into twelve subtopics, each narrated through materials in such a way as to emphasise legal doctrine and legal principles.[114] To take another example, Bacon introduced the topic of the jury by means of a brief historical and politico-constitutional definition before dividing this subject, too, into multiple subheadings. Here information regarding the jury emerged by way of questions that might occur, and proceeding in greater detail. If one considered '(D) In what Cases and in what Manner special Juries are appointed,' the text seems to suggest, one might then wonder '(E) Who are to be returned; and therein of the Qualifications and several Causes for which they may be challenged.'[115] The logic underlying this series of questions reveals the adherence to past practice as well as that interest in agency, capacity and the potential for bias that was evident in commonplace entries on jury and jurors. It is indicative of an approach that emphasised precedent and procedure but also analogous to the expository and explanatory approach of an encyclopedia entry. 'With systematic subdivision may go attempts to state the law by direct exposition, rather than by stringing together digests of cases,' Brian Simpson explains. 'If this is attempted, the "authorities" move out of the text and into the notes.' 'The first full abridgment illustrating this process,' Simpson concludes, 'is Bacon's *Abridgment* (1736–59).'[116]

There are similarities among Bacon's, D'Anvers' and Nelson's abridgments in terms of the choices made about alphabetical organisation, marginal citation and cross-referencing. All three authors, like the compilers of commonplace books, dictionaries and encyclopedias, experimented with the ordering of knowledge and reflected on the usefulness of their texts. All three

112 Yeo, *Encyclopaedic Visions*, 12, on vernacular encyclopedia.

113 McIntosh, 'Eighteenth-Century Dictionaries', 3–4, 8–10.

114 Matthew Bacon, *A New Abridgment of the Law*, vol. 1 (London, 1736), 1.

115 Bacon. *New Abridgment*, vol. 3 (London, 1740), 231.

116 Simpson, 'Rise and Fall of Treatise', 640. And cf Michael Lobban's recognition of the ways in which 'reporting culture fed into the treatise culture', Lobban, 'English Legal Treatise and English Law', 84.

also demonstrated adherence to traditionalism and precedentialism, and attempted to transmit the vast accumulated wisdom and practice of common law. Yet, as Simpson's statement intimates, Matthew Bacon's abridgment has long been regarded as an improvement upon Nelson and D'Anvers, in part because of his use of systematic subdivision. Bacon's methods of organisation and exposition are usually said to indicate an advance, the end-point in a history of progress in systematisation and organisation which ultimately lead to the modern legal treatise and the modern legal encyclopedia.[117] This same progress towards specialisation and treatise-writing by the end of the eighteenth century is said to take place in the literature of science as well as law. So, the *Encyclopaedia Britannica* has been described by Richard Yeo and others in much the same way as scholars have described Bacon's *New Abridgment*: as a set of treatises on major subjects still arranged alphabetically.[118]

The fact that Bacon's volumes were produced over many decades, and involved later compilers, informs scholars' sense of his work as transitional and modern.[119] Even more, Bacon's reputation is bound up with their assessment of two other key contemporary legal figures, Charles Viner and Geoffrey Gilbert. Viner and Gilbert are conventionally regarded as important predecessors to William Blackstone, who authored that famous treatise, the *Commentaries on the Laws of England* (1765–69). Yet Viner's *A General Abridgment of Law and Equity* (1741–53), a 'monumental' twenty-three volume continuation of D'Anvers and Rolle, was outdone by Bacon's *New Abridgment*.[120] Bacon's abridgment was extremely popular, going through seven English editions, two Irish editions and multiple American editions into the nineteenth century. Some of the explanation for this popularity has, again, been attributed to Bacon's partial adoption of the treatise form.

Contemporary competitors, like Viner and Blackstone, speculated that Matthew Bacon adopted the treatise form, and achieved this popularity, by lifting 'considerable parts' of the *New Abridgment* from the published monographs and unpublished manuscripts of Geoffrey Gilbert. This allegation has since been repeated by modern scholars, like Michael Macnair, who attach

117 Holdsworth, *A History of English Law*, vol. 5 (London, 1924), 377; Simpson, 'Rise and Fall of Treatise', 640; Cowley, *Bibliography*, lx.

118 Yeo, *Encyclopaedic Visions*, xv–xvii, and ch. 7.

119 The first three volumes written by Bacon, but published anonymously, appeared between 1736 and 1740; Bacon died before completing the fourth volume, and these last two volumes were compiled by other authors, appearing in 1759 and 1766. Peter R. Glazebrook, 'Bacon, Matthew', in Simpson ed., *Biographical Dictionary of Common Law*, 27; N.G. Jones, 'Bacon, Matthew', *ODNB*; Cowley, *Bibliography*, lxiii–lxiv.

120 Baker, *Introduction to English Legal History*, 186; note he, unlike most others, regards Viner as the culmination of the abridgment tradition. Profits from sales of Viner's *Abridgment* formed part of Viner's bequest to the University of Oxford in order to fund the first professorship of common law; Blackstone, of course, was the first occupant of the Vinerian chair in English law.

it to claims about the significance of Gilbert's work.[121] Geoffrey Gilbert, the author of treatises on topics such as evidence, uses and trusts, dower, Exchequer and Chancery, served on the Kings Bench and Exchequer courts in Ireland between 1715 and 1722, before he was transferred to the English bench. Since Matthew Bacon was an Irishman, and apparently remained in Ireland until he was admitted to the Inner Temple in May, 1726, rumour held that Bacon might have had access to Gilbert and his manuscripts in the early 1720s.[122] Bacon's *New Abridgment* is usually assessed, then, in relation to Gilbert's treatises and, more broadly, in the terms of a progressive narrative towards nineteenth-century reform.[123] In this way Bacon's work also plays an ambiguous role in the assessment of Irish contributions to jurisprudence: he is simultaneously portrayed positively, as a modern proto-treatise writer, and negatively, as even less original or conscientious than other compilers. Although the notion of plagiarism is very different in these abridgment texts, where the norm is of compilation and the reproduction of others' words, repetition of this rumour about the relationship between Bacon and Gilbert clearly replicates eighteenth-century views about the superiority of English culture over Irish learning.

This depiction of Bacon as treatise writer – and as treatise thief – also perpetuates an anachronistic understanding of the early eighteenth-century abridgment literature. Like other early eighteenth-century law authors, Bacon did not in fact share this view that privileges the legal treatise over the abridgment. Indeed Bacon expressed a preference for the abridgment, and in his earlier *A General Abridgment of Cases in Equity* (1732) he defended the usefulness of this kind of text:

> The Principal Design of it, is to collect and dispose, by Way of Abridgment, under proper Heads, all such Cases adjudged in the Courts of Equity, as are any where in Print; and this is conceived to be a better Method than composing a regular Institute of those Matters: In the Way of Institute, much must always be taken from the private Opinion of the Writer; in this of an Abridgment, Knowledge flows from the Points adjudged, and authentick Resolutions which the Reader has before him.[124]

121 Simpson, 'Rise and Fall of Treatise', 654–5; Michael Macnair, 'Sir Geoffrey Gilbert and his Treatises', *Legal History*, 15, 3 (1994): 258; Macnair, 'Gilbert, Sir Jeffray', *ODNB*; 'Bacon, Matthew' *ODNB*; Cowley, *Bibliography*, lx-lxiii.; Bacon, *New Abridgment*, vol. 1 (London, 1778), iv.

122 'Bacon, Matthew' *ODNB*. Many Irishmen matriculated at the Inns in this period: training in English common law at the Inns of Court was a prerequisite for lawyers practising at the Irish Bar. Lemmings, *Gentlemen and Barristers*, 18.

123 Simpson, 'Rise and Fall of Treatise', 651–68; Macnair, 'Gilbert and his Treatises', 258–61.

124 Bacon, *General Abridgment of Cases in Equity*, preface 1st page; cf also the preface to Bacon's *The Compleat Arbitrator, Or, Law of Awards and Arbitraments* (London, 1731), iv,

Bacon's statement is an indication of the centrality of past practice and the role of judicial decisions in his conception of law. He regarded the compilation of specific examples and prior practice as a surer basis for knowing, and understanding, the law – even the law administered in courts of equity where common law precedent and procedure did not apply.

Bacon's statement is also an expression of his ideas about the retrieval, collection and transmission of information. Bacon, like Nelson, D'Anvers and others, believed in the efficacy of his methods and his work should not simply be judged as part of a linear progression away from the older forms. The *New Abridgment* certainly differs from the simple digest or citing of cases that typified Nelson's and D'Anvers' work and although others, like Giles Jacob, also offered definitions and conveyed information through reasoned and readable prose, Bacon's work was much more comprehensive. Yet the exposition through multiple and often connected sub-headings, the collection and citation of multiple authorities, and the defence of the abridgment project, are not very different in Bacon's work. This preference for the abridgment form was shared by fellow law book authors, like Nelson and D'Anvers, and by encyclopedists, like Diderot, who were attracted to 'the simplicity of alphabetical entries over large treatises' because they believed that a coherent and systematic knowledge of a subject could be profitably conveyed in this way.[125]

Just a few years after Matthew Bacon expressed his preference for the abridgment, Giles Jacob articulated a similar proposal for an abridgment of the common law. In a preface to his edition of the case reports of Chief Justice Holt, Jacob hearkened back to the great books of Roman law, calling for a Digest of the common law that would contain the collective knowledge of the legal community:

> To write a compleat Abridgment of the Common Law, may justly, at this Time of Day, be thought a Work too extensive for any one Person to undertake. Such a Work, or rather a *Digest* of our Laws, is worthy of a *Juncto* of the first Men in the Profession; of an English *Tribonian* and his Fellows. When that shall be effectually performed, the seeming Contradictions of the Reports shall be reconciled, and those Cases shall be thrown aside which have been denied by later Authorities, and upon better Reasons: And then the recorded *Dicta* and *Responsa* of *Hale*, *Holt*, and *Lee*, will be written down for Text-Law; as in the *Roman Digest* we find those of *Paulus*, *Ulpian*, and *Papinian*.[126]

on the value of both 'general Abridgments' and 'particular Treatises on some general and useful Head of the Law' in bringing 'Order' to 'Confusion' and 'Intricacy'.

125 Yeo, 'Encyclopaedism and Enlightenment', 358, citing Diderot's statement in a prospectus of 1750. And cf McIntosh, 'Eighteenth-Century Dictionaries', 8, citing D'Alembert's preface to the 1751 edition of the *Encyclopedie* which stated the author's 'intentions of summarizing, clarifying and arranging all knowledge'.

126 Giles Jacob, ed. (?), *A Report of all the Cases Determined by Sir John Holt, Knt. From*

Jacob's proposal sounds similar to the eighteenth-century encyclopedic projects of Harris, Chambers and others. It even anticipates later encyclopedias, like the third and subsequent editions of the *Britannica*, in suggesting this 'Juncto' of multiple authors.[127] In calling upon the example of Roman law Jacob misleads the reader at first, since he is not calling for an institute, a systematic treatise or textbook of law. Jacob was, however, attracted to a comparative approach to law like that pursued by Thomas Wood, whose work he and others admired. Wood's *Institute of Civil Law* (1704), an important contribution to the Roman and natural law traditions, offered side-by-side comparisons of civil and common law, and Jacob may have been proposing an extension of this kind of work.[128] Jacob, like Wood and Bacon, adhered to contemporary notions about reasoning through examples, comparisons and juxtaposition, and through a combination of the alphabetical and thematic organisation of information. In Jacob's mind the dicta and responsa of jurists would become text law still recorded as cases and arguments rather than in treatise form. Analysis of law would remain inductive, rules and reasons would be derived from cases and remedies. In this way Jacob's conception of abridgment confirmed the wisdom of common law as the accretion of tradition, and portrayed the evolution of common law through the decisions of judges, like Holt, who worked within the stable structures of that system.

The collection of Holt's reports that follows Jacob's proposal is a large reference work, more than seven hundred folio pages arranged alphabetically from abatement to writs, with extensive tables of titles, cases and principal matters appended at the front and back. Jacob's *New Law Dictionary* (1729) is similarly large and aimed to be even more comprehensive than his other works. This dictionary is most like the work of Chambers and Harris and other encyclopedists both in terms of its layout (small print in double columns in two volumes of unpaginated folios), and in terms of its attempt at accessibility and communication with a wide audience. Jacob's dictionary reached a sizable audience not only in Britain but also in colonial America where it was 'the most widely used English law dictionary', and could be

1688 to 1710, During which Time he was Lord Chief Justice of England (London, 1738), ii–iii. The attribution of this edition of reports to Jacob is generally accepted, and appears in Charles C. Soule, *The Lawyer's Reference Manual of Law Books and Citations* (Boston, 1883), *The Catalogue of the Hampton L. Carson Collection: Illustrative of the Growth of the Common Law*, 2 vols. (Boston, 1962), as well as the catalogues of law libraries such as the Diamond Law Library at Columbia University, and the Harvard Law Library.

127 Yeo, *Encyclopedic Visions*, 183.

128 Thomas Wood, *A New Institute of Imperial or Civil Law ... Shewing in some Principal Cases, amongst other Observations, how the Canon law, the Laws of England, and the Laws and Customs of Other Nations Differ from it* (London, 1704). See further discussion of Wood's texts below, chapter 5.

found in the collections of Thomas Jefferson, John Adams, and in many other law libraries.[129]

The *New Law Dictionary* was probably Jacob's most successful work, but it was only one among the many practical legal, political and literary works he produced in the first few decades of the eighteenth century. Jacob, like his fellow compiler William Nelson, produced a large number of legal texts on conveyancing, Chancery practice, local courts and officers, military, commercial, criminal and constitutional law, as well as his law dictionary.[130] Jacob's first works on court keeping, conveyancing, and the responsibilities of modern justices of the peace claimed, like the abridgments, to be comprehensive and up-to-date surveys of practice and collections of precedents.[131] He also made his mark early on with his alphabetical digest of statute law, A *Review of the Statutes* (1715). Accessible and portable, these texts advertised themselves as 'an itinerant Library or Office' useful for the practitioner but aimed at non-lawyers as well.[132] Jacob's own practical experience, he said, as steward and secretary to the politician William Blathwayt, gave him particular insight into what would be the most useful information to include. This service to a prominent official, an apprenticeship to an 'eminent attorney', extensive reading and self-education were the bases of Jacob's education in the law.[133] Unlike Nelson, D'Anvers and Bacon, Jacob did not matriculate at one of the declining Inns of Court, nor was he called to the bar. But Jacob's

129 McDowell, 'Politics of Meaning: Law Dictionaries and Liberal Tradition', 261.

130 Jacob was the most prolific, producing upwards of 30 texts, while Nelson published his abridgment, as well as a number of other works and an updated edition of Thomas Blount's A *Law Dictionary*, 3rd edn (London, 1717). Nelson was also perhaps the editor of the last edition of John Cowell's dictionary *The Interpreter*. See Lobban, 'Blackstone and Science of Law', 314; Cowell, *Bibliography*, lxxxviii–ix, xc, 103–4; 'Nelson', *ODNB*.

131 Giles Jacob, *The Compleat Court Keeper; Or Land-Stewards Assistant* (London, 1713); Jacob, *The Accomplished Conveyancer*, 3 vols (London, 1714–15); Jacob, *The Court Keeper's Companion* (London, 1717); Jacob, *The Modern Justice: Containing the Business of a Justice of Peace in All its Parts* (London, 1716); Jacob, *The Compleat Parish Officer* (London, 1718). Almost all of these texts went through multiple editions.

132 Giles Jacob, *The Grand Precedent, Or the Conveyancer's Guide and Assistant* (1716); see also Jacob, *Lex Mercatoria, Or the Merchant's Companion* (1718); Jacob, *Court Keepers Companion* (1717). And compare the preface to *The Clerk's Magazine or Law Repository* (Dublin, 1749), where another author refers to public interest in conveyancing: 'To which End a *Manual* is here compiled from the best Authors, and no Pains spared to make it, what we hope will be thought, of Service to Practitioners, who, tempted by the Cheapness and compendious Size of it, as well as by its useful Contents, may condescend to take it into their *Portmanteaux*.' This author further points to the usefulness of the text for laymen who, by consulting the volume, might be able to avoid the expense of hiring a lawyer for small matters.

133 Jacob, *Compleat Court Keeper*, vii–viii; 'Jacob', *ODNB*. Note that before he was land steward to Blathwayt, Jacob served as assistant to Richard Dibben, and as land steward to Thomas Lord Arundel and to Thomas Freke.

legal education was typical for his time, and it enabled him to understand what kinds of practical texts would be most helpful to the young lawyer.

Two of Jacob's texts spoke directly to the matter of legal education, and its relation to the commonplace tradition. Jacob's *Student's Companion*, and his *Common Law Common-placed* were published in 1725 and 1726, the same years as Nelson's volumes, and also went through multiple editions. They are organised alphabetically and, like the abridgment and commonplace books, aimed to serve as useful reference texts. Here Jacob openly signalled an indebtedness to the commonplace tradition by manipulating the familiar image of the commonplace writer as a bee harvesting nectar from multiple flowers. Jacob's assertion that he was laying out a new path of legal knowledge was tempered by an admission that he was also 'obliged to our greatest Writers on the Subject for some of my choice Flowers of Reason'.[134] The title *The Common Law Common-placed* is an even more obvious tribute to the manuscript tradition. In this text Jacob adhered closely to the commonplace headings from abatement to writ, and to the commonplace and abridgment practices of marginal citation and cross-referencing. Jacob acknowledged that he consulted the abridgments of both D'Anvers and Lilly and claimed that he would be content if this text 'should be construed a short methodical Abridgment either of Coke's *Institutes*, Danvers, Wood or Lilly'.[135] Jacob made a similar connection between the student's work of commonplacing and his work in publishing his abridgments in the preface to his earlier *Statute Law Common-plac'd* (1719). Here Jacob asserted that his own failure to prosper in the practice of law made him peculiarly well equipped 'to do some Service to others, at least in assisting their Memories, if not improving their Judgments, by reducing the several Branches of the Law to a proper Bounds, freeing them from a Confusion of Method, and perfecting what I find little more than begun by my industrious Predecessors'.[136] The success of his guides to court keeping and to the statutes, Jacob often claimed, led many practitioners and publishers to request further editions and this in turn encouraged him to compile other legal texts.

Giles Jacob produced narrowly topical as well as broadly comprehensive

134 Jacob, *Student's Companion*, v.

135 Jacob, *The Common Law Common-placed: Containing the Substance and Effect of all the Common Law Cases Dispersed in the Body of the Law, Collected as well from Abridgments as Reports, in a Perfect New Method* (London, 1726), preface 2nd page.

136 Giles Jacob, The *Statute Law Common-plac'd: Or a Second General Table to the Statutes* (London, 1719), A3v. In this preface Jacob's request for patronage includes not only the usual claims for modesty of performance but also alludes to the hardship Jacob faced in training and practice: '… I think it consistent with my Duty to make an Apology for my very great Presumption in prefixing the Names of the Right Honourable the Lord Chancellor the Judges (the Ornaments of the Law, and Distributers [sic] of Justice) in the Front of this small Performance; and it would be wholly unpardonable, were it not to implore a *Protection*, which a Person bred to the Law, by a Train of Misfortunes may otherwise want.'

works organised both alphabetically and non-alphabetically. He experimented with different methods of communicating information and quite often presented the same material in different formats, producing multiple texts for different segments of his audience. He wrote for lawyers, local officers, merchants, students, clerks and stewards. Jacob also wrote for poets, playwrights and gentlemen of taste, and his literary works were similarly varied, including essays, memoirs, plays and poems as well as the *Poetical Register* (1719–20), a broad anthology of collective biography in two volumes.[137] The *Poetical Register* especially betrays Jacob's persistent concern with the organisation of knowledge: here, Jacob takes part in an 'ordering of the arts' that has been described as a product of an Enlightenment interest in a history of the arts and in standards of taste and genre.[138] Jacob's *Poetical Register*, his *Law Dictionary* and his many comprehensive abridgments and guides to the law share similar concerns, and may even have been influenced by a contemporary philosophical analysis of the intersections between language, knowledge and civility.[139] These multiple venues for reflection, and the comparisons naturally to be made between his own varied works, enabled Jacob to question and experiment with the organisation and communication of knowledge.

Abridgment was clearly a favorite form and Jacob often defended this approach for its accessibility, clarity and ease of use. His arguments repeated the claims made for collections, or 'libraries', in multiple fields.[140] 'Abridgments of large and copious Writings have ever been held in Esteem, as they are accounted useful to Persons of every Profession, especially that of the Law, wherein so many considerable Volumes have been publish'd,'

137 Giles Jacob, *The Poetical Register: or the Lives and Characters of the English Dramatick Poets. With an Account of their Writings* (London, 1719); Jacob, *An Historical Account of the Lives and Writings of Our Most Considerable English Poets, whether Epick, Lyrick, Elegiack, Epigrammatists, Etc.* (London, 1720). Both volumes were reissued in 1723.

138 McLaverty, 'Pope and Giles Jacob', 24; Brewer, *Pleasures of Imagination*, ch. 11.

139 See, for example, the opening of Jacob's *The Common Law Common-placed*, 1: 'The Great and Commendable Learning of the Laws of one's Country, if rightly considered, is equal with any other Learning, even the Politest of the most flourishing Kingdoms, tho' it is not commonly so accepted; as it points out to us Justice between Man and Man, and the Means that secure all Men from Injustice; And if Knowledge, in general, is to be estimated by the Difficulty in its attaining, that of the Law, beyond any other, merits our Approbation.' And cf McDowell, 'Politics of Meaning: Law Dictionaries and Liberal Tradition', 268–70.

140 Chartier, *Order of Books*, 65–6. Compare Jacob's statement with Gabriel Naude in his *Advis Pour Dresser une Bibliotheque* (1627) quoted by Chartier: 'In the first place they save us the trouble of seeking out an infinite number of highly rare and curious books; secondly, because they leave space for many others and give relief to a Library; thirdly, because they condense for us in one volume and commodiously what we would have to seek with much trouble in several places; and finally, because they bring with them a great saving, being certain that it requires few testons … to buy them than it would require ecus if one wanted to have separately all the [works] that they contain.'

Jacob asserted in the preface to his *Catalogue of Writs and Processes* (1717). Written for the attorney, clerk and student, texts such as this, Jacob added, when they are 'well finished, and are not so concise but that they contain sufficient Explanations, they are certainly of greatest Use, as they immediately introduce the reader to the desired Information in a shorter Time, and thereby save him a great deal of Trouble in turning over many larger Volumes.'[141] Jacob abridged the learning of the common law in a number of different texts but all of the texts – whether alphabetical or non-alphabetical, large or small, written for the novice or the experienced practitioner – included 'sufficient explanation' of the legal topic at hand, along with the usual digest of precedents. So, for example, in *The Common Law Common-placed* each entry opens with a brief definition followed by a series of discrete points deduced from the usual authorities.[142] Although each point is accompanied by marginal references to named case reports, statutes, the works of Coke, Fitzherbert and other authorities, information is not presented simply as cases in digest form but is narrated as principles or rules of law.

On the basis of these texts, surely, Jacob cannot be held up as the symbol of the inaccessibility of the common law implied in Pope's *Dunciad*. Indeed, even in those texts, such as his *The Statute Law Common-plac'd* (1719), that are similar to the digest form prevalent in other abridgments and commonplace books, Jacob addressed the issues of accessibility and comprehensibility. *The Statute Law Common-plac'd* begins with a brief discursive introduction defining statute and analysing Magna Charta, 'the Basis and Foundation of our Statute Law.' The subsequent alphabetical entries from abatement to wreck then proceed as a simple compilation of statutes listed under the relevant heads.[143]

There is a resemblance here between Giles Jacob's and Matthew Bacon's texts since both authors often begin with a brief discussion of the meaning of the law term and history of the practice under consideration.[144] In fact Jacob and Bacon criticised, and tried to rectify, the general obscurity of

141 Giles Jacob, A *Catalogue of all the Writs and Processes that Issue Out of the Several Courts at Westminster &c. With great Variety of Cases Relating to the Same. Together with a Full and Exact Account of their Nature and Use*. (London, 1717), A2r–v.

142 So, for example, an entry on 'baron and feme' proceeds from an initial definition of coverture, through various points concerning a wife's capacity and liability with regard to property, contract and other actions at law. Jacob, *Common Law Common-placed*, 62–5.

143 Cf also *The Rules of Practice Common-plac'd: With Remarks* (London, 1740), a text that sets out information on process in Kings Bench and Common Pleas in a way that echoes both D'Anvers and Jacob.

144 See, for example, entries in Jacob's, *Common Law Common-placed*; Jacob, *Student's Companion*; Jacob, *Review of Statutes*; Jacob, *Modern Justice of the Peace*; Jacob, *Catalogue of Writs and Processes*; and Jacob, *Accomplished Conveyancer*. Jacob's *Compleat Court Keeper* is slightly different in that it includes a separate introduction and conclusion which define and explicate legal practices and personnel, while the intervening text is composed mainly of precedents and forms.

legal literature. Using the metaphor of darkness and light, they promised to rescue the reader who, in Jacob's words, was 'like a Traveller in a Wood without a Guide', 'lost' in the 'Wilderness'. Bacon's lament that 'the Way to the Knowledge of [our laws] is so dark and rugged, so full of Windings and Turnings', repeated the words used by Thomas Wood in his defence of the aims of his *Institute of the Laws of England.*[145] And all three of these authors relied on an image most likely derived from that authoritative source, Sir Edward Coke, in order to assert the value of their contribution.[146]

At the same time as they staked a claim to significance and novelty by criticising the available case reports, or the classic texts of Bracton, Littleton and Coke, Matthew Bacon and Giles Jacob carefully positioned their own contributions within that broader tradition needing improvement. They did not abjure the common law emphasis on pleading, practice and prescription. Rather 'the Method of writing general Abridgments, or particular Treatises', Bacon explained, would be improved by the application of proper form. And a suitable method, Jacob promised in his *Student's Companion*, would 'bring Things into the Light':

> My Method is something in the Nature and Manner of Case, and Opinion, or brief Commentary; Under what I call Case, is a Short Body of the Law in general, in its most useful and essential Points, which I have carefully gathered from our most valuable Authors of the best Reputation; And at the Foot of it is the Opinion, containing the Powerful Reason and Foundation of it.[147]

Jacob, like other law authors, did not see the commonplace or abridgment form as antithetical to the expression of rational legal principles.[148] The structural as well as conceptual emphasis on the particular and the prescriptive was essential to legal thought, to a jurisprudence that founded the authority of law in past practice. But the particularistic and alphabetical or commonplace organisation of information was not only that. It was also part of a broader enlightened interest in the management and cogent expression of knowledge.

Wide-ranging, accessible and formatted for ease of use Jacob's texts share many characteristics with the other abridgments and should, similarly, be understood within the multiple contexts of encyclopedia, abridgment and commonplace traditions. While there are some significant differences, Jacob is not simply a 'hack' or an outlier, and his work should be included in the

145 Bacon, *Compleat Arbitrator*, iii. Wood, Thomas, *An Institute of the Laws of England; Or, the Laws of England in their Natural Order, According to Common Use*, 2nd edn (London, 1722), iv.

146 Edward Coke, *The Third Part of the Institutes of the Laws of England: Concerning High Treason and Other Pleas of the Crown, and Criminal Causes* (London, 1644), B1r.

147 Jacob, *Student's Companion*, iv–v.

148 Ibid., i–iii.

study of eighteenth-century legal education, legal literature, enlightened encyclopedism and print culture. In thinking about comparative differences, for example, it is true that with regard to sheer size Jacob's texts are far less imposing than the folio volumes of Bacon, D'Anvers and Wood. Most of Jacob's books are quarto or octavo sized, and many of them are conceived of as portable surveys of legal practice rather than as comprehensive and technical reference texts. The size of these books, however, cannot simply be taken as an indication of their lack of seriousness or their popular rather than professional nature. There are many examples of respected law books, such as William Hawkins' *An Abridgment of the First Part of my Lord Coke's Institutes* or Robert Gardiner's *Instructor Clericalis*, that also stressed their portability and usefulness. Hawkins, like Jacob and Bacon, also criticised the obscurity of many contemporary legal texts and emphasised the usefulness of abridgments such as his that relayed the 'common Grounds' of law.[149] These kinds of smaller, portable books were equally important as the larger volumes, and 'were another form of "library" produced by the books trade'. While collected libraries, or bibliotheques, like the encyclopedia and dictionary, were one form of response to the proliferation of print and the problem of collection, Roger Chartier explains, these 'had a counterpoint in the eighteenth century in a vast number of equally popular small, concise and easily handled volumes named *extraits*, *esprits*, *abreges*, *analyses*, and so forth.'[150]

The value of the portable abridgments for practitioners as well as students becomes clear when Jacob's work is compared not only to other technical or professional works, but also to several popular legal texts. In fact, even if we compare Jacob's own more general *Every Man his Own Lawyer* (1736) with the unattributed *The Young Lawyers Recreation* (1694) we can see that Jacob's work remained useful for the professional. Both texts are intended to shed light on the legal profession for ordinary readers, both proceed topically with some interconnected entries, and both authors express a desire to entertain while offering instruction. Yet *The Young Lawyers Recreation* is on the whole much more amusing and, at times, sensational. Although the text opens with an alphabetical table of familiar headings, includes a brief reflection on the definition of the common law, and relies upon the usual case reports, statutes and respected authorities for its entries, a good deal of prurient material is also included. Frequent attention is given to sexual

149 William Hawkins, *An Abridgment of the First Part of my Ld Coke's Institutes* (London, 1711), iii–iv.

150 Chartier, *Order of Books*, 68. An indication of the prevalence of these small volumes may be found in the sale catalogue of the library of the eighteenth-century lawyer, William Carr, where the list of 'practical' law books in octavo owned by Carr runs for four pages. Daniel Browne, *A Catalogue of the Libraries of the Honourable William Carr, of Lincoln's-Inn, … And of the Reverend Mr. John Herbert* (London, 1721), 21–5.

matters, including more than one reference to the notorious Castlehaven case, and to a case involving a 'woman indicted for copulating with a dog'.[151]

Giles Jacob also makes the claim that unusual and instructive information is to be found within his *Every Man his Own Lawyer*, but his text is instead a robust survey of main points of legal process and personnel, estates, marriage and inheritance, and even of constitution and statute. Information that appears in Jacob's other works is included here, fitted for readers 'of every capacity' and with the hope expressed that such information might have a positive impact on the prosecution of suits during this period of law reform.[152] Unlike the author of another contemporary text, *The Attorney's Pocket Companion*, Jacob did not fear that popular understanding – promoted by the burgeoning print culture and by changes in legal language – would lead to abuse of the law and erosion of professional authority. In an 'Age of Inquiry into Things', as Jacob put it, knowledge can be organised and communicated in such a way as to be beneficial to an inquiring public but also '[afford] a very just Instruction' to legal professionals.[153]

Thus Giles Jacob participated in the expansion and popularisation of print that was a marked feature of legal practice, like other professional practices such as medicine, in the eighteenth century. But Jacob also published a number of more technical law books aimed directly at the practitioner. These works fall into the category of texts on pleading and process, one of the most numerous and most important types of practical legal literature produced in this period.[154] Books on pleading were mainly composed of exemplary precedents to be used by the lawyer in the course of a suit, such as specimens of declarations, common counts and actions. In addition, they gave information about the art of pleading through discussion of different forms that might be used, and of choices to be made in the order of pleading.[155] These books developed out of older books of specimen writs and

151 In this text even entries about mutability of contract, or bequests of estates to church, are treated in a humourous fashion, *The Young Lawyer's Recreation. Being a Choice Collection of Several Pleasant Cases, Passages and Customs in the Law* (London, 1694), 10–11, 42, 87, 194.

152 Jacob, *Every Man his Own Lawyer: Or a Summary of the Laws of England in a New and Instructive Method* (London, 1736), vi; and cf the preface to *The Attorney's Pocket Companion: Or a Guide to the Practisers of the Law*, 2 vols (London, 1733) where the author warns against popular knowledge of law (here directed against legislation ending law Latin) because it will lead to frivolous and expensive suits.

153 Jacob, *Every Man his Own Lawyer*, v–vi.

154 Holdsworth, *History of English Law*, vol. 12, 356, vol. 6, 603.

155 Baker, *Introduction to English Legal History*, ch. 11. Important works on pleading in this period include, William Brown, *Methodus Novissima Intrandi Placita Generali, Or a New, Compleat and Exact Method...of Drawing and Entring Declarations, Pleas, Issues ... To Which is Added a Compleat Analysis of the Science of True and Correct Pleading* (London, 1699); Robert Gardiner, *Instructor Clericalis* (multiple parts and edns, London, 1693–1727); *Regula Placitandi: a Collection of Special Rules for Pleading* (London, 1691); George

entries, and they met a real need among students, novice lawyers, and court clerks. They were also an important reference tool for more experienced practitioners, some of whom closely studied and annotated these texts, or produced their own extensive manuscripts of precedents of pleading.[156]

One of the most comprehensive of these printed works on pleading and procedure was the *Instructor Clericalis*, a multi-volume work first appearing in 1693 and reissued in various volumes and editions up until 1727.[157] Each volume contained useful information regarding practice, such as proper abbreviations, methods of entering judgments and of drawing up declarations, as well as many 'choice and useful precedents for pleadings'. These were small, portable texts, initially compiled by Robert Gardiner, a clerk in the court of Common Pleas, and meant for easy reference. Information was generally presented thematically rather than alphabetically in these volumes, although occasionally topics were treated in alphabetical order and each volume also had a copious alphabetical index.[158] Holdsworth described *The Instructor Clericalis* as 'a miscellaneous book, not very well arranged', yet Gardiner's contemporaries evidently found it useful and recognised that combination of thematic exposition with the help of alphabetical organisation characteristic of the encyclopedia and commonplace books.[159] After 1731 these printed books on pleading were considered to be particularly valuable because once the change was made to the use of English in the

Townesend, *A Preparative to Pleading, Being a Work Intended for the Instruction and Help of Young Clerks of the Court of Common Pleas* (London, 1675); John Lilly, *Modern Entries, Being a Collection of Select Pleadings in the Courts of Kings Bench, Common Pleas and Exchequer*, 2 vols (London, 1723); William Bohun, *Declarations and Pleadings in the Most Usual Actions Brought in the Central Courts of Kings Bench and Common Pleas at Westminster* (London 1733). Also note that earlier texts, like Samson Euer's *Doctrina Placitandi, Or L'Art & Science De Bon Pleading* (London, 1677) or Anthony Fitzherbert's *La Nouvel Natura Brevium* (London, 1583), were still used and also published in new editions.

156 See for example William Brown's preface to his *Praxis Almae Curiae Cancellariae: A Collection of Precedents by Bill and Answer, Plea and Demurrer* (London, 1694; and subsequent editions in 1705, 1725) where he states that his main purpose is to help common law clerks, also called 'country practisers', who live far from London, without opportunity for apprenticeship and experience. Examples of practitioners who compiled their own manuscript books of pleadings include: HLS, 1055, 1166 (and note that such manuscripts cite Gardiner's *Instructor Clericalis*, among other authorities).

157 Holdsworth, *History of English Law*, vol. 6, 602, vol. 12, 357.

158 For example, in the second volume, after actions/deed, the text proceeds alphabetically to take up covenant, debt, detinue, ejectment, prohibition, trespass, trover, waste. The alphabetical index in the first volume was also divided jurisdictionally, between Kings Bench and Common Pleas.

159 See Gardiner, *Instructor Clericalis* preface to Part I of the edition of 1707, for example, which notes the necessity of producing multiple editions because of the popularity of this text. Holdsworth went on to admit that the *Instructor Clericalis* 'contains a mass of useful information on practice and pleading, and more especially on pleading.' Holdsworth, *History of English Law*, vol. 12, 358.

courts there were new uncertainties about proper pleading.[160] The author of *The Attorney's Pocket Companion* expressed worry about this uncertainty, and what he saw as a new hardship for practitioners, and presented his work as a useful remedy. In a critique of the overreach of the statute mandating the use of the vernacular, the author also expressed doubts that this change in language actually made the law any more comprehensible to laymen in England and, even more doubtfully, to those in Wales or Scotland.[161] Yet the author also capitalised on these changes in legal practice and print culture by publishing his own helpful 'pocket companion'.

Giles Jacob's two-volume *The Compleat Attorney's Practice* (1737) included large sections of text focused on pleading but he did not produce a separate text on this topic.[162] The focus of most of Jacob's works for practitioners was, instead, conveyancing, that is the methods for the transfer of property that were at the core of common law knowledge. Conveyancing was of particular use to provincial attorneys and solicitors in the eighteenth century as they began to focus more on such business activities and less on litigation in the central courts.[163] Jacob's books on conveyancing were arranged thematically and similarly stuffed with exemplary precedents. Texts such as Jacob's *The Accomplish'd Conveyancer* (1714–15), and his *The Grand Precedent: or the Conveyancer's Guide and Assistant* (1716), provided precedents of deeds and instruments, including bargain and sale, gifts and grants, or mortgages and surrenders, and covered the conveyance of stocks, bonds and annuities as well as of real and personal estates. These texts also offered 'practical information as to the significance of the usual clauses in conveyances', observations on the legal principles involved, and additional information on procedure.[164] Some other such texts, like John Lilly's *Practical Conveyancer*,

160 Baker *Introduction to English Legal History*, 87, Holdsworth, *History of English Law*, vol. 12, 356.

161 *Attorney's Pocket Companion*, preface. This defence of law language by an argument from the 'British' perspective was joined by other arguments about how this legislation would benefit defendants rather than plaintiffs, and how it could also possibly harm commercial interests.

162 Giles Jacob, *The Compleat Attorney's Practice in English, in the Courts of Kings Bench and Common Pleas* (London, 1737) includes sections on pleading in the two Westminster courts. Note also that some information on pleading is also conveyed in Jacob's *Catalogue of Writs and Processes* which proceeds as an alphabetical abridgment of writs and includes a 'concise Account of their Nature and Use'.

163 Horwitz, 'Changes in the Law and Reform', 310; Henry Horwitz and Lloyd Bonfield, 'The "Lower Branches" of the Legal Profession: A London Society of Attorneys and Solicitors of the 1730s and its "Moots"', *Cambridge Law Journal*, 49 (November, 1990): 461–4, 472.

164 Jacob, *Grand Precedent or Conveyancer's Guide and Assistant*; Jacob, *Accomplished Conveyancer*, vol. 1; John Lilly, *The Practical Register: Or A General Abridgment of the Law*, 2 vols (London, 1719), part 1; Holdsworth, *History of English Law*, vol. 12, 376. Cf also *The Second part of the Modern Conveyancer, Or Conveyancing Improved, in Two Volumes. Being a Choice Collection of Presidents on Most Occasions … to Which are Added*

provided this information under alphabetical heads, and used the marginal citations and cross-referencing typical of the commonplace and abridgment. Jacob's volumes on conveyancing proceeded topically and in more expository prose, but the format of his volumes was also recognisable and aimed at accessibility and ease of use like the abridgments and encyclopedias.

The self-proclaimed goal of Jacob's *The Accomplish'd Conveyancer* was to create a 'directory' for practitioners 'so as to draw any Deed or Conveyance in the most effectual manner', thus ensuring a successful practice for the lawyer and security for his client.[165] Jacob similarly conceived of *The Grand Precedent: or the Conveyancer's Guide and Assistant* as a portable library which might function as an aid to memory for the young practitioner drawing up deeds. The reader was reminded to use these precedents with care however, and cautioned against simple and slavish reproduction. The forms, customs and precedents of common law were useful only when understood, Jacob insisted, and not when they were emptied of meaning. Here Jacob presented himself as an example to be emulated, recommending a course of diligence and experience.

Although he did not have the same kind of reputation or stature as some other authors of law books, Jacob's intermediary position between popular and professional allowed him to more easily identify with the student, the professional, and the common reader. It is vital to appreciate Jacob's intentions with regard to his readers because then we take an important step towards understanding the multiple audiences for these texts, the strategies lawyers used in reading them, and the similarities between this practical legal literature and the many abridgments, compilations, and libraries produced for readers in other fields.

Owning, commonplacing, annotating: trends in legal thinking

Giles Jacob's works on law, like the rest of the practical legal literature produced by Nelson, Bacon, D'Anvers, Lilly and others, were conceived of as reference works and repositories, and as a means of collecting, selecting, and often condensing the learning of the common law. This was the sense in which they were 'practical' books, to be used selectively, in study and practice, for the retrieval of information. But many of these law books were also intended to be used in their entirety, as coherent books to be read, not just consulted. Here the same insights into intentionality and authorship that scholars have brought to bear on the analysis of eighteenth-century dictionaries, libraries and encyclopedias apply to many of the law books too:

Opinions of Several Learned Council, Relating to Conveyancing and other Matters in Law, 2 vols (London, 1704).

165 Jacob, *Accomplished Conveyancer*, v, vii.

they 'promised to replace other books, condensing knowledge … [and] they were conceived as having a structure or design, planned by an author.'[166] These books were intended to provide information and instruction in an area of the law – or in the case of the large abridgments, in the entirety of the common law – not only for students and novices but also for experienced practitioners who needed help in confronting the burgeoning literature of the law.

Embedded in this conception of an audience made up of novices and of experienced attorneys is a particular conception of expertise. Legal expertise was thought to consist of a mastery of the material, but also an ability to consult multiple sources and retrieve valuable information, an ability to read these texts and use these sources intelligently and not 'slavishly' with simple repetition rather than reasoning. The act of reading (and gaining expertise) was envisioned in much the same way as the act of commonplace composition, not simply as copying information but as a way of conceiving, organising and generating knowledge. In the development of these reading and commonplace practices we see the further evolution of what John Baker has described as a transition from 'common erudition' to 'common opinion' which was so important to the emergence of a jurisprudence focused on case law.[167]

If these were some of the intentions behind the composition of the law books, what are the indications of reader expectations and approaches? Information about readers and reading strategies can be found in legal commonplace books, lawyers' notes written in preparation for trial or other elements of practice, catalogues of lawyers' libraries and subscriber lists, and in the annotated law books themselves. In such sources we can see who actually read all these books, and whether the audience for these books matched the audience conceived of by authors and compilers. We also find evidence about the real usefulness or accessibility of these books; and, although more difficult to ascertain, evidence of readers gathering knowledge as well as information, or engaging in jurisprudential reflection as well as memorising facts.

Such evidence has survived from the period studied here, the later seventeenth and early eighteenth centuries, but it is important to be aware that those traces of reading were themselves read and used and valued by successive generations of readers. This is further indication of the intersections between manuscript and print, and between composition and consumption.[168] It is clear from these records that law texts were used as authorities

166 Yeo, 'Encyclopedic Knowledge', 210. Cf Chartier, *Order of Books*, 64–6.

167 Baker, *Law's Two Bodies*, 86.

168 Note inscriptions of owners' names dated well into the nineteenth century, for example in copies of Fitzherbert's *La Graunde Abridgment* (London, 1516 and 1577) FLP, Carson LC 4 210, LC 4 214, or *Attorney's Pocket Companion* (London, 1733) FLP, Carson LC 1537. The fact that interleaving of books is noted by contemporaries who compiled

to be cited in students' notebooks and lawyers' arguments. These books were also used *as* commonplace books, books that could be annotated, interleaved, and turned into a hybrid between textbook and notebook, reminding us of the instability of the text 'written' by an author.[169] Early modern annotation, like commonplace, practices were 'modeled on those of the classical grammarians and editors', H.J. Jackson explains. These practices included 'textual collations and corrections, explanations of hard words and obscure passages, references to sources, and illustrative examples'.[170] There was little expression of personal opinion, Jackson confirms, yet even if it is unclear what the individual reader made of a text, recognising the particularities of legal reading strategies can still provide insights into the evolution of a defence of the common law.

The audience for these books was, indeed, essentially the same as the audience conceived of by the authors. Students, attorneys, clerks and judges read these books. The nominative case reports were collected and highly-valued, but the abridgments were also purchased and well-used. D'Anvers' *General Abridgment of the Common Law*, for example, boasted a long list of subscribers which included men called to the bar of the Middle and Inner Temples, men identified with other Inns, as well as a sizable number of booksellers.[171] The library lists of eminent men, such as Lord Chancellor William Cowper or Justice Martin Wright, indicate that they collected abridgments along with many other practical legal texts. Cowper's library included 'Nelsons collection 2 vols', Wingate's and Washington's abridgments of the statutes, Fitzherbert's *Graunde Abridgment* as well as his *Natura Brevium*, and Statham's *Abridgment*.[172] These volumes were not only passed down after the lord chancellor's death, but his collection practices were emulated during his lifetime by a nephew who admired the accomplished uncle's great learning and wealth. This young man sought Cowper's advice, and asked for funds so that he could purchase Rolle's Abridgment, and other 'good ones', to begin 'a proper collection of the larger sort.'[173] Martin Wright, who was a baron

inventories of eighteenth-century libraries is another indication of the value of readers' notes.

169 Chartier, *Order of Books*, 9–10.

170 H.J. Jackson, *Marginalia: Readers Writing in Books* (New Haven, 2001), 50.

171 D'Anvers, *General Abridgment of the Common Law*, vol. 1 (London, 1705), FLP, Carson LC 4 246.

172 Inventory of William Cowper's Library, HALS, Panshanger MS D/EP F214. Studies of the formation and significance of private libraries include Robin Myers and Michael Harris eds, *Property of a Gentleman: The Formation, Organization and Dispersal of the Private Library 1629–1920* (Winchester, 1991); Margaret Willes, *Reading Matters: Five Centuries of Discovering Books* (Yale 2008); Giles Mandelbrote, 'Personal Owners of Books', in Giles Mandelbrote and K.A. Manley eds, *Cambridge History of Libraries in Britain and Ireland, Volume 2, 1640–1850* (Cambridge, 2006), 173–89.

173 Letter from nephew to Earl Cowper, 31 May 1711, HALS, Panshanger D/EP F58, fols 84–6. This nephew William, the son of the lord chancellor's brother Spencer

of the court of the Exchequer, then a judge on the Kings Bench, and a legal writer himself, owned even more of the abridgments.[174] Wright's library catalogue lists the abridgments of Brooke, Statham, Fitzherbert, Rolle, Nelson, D'Anvers, Cay, Bacon and Viner, as well as the *General Abridgment of Cases in Equity* attributed to Bacon, Robbins' *Abridgment of Irish Statutes* and *Hawkins' Abridgment of Coke*. Although Giles Jacob's abridgments were not listed among these other volumes, Wright's library did include Jacob's *Law Dictionary* (1732 edition), *Lex Mercatoria*, *City Liberties*, and the collection of Holt's reports edited by (although not here attributed to) Jacob.[175]

The catalogue of another attorney, William Carr, printed in anticipation of the sale of books and manuscripts from his library, also lists many abridgments and some of Jacob's texts among the enormous number of law books for sale. William Carr, 'of Lincoln's-Inn, Esq; Late one of the Commissioners of the Excise; Of an Eminent Counsellor at Law', apparently owned the abridgments of Rolle, Fitzherbert, Brooke, Statham, Sheppard, Wingate and Washington, an abridgment of the Irish Statutes, and various abridgments of Coke's Reports and Coke on Littleton.[176] This library – like Cowper's and Wright's – included the 'classics' of law written by Coke, Fortescue, St German or Hale. However Giles Jacob's *Catalogue of Writs and Processes*, *Compleat Court-keeper*, *Conveyancer's Guide and Assistant*, *Laws of Appeal and Murder* and *Gentleman's Law* were for sale on Carr's list along with the works of many others legal compilers like Gardiner, Blount and Euer. The catalogue of Carr's library also listed a selection of law manuscripts for sale; these included manuscript notes and reports, and manuscript copies of published as well as unpublished texts.[177] Both Carr's and Wright's lists

Cowper, became clerk of the parliaments after the Hanoverian accession. Another letter from him, 5 July 1711, HALS, Panshanger D/EP F58, fols 87–8, mentions the copy of Coke's Reports which his father Spencer has just passed on to him, before focusing on the main subject of the letter – a denial of his intention to marry, despite rumours about his romantic liasons that might have reached Earl Cowper and incurred his disapproval.

174 J.H. Baker, 'Wright, Martin', *ODNB*; Edward Foss, *The Judges of England*, vol. 8 (London, 1864; reprint New York, 1966), 177–8; Holdsworth, *History of English Law*, vol. 12, 369. Wright was the author of *An Introduction to the Law of Tenures* (London, 1729).

175 Catalogue of Sir Martin Wright Library 1769, IT, Barrington 63.

176 Browne, *Catalogue of the Libraries of Carr and Herbert*. Although the catalogue does not distinguish between the libraries of these two men, I am assuming that Carr was the owner of the common law texts. These abridgments of law were not the only abridgments listed in this catalogue; volumes for sale from the combined libraries of Carr and the Reverend John Herbert included many other texts produced in this period of abridgment, encyclopedia, library and dictionary, such as abridgments of Boyle's philosophical works, of Collier's dictionary, of Raleigh's *History of the World*, and of Plutarch's *Morals*.

177 Browne, *Catalogue of the Libraries of Carr and Herbert*, 41–2. Examples of manuscript copies of printed law books include: FSL, v.b.64, a handwritten copy of *Obsborne's Short Compendium of Exchequer Practices*, which was owned by Chief Baron Parker, and passed along as a prized possession by John [Webb] in November 1747; and FLP, Carson, LC 14.45, a manuscript copy of *Lord Keeper Guilford on Pardons*, and the first tract in a care-

further indicated which printed volumes were interleaved with manuscript notes, demonstrating another facet of the intersections between print and manuscript, reading and writing.

This practice of interleaving a book entailed binding or rebinding the printed text with additional blank pages which were to be used for note-taking and commentary. Examples of texts used in this way in Carr's library include 'Perkins Law interleaved', 'Method of Passing Bills in Parliament interleaved', and 'Compleat Justice interleaved with large notes'.[178] Martin Wright owned interleaved copies of Finch's *Discourse of the Law* (2 vols 1627), Euer's *Doctrina Placitandi* (1677), and 'four volumes of D'Anvers' *Abridgment* (1701) with manuscript notes'.[179] Another example of an extensively interleaved and annotated copy of Euer's *Doctrina Placitandi* is to be found in the library of Henry Singleton, an Irish Tory politician and lawyer who served first as chief justice of the Irish court of Common Pleas, and then as master of the rolls in Ireland, throughout the 1740s and 50s.[180] Singleton's copy of *Doctrina Placitandi* is a massive text: the printed work of over four hundred pages, quarto-sized and in law French, is bound with hundreds of folio-sized pages of manuscript notes in a small and remarkably consistent hand, generally written in English. The first pages consist of manuscript notes on pleading, written in two columns on each folio page and as a series of enumerated points, with references to Euer's text, to his own marginalia, and to other authorities (mostly the nominative reports) noted at the end of each line. After a series of blank interleaved pages, the printed text of *Doctrina Placitandi* begins. Additional manuscript notes with citations and cross-references to this text, as well as to the annotator's notes in other law texts, appear on the printed quarto pages. Moreover, the annotator frequently re-orders and renumbers the printed text. The manuscript notes on the interleaved folio pages continue the discussion of material that

fully transcribed presentation copy that also included *The Judgment of the Court of Kings Bench in the case of Middleton and Croft On a Prohibition to the Consistory Court of the Bishop of Hereford Michaelmas Term 10th Geo: 2d 1736*, *Observations On the Three Acts of Parliament 3d Geo: 1st by which the Aggregate South Sea and General Funds are Established*, and a case report regarding the question of future payments from London's Orphans' Fund.

178 Browne, *Catalogue of the Libraries of Carr and Herbert*, 16, 18, 22.

179 IT, Barrington 63.

180 DLL, Singleton 43. Other examples of interleaved texts in the Singleton collection include Matthew Hale's *Pleas of the Crown: Or, a Methodical Summary of the Principal Matters Relating to that Subject* (London, 1707), DLL, Singleton 41, and William Hawkins' A *Treatise of the Pleas of the Crown, Or a System of the Principal Matters Relating to that Subject*, 2 vols (London, 1716–21), DLL, Singleton 40. The attribution of notes in these and other texts to Henry Singleton is not conclusive. Yet another example of an interleaved and annotated copy of Euer's *Doctrina Placitandi*, with manuscript notes said to be written by Francis Hargrave, is BL 1144.k.15; another copy of Euer's text which is not heavily annotated is FLP, Carson LC 6 130.

appears on the printed page and include topic headings which translate and change the printed headings.[181] This is a dramatic example of deep engagement with the law text, and of the ways in which commonplace practices were brought to bear on the printed page.

A well-worn copy of Rolle's two-volume *Abridgment* (1668), passed down from owner to owner as late as 1828, provides one more example of a massive and extensively interleaved printed text.[182] In this copy each page of the folio printed text is interleaved with a folio page to be used for manuscript notes. Each volume is also interleaved at front and back with pages of manuscript commonplace headings which served as an alphabetical index to both the printed and manuscript texts. Here the annotators provided a commonplace for a book already organised alphabetically, although these additional pages often provided more specific indications of just what topics were discussed in the text. The first volume opens with an initial page of notes written in English, law French and Latin, and subsequent manuscript notes are similarly varied, written in multiple hands and languages by multiple generations. These manuscript notes appear as enumerated points, as simple references to statutes, decrees and relevant cases, and as maxims of the common law. The entry on 'Chancery' in volume one, for example, is annotated in the margins with notes in law French and a reference to a 1718 decree by Lord Chancellor Macclesfield, as well as references to named cases and the nominative reports. This entry also includes interleaved pages with references to other cases, statutes and maxims such as 'He that will have equity must doe equity' or 'Equity sequitur Lege[m]'.[183]

The owners and annotators of these books seem to have taken Giles Jacob's advice to heart, understanding that where 'the Treatise be large, and your Memory treacherous, it will be necessary to make Remarks as you proceed, or at the end of every Chapter.'[184] These interleaved texts give us a real sense of the intertwined practices of reading and writing, and they give us a sense of the impact a text could have on its reader. The mutual influences of the commonplace book and the printed law book in their general format, and even in the specific layout of the page, shaped reader, author and publisher practices. These books looked familiar to the reader,

[181] The techniques of interleaving and note-taking here are similar to those used on other texts in the Singleton collection, especially the heavily annotated copy of Hale's *Pleas of the Crown*.

[182] Henry Rolle, *Un Abridgment des Plusiers Cases et Resolutions del Common Ley* (London, 1668), Biddle Law Library, University of Pennsylvania Law School, Philaldelphia, PA, KH/KD 295 R64 1668. Owners' inscriptions on the title page include Jacob R. Howell 1785(?), Richard C. Wood 1816 and W. Bouvier Sept. 19 1828. Another example is the copy of Rolle's abridgment annotated by Baron Price, IT, Misc. MSS 125–30. And an example of an annotated, but not interleaved, copy is Henry Rolle, *Un Abridgment des Plusiers Cases* (London, 1668), FSL, 143- 353f, vols 1–2.

[183] Rolle, *Un Abridgment*, Biddle Law Library, 370–7, esp. 371.

[184] Jacob, *Student's Companion* vi–vii.

with marginal citations, enumerated points, and topic headings. Readers were guided and constrained by this format but they were also, in part, the creators of these structures through their notes and commonplace books.[185] These copiously annotated and interleaved texts offer another indication that this growing practical literature was supplementing and perhaps even replacing the manuscript practice of composing a legal commonplace book. Printed texts like Rolle's *Abridgment* and Euer's *Doctrina Placitandi* were viewed as essential volumes that could be rendered even more useful as commonplace books. This practice of interleaving and transformation was advocated for other essential texts, like Blackstone's *Commentaries*, into the nineteenth century.[186]

Interleaved texts also provide evidence of reader independence and creativity through examples of explanatory or expository notes. The Singleton Collection's copies of *Doctrina Placitandi*, or of Hawkins' and Hale's *Pleas of the Crown*, for example, include complex summaries, historical narratives and legal analysis of the printed text composed by readers. The manuscript notes in these and other interleaved texts also reveal aspects of that 'interpretive grid' readers brought to their books, indicating areas of lawyer interests, influences and concerns.[187] That general law-reader's interest in conveyancing and the adjudication of property disputes, for example, is evidenced by the fact that the chapter on 'devises' is one of the most heavily annotated sections of an interleaved copy of Matthew Bacon's *General Abridgment of Cases in Equity*.[188] In all of these examples, readers are engaged in dialogue with texts – adding, disagreeing, emphasising, comparing, contrasting – and in dialogue with other readers, as this intergenerational community bequeaths texts, notes and reader practices. There was, then, dialogue and debate as well as memorisation and repetition in these practical tomes. The activities of reading, and writing, from the specific to general, from remedies to rules – and indeed the whole emphasis on citation of precedents, statutes and authorities – are indicative of that common law belief in the accretion of custom and the authority of tradition. These reading and writing practices are, however, also indicative of the kinds of reading strategies deemed useful in approaching texts such as the Enlightenment encyclopedias. Readers of law books were ideal examples of what Richard Yeo, following the eighteenth-century writer Isaac Watts,

185 Chartier, *Order of Books*, 23.

186 Hoeflich, 'Lawyer Pragmatic Reader', 109; Yeo, 'Encyclopedism and Enlightenment', 360.

187 Moss, *Printed Commonplace Books*, 136.

188 This copy of Bacon, *General Abridgment of Cases in Equity* (1732), FLP, Carson LC8 106, was owned by the Scottish lawyer Alexander Hume Campbell (1708–1760), descendant of Campbell (1675–1740), Lord of the Scottish Sessions.

calls 'active readers' who properly drew out the system and coherence of such books.[189]

Other examples of annotated law books have survived that are not as heavily over-written or interleaved. The reader practices here appear more muted and detached, although like the interleaved texts these manuscript annotations appear in multiple hands and multiple languages, and continue the familiar use of headings, enumerated lists, and cross-references. Marginal annotations appear in copies of practical texts such as *The Attorney's Pocket Companion*, *Instructor Clericalis*, Hawkins' *Abridgment of the First Part of … Coke's Institute*, *Hughes' Quaeries* and Fitzherbert's *La Graunde Abridgment*.[190] Often the notes in these books are minimal and consist simply of underlining or otherwise noting important passages, or they are corrections of errata. There are also, however, manuscript notes that aim to clarify the printed text, and notes that distill or summarise the text. Many times the notes indicate a reader's attempt to make these books useful, by adding topical headings in the margins for example, or again to make these books a type of commonplace, by adding marginal references to other texts, cases, statutes or maxims.[191]

Finally there are, of course, many other surviving copies of abridgments, works on pleading and process, law dictionaries and other useful texts that were not annotated or interleaved. One reason was the impracticality of obtaining pen and ink in order to annotate those portable texts by Jacob, and others, which served as an 'itinerant library'. Also, readers would not be likely to annotate the large abridgments of Bacon, Nelson or Jacob if they used them primarily as a directory or dictionary. And if some of these abridgments served as readers' ready-made commonplace books, the printed text itself performed the function of composition and citation. Even without manuscript notes on the printed page of the abridgments, however, traces of reader practices can be found in the citation of these and other practical texts in lawyers' commonplace books and notebooks of precedents of pleading. The early eighteenth-century commonplace book of Sydenham Fowke, nephew of Henry Singleton, for example, relied on *Style's Practical*

189 Yeo, 'Encyclopaedism and Enlightenment', 360–1.

190 Annotated copies consulted: *Attorney's Pocket Companion*, 2 vols (London, 1733) FLP, Carson LC15 37; William Hawkins, *Abridgment of the First Part of Lord Coke's Institutes* (London 1711) Biddle Law Library, KH/KD 600 C65 1711, and (London, 1736) FLP Carson LC6 52; *Hughes' Quaeries* (London, 1675) FLP, Carson LC8 144; Fitzherbert, *La Graunde Abridgment* (London, 1516) FLP, Carson LC4 210 and (London, 1577) FLP, Carson LC4 214; Gardiner, *Instructor Clericalis* (London, 1695), HLS, Harvard Rare Wing G241, and (London, 1697–1722) HLS UK 017 GAR, and (London, 1727) HLS, Rare Treatises G.

191 For notes that distill or summarise, and add marginal references, see, for example, the heavily annotated portions of Fitzherbert, *La Graunde Abridgment* (London, 1516) FLP, Carson LC4 210, vol. 1 on 'Accion sur case', 'Barre', vol. 2 on 'Dette'; and (London, 1577) FLP, Carson LC4 214 on 'Corone et plees de corone'.

Register, while John Strange tended to cite its successor, *Lilly's Practical Register*, in his commonplace book.[192] Citations to abridgments by Bacon, Lilly and Viner, as well as Euer's *Doctrina Placitandi*, appear frequently in a small commonplace book composed in the late eighteenth and early nineteenth centuries.[193] Those notebook collections of precedents of pleading also relied upon abridgments by D'Anvers, Lilly, Viner and Bacon as well as Gardiner's *Instructor Clericalis*.[194] And these texts appear more frequently and silently in the citation of cases and precedents in other commonplace books, since it could have been more useful to cite the case or statute or treatise, rather than the abridgment, for future reference and retrieval. Indeed, legal commonplace books demonstrate a certain continuity over time in the citation of statutes, of case reports, and of a handful of canonical texts such as the works of Coke, Littleton, Rolle, St German's *Doctor and Student* and, somewhat less frequently, the works of Bracton and Fitzherbert. In the later eighteenth and early nineteenth centuries the newer treatises, such as those written by Gilbert and Blackstone, begin to be cited.[195]

Lawyers continued to compose commonplace books well into the nineteenth century.[196] Abridgments continued to be used, and attempts were still made to make legal learning manageable and comprehensible. There was a persistence of this legal learning and thinking that remained part of a developing common law jurisprudence. This emphasis on citation of precedents and authorities, and this legal reasoning that developed through enumeration, comparison and cross-reference, was not simply backward-looking. Nor was it simply a rejection of some rationalist, abstract, Enlightenment ideals. Rather the legal literature and legal learning of the early eighteenth century was fully part of humanist traditions of scholarship, and fully part of more widespread enlightened approaches to the mastery and communication of knowledge.

192 FLP, Carson LC.14.86; DLL, Singleton 37; cf also reliance on William Style in FLP, Carson LC.14.98.

193 HLS, 6020.

194 HLS, 1055, 1166.

195 HLS, 1055, 4011, 6020; DLL, Singleton 37.

196 See examples of nineteenth-century lawyers' commonplace books in HLS, 6019, 6020, FLP, Carson LC 14 100.

3

Expertise and Evidentiary Practices in Science and Law

Scientific and medical books, like law books, proliferated in the early eighteenth century. This 'ocean of books' had also begun to swell in the late sixteenth and seventeenth centuries, with the advent of printing and the establishment of the Royal Society, but took on certain characteristic forms in the eighteenth century. For example periodicals, like the Royal Society's *Philosophical Transactions*, became a favoured and flourishing medium for circulating new research and information. In addition large, expensive, multivolume reference works were produced, again with the approval or even encouragement of an authoritative body like the Royal Society whose printer in the 1690s, Samuel Smith, pioneered methods that made publication and distribution of such volumes affordable and even profitable.[1] Both law books and science books and journals benefited from such kinds of official support even though Britain's was an unregulated printing regime after 1695.[2] Beyond such official or corporate control, more modest vernacular medical books formed a third, and very popular, mode of publication of natural knowledge in this period. These medical books became an important means by which a wide range of practitioners established a reputation by offering their own techniques and remedies in print. Such popular texts were consulted by other practitioners, including members of the College

1 Johns, 'Science and the Book', 274–5. The phrase 'ocean of books' appears in numerous contemporary texts. Johns, 'Print and Public Science', 542–3; Thomas H. Broman, 'Periodical Literature', in Marina Frasca-Spada and Nick Jardine eds, *Books and the Sciences in History* (Cambridge, 2000), 225–38. As Richard Yeo notes, the review of a multivolume dictionary of science like John Harris' *Lexicon Technicum* in the *Philosophical Transactions* affirmed its value not only in defining terms but also in conveying scientific information. Richard Yeo, 'Classifying the Sciences', in Roy Porter ed., *The Cambridge History of Science, Volume 4: Eighteenth-Century Science* (Cambridge, 2003), 255; and cf Yeo, 'Encyclopaedic Knowledge', 208.

2 On royal patents and legal publishing see below, chapter 4. On the Royal Society as a 'corporate licenser' and 'corporate publisher' see Adrian Johns, 'History, Science, and the History of the Book: The Making of Natural Philosophy in Early Modern England', *Publishing History*, 30 (1991): 14.

of Physicians and of the Royal Society, as well as by ordinary readers who sought advice on self-diagnosis and recipes for useful cures.[3]

All of these kinds of scientific and medical publications shared a common goal with eighteenth-century law books, such as the abridgments, because they too attempted to disseminate, in more accessible forms, a growing body of knowledge. Natural knowledge was condensed and popularised in the vernacular medical literature, and in newer encyclopedic works like John Harris' *Lexicon Technicum*. Periodicals like the *Philosophical Transactions* also furthered these developments by including notices, reviews and abridgments of books within their pages. Students and practitioners of science, like those in law, could thus avoid labouring over 'a long and ponderous treatise' but still discover what useful knowledge lay within. Here these publications illuminate the shared educational and reading practices of eighteenth-century men of science and men of law, and allow us to see the cultural norms that shaped individual, and in this case also professional, practice.[4] Scientific readers, like law readers, tried to follow the advice on note-taking, commonplacing and indexing offered by their teachers and trusted advisors. For English doctors especially whose education, like lawyers', consisted of apprenticeship and private study more than university training, such advice on how to read was indispensible.[5] Reading also took place in public spaces: the classic eighteenth-century example is the coffeehouse, where combined conversation and reading, shared print (especially periodicals), and mixed company, generated new expectations for the circulation of information.[6] Finally, reading and writing were activities that remained closely tied to the scientific practice of observation. 'In addition to the fact that note-taking in the lab and in the field derived from note-taking on books,' Lorraine Daston explains, 'the processes by which attention was channeled and held, and by which seeing was converted first into writing (and drawing) and then into reading, are suggestive of how nature was made intelligible by being made legible.'[7]

3 Johns, 'Science and the Book', 283–4; Fissell and Cooter, 'Exploring Natural Knowledge', 146–51; Fissell, *Vernacular Bodies*. Note for example the transcription of many remedies for ailments such as 'mad dog bite', 'gout', 'pissing blood', 'infection from small pox', 'hystericks and melancholy' in FSL, MS V.a. 260.

4 Broman, 'Periodical Literature', 225, 229; Ann Blair, 'An Early Modernist's Perspective', *Isis*, 95, 3 (2004): 421.

5 Blair, 'Annotating and Indexing Natural Philosophy'; Blair, 'Humanist Methods in Natural Philosophy'. Thomas H. Broman, 'The Medical Sciences', in Roy Porter ed., *The Cambridge History of Science, Volume 4: Eighteenth-Century Science* (Cambridge, 2003), 465; Rosemary O'Day, *The Professions in Early Modern England 1450–1800: Servants of the Commonweal* (New York, 2000), 222–36.

6 Johns, 'Print and Public Science', 553–4.

7 Lorraine Daston, 'Taking Note(s)', *Isis*, 95, 3 (September, 2004): 446. See also Scott Mandelbrote, 'Professional Collections: Libraries for Scientists and Doctors', in Giles Mandlebrote and K.A. Manley eds, *Cambridge History of Libraries in Britain and Ireland*,

Evidence that reading, note-taking and commonplacing remained essential activities for scientists in the eighteenth century – even after the advent of experimentation, observation and mathematical investigation as dominant methods of discovery – is to be found in their surviving manuscript notebooks, as well as their annotations and marginalia in printed books. Moreover these notes became valued possessions and were, like annotated law books and legal commonplace books, sold to other members of the scientific community or passed down to the next generation of scholars.[8] A particularly interesting example of this kind of bequest, and worth attributed to notes, can be found in the collection of books annotated by Sir Isaac Newton. Scholars focused on Newton's use of cross-referencing, commentary, correction and highlighting, have discerned changing patterns within his scholarly practices and professional interests.[9] Less attention has been paid, however, to the fact that many of Newton's annotated books and manuscripts ended up in the library of the Earls of Macclesfield – a fact that offers another indication of the commonalities between legal and scientific print cultures in the eighteenth century. The founder of this library, the first earl of Macclesfield, was not only a prominent judge but he was also a member of the Royal Society and a man of wide-ranging intellect, closely acquainted with a physician-philosopher like Bernard Mandeville and a scientist like Newton.[10] The inclusion of hundreds of Newton's books and manuscripts in the Macclesfield library likely came about through this personal relationship and, even more importantly, through the bequest of two other scientists and mathematicians associated with Newton, John Collins and William Jones, whom the first earl and his son studied with, supported and befriended. It is worth noting too that Jones's son was the later eighteenth-century linguist and judge whose legal commonplace book was discussed in the previous chapter. The importance of reading, note-taking, conversation and correspondence is evident in the careers of all these men of science and of law.[11]

Volume 2, 1640–1850, 158–72, on the relationship between texts and equipment in collection and education.

8 Blair, 'Early Modernist's Perspective', 423–7; Daston, 'Taking Note(s)', 447; see discussion above pp. 45–6, 76–80.

9 Blair, 'Early Modernist's Perspective', 423; John Harrison, *The Library of Isaac Newton* (Cambridge, 1978), 15–27; Scott Mandelbrote, *Footprints of the Lion: Isaac Newton at Work*, Cambridge University Library Exhibition, http://www.lib.cam.ac.uk/Exhibitions/Footprints_of_the_Lion/index.html.

10 A.A. Hanham, 'Parker, Thomas', *ODNB*, and see chapter 6 below. Both Hanham and Paul Quarrie, 'The Scientific Library of the Earls of Macclesfield', *Notes and Records of the Royal Society*, 20 (2006): 5–24, pointedly note that the first earl served as a pall-bearer at Newton's funeral.

11 Newton left some of his papers and books to Cambridge University, and more eventually came to the University in the nineteenth century as a result of an initial bequest of materials to Newton's niece, but an enormous amount remained in the Macclesfield Library at Shirburn Castle. As late as the 1990s an 'archive of scientific

These connections and comparisons provide, in part, an elaboration of my argument about the relevance of humanist commonplace practices and enlightened encyclopedism to the analysis of an early eighteenth-century practical legal literature. Legal print culture and legal education, like scientific print culture and education, were part of that Enlightenment of communication, organisation and conversation. And yet there are also differences between these scientific and legal print cultures in the eighteenth century that must be explored.[12] For example, scientific publications were most frequently aimed at a transnational audience and debate, and law books generally were not. While there was certainly interest in comparing the laws, procedures and institutions of different jurisdictions within the British Isles, the value of a common law abridgment was greatest for a student or practitioner in England. An exception, of course, was the important market for English law books in the North American colonies.[13] For the early eighteenth century we can describe this legal print culture as a trans-regional one, although, when it persisted after 1776, it too became a transnational legal print culture.

A second area of some complexity lies in contemporary attitudes towards the originality and authenticity of printed texts. At the same time that works of natural knowledge, like legal knowledge, were being printed in large numbers and in a greater variety of forms, the authors, publishers and

papers of Sir Isaac Newton' was 'actually in a cupboard in the library, with a mass of other papers'. Quarrie, 'Scientific Library of Earls of Macclesfield', 6, 11–16; Peter Fox 'Foreword' and Scott Mandelbrote, 'Introduction', *Footprints of the Lion*. Quarrie adds that 'intellect and determination' enabled Jones, Hardwicke, Macclesfield and Newton all to escape their modest origins and to achieve fame and wealth.

12 The recognition of multiple Enlightenments, and of this 'media-driven concept of Enlightenment', also entails a recognition of multiple print cultures in the eighteenth century. Adrian Johns offers support for this contention: 'It seems clear enough,' he asserts, 'that the press, like other technological devices, can be subjected to different practical uses, and that as a result it can generate a variety of cultural consequences.' Johns, 'Print and Public Science', 538. While Johns is referring to different regional or national print cultures, I'm positing as well different professional or topical print cultures.

13 Mary Sarah Bilder, 'The Lost Lawyers: Early American Legal Literates and Transatlantic Legal Culture', *Yale Journal of Law and the Humanities*, 11, 1 (Winter, 1999): 47–117; Karen S. Beck, 'One Step at a Time: The Research Value of Law Student Notebooks', *Law Library Journal*, 91, 1 (Winter, 1999): 29–49; Alfred L. Brophy, 'Book Review: The Law Book In Colonial America: A History of the Book in America: The Colonial Book in the Atlantic World', *Buffalo Law Review*, 51 (Fall, 2003): 1119–43; Howell J. Heaney, 'A Signer of the Declaration of Independence Orders Books from London: Two Documents of George Read of Delaware in the Hampton L. Carson Collection of the Free Library of Philadelphia', *The American Journal of Legal History*, 2, 2 (April, 1958): 172–85; John H. Langbein, 'Chancellor Kent and the History of Legal Literature', *Columbia Law Review*, 93, 3 (April, 1993): 547–94; Eben Moglen, 'Taking the Fifth: Reconsidering the Origins of the Privilege Against Self-Incrimination', *Michigan Law Review*, 92 (March, 1994): 1095–1125.

printers of scientific texts sought to preserve their claims to originality and priority. As Adrian Johns notes, the frequent publication of pirated works was seen as a serious problem by these men. And they defined the problem of piracy quite broadly: a pirated text might be a work printed without authorisation, in a region different from the place of original publication, or it could be the extra copies printed, for extra profit, by an authorised printer; a pirated text might be one that imitated, abridged or translated another text, or one that reported on meetings of the members of a scientific group, like the Royal Society, that never actually occurred. Johns traces the steps taken by members of this scientific print culture to preserve the authenticity of their publications, and regards them as a crucial part of the development of an Enlightenment print culture of civility.[14]

Within this Enlightenment print culture, however, the authors, printers and publishers of law books expressed some different opinions regarding originality, primacy and facticity. First, in an eighteenth-century legal literature largely based on compilation, collection and abridgment the matter of new discovery and originality was not so critical. Authors like Knightley D'Anvers or Giles Jacob openly acknowledged their reliance on earlier abridgments, and emphasised the usefulness and comprehensiveness more than the novelty of their texts. Indeed the mastery of tradition, and of well-established practice, was at the heart of their enterprise. And yet, legal authors and publishers did register similar complaints against pirated texts printed in other jurisdictions – a law book published in London, for example, might caution against the purchase of an inauthentic and inaccurate copy produced in Dublin.[15] This kind of complaint was evidence of a concern about Irish competition, and a desire to maintain monopolistic control over legal publishing. It was also evidence of a concern with authenticity. The producers of legal and scientific books might differ on the questions of imitation and abridgment, yet they certainly shared the goals of authenticity and accuracy. Both promised their readers essential knowledge, and the tools for professional expertise.

But just what was accurate knowledge? What was the nature of 'fact' and 'truth'? The contradictory impulses within legal and scientific Enlightenment print cultures – towards dissemination, abridgment, popularisation, but also restriction and authorisation – is one indication that these questions remained unresolved, and were continuously debated in this period. Another indication is to be found in contemporary legal and natural-

[14] Johns, 'History, Science and History of the Book', 10, 14. Johns, 'Print and Public Science', 537, 539, 541–6; Johns' article concludes by tracing the eventual replacement of this culture of civility by a legalistic culture of copyright.

[15] See for example the preface to Geoffrey Gilbert, *The History and Practice of the High Court of Chancery … By the late Lord Chief Baron Gilbert. Printed from a Correct Manuscript Copy, Free from the Numerous Errors and Omissions of the Irish Edition* (London, 1758). See also Raven, 'The Book Trades', 17–18.

philosophical discussion about testimony, proof and fact. There was a wide range of such early modern ideas about witnessing and proof, probability and fact. And many scholars have charted the development of these ideas, providing newly historicised accounts of the concepts of rationality, truth and objectivity.[16] Here historians of science, interested in challenging the traditional narrative about the Scientific Revolution, have been affected by those methodological debates about the value of an internalist versus an externalist approach. As a result of their willingness to question an internalist story about scientific logic and rationality progressing towards greater truths, they have developed a better understanding of the history of fact and truth.[17] This area of scholarship has also been furthered because of a similar desire among legal historians to challenge the conventional and progressive

16 See for example Barbara J. Shapiro, *Probability and Certainty in Seventeenth-Century England: A Study of the Relationships Between Natural Science, Religion, History, Law and Literature* (Princeton, 1983); Shapiro, 'To A Moral Certainty: Theories of Knowledge and Anglo-American Juries 1600–1850', *Hastings Law Journal*, 38, 1 (1996): 153–93; Shapiro, *Beyond 'Reasonable Doubt' and 'Probable Cause': Historical Perspectives on the Anglo-American Law of Evidence* (Berkeley, 1991); Shapiro, 'The Concept "Fact": Legal Origins and Cultural Diffusion', *Albion*, 26, 1 (Spring, 1994): 1–26; Shapiro, *Culture of Fact*; Lorraine Daston, *Classical Probability in the Enlightenment* (Princeton, 1988); Daston, 'Probability and Evidence', in Daniel Garber and Michael Ayers eds, *The Cambridge History of Seventeenth-Century Philosophy*, vol. 2 (Cambridge, 1998), 1108–44; Daston, 'Marvelous Facts and Miraculous Evidence in Early Modern Europe', and 'Historical Epistemology', in James Chandler, Arnold I. Davidson and Harry Harootunian eds, *Questions of Evidence: Proof, Practice and Persuasion Across the Disciplines* (Chicago, 1994), 243–74, 282–5; Daston,'Attention and the Values of Nature in the Enlightenment', in Lorraine Daston and Fernando Vidal eds, *The Moral Authority of Nature* (Chicago, 2004), 100–26; Peter Dear, *Discipline and Experience: The Mathematical Way in the Scientific Revolution* (Chicago, 1995); Steven Shapin, *A Social History of Truth: Civility and Science in Seventeenth-Century England* (Chicago, 1994). Other scholars, like James Franklin, *The Science of Conjecture: Evidence and Probability before Pascal* (Baltimore, 2001) or R.W. Serjeantson, 'Testimony and Proof in Early Modern England', *Studies in the History and Philosophy of Science*, 30, 2 (June, 1999): 195–236, have also contributed to this field; see Serjeantson for a useful bibliography of some of these other works.

17 Paula Findlen, 'The Two Cultures of Scholarship?', *Isis*, 96, 2 (June, 2005): 230–7; Katharine Park, 'Women, Gender and Utopia: *The Death of Nature* and the Historiography of Early Modern Science', *Isis*, 97, 3 (September, 2006): 489–91; Steven Shapin, 'Discipline and Bounding: The History and Sociology of Science as Seen through the Externalism-Internalism Debate', *History of Science*, 30 (1992): 333–69; Deborah Harkness, 'Review: Entering the Labyrinth: Exploring Scientific Culture in Early Modern England', *Journal of British Studies*, 37, 4 (October, 1998): 446–50; Lorraine Daston, review of Steven Shapin *A Social History of Truth*, *The Journal of Philosophy*, 92, 7 (July, 1995): 391–2; Lorraine Daston and Peter Galison, 'The Image of Objectivity', *Representations*, 40 (Autumn, 1992): 81–128. See also, for example, Margaret J. Osler ed., *Rethinking the Scientific Revolution* (Cambridge, 2000); Steven Shapin, *The Scientific Revolution* (Chicago, 1996), H. Floris Cohen, *The Scientific Revolution: A Historiographical Inquiry* (Chicago, 1994); Roy Porter and Mikulas Teich eds, *The Scientific Revolution in National Context* (Cambridge, 1992).

view of the Anglo-American trial by jury as another hallmark of modernity and engine of truth; there has also been ongoing interest in recounting an internal history of the common law doctrine of evidence.[18]

These historians of science and of law have been particularly concerned to explain how and why enduring concepts of fact, truth and objectivity emerged in England and Europe between the sixteenth and eighteenth centuries. And a major element of this scholarship has been its emphasis on the influence of legal thought and practice on natural philosophy.[19] Moreover, while scholars have demonstrated the ways in which Romano-canonical process shaped the common law of evidence, they have also attributed particular importance to the early modern development of jury, rather than inquisitorial, trial in the formulation of methods of proof and standards of certainty. Scholars like John Langbein have argued that the increasingly adversarial nature of English jury trials, and the eventual admission of defence attorneys in criminal matters, underscored the necessary and growing reliance on witness testimony, furthering reflection on credibility and epistemology.[20] Other aspects of early modern society and culture have also been regarded as influential in this process. Historians have focused on the 'gentlemanly' social milieu that fostered practices of truth-telling and levels of trust; they have traced changes in educational practices and 'disciplinary culture' that contributed to a new conception of the status of testimony; and they have analysed similar developments in early modern casuistry or, more broadly, theological doctrine and matters of conscience, that also had a considerable impact on the history of proof and fact.[21]

18 James Q. Whitman, *The Origins of Reasonable Doubt: Theological Roots of the Criminal Trial* (New Haven, 2008); Langbein, *Torture and the Law of Proof* and Langbein, *Origins Adversary Trial*, are especially interested in uncovering the limitations of jury trial; see also Gary Edmond, 'Whigs in Court: Historiographical Problems with Expert Evidence', *Yale Journal of Law and the Humanities*, 14, 1 (Winter, 2002): 123–75. For recent legal-historical research into the development of evidence law see, for example, T.P. Gallanis, 'The Rise of Modern Evidence Law', *Iowa Law Review*, 84 (March, 1999): 499–560, Stephan Landsman, 'From Gilbert to Bentham: The Reconceptualization of Evidence Theory', *Wayne Law Review*, 36 (1990): 1149–86; John H. Langbein, 'Historical Foundations of the Law of Evidence: A View from the Ryder Sources', *Columbia Law Review*, 96, 5 (June, 1996): 1168–1202.

19 Barbara Shapiro's work has moved from interest in 'interactions' between ideas about evidence and proof in law and other disciplines, to stronger claims about law 'shaping' these other disciplines. See also Daston, *Classical Probability*, ch. 1; Daston, 'Probability and Evidence', 1112–13, 1120–22; Serjeantson, 'Testimony and Proof', 195.

20 Langbein, *Origins Adversary Trial*, ch. 1.

21 Shapin, *Social History of Truth*; Serjeantson, 'Testimony and Proof'; Whitman, *Origins of Reasonable Doubt*. And cf Lorraine Daston's scholarship on the significance of an early modern approach to miracles and prodigies within this debate about evidence and fact, in Daston 'Marvelous Facts and Miraculous Evidence', and Daston and Katherine Park, *Wonders and the Order of Nature, 1150–1750* (Cambridge, Mass., 2001).

Modern analyses of early eighteenth-century approaches to the valuation and dissemination of knowledge clearly emphasise the importance of legal ideas, practice and culture. But they have paid little attention to the role of common law jurisprudence in the history of these developments. How did ideas about fact and truth, especially legal fact and truth, stand in relation to ideas about the justice of custom, precedent and prescription? In what ways were these common law ideas, and practices, understood to conform to but also challenge emergent criteria of credible truths? These questions are vital to the project of reconceptualising the relationship between common law and Enlightenment. And they are questions that will further the project of historicising Scientific Revolution as well as pluralising Enlightenment since, despite recent historiographical trends, there is still some tendency to identify Enlightenment with the elevation of scientific or natural knowledge.[22] Finally, these questions will help to make sense of a fascinating criminal trial that took place in England in 1699, and that involved prominent men of science and influential men of law. By focusing on a case study, and drawing attention to these legal practitioners, it will become possible to extend the contributions scholars have made to our understanding of common law within such broad intellectual and cultural contexts. Even more, a history of both practices and concepts will enable us to disentangle the constitutive elements of the construction of legal and scientific truths.[23] It is also salutary, of course, to focus on a criminal trial since that is an area of the law that has been recognised as undergoing significant change over the course of the eighteenth century.

The trial of Spencer Cowper, Ellis Stephens, William Rogers and John Marson for the murder of Mrs. Sarah Stout took place at the Hertford assizes in July 1699. The controversy surrounding the case, as well as ongoing legal machinations and scientific speculation, continued in print, in the courts, and in public discourse for some years afterwards. These controversies and debates were focused, among other things, on questions about the function of respiration, and about the reliability of autopsy and experiment. Not only did each side challenge the other's adherence to established scientific and legal procedures, but they also engaged in explicit discussion about the rela-

22 John Henry, 'Science and the Coming of Enlightenment', in Martin Fitzpatrick, Peter Jones, Christa Knellwolf and Iain McCalman eds., *The Enlightenment World* (New York, 2004), 10–27; Peter Hanns Reill, 'The Legacy of the Scientific Revolution', in Roy Porter ed., *The Cambridge History of Science, Volume 4: Eighteenth-Century Science* (Cambridge, 2003), 23–4; Johns, 'Print and Public Science', 536.

23 See Findlen, 'Two Cultures', 233–5 on microhistorical trends in the history of science, and the continuing challenge 'to construct a "big picture" from this mass of detail'; and Gianna Pomata, '*Praxis Historialis*: The Uses of *Historia* in Early Modern Medicine', Donald R. Kelley, 'Between History and System', both in Gianna Pomata and Nancy G. Siraisi eds, *Historia: Empiricism and Erudition in Early Modern Europe*, (Cambridge, Mass., 2005), 105–46, 211–38.

tive value of science and law. Indeed, precisely because it was not framed as a simple contest between 'new' 'experimental' science and 'traditional' legal authority, the Stout murder case provides important evidence of contemporary approaches to the relationship between legal and scientific ideas and practices. It also provides important evidence of the jurisprudential implications of concerns about truth and proof articulated as part of the development of the adversarial trial. The use of expert witnesses in this trial, and the focus on competing scientific facts, fostered doubts and debates about the veracity of scientific knowledge, and about the justice of common law trial.

Concerns about print and authenticity are also relevant here, first because of the interesting connections contemporaries made between norms of experimentation and publication, and assertions regarding justice. Second, participants in the trial, both scientists and lawyers, insisted upon the authority of citation and had occasion to defend their recourse to established texts and ancient authors. Third, William Cowper, a central author of the defence for his accused brother Spencer, employed those enlightened reading and note-taking practices when compiling his legal claims. William Cowper pursued these practices in other areas too and the evidence of some of the letters and notebooks in his collection, incorporating references to contemporary travel and epistolary literature, is another indication that he was affected by the development, and disquiet, about truth and fact that characterised eighteenth century print cultures.[24]

Broad disquiet about truth and fact, and specific concerns about biased witnessing, arose in this trial not only with regard to scientific evidence but also with regard to the criminal appeal process itself. An appeal of felony had developed in the early common law as a way in which to initiate criminal prosecution, but by the time of this trial it was more often used 'as a means … of obtaining a new trial where an indictment for homicide had failed'.[25] Sarah Stout's mother, Mary Stout, used the procedure in this appellate fashion, aiming to secure a rehearing after the defendants had been acquitted of the murder indictment brought by the crown. Although this case took place at the very earliest stage of the developing adversary trial it demonstrates some of the challenges of that system, not least in this recourse to appellate review. Since each side was responsible for producing

24 HALS, Panshanger D/EP F82. Daniel Carey, 'Travel, Geography and the Problem of Belief: Locke as a Reader of Travel Literature', in Julia Rudolph ed., *History and Nation* (Cranbury, NJ, 2006), 97–136; Larry Wolff, 'Discovering Cultural Perspective: The Intellectual History of Anthropological Thought in the Age of Enlightenment', in Larry Wolff and Marco Cipolloni eds, *The Anthropology of the Enlightenment* (Stanford, 2007), 3–32.

25 Baker, *Introduction to English Legal History*, 504; Daniel R. Ernst, 'The Moribund Appeal of Death: Compensating Survivors and Controlling Jurors in Early Modern England', *The American Journal of Legal History*, 28, 2 (April, 1984): 165, 177–80.

witnesses and proofs, Stephan Landsman explains, this developing adversary system needed to come up with some rules to monitor participants' behaviour and to 'guard the integrity of the process'. 'One of the most important consequences of this aspect of adversarial structure,' Landsman concludes, 'is that it creates a demand for some sort of process of review to guarantee that the participants have honored the rules regulating the contest.'[26] Mary Stout sought this review, and her use of the appeal highlights another facet of the adversarial trial that had jurisprudential as well as jurisdictional implications. If common law criminal trial ended with an unjust result was there any remedy? Who would judge the prior result? In the Stout murder case advocates presented arguments in defence of the justice of adherence to common law procedure and precedent. In fact, Chief Justice Holt also advanced this kind of argument in commenting upon the final verdict in this case: although Holt and the other judges rejected Mary Stout's attempt at appeal on technical grounds, Holt recognised her legal standing and her right of criminal appeal concluding, with rhetorical flourish, that the appeal was 'a noble prosecution, and a true badge of English liberties'.[27]

Judge Holt's defence of the criminal appeal is still remembered today, but the case that prompted it – and the people and concerns and contexts that fuelled it – has either been ignored, or too narrowly interpreted.[28] When this case has been discussed it has been characterised as an instance of political bias and religious conflict at work in the courtroom, or simply cited as an example of the use of forensic evidence and expert witnessing in early modern England.[29] With the exception of my own work on gender norms

26 Stephan Landsman, 'The Rise of the Contentious Spirit: Adversary Procedure in Eighteenth-Century England', *Cornell Law Review*, 75 (March, 1990): 501.

27 Jacob ed. (?), *A Report of all the Cases Determined by Sir John Holt, Knt.*, 483; *Stout v. Towler*, 12 Mod. 372, 88 *English Reports*, 1387–89; *Rex v. Toler*, 1 Ld Raym 555, 91 *English Reports* 1270–2.

28 References to Holt's statement appear, for example, in Baker, *Introduction to English Legal History*, 504 n. 23; Lieberman, 'Mapping Criminal Law', 155, n. 54.

29 Vanessa McMahon, 'Reading the Body: Dissection and the "Murder" of Sarah Stout, Hertfordshire, 1699', *Social History of Medicine*, 19, 1 (2006): 19–35; David Lemmings, 'Cowper, Spencer', *ODNB*; Langbein, *Origins Adversary Trial*, 24 n. 73; Anne Kugler, *Errant Plagiary: The Life and Writings of Lady Sarah Cowper 1644–1720* (Stanford, 2002), 38–9; Alan Wharam, *Murder in the Tower: And Other Tales from the State Trials* (Aldershot, 2001), ch. 13; R.B. Blake, 'Challenges for Cause, Stand-Asides, and Peremptory Challenges in the Nineteenth Century', *Osgoode Hall Law Journal*, 38 (Fall, 2000): 456–62; Beverly Ann Adams, 'The Body in the Water: Religious Conflict in Hertford 1660–1702' (Ph.D. diss., University of London, 2000); Michael J. Saks, 'Merlin and Solomon: Lessons from the Law's Formative Encounters with Forensic Identification Science', *Hastings Law Journal*, 49, 4 (1998), 1069; D. Michael Risinger with Michael J. Saks, 'Science and Nonscience in the Courts: Daubert Meets Handwriting Identification Expertise', *Iowa Law Review*, 82, 1 (October, 1996), 21; Ernst, 'Moribund Appeal of Death', 181; Albert Rosenberg, 'The Sarah Stout Murder Case: An Early Example of the Doctor as an Expert Witness', *Journal of the History of Medicine and Allied Sciences*,

and forensic practice in this case, Spencer Cowper's trial has been portrayed as an unfair attack on an innocent man, and Mary Stout's appeal dismissed as the work of a vengeful mother intent on restoring the reputation of her lovesick and suicidal daughter.[30] This chapter will continue the work of reinterpretation begun elsewhere by considering the whole of the Stout murder case, and by connecting the trial arguments regarding scientific and legal truth with the appeal arguments regarding common law justice. A closer study of the trial of Spencer Cowper and the death of Sarah Stout will address those questions about the historical development of concepts of fact, truth, precedent and justice, and thus lead to a better understanding of the complex evolution of common law jurisprudence in the eighteenth century.

Expertise and truth

On the morning of 14 March 1698/9, the first day of the Lent assizes in Hertford, the dead body of Sarah Stout was found in the local river, close by to James Berry's mill.[31] This discovery triggered a set of events, and a series of publications, that lasted from 1699 to 1701. Other publications relating to the case appeared almost three decades later, and some versions of the case were reprinted well into the nineteenth century.[32] First in the

12 (1957), 61–70; Frederick Edwin Smith, *Famous Trials of History* (New York, 1926), 91–101; John Paget, *Paradoxes and Puzzles, Historical, Judicial and Literary* (London, 1874), 387–410; Baron John Campbell, *The Lives of the Lord Chancellors and Keepers of the Great Seal of England*, vol. 5 (London, 1868), 235–7; T.B. Macaulay, *The History of England from the Accession of James II*, vol. 8 (New York, 1866), 248–9.

30 Julia Rudolph, 'Gender and the Development of Forensic Science: A Case Study', *The English Historical Review*, 123, 503 (August, 2008): 924–46, especially 944–5.

31 *The Trial of Spencer Cowper, esq., John Marson, Ellis Stevens, and William Rogers, gent., Upon an Indictment for the Murther of Mrs. Sarah Stout, a Quaker, State Trials*, vol. 13, 1116.

32 Manuscript material – such as William Cowper's notes for the defence, or Sarah Cowper's references to the case in her diary –remain in the Hertfordshire Archives and Local Studies collections. And detailed versions of events appeared in print 1699–1701: *The Trial of Spencer Cowper, esq., John Marson, Ellis Stevens, and William Rogers, gent., Upon an Indictment for the Murther of Mrs. Sarah Stout, a Quaker* (London, 1699), *An Account of the Full Tryal and Examination of Spencer Cowper, Esq.* (London, 1699), *The Case of Spencer Cowper Esq., John Marson, Ellis Stephens, and William Rogers Gentlemen* (London, 1699?), *The Hertford Letter: Containing Several Brief Observations on a Late Printed Trial, Concerning the Murder of Mrs. Sarah Stout* (London, 1699), *A Reply to the Hertford Letter: Wherein the Case of Mrs. Stout's Death is More Particularly Considered* (London, 1699), *A Dialogue between a Quaker and his Neighbour in Hertford, about the Murder of Mrs. Sarah Stout* (London, 1699), *The Case of Mrs. Mary Stout, Widow* (London, 1699, 1700), *Some Observations on the Tryal of Spencer Cowper, J. Marson, E. Stevens, W. Rogers: that were tried at Hertford about the Murder of Sarah Stout* (London 1701). Most of these were also reprinted in the nineteenth century in Cobbett's *State*

series of events and debates that immediately ensued in March 1698/9 was the coroner's inquest. Since Sarah's death was sudden, and possibly suspicious, Hertford's coroner quickly impaneled a jury to examine the body, and to consider any other evidence indicating the cause of death. A typical coroner's jury consisted of twelve to sixteen men assembled by the local sheriff, sworn to provide truthful testimony by the coroner, and given the task of examining the naked body for external signs of death by unnatural causes.[33] This Hertford inquest followed the norm, and included numerous local men and women who testified about what they had witnessed, as well as their impressions upon inspection of the corpse.[34] At this time the body was also examined by a midwife and two surgeons who were summoned by Sarah's mother, Mary Stout. These witnesses testified to the coroner as to the marks, bruises and swelling that they had observed. The midwife Sarah Peppercorn provided evidence at that time that Sarah Stout's body showed no signs of pregnancy. Peppercorn examined Sarah Stout's body '[t]o know if she was with child; for it was reported she had drowned herself because she was with child; and so her mother desired me to come to give an account that it was not so; and I found that it was not so.'[35] Clearly Mary Stout was concerned to have a full accounting of her daughter's death and, it seems, to quell any nasty rumours that had already begun to circulate.

The Stout family was a well-established and respected presence in Hertford. They were prominent leaders of the local Quaker community, and prosperous maltsters who enjoyed a 'great intimacy' with the powerful Cowper family.[36] The Cowpers were landowners, lawyers and well-connected Whigs who served as MPs for Hertford in 1679–81 and 1689–1700. Sarah Stout's father, Henry, had been active in marshalling Quaker support for the Cowper's political interest in the 1680s and 90s, before his death. Sarah's stepbrother John also supported the Cowpers before 1699, and the two families had regular contact.[37] At the time of Sarah Stout's death Sir William

Trials. Another version of the case was included in the *Newgate Calendar*. And satirical verse versions of events were printed at the time of Spencer Cowper's death, 1728–9: Charles Beckinham, *Sarah, the Quaker, to Lothario, Lately Deceased, on Meeting him in the Shades* (London, 1728), Beckinham, *Lothario's Answer to Sarah the Quaker, in the Shades* (London, 1729).

33 T.R. Forbes, *Crowner's Quest, Transactions of the American Philosophical Society*, 68, 1 (1978), 6; R.F. Hunnisett, *Sussex Coroners' Inquests 1558–1603* (Kew, 1996), xix–xlvi; Hunnisett, *Sussex Coroners' Inquests 1603–1688* (Kew, 1998), xiv–xxvi.

34 *Trial of Spencer Cowper*, 1111, 1116–26, McMahon, 'Reading the Body', 25; Rudolph, 'Gender and Forensic Science', 929.

35 *Trial of Spencer Cowper*, 1122–5; *Case of Spencer Cowper, State Trials*, vol. 13, 1191.

36 *Some Observations on the Trial, State Trials*, vol. 13, 1238. Henry Stout Will, NA, Prob/11/429 gives some indication of Stout's wealth. Beverly Adams, '"The Durty Spirit at Hertford": A Falling Out of Friends,' *Journal of Ecclesiastical History*, 52, 4 (October, 2001): 664, 667–8; Adams, 'Body in Water', 64–5, 101, 137, 139–40, 148, 179–80.

37 Campbell, *Lives of the Lord Chancellors*, 223; *Some Observations on the Trial*, 1238,

Cowper, second baronet, and his eldest son William Cowper, king's counsel and prominent barrister, were serving as Hertford's MPs. The second son, Spencer Cowper, was also a barrister with professional interests in London, serving as comptroller of the Bridge House estates in Southwark.[38] Spencer arrived in Hertford from London on 13 March 1698/9, and planned to keep company with his brother during the work of the assizes. But on that day he went from his lodgings in town to dine with Sarah Stout, and returned to visit with her later that evening.[39] Spencer Cowper was the last person to see Sarah Stout alive.

The next day Spencer Cowper was questioned along with the other deponents during the coroner's inquest. The inquest concluded that day with a finding that Stout had committed suicide, being *non compos mentis*.[40] But questions persisted because the verdict of suicide generated speculation about the motivations for Sarah Stout's actions. That speculation was shaped by norms regarding female chastity, male honour, and general beliefs about female irrationality. Most of the speculation centred on the possibility of an adulterous affair between Spencer Cowper and Sarah Stout. Suspicions remained about Sarah's mental state as well as her physical and moral behaviour, and thus the reliability of testimony at the coroner's inquest was called into question. If Spencer and Sarah had an illicit relationship Sarah might have killed herself out of despair, some concluded. But it was also possible that Sarah might have been murdered to keep her from revealing the affair, or even to conceal physical evidence – specifically pregnancy – resulting from the affair. Such speculation was fuelled not only by salacious rumours about Sarah, or even about Spencer, but also because of gossip about Spencer's older brother William. William Cowper had fathered a child in 1697 (and would father a second in 1700) in his own adulterous relationship.[41]

Finally there was added suspicion that financial misconduct was involved. Sarah's father had been a well-to-do maltster, like many Quakers a part of

Adams, 'Body in Water', 201, 276; Rudolph, 'Gender and Forensic Science', 934–5. Henry Stout's will was dated 9 September 1695, NA, Prob/11/429. See also the trial testimony given by William Cowper's wife, Judith, regarding the social relationship between Sarah Stout, Judith, and Spencer's wife, Pennington Cowper. *Trial of Spencer Cowper*, 1167, 1171–5; *Some Observations on the Trial*, 1238–9, 1241.

[38] 'Cowper, Spencer', *ODNB*; Campbell, *Lives of the Lord Chancellors*, 223–5, Kugler, *Errant Plagiary*, 24–6.

[39] *Trial of Spencer Cowper*, 1112–13, 1149–50.

[40] *Case of Spencer Cowper*, 1191; copy of inquest postmortem, HALS , Panshanger D/EP F 96.

[41] Kugler, *Errant Plagiary*, 30; Campbell, *Lives of the Lord Chancellors*, 221; but cf Geoffrey Treasure, 'Cowper, Williiam', *ODNB* which discounts the story of this affair. Letters from these children to William Cowper are held in HALS, Panshanger D/EP F85; see also the article on Elizabeth Culling, HALS, William Blyth Gerish Collection, D/EGr 43. And see the comments about Spencer Cowper's reputation in *Dialogue Between a Quaker and his Neighbour*.

'the comfortable middle section of the county community' and 'wealthier than the general population', and he left his daughter with a good inheritance.[42] According to one account Sarah was left as her father's 'sole executrix, and [he] gave her most part of his personal estate', and she was active in investing and managing this inheritance.[43] Spencer Cowper advised Sarah on her investments and supporters of the Stouts questioned his honesty, suggesting that Sarah was murdered for her money.[44] A slightly different narrative posited that Spencer had mismanaged the money Sarah entrusted to him. In this narrative Spencer was depicted promoting speculation and promising wealth – the epitome of that Whig 'monied man' who was viewed with suspicion in much contemporary literature.[45] Spencer's own testimony acknowledged that Sarah had refused to sign a receipt he presented to her the night that she died 'which plainly shewed,' one commentator insisted, 'her dissatisfaction, and that there was more due to her, else she would never have refused it.'[46] The account of a misuse and loss of monies, like the narrative of an adulterous affair, could be used to support arguments for suicide or for murder.

Mary Stout had her daughter's body exhumed and dissected in late April 1699 in order to counter both rumours of adultery and suicide. In this case the recourse to autopsy took place six weeks after the physical examination of the body at the coroner's inquest. Six men participated in this second, more extensive examination. At least one of them, Dr Coatsworth, came from out of town, but three men were well-known local surgeons: Robert Dimsdale, his son John Dimsdale, and grandson John Dimsdale junior were part of a family dynasty of medical practitioners who were members of the local Quaker community, and active burgesses in the Hertford corporation.[47] These surgeons' affidavit of 28 April affirmed that they 'found the uterus perfectly free and empty, and of the natural figure and magnitude, as usually in virgins.'[48] In addition to certifying Stout's virginity, the affidavit

42 Barry Reay, 'The Social Origins of Early Quakerism', *Journal of Interdisciplinary History*, 11, 1 (Summer, 1980): 67; Adams, 'Body in Water', 101, 148, 179–80.

43 *Some Observations on the Trial*, 1238; NA, Prob/11/429.

44 *Dialogue Between a Quaker and his Neighbour*; *Hertford Letter*, *State Trials*, vol. 13, 1214.

45 *Some Observations on the Trial*, 1238–9. For analysis of these kinds of 'country' critiques of new money see, for example, Pocock, *Virtue, Commerce, and History*, Shelly Burtt, *Virtue Transformed: Political Argument in England 1688–1740* (Cambridge, 1992), Bruce Carruthers, *City of Capital: Politics and Markets in the English Financial Revolution* (Princeton, 1996).

46 *Some Observations on the Trial*, 1242.

47 *Reply to Hertford Letter*, *State Trials*, vol. 13, 1216; Adams, 'Body in Water', 193, 282; Andrea Rusnock, 'Dimsdale, Thomas', *ODNB*. The surgeons listed on the affidavit were John Dimsdale, sen., Robert Dimsdale, John Dimsdale jun., William Coatsworth, Samuel Camlin and Daniel Phillips.

48 *Reply to Hertford Letter*, 1216.

insisted that the findings of the autopsy necessitated the conclusion that Sarah Stout did not drown. This new information led to a new summons for all of the accused to appear before Chief Justice Holt in London. Marson, Stephens and Rogers were soon released on bail. Although these men were suspected of assisting Spencer Cowper in some way, Cowper remained the main focus of investigation and he would be the principal defendant at the upcoming trial. In late May 'the lord cheif [sic] justice Holt committed to the kings bench prison Spencer Cowper, esq., barrister at law, on suspition of murthering a quaker woman at Hartford,' and Cowper remained imprisoned for close to two months until the trial at Hertford took place.[49] The new information fuelling this suspicion must have been compelling enough for a grand jury indictment but Spencer Cowper claimed that there was no action taken for him to be moved for trial until he made out a writ himself.[50]

The Hertford trial took place at the very beginning of a period of change in English criminal trial procedure. As historians like John Langbein and Stephan Landsman have shown, over the course of the eighteenth century the modern adversarial or 'lawyer-dominated' trial took shape. Both scholars agree that significant change was effected by the 1730s, when the criminal trial began to be characterised by the active involvement of prosecution and defence counsel engaged in a contest of proofs. Langbein points to the 1690s treason trials, which catalysed an elite push for defence counsel, as the origins of this change. By contrast, Landsman credits the increasing activities of professional thief-catchers in the first decades of the eighteenth century, whose aggressive evidence-gathering tactics motivated judges to allow 'a more robust defense'.[51] While defence counsel had earlier been allowed in cases of criminal, and civil, misdemeanor, this admission of counsel for defendants charged with felony and treason led to new expectations for, and reliance, on counsel. The resulting shift toward adversarial contest was a key factor in the evolution of rules of evidence, specifically the exclusionary rules that distinguish the Anglo-American system.[52]

These changes in the common law criminal trial accord with the kind of movement towards modernisation and rationalisation that is typically asso-

[49] Narcissus Luttrell, *A Brief Historical Relation of State Affairs from September 1678 to April 1714*, vol. 4 (Oxford, 1857, reprint, Wilimington, DE, 1974), 518. *Case of Spencer Cowper*, 1191–2.

[50] *Hertford Letter*, 1212. Shapiro, *Beyond Reasonable Doubt*, 54–78. Note that the *Case of Spencer Cowper*, 1192, makes the claim that the judges were split over the decision whether to allow him bail along with the other defendants.

[51] Landsman, 'Rise of Contentious Spirit', 503, 572–81; Langbein, *Origins Adversary Trial*, 67–105. See also Langbein, 'The Criminal Trial before the Lawyers', *University of Chicago Law Review*, 45, 2 (Winter, 1978): 263–316.

[52] Gallanis, 'Rise of Modern Evidence Law'; Langbein, *Origins Adversary Trial*, 249–50 and, more generally, ch. 4; J.M. Beattie, 'Scales of Justice: Defense Counsel and the English Criminal Trial in the Eighteenth and Nineteenth Centuries', *Law and History Review*, 9, 2 (Autumn, 1991): 221–67.

ciated with Enlightenment ideals, yet these changes were not the product of such ideals. Moreover, in Cowper's 1699 homicide trial such rules did not apply and, since it took place well before the years of fundamental change, many features of an earlier form of trial were still in place. For example, judicial control of the courtroom was expected and in Hertford the presiding Judge Hatsell played an active role in the trial. Rather than functioning as a neutral decision-maker, Hatsell interrogated witnesses and expressed his own opinions during the proceedings.[53] However there were some features of the emerging adversarial trial already operating in this case. First, Spencer Cowper performed as his own defence counsel in the courtroom, and he was aided behind the scenes by another counsellor, his brother William Cowper. Second, both prosecution and defence brought proofs and paid for witnesses as they mounted a contest of evidence. Medical experts marshalled scientific facts in order to make the case for a prosecution or defence version of the truth that was meant to lead to a just verdict. Since he was an elite defendant who could afford to present a robust defence, Cowper had a good chance of succeeding in this adversarial setting where truth-seeking was subordinated to the demands of a courtroom contest. In this way, the Hertford trial demonstrates those 'characteristic shortcomings of adversary procedure' described by John Langbein as a 'wealth effect' and a 'combat effect'. [54] Indeed, in order to make their arguments appear even stronger Cowper's defence emphasised the contrast between the social status and political standing of their own witnesses and those of the prosecution. They attacked the surgeons, sailors, servants and other eyewitnesses who testified for the prosecution, characterising them as 'obscure and poor men' whose testimony was coached by their superiors.[55]

The influence of wealth and the nature of truth-seeking were further complicated in this trial. The Stouts, as has been noted, were a family of some means and Mary Stout was also able to pay for evidence-gathering and witnessing. The Stouts' expert surgeons who testified at the trial were pitted against the Cowpers' expert physicians, and the contest of evidence became a contest about professional stature as well as socio-economic place. One way to understand the recourse to expert medical and scientific testimony, then, is to view it within the context of competition between members of the medical profession. This was a period of 'the decline of the old medical order' and of growing emphasis on empirical knowledge, scientific inquiry and expertise which was bound up, as we have seen, with the development

53 Landsman, 'Rise of Contentious Spirit', 513–14; Langbein, *Origins Adversary Trial*, 28–33, 311–314.

54 Langbein, *Origins Adversary Trial*, 102–5; Stephan Landsman, 'Of Witches, Madmen and Product Liability: An Historical Survey of the Use of Expert Testimony', *Behavioral Sciences and the Law*, 13, 2 (Spring, 1995): 131–57.

55 *Trial of Spencer Cowper*, 1144.

of scientific print culture.[56] And here in fact we can recognise some ways in which so-called Enlightenment rationalism and empiricism did play a part in the emerging adversarial trial. As Barbara Shapiro and other scholars have demonstrated, continental inquisitorial norms and Roman law concepts regarding witnessing and proof had for some time influenced English criminal trial proceedings. Now shifts in trial procedures, and in expectations of juries, further encouraged a reliance on witnessing which contributed to concerns about credibility and epistemology. Evidentiary standards became stricter as legal reasoning grappled with epistemological and logical problems in common with other enlightened disciplines and discourses.

Prosecution and defence in this case sought to align themselves with the rise of the new science. Witnesses presented detailed evidence about the anatomy of Sarah Stout's body, of the body of a local child who had drowned in the same river, and of the bodies of drowned sailors, Negroes and dogs. Technical discussion of the function of respiration was emphasised, and repeated in the pamphlet debate, since it was considered to be directly relevant to the question of murder. Was Sarah Stout alive when entering the river, and did she inhale water? How much water was necessary to drown a person, and how much should be expected to be found in the body? If water had initially been in Stout's drowned body would examiners be able to tell six weeks later (and after burial)? The prosecution surgeons testified to such matters from the evidence provided by the dissection of Stout's body, and they insisted that the absence of water meant that Sarah Stout was not drowned. '[A]nd so we did open her,' Dr Coatsworth explained,

> and as soon as she was opened we perceived the stomach and guts were as full of wind as if they had been blown with a pair of bellows; we put her guts aside and came to the uterus,...and after that, we put the intestines into their places; and we bid him open the stomach, and it was opened with an incision-knife, and it sunk flat, and let out wind, but no water; afterwards we opened the breast and lobes of the lungs, and there was no water: then we looked on each side and took up the lobes of the lungs too, to see if there was no water in the diaphragm, and there was none but all dry. Then I remember I said, this woman could not be drowned, for if she had taken in water, the water must have rotted all the guts.[57]

In addition to these surgeons the prosecution called 'gentlemen that are doctors of skill, to know their opinions of them that are found floating

56 Harold J. Cook, *The Decline of the Old Medical Regime in Stuart London* (Ithaca, 1986); Cook, 'Good Advice and Little Medicine: The Professional Authority of Early Modern Physicians', *Journal of British Studies*, 33, 1 (January, 1994): 1–31; Steven Shapin, 'The Image of the Man of Science' in Roy Porter ed., *The Cambridge History of Science, Volume 4: Eighteenth-Century Science* (Cambridge, 2003), 159–83; Johns, 'Science and the Book'.

57 *Trial of Spencer Cowper*, 1127.

without water in them, how they came by their death'.[58] These men spoke from their experience in the observation of drowned bodies all of which were, they maintained, full of water. Following these witnesses, several sailors testified, calling upon examples from their own experience, to show 'that all men swim if they be dead before they come into the water'.[59] These comparisons made to other floating bodies was a species of circumstantial evidence which was deemed necessary in trying 'secret' crimes like hidden murder, 'done in the dark'. This kind of evidence could, however, also be valued as a species of eyewitness testimony to apparently similar events.[60]

The most significant scientific evidence in the trial was this evidence derived from dissection. These were proofs brought from the autopsy performed on Stout's exhumed body and, later in the trial, from the dissection of dogs drowned in a series of experiments performed by Cowper's witnesses. This kind of evidence epitomised the contemporary focus on nature, rational inquiry and universalisable principles. 'The study of anatomy was in the forefront of the new philosophical regime,' Jonathan Sawday concurs. 'Indeed for some it *was* the new science.'[61] Although the recourse to autopsy was not a fully established part of forensic practices at this time – nor was exhumation of bodies for dissection regular practice – dissection was certainly a well-known procedure that generated interest in both elite and popular circles. As recent work has shown, despite the infrequency of public university-sponsored dissections there were other venues where autopsy and anatomical study took place. The frequency and broad popularity of such practice contributed to what has been described as a 'culture of dissection' in early modern England and Europe.[62]

Autopsy or dissection became increasingly important to forensic practice over the course of the eighteenth century, gradually supplanting reliance on the coroner's clinical evidence.[63] Cowper's trial took place at this formative

58 Ibid., 1131.

59 Ibid., 1134.

60 Shapiro, *Beyond Reasonable Doubt*, 214–17. This example does not fall neatly into either of Shapiro's categories (circumstantial/presumptive and direct); and although this case may be considered a part of the general 'receptivity' to circumstantial evidence at the end of the seventeenth century it also indicates that the later elevation of circumstantial evidence may have been more complex, since circumstances (related by experts) might in fact lie.

61 Jonathan Sawday, *The Body Emblazoned: Dissection and the Human Body in Renaissance Culture* (London, 1995), 231.

62 Sawday, *Body Emblazoned*, 2ff, 54–66; Hillary M. Nunn, *Staging Anatomies: Dissection and Spectacle in Early Stuart Tragedy* (Aldershot, 2005); cf also Katherine Park, *Secrets of Women: Gender, Generation and the Origins of Human Dissection* (New York, 2006) on the earlier medieval roots of such practices.

63 David Harley, 'The Scope of Legal Medicine in Lancashire and Cheshire, 1660–1760', and Catherine Crawford, 'Legalizing Medicine: Early Modern Legal Systems and the Growth of Medico-Legal Knowledge', both in Michael Clark and Catherine Crawford

moment in forensic science as well as adversarial trial, and again it betrays aspects of later developments. The trial was one of a cluster of high-profile homicide trials taking place at the end of the seventeenth century that used expert medical testimony and forensic science.[64] As these trials indicate, this was a period in which there was beginning to be 'a subtle but perceptible increase in the authority ascribed to medical evidence', and indeed a time in which evidentiary claims in general began to be of more interest to judges, as well as plaintiffs and defendants, because the courts began to recognise them as one of a number of valid reasons underlying a motion for a new trial.[65]

Mary Stout's insistence upon an autopsy of her daughter is an indication of her participation in this culture of dissection. Mary was an educated woman who took an interest in broader intellectual, religious, economic and legal trends and opportunities. She and her husband were Quaker community leaders, prominent contributors to the building of the meeting-house at Hertford and longtime friends of George Fox.[66] They were part of the 'middling sort' whose importance in understanding local governance, the relationship between rulers and ruled, and between elite and popular culture, has been emphasised by scholars.[67] Mary was also a skilled writer who had contributed to published polemical debates between Quakers and Congregationalists in Hertford in the 1670s.[68] And Mary Stout was clearly conversant with developments in medicine and law as well as religion and

eds, *Legal Medicine in History* (Cambridge, 1994), 45–63, 89–116; T.R. Forbes, *Surgeons at the Bailey, English Forensic Medicine to 1878* (New Haven, 1985), ch. 1.

64 Other examples include *The Trial of Philip Earl of Pembroke and Montgomery at Westminster for the Murder of Nathaniel Cony* (1678), *State Trials*, vol. 6, 1310–49; *The Trial of Robert Green, Henry Berry, and Lawrence Hill at the King's Bench, for the Murder of Sir Edmundbury Godfrey* (1679), *State Trials*, vol. 7, 150–230; *The Trial of Charles Lord Mohun before the House of Lords, for the Murder of Richard Coote, esq.* (1699), *State Trials*, vol. 13, 1033–60.

65 Stephan Landsman, 'One Hundred Years of Medical Rectitude: Medical Witnesses at the Old Bailey 1717–1817', *Law and History Review*, 16, 3 (Autumn, 1998): 445–93; Baker, *Introduction to English Legal History*, 84–5; *Pritchard v. Boyle* (1696) in W. Hamilton Bryson ed., *Samuel Dodd's Reports 1678–1713 and Miscellaneous Exchequer Cases 1671–1713* (Durham, 2000), 167–8. And, as will be discussed below, Mary Stout did attempt an appeal based on claims to new evidence.

66 Adams, '"Durty Spirit at Hertford"', 664, 667–8; Adams, 'Body in Water', 64–5,137, 139–40.

67 Tim Harris, 'Problematising Popular Culture', in Tim Harris ed., *Popular Culture in England, 1500–1800* (New York, 1995), 15–18, 219 n. 42.

68 Adams, 'Body in Water', 166–7. It is notable that part of Mary's polemic is a defence of women's activism among Quakers. Mary Stout's texts appear as portions of John Crook, *Rebellion Rebuked, In an Answer to a Scandalous Pamphlet Entitled, The Quaker Converted to Christianity, &c* (London, 1673), 55–6, and *The Testimony of the Hartford Quakers for the Man Christ Jesus, Vindicated.... With a Brief and Serious Reply by Mary Stout* (London, 1676), 40–55.

politics. The Quaker community had shown particular interest in the new science and this broader Quaker involvement may be relevant to understanding Stout's recourse to medical experts.[69] Mary's middling status and local stature also afford explanation for her access to such resources.

Mary Stout's decision to have her dead daughter's body exhumed and dissected can be understood as a choice to take part in contemporary medico-legal trends. This interest in providing clear empirical evidence of the 'secrets' of her daughter's body was matched by a commitment to defending her daughter's reputation. And both of these impulses fit with what scholars have documented as the rise of male medical expertise and erosion of female medical authority in early modern England and Europe.[70] The approach to and documentation of Sarah Stout's body is an example of the increasingly medicalised, objectified and sexualised understanding of the female body that was dominant by the sixteenth and seventeenth centuries. However, there are also important ways in which Mary Stout's use of autopsy and anatomical evidence-gathering should be understood as continuous with older practices of dissection – practices in which female medical expertise was valued, and practices in which scientific inquiry was furthered by women and congruent with familial and religious values.[71] The opening of Sarah's body did not just take place in the context of male science, under the 'male gaze', but it also furthered older cultural practices of dissection.

Despite the fact that Sarah's body was exposed in the context of public scandal, some structures of her dissection were characteristic of the kind of medieval and early modern 'intimate anatomies', especially of mothers and children, described and analysed by Katherine Park. First, Sarah Stout's body was dissected at the request of her family and at her family home.[72] Her autopsy was performed by surgeons but initiated by a woman; moreover the surgeons' evidence specifically regarding the state of Sarah Stout's uterus was matched by expert evidence provided by other women, like midwife Pepper-

69 Geoffrey Cantor, 'Quakers in the Royal Society, 1660–1750', *Notes and Records of the Royal Society of London*, 51, 2 (1997): 175–93.

70 Rudolph, 'Gender and Forensic Science', 946. Sawaday, *Body Emblazoned*, especially ch. 8.

71 Katharine Park's *Secrets of Women* provides an insightful account of the role of women in a history of dissection. She details complexities in this change to a medicalised view, and exposes important continuities between new and older practices invested in women's knowledge of the female body. Further, by emphasising the intersections, rather than separation, between religion and science, scholars like Park, or Lucia Dacome, 'Resurrecting by Numbers in Eighteenth-Century England', *Past & Present*, 193 (November, 2006): 73–110, make an important contribution to the reevaluation of earlier narratives about scientific revolution and Enlightenment.

72 Dr Coatsworth explained that when he was summoned to Hertford he was told that 'there was a suspicion [Sarah Stout] was murdered, and that her relations were willing to have her taken up and opened'. *Trial of Spencer Cowper*, 1126. Compare to depictions of domestic autopsies of elite Florentine matrons in Park, *Secrets of Women*, ch. 3.

corn, regarding Sarah's reproductive health. The significant participation of the midwife and other women in this case as a whole was unremarkable and an indication of the role women generally played in attending to women's bodies and, more generally, preparing bodies for death as well as birth.[73] The recourse to expert medical testimony by midwife and surgeons regarding questions about conception and virginity was especially typical. Here this case is in line with early and continuous examples of testimony provided by midwives and matrons and employed in English cases concerning illegitimacy, infanticide and rape – what the influential thirteenth-century legal authority Bracton called the 'examination of the belly'.[74]

Second, the surgeons performing the dissection focused on Sarah's abdomen and chest, and so did not cause a total disfigurement of, and dishonour to, her body. It is true, of course, that the bruising around Sarah's neck and chest which was noted at the coroner's inquest, and the putrefaction of Sarah's head and neck resulting from six weeks of interment, were important indications of violation.[75] However both surgeons and midwife, as well as other women who examined Sarah's body during preparation for burial, pointedly remarked on the 'soundness' and health of her body.[76] These aspects of Sarah Stout's autopsy were also essential features of earlier intimate or domestic anatomies, typical of the dissections of suspected victims of murder, and of women who died in childbirth. Those kinds of 'domestic anatomies,' Park explains, 'helped to allay the distress and satisfy the curiosity of relatives of people who … died mysteriously or unexpectedly.'[77] Privacy and respect for the corpse were crucial features of this older cultural practice of dissection. And in this instance in 1699 such respect had a particular significance for Sarah's mother, providing an effec-

73 Malcolm Gaskill, *Crime and Mentalities in Early Modern England* (Cambridge, 2000), 256. Gaskill asserts that women's expertise in preparing the body also came into play after burial: 'At exhumations it was common for the grave-digger to stand aside once the coffin had been opened to allow women to unwrap the winding sheet around the corpse'. See also Fissell, *Vernacular Bodies*, and Laura Gowing, *Common Bodies: Women, Touch and Power in Seventeenth-Century England* (New Haven, 2003), on the importance of communities of women for medical and legal practices

74 Forbes, *Surgeons at the Bailey*, 27, citing Henri de Bracton, *De Legibus et Consuetudinibus Angliae*. Gaskill, *Crime and Mentalities*, 255–6; Harley, 'Scope of Legal Medicine', 50–4; Mark Jackson, *New-Born Child Murder: Women, Illegitimacy and the Courts in Eighteenth-Century England* (Manchester, 1996), 103–4; Roger Smith, *Trial by Medicine: Insanity and Responsibility in Victorian Trials* (Edinburgh, 1981), 213–14 n. 27; James C. Oldham, 'On Pleading the Belly: A History of the Jury of Matrons', *Criminal Justice History*, 6 (1985): 1–64. Cf also the role of midwives in the examination and prosecution of suspected witches, discussed by Clive Holmes, 'Women: Witnesses and Witches,' *Past & Present*, 140 (August, 1993): 65–75.

75 *Trial of Spencer Cowper*, 1127–31; Park, *Secrets of Women*, 15–16.

76 *Trial of Spencer Cowper*, 1125–7.

77 Park, *Secrets of Women*, 124.

tive counter to her daughter's exposure at the coroner's inquest, and ensuing submission to public science and the male gaze. The autopsy of Sarah Stout offers evidence of the role of the new science in this seventeenth-century courtroom, but it is also points to the ways in which Mary Stout reclaimed her daughter's body and used the culture of dissection to her own ends.

The defendant, Spencer Cowper, challenged this practice of domestic anatomy through a claim to legal process. Cowper questioned whether Stout's autopsy was admissible evidence since the exhumation of the body had taken place without legal warrant. 'Had you a Melius Inquirendum or any lawful warrant for making this inspection?' Spencer Cowper asked his accusers. A warrant, he suggested, would have made the autopsy public and subject to scrutiny: 'if [a body] is to be taken up, it is to be done by some legal authority; for if it be otherwise, any gentleman may be easily trepanned: for instance, if they should have thought fit, after a coroner's view, to have broken the skull into a hundred pieces, this was a private view altogether among themselves.'[78] Here Cowper echoed one premise of contemporary scientific practice, the insistence upon transparency, and in his argument this was directly related to legal authority. In similar fashion the prosecution surgeons emphasised the agreement between the integrity of their autopsy evidence and the legality of their actions. No affidavit could be signed, they explained, until they had viewed the body.[79]

Cowper's courtroom defence was largely premised on such claims about the identity between legal and scientific proofs, and on an insistence that professional medical science and law were bound together. There is no sense here of a conflict or contrast between the new experimental science and customary legal authority. Indeed the conception of justice articulated here incorporated both natural-philosophical truths and traditional order and rules. Both were required for common law justice to be achieved.

Thus Spencer Cowper's next response to the prosecution reliance on dissection and scientific evidence-gathering was to introduce his own more famous medical and scientific experts into the legal proceedings:

> Mr. *Cowper*. My Lord, if your lordship pleases, I have some physicians of note and eminency that are come down from London; I desire they may be called into court to hear what the surgeons say?
> Baron *Hatsell*. Ay, by all means.
> Mr. *Cowper*. My lord, there is Dr. Sloane, Dr. Garth, Dr. Morley, Dr. Gilstrop, Dr. Harriot, Dr. Wollaston, Dr. Crell, Mr. William Cowper, Mr. Bartlett, and Mr. Camlin –
> [Who respectively appeared in court.][80]

78 *Trial of Spencer Cowper*, 1127.
79 Ibid., 1130.
80 Ibid., 1123.

The status of Cowper's witnesses was only highlighted when prosecution expert witness John Dimsdale Jr. was asked to resume his testimony and was immediately interrupted once again, this time by Judge Hatsell. 'You are a physician, I suppose, Sir?' Hatsell inquired, to which Dimsdale had to reply 'A surgeon, my Lord.'[81] Cowper's witnesses were, by contrast, elite members of the Royal Society present, perhaps, at the behest of Spencer's brother William who was associated with the president of that body, John Somers. When William Cowper marshalled prominent men of science to serve as expert witnesses for his brother he not only indicated his political and social status, but also his participation in that Enlightenment of correspondence and conversation, observation, experimentation and rationalism. Since several of these experts had published accounts of dissections they had performed in the *Philosophical Transactions* – where numerous such accounts provide further indications of that culture of dissection – their testimony had a special value.[82]

81 Ibid.; and there is a similar exchange between Spencer Cowper and the prosecution witness, Mr Babington, a surgeon a little later in the trial, 1132. The jockeying for authority in the courtroom is also an indication of that broader competition taking place within the medical profession between bodies like the College of Physicians, the Society of Apothecaries and the Company of Barber-Surgeons over the scope of their authority, prestige and practice. Indeed, two of Cowper's expert physicians, Samuel Garth and Hans Sloane, were actively involved in challenges to the Society of Apothecaries. Sloane defended physicians' practical knowledge of drugs against apothecaries' insults; and both Sloane and Samuel Garth proposed that the College of Physicians should directly confront the Society of Apothecaries by establishing a public dispensary where impoverished men and women could receive discounted medicines and free medical advice. Arthur MacGregor, 'Sloane, Hans', *ODNB*; Samuel Garth, *The Dispensary: A Poem* (London, 1699).

82 See, for example, William Cowper, 'A Letter from Mr. William Cowper, Giving an Account of a Very Large Diseased Kidney, Found on the Dissection of a Lady, with the Symptoms of the Disease before Her Death, and an Explanation of Their Phaenomena', *Philosophical Transactions*, 19 (1695–1697): 301–9; William Cowper and Hans Sloane, 'An Account of what Appeared on the Dissection of the Body of Mr. - Dove. By the Late Mr. William Cowper, Surgeon, F. R. S. In a Letter Communicated by Dr. Hans Sloane, R. S. Secr.', *Philosophical Transactions*, 27 (1710–1712): 512–14. The many accounts of dissection in contemporary issues of the *Philosophical Transactions* included, for example, Edmond King, 'A Relation of a Petrified Glandula Pinealis, Lately Found in the Dissection of a Brain: Communicated by Sr. Edmond King Knt. M. D. and Reg. Soc. S.', *Philosophical Transactions*, 16 (1686–1692): 228–31; Henry Sampson, 'A Relation of One Hannah Taylor, a Very Extraordinary Child of about Six Years of Age, Who in Face, etc. Was as Large as a Full Grown Woman; and of What Appeared on the Dissection of Her Body: By Dr. Hen. Sampson, Fellow of the Colledge of Physicians, London', *Philosophical Transactions*, 19 (1695–1697): 80–2; Charles Preston, 'An Anatomical Account of Some Remarkable Things, Found on the Dissection of a Woman, Who Dyed of the Dropsie, after the Paracentesis Was Performed, with a Small Reflection on the Causes of the Dropsie', *Philosophical Transactions*, 19 (1695–1697): 330–2; Preston, 'An Account of a Child Born Alive without a Brain, and the Observables in It on Dissection', *Philosophical*

Hans Sloane, for example, was surely an impressive witness. By 1699 he had served as secretary of the Royal Society for four years, and had published his first book as well as a number of observations in the *Philosophical Transactions*.[83] The defence expert even more renowned for his important public and experimental research was the surgeon William Cowper (no relation). Already a member of the Company of Barber-Surgeons, Cowper was elected to the Royal Society in January 1698/9 and soon became an active member of that society. Cowper was the author of many essays in the *Philosophical Transactions* as well as important treatises on anatomy.[84] His publications and his surgical experience made him a particularly important witness to respond to the prosecution account of dissection and explanation of respiration. Cowper, Sloane, Garth and other experts provided a steady, increasingly complex and remarkably consistent set of responses to the prosecution's witnesses.

First, Hans Sloane answered the questions about drowning and respiration through references to his own observations as well as to common sense:

> As to my opinion of drowning, it is plain, that if a great quantity of water be swallowed by the gullet into the stomach, it will not suffocate or drown the person: Drunkards, who swallow freely a great deal of liquor, and those who are forced by the civil law to drink a great quantity of water, which in giving the question (as it is called) is poured into them by way of torture to confess crimes, have no suffocation or drowning happen to them: But on the other hand, when any quantity comes into the windpipe, so as it does hinder or intercept the inspiration, or coming in of the air, which is necessary for respiration, or breathing, the person is suffocated. Such a small quantity will do, as sometimes in prescriptions, when people have been very weak, or forced to take medicines, I have

Transactions, 19 (1695–1697): 457–67; Samuel Doudy, 'A Relation of a Strange Symptom Attended an Hydrops Pectoris, and the Reason of It, as It Appeared on Dissection of the Body', *Philosophical Transactions*, 19 (1695–1697): 390–1; William Clerk and Charles Preston, 'An Account of a Stone Found in the Stomach of a Lady on Dissection, Another in the Left Kidney, and Some Smaller Ones in the Gall-Bladder', *Philosophical Transactions*, 2, (1699): 95–100; Henry Vaughan, 'Part of Two Letters from Mr Henry Vaughan to the Publisher, Containing Some Uncommon Observations Made upon the Dissection of Some Morbid Bodies', *Philosophical Transactions*, 23 (1702–1703): 1244–6; James Keill, 'An Account of the Death and Dissection of John Bayles, of Northampton, Reputed to Have Been 130 Years Old', *Philosophical Transactions*, 25 (1706–1707): 2247–52; J. Douglas, 'An Account of the Dissection of a Person, Who dy'd of an Ulcer in the Right Kidney', *Philosophical Transactions*, 27 (1710–1712): 32–5. There are also numerous accounts of the dissection of animals, some in the course of experimentation and others, as with the human examples, as part of the investigation of disease or 'peculiarity.'

83 Hans Sloane's book, *Catalogus Plantarum quae in Insula Jamaica Sponte Proveniunt* (London, 1696), was dedicated to the College of Physicians and the Royal Society, signalling the importance of both medical practice and natural philosophy.

84 William Cowper, *The Anatomy of Humane Bodies* (London, 1698); Cowper, *Myotomia Reformata, or, A New Administration of all the Muscles of Humane Bodies* (London, 1694).

> observed some spoonfuls in that condition (if it went the wrong way) to have choaked or suffocated the person.[85]

Sloane's use of the example of simulated 'near-drowning', drawn from the practices of judicial torture, is striking. It was, perhaps, not only a useful image for comparison with the two drowned bodies – Sarah Stout and the Kimpson infant – described in the courtroom, but also a deliberate indication of Sloane's familiarity with the evidentiary procedures of Romano-canon law.

Samuel Garth was also already well known for his wide-ranging knowledge and for his specific expertise on the subject of respiration. Garth spoke on the topic of respiration when he delivered the yearly Goulstonian lecture at the Royal College of Physicians in 1694. Moreover, Garth was recognised as the author of a popular poem that was part of contemporary debate over professionalisation and medical care, and in this way gained a reputation for wit as well as for medical skill. A member of literary as much as scientific circles, Garth brought the prestige of the public and polite man of science to Cowper's defence.[86] Garth built upon Sloane's testimony, and made the case for Sarah Stout's suicide, by reference to precise calculations and observations recorded in his explication of respiration – providing a good example of those ways, described by Daston, in which 'nature was made intelligible by being made legible':

> I believe when she threw herself in, she might not struggle to save herself, and by consequence not sup up much water. Now there is no direct passage into the stomach but by the gullet, which is contracted or pursed up by a muscle in nature of a sphincter: for if this passage was always open like that of a wind-pipe, the weight of the air would force itself into the stomach, and we should be sensible of the greatest inconveniences. I doubt not, but that some water fell into her lungs, because the weight of it would force itself down; but if we consider the windpipe with its ramifications as one cylinder, the calculation of its contents will not amount to above twenty-three or twenty four solid inches of water, which is not a pint, and which might imperceptibly work and fall out.[87]

William Cowper provided a similarly technical and even more detailed description of respiration and drowning:

> Nor is a greater quantity of water in the windpipe necessary to choak any person, if we do but reflect what an ebullition is caused by its meeting with the air which remained in the lungs, whereby a small quantity of water is converted into froth, and the channel of the windpipe, and those of the bronchia, are filled with it,

85 *Trial of Spencer Cowper*, 1156.
86 Shapin, 'Image of Man of Science', 167–78.
87 *Trial of Spencer Cowper*, 1158; Daston, 'Taking Notes', 446.

> insomuch that no air can enter the lungs for the office of respiration. After a suffocation is thus commenced (I am apt to think) all regular animal actions are perverted, and particularly that of swallowing (or deglutition); and what water flows into the lungs at the instant, or after this suffocation, is from its own weight, which is more or less as the body is farther under or nearer the surface of the water.[88]

These testimonies offer some indication of the new mechanised physiology, which adhered to natural philosophy's focus on matter in motion and 'presented the human body as a vast mechanical contrivance'.[89] The concurrent discussion in the case about the physics of floating bodies is also indicative of the influence of the mechanised understanding of nature. An elevated debate about anatomy and respiration continued in two pamphlets, *The Hertford Letter* and *A Reply to the Hertford Letter*, published soon after the trial. The author of the first (signed 'P.D.') explicitly challenged the anatomist William Cowper's expertise by describing the form and operations of the lungs in even greater detail, and referring to the work of a 'microscopical anatomist' who revealed such portions of the lungs 'not yet described by anatomists'. Moreover, the author cited the findings of 'a treatise of Robert Boyle, esq, called New Experiments Physical-Mechanical, touching the spring of the air', in order to make his argument that Sarah Stout was no longer breathing when she entered the water, and so did not drown.[90] The text is likely referring here to Boyle's notion of 'vital spirit' in the air, as well as his description of the porousness of the membrane of the lungs. Boyle's experiments contributed to contemporary understanding of respiration as a mechanical process, and appreciation for the necessity of aerated blood to life.[91] Respiration was, in fact, a focus for reflection on the implications of a mechanical understanding of nature. John Locke, for example, wrote an early essay, *Respirationis Usus* (c.1666–67), in which he posited a chemical explanation for the function of respiration against Boyle's mechanical theory.[92] There is evidence in these Hertford pamphlets as well of continued debate over whether mechanics could provide sufficient

88 *Trial of Spencer Cowper*, 1161–2.

89 Broman, 'Medical Sciences', 469.

90 *Hertford Letter*, 1204.

91 Roy Porter, *Flesh in the Age of Reason: The Modern Foundations of Body and Soul* (New York, 2004), 52–3, 90–1; Steven Shapin and Simon Schaeffer, *Leviathan and the Air Pump: Hobbes, Boyle and the Experimental Life* (Princeton, 1989). See also William Musgrave, 'Part of a Letter from Dr William Musgrave, Fellow of the College of Physicians and R.S. to Dr Sloane, Concerning the Cause of Necessity of Breathing', *Philosophical Transactions*, 20 (1698): 178–81, for another contribution to the debate regarding aerated blood.

92 Jonathan Walmsley, 'Locke's Natural Philosophy in Draft A of the *Essay*', *Journal of the History of Ideas*, 65, 1 (January, 2004): 17–18, 20. Cf Kenneth Dewhurst's medical biography of Locke, *John Locke 1632–1704, Physician and Philosopher: A Medical Biography with an Edition of the Medical Notes in his Journals* (London, 1963).

explanation for the inner workings of the body. The range of propositions offered by these medical men included ideas about bodily temperament and body chemistry.[93]

A significant portion of expert testimony in the courtroom concerned experimentation, and this evidence was further debated in the pamphlet literature. In the pursuit of authentification these experts were participants in print culture as well as the culture of dissection: they performed experiments on numerous drowned dogs, and publicised the results, as a means of interpreting the evidence derived from the dissection of Stout's body.[94] 'We last night drowned a dog, and afterwards dissected him,' the defence Dr Morley testified, 'and found not a spoonful of water in his stomach, and, I believe, about two ounces in his lungs; while we were doing this we drowned another.' Dr Cowper referred to additional experiments with dogs, one similarly alive and 'suddenly plunged under water till [it was] stifled', another 'hanged and [then] put into the water'. Dr Cowper subtly reaffirmed the reliability of his methods by admitting 'how fallacious the first experiment was' with yet another dog, a spaniel whose long hair might have interfered with the process of sinking.[95] Cowper demonstrated his awareness of the need to meet methodological challenges, thus reminding listeners of his prior experience and reputation, but he was not able to wholly deflect attacks on his experiments in this case as 'clandestine' and doubtful. 'The verity of his private experiments, I doubt, because when he made a public one, it infinitely contradicted his clandestine ones,' the author of *The Hertford Letter* remarked, adding, that 'there is a vast difference in drowning a creature in a tub, and in a river; in sinking him with a weight tied to him, and permitting him to sink by his own gravity.'[96] To answer such criticisms, the respondent to the author of *The Hertford Letter* performed further experiments after the conclusion of the trial. 'I sent for a dog, and…procured the use of a distiller's back, which, if I may call it so, is a sort of trough, containing in dimension thirty foot of length, and half as much of breadth: into this, when filled with water, I caused the animal to be cast,' he explained, 'having before ordered his forefeet to be tied together.'[97] After a lengthy description of thirty minutes' worth of canine struggling the pamphlet recorded the findings of the autopsy performed on the dog, and also listed the names of other witnesses who would vouch for this experiment's veracity.

The debate over these experiments, like the courtroom debate over the domestic anatomy performed on Sarah Stout, focused on the ideal of transparency and connected it to the principle of procedural regularity. Regular

93 On chemical qualities, and bodily 'juices', *Hertford Letter* 1204; Broman, 470.

94 *Trial of Spencer Cowper*, 1133–4, 1155, 1159–64; *Hertford Letter*, 1206, 1215–16; *Reply to Hertford Letter*, 1220–3, 1225.

95 *Trial of Spencer Cowper*, 1159, 1162.

96 *Hertford Letter*, 1210.

97 *Reply to Hertford Letter*, 1222.

process was understood to include standards regarding the replicability of experiment, and regarding the authority of those summoned to guarantee public oversight.[98] Competition among these medical practitioners, and the defensiveness about integrity and skill that are apparent in this case, were part of broader debates over witness credibility, the originality of knowledge, and the authenticity of scientific publication. In this period there was conflict among physicians themselves about the rise of the new science and the new focus on empirical knowledge. Anxiety was expressed about the possible decline in the authority of classical academic medical knowledge, as well as about the site of such knowledge, after the emergence of the Royal Society in 1660.

The Cowper case is clearly unusual in the sheer extent of expert testimony offered during the trial and its aftermath, and in the serious attention given to the question of the relationship between law and science. Despite this singularity, however, participants' attitudes towards medical expertise in this case suggest that we should question the traditional claim that 'Britain lagged nearly two centuries behind continental Europe in developing a science of forensic medicine'.[99] Moreover, the accepted model of English insularity in forensic practices is undermined by indications here that participants were conversant with continental literature, for example citing the works of Ambroise Paré and Paolo Zacchia. Members of the Royal Society, like Hans Sloane and William Cowper, were part of an international community and could be expected to have encountered these works. But the wider familiarity with this literature shown in this courtroom suggests that such trials were another avenue by which practices in continental law influenced English evidentiary concepts.[100]

The references to Paré and Zacchia were made as part of the broad debate among these medical experts about the nature of scientific reasoning and its relationship to law. Citation of relevant passages from these texts in *The Hertford Letter*, for example, was used to demonstrate the unreliability of defence witnesses testifying 'on parole' by contrast with the prosecution witnesses who appeared under oath.[101] During the trial, Paré and Zacchia were specifically cited as part of an argument about the value of expertise which was based both upon established authorities and upon experimentation. The defence Dr Crell proposed

98 The author of the *Reply to Hertford Letter* further associated the defence's evidence with public, male, science by ridiculing female testimony offered in the courtroom, and emphasising an objectified and sexualised image of Sarah Stout. *Reply to Hertford Letter*, 1231, 1237.

99 Crawford, 'Legalizing Medicine', 89. Cf Forbes, *Surgeons at the Bailey*, 40; Carol A.G. Jones, *Expert Witnesses: Science, Medicine and the Practice of Law* (Oxford, 1994), 22. *Trial of Spencer Cowper*, 1127–8, 1131, 1155, 1157–8.

100 *Trial of Spencer Cowper*, 1163; *Hertford Letter*, 1209–10.

101 *Hertford Letter*, 1210.

> Now, my lord, I will give you the opinion of several ancient authors.
> Baron *Hatsell*. Pray, doctor, tell us your own observations.
> Dr *Crell*. My lord, it must be reading, as well as a man's own experience, that will make any one a physician; for without the reading of books of that art, the art itself cannot be attained to: besides, my lord, I humbly conceive that in such a difficult case as this, we ought to have a great deference for the reports and opinions of learned men: Neither do I see any reason why I should not quote the fathers of my profession in this case, as well as you gentlemen of the long robe quote Coke upon Littleton in others.[102]

When Crell called for 'a great deference for the reports and opinions' he aligned natural philosophy with precedent and prescription as the basis for a truthful and just verdict. Although this case provides striking evidence of the developing emphasis on scientific inquiry and expertise, Crell's, and others', defensiveness or self-consciousness also demonstrates a perceived need to justify the use of such knowledge.[103]

Remedies and liberties

Contemporaries did not assume that the new experimental science could simply be valued as superior to, or apart from, traditional legal authority. Instead they regarded the combination of natural knowledge and legal custom as necessary for truth, and as the proper foundation for justice. Cowper's courtroom defence was largely premised on such claims about the identity between legal and scientific proofs, and on an insistence that professional medical science and law were bound together. The more defensive justifications of experiment and medical expertise offered in this period did, however, contribute to the self-promoting and self-aggrandising tendencies of the new science. And this, in turn, contributed to the later development of that powerful conception of an Enlightenment reason and science that excluded common law thought.

Modern scholars' belief in the justice of Spencer Cowper's acquittal, and in the value of expertise underlying the verdict, is informed by this enduring view. Over the course of this trial there developed a Cowper, and Whig, narrative of an impartial, scientific and truthful defence made triumphant against an onslaught of prejudiced, conspiratorial and delusional Tories, Quakers and women. Historians like T.B. Macaulay in the nineteenth century, or David Lemmings and Anne Kugler in the twentieth, reaffirmed this powerful narrative by delineating a sharp contrast between what they

102 *Trial of Spencer Cowper*, 1163.

103 See also Samuel Garth's and William Cowper's repetitive insistence on the objective value of scientific experimentation and technical knowledge, *Trial of Spencer Cowper*, 1157, 1161–2.

saw as the reasoned impartiality of Cowper's defence, and the irrationality of a prosecution fuelled by religion, politics, and notions of female honour. Kugler, for example, articulated this typical interpretation of the case when she asserted that the Stout prosecution was 'clearly perpetuating a malicious attack on Spencer Cowper', and dismissed their so-called 'experts' as inferior to Cowper's 'battery of expert witnesses, seven respected London physicians including Dr. Garth and Dr. Sloane'.[104] The assumptions underlying this scholarly consensus exemplify what has recently been described as a modern whiggish approach to evidentiary contests: that is, a tendency to 'draw upon idealized images of scientific knowledge and practice' and 'to accept the value accorded to the evidence at the close of the proceedings, trivializing the contingent and strategic processes involved in its production, articulation and assessment'.[105] The roots of this approach lie in the eighteenth century.

As we have seen, of course, seventeenth and eighteenth-century men and women well understood the strategic and contestable nature of their evidence. And they voiced epistemological concerns about that evidence because of the jurisprudential implications of remaining doubts about expert testimony. What exactly was the nature of justice in a common law trial founded on competition and uncertainty? Part of the answer, for both prosecution and defence in this case, lay in an insistence upon legal precedent and prescription as essential to justice. When Mary Stout challenged the 'not guilty' assize verdict by pursuing an appeal of felony, the focus of debate regarding Spencer Cowper's guilt shifted to a concern with rules of pleading, statutory definition, case law, precedent and the nature of legal reasoning. Yet this debate still encompassed those ongoing concerns about integrity, witnessing, knowledge, reason and fact. It was understood that strategy and contest could influence common law procedural practices as much as forensic practices and this provoked some, like Chief Justice Holt, to reaffirm common law justice.

Mary Stout followed required process for the appeal of felony in the months after Spencer Cowper's acquittal by seeking out Sarah's next living male heir. This heir was the twelve-year-old son of Ralph Allerton and Elizabeth Stout, granddaughter of Mary's deceased husband Henry Stout. Mary took steps to be made legal guardian of this child, also named Henry Stout, who 'chose the Deceased's Mother for his Guardian, before Holt C.J. in his

104 Kugler, *Errant Plagiary*, 38–9. Kugler refers to the Stout witnesses with facetious punctuation as 'experts' while simply stating that Sloane and the others were in fact expert witnesses. Other modern narratives that endorse this kind of interpretation include: Lemmings, 'Cowper, Spencer', *ODNB*, Rosenberg, 'Sarah Stout Murder Case', Smith, *Famous Trials*, Wharam, *Murder in the Tower*. See also Macaulay, *History of England*, vol. 8, 248–51; Campbell *Lives of Lord Chancellors*, 235–7; Foss, *Judges of England*, vol. 8, 20–1, 115–18.

105 Edmond, 'Whigs in Court', 149; cf Jones, *Expert Witnesses*, 11.

Chambers, and she was then and there accordingly admitted'.[106] Mary then attempted to dispute the assize trial verdict by bringing a criminal appeal on the child's behalf. Here she made use of that dual purpose in the law of appeals, whereby the appeal was 'frequently us'd in the Common and Civil Law, on the Removal of a Cause from an inferior Judge to a Superior; but more commonly for the private accusation of a Murderer, by a Person who had Interest in the Party kill'd'.[107] Through an appeal Mary Stout could pursue the private accusation of murder, and have the case reheard; she could not, however, act as the appellant herself since, according to law, only the male heir or widow of the victim could appeal the wrong done.[108] So, having been appointed guardian of Sarah's male heir, Mary had the writ of appeal sued out and then pursued this appeal on the infant's behalf, appearing 'personally in the court of King's-bench' on the first day of Easter term, April 15 1700.[109]

The records of this appeal in the printed reports, in the partisan pamphlets *The Case of Mrs. Mary Stout, Widow* and *The Case of Spencer Cowper, esq.*, and in William Cowper's handwritten notes, indicate Mary Stout's determination and continued activism. In attempting this criminal appeal, and earlier during the Hertford trial, Mary relied upon her own prior legal experience; she also benefited from the broader legal experience and counsel available within the Hertford Quaker community.[110] Like many Quakers, Mary Stout and her family had experience with the law because they had suffered harassment under the penal laws of the 1660s and 70s. Mary, for example, had been fined for failing to conform to the Second Conventicle Act of 1670. Her husband Henry had earlier faced prosecution for his refusal to sign the Oath of Allegiance, as well as for his non-attendance at church, and he finally endured imprisonment for his attendance at Quaker meeting. Mary's stepson John Stout actively invited legal action by mounting public oral attacks on the mayor and aldermen of Hertford, and he faced prosecution at the Quarter Sessions in 1695.[111] The Stouts were clearly conversant with the law, but the fact that Mary was able to negotiate complex

106 *Stout v. Towler*, 12 Mod. 373–4, 88 *English Reports*, 1387–89; Jacob, *Report of all the Cases Determined by Sir John Holt*, 483.

107 Giles Jacob, *The Laws of Appeals and Murder* (London, 1719), 1, and citing Edward Coke; Ernst, 'Moribund Appeal of Death', 168–9.

108 Jacob, *Laws of Appeals and Murder*, 4.

109 *Case of Mary Stout*, *State Trials*, vol. 13, 1197.

110 Craig Horle, *The Quakers and the English Legal System 1660–1688* (Philadelphia, 1988); David L. Wykes, 'Friends, Parliament and the Toleration Act', *Journal of Ecclesiastical History*, 45, 1 (January, 1994): 42–63; Wykes, 'Quaker Schoolmasters, Toleration and the Law, 1689–1714', *Journal of Religious History*, 21, 2 (June, 1997): 178–92.

111 Evidence that Henry Stout was conversant with the law appears in the record of his refusal to plead and his public recitation from the borough charter in his 1664 trial, as well as the record of his recourse to legal complaint in a business dispute in 1674. Adams, 'Body in Water', 87–8, 97–9, 108, 113, 274.

legal processes such as the appeal – which had 'notoriously difficult pleading requirements' – led the Cowpers to suspect that she was receiving expert legal advice, perhaps from the prosecutors who had served in the murder trial.[112] Mary Stout flatly denied such influence, and the additional political and pecuniary motives that were attributed to her. She insisted that the goal of her appeal was simply to pursue justice in the case of her daughter's murder.[113]

While Mary may have had some legal experience, and may have received professional legal advice, she still faced formidable legal adversaries. The records of this appeal, along with other Cowper materials, provide insight into the nature and scope of the Cowpers' legal learning. The brothers had been trained at the Middle Temple where William was called to the bar in 1688, and Spencer in 1693.[114] By the time of the trial both men enjoyed successful legal careers, but William was the more prominent of the two and he used his legal and political connections on Spencer's behalf. As a member of parliament William had already been involved in some significant public trials, and had received positive attention for his oratorical skills and effective legal advocacy.[115] William had also formed a close relationship with John Somers on the basis of his early and well-received appearances before the lord chancellor in the court of Chancery.

In addition to the printed records of William's distinguished courtroom arguments and parliamentary speeches, his notebooks, correspondence and library inventories offer further evidence of his extensive training and practice in law. The catalogue of William Cowper's library, for example, indicates that he owned classic legal texts like Littleton, Coke and Bracton, and great numbers of legal abridgments, reports, statute collections, and manuals of pleading and precedent. This catalogue also demonstrates William Cowper's broader interests, and the depth of his learning in areas outside of the law. There are works of poetry by authors like Waller, Milton and Settle (as well as Samuel Garth's poetic attack on apothecaries, *The Dispensary*), histories of places like Portugal and Lapland as well as England and France, collections on morals like the popular volumes by La Rochefoucauld, along with texts on a multitude of other subjects such as religion, travel, architec-

112 Ernst, 'Moribund Appeal of Death', 170, and see 181 where he repeats this suggestion (with some misstatement of fact) that the appeal against Spencer Cowper was politically motivated. *Case of Spencer Cowper*, 1192–3, 1196.

113 *Case of Mary Stout*, 1201. See Ernst, 'Moribund Appeal of Death', 171–2, on early use of appeal as way to extort compensation.

114 Campbell, *Lives of Lord Chancellors*, 220, 222; Foss, *Judges of England*, vol. 8, 19, 115. Spencer's son William Cowper's letters to his uncle asking for advice regarding his legal studies at the Middle Temple, cited in chapter 2 above, indicate that he too followed in this tradition. HALS, Panshanger D/EP F58, fols 84–8.

115 Campbell, *Lives of Lord Chancellors*, 227; Foss, *Judges of England*, vol. 8, 20–1.

ture, art, geography, mathematics, economics and natural philosophy.[116] Like other prominent lawyers and judges, Cowper was engaged in many aspects of enlightened culture: Cowper 'became an elegant scholar,' his biographer Campbell asserts, 'and he acquired a taste for polite literature, which adhered to him through life.'[117]

The many pages of notes that William Cowper compiled as case reports and legal memoranda, including his detailed notes on his brother Spencer's case, are an important record of William Cowper's legal strategies. They must also, however, be seen in this broader context of reading, note-taking and study. These notes show William Cowper following the norms of professional practice, using compilation and collection, listing and citation, in order to present the Kings Bench judges and Lord Keeper Wright with copious legal argument from case law, statute and rules of pleading.[118] Several of these arguments also appear in the defence publication *The Case of Spencer Cowper*. This pamphlet and William's notes may usefully be compared to contemporary tracts like Giles Dunscombe's *Tryals per Pais*, or Giles Jacob's *The Laws of Appeals and Murder*, which similarly used collection and enumeration to explain appeals procedure and evidentiary standards. William Cowper's manuscript notes are an important supplement to such printed tracts because they provide insight into the way an influential legal figure marshalled his sources, organising and evaluating his materials.[119] Indeed this controversy affords an unusual moment in which to study a number of prominent actors recorded in a courtroom setting, their arguments made not through treatise, parliamentary speech or judicial opinion, but rather through testimony, practical notes, and pamphlets. Here is an opportunity to regard doctrine and practice, enabling us to see some of the ways in which norms of fact and truth in law as well as science were understood, contested and manipulated.

A fundamental part of Cowper's argument against Stout's legal maneuvers lay in analysing the criteria for criminal appeal. Cowper addressed the general definition of appeal of felony, explaining why it was instituted and

116 HALS, Panshanger D/EP F214. On personal and professional book collecting see Scott Mandelbrote, 'Professional Collections', and Giles Mandelbrote, 'Personal Owners of Books'.

117 Campbell, *Lives of Lord Chancellors*, 220.

118 William Cowper's notes made in preparation for the hearing include 'Argument for my Bro Spenser at Ld Keeper Wrights Chamber in the Inner Temple May 27 1700', 'Reasons + auth. Agt a New Writ', and 'Notes Wch may be of use in Bro. Appeal', HALS, Panshanger D/EP F96, fols 78–81, 84–6.

119 These notes are also helpful in elucidating how judges might have evaluated a dispute, and come to their decisions; Cowper's practice notes thus have a similar function as the judges' notes that James Oldham points to in corroborating but also elaborating on the printed reports. James Oldham, 'Eighteenth-Century Judges' Notes: How they Explain, Correct and Enhance the Reports', *The American Journal of Legal History*, 3, 1 (January, 1987): 9–42.

in what cases justified, in order to argue that his brother's case did not merit appeal:

> Bec[ause] the Def[endan]ts were all found not guilty on an Indictment after a long + a full trial, to the satisfaction of all that heard it: And though by Stat[ute] of 3.H.7.c.1 this be now no Barr to an Ap[peal] (as it was at the Common Law) yet tis plain from the penning of said Stat[ute] that the reason of... alt[e]ring it Co:L in that particular was only this; that the Stat[ute] having enacted that the K[ing] might... on an Indictment within the year and a day (which before was not used) it... was forseen that an acquittal might be procured on an Indictment + a feigned prosecution, or the offender, if attaint, might be pardoned, for the reason of which the appeal is saved: but where a man is acquitted after an unfeigned + violent prosecution, though he may be again tryed on ap[peal] within a year + day according to the general purview of that Stat[ute] yet that case was not within the design and reason on which the Lawmaker went in that alteration of the Com[mon] Law. the Equity of which is yet remaining that no man ought to be twice tried in good earnest + him put in jeopardy of his life for the same offense.[120]

In Cowper's account of the historical development of the appeal, statute refines and preserves the reason of the king's common law. The intention of that law was to provide a full and fair trial, ensuring a just result. And so the appeal was preserved, even after an initial prosecution and acquittal, as a further guarantee of just prosecution. This Tudor statute, Cowper explained, was enacted in order to provide safeguards against the potential erosion, or evasion, of that reason of the law. Here Cowper's analysis of the statutory revisions of common law practice accords with modern scholars' emphasis on the crown's interest, after the War of the Roses, in punishing wrongdoing and preserving the peace.[121]

The principle of justice, termed equity by Cowper in this passage, was the foundation of his argument against the use of the appeal in his brother's

120 'Reasons + auth. Agt a New Writ', HALS, Panshanger D/EP F96, fol. 84. In quoting from manuscript sources I have kept the original spelling and, where necessary, have completed abbreviated words (additions appear in brackets) in order to aid the reader. See also 'Arguments for my Bro Spenser', HALS, Panshanger D/EP F96, fol. 79 for a discussion of the history of the Statute of Gloucester, 3 H 7, and reasons for changes over time. Similar arguments appear in the defence pamphlet *Case of Spencer Cowper*, 1196, although in this printed text the arguments against double jeopardy were not repeated. Finally, compare Cowper's arguments elsewhere regarding the two-witness rule in cases of treason where he lays a similar emphasis on statutory history and arguments about jurisdiction, 'Proceedings against Sir J Fenwick upon a Bill of Attainder', in *Cobbett's Parliamentary History of England, from the Norman Conquest in 1066 to the year 1803*, vol. 8 (London, 1806–12; reprint New York, 1966), 1143.

121 Ernst, 'Moribund Appeal of Death', 173–5.

case. In this instance, he asserted, the statute would not ensure fair prosecution and punishment but rather open the defendant to an unfairly doubled risk of conviction. By pointing to the maxim 'that no man ought to be twice tried in good earnest + him put in jeopardy of his life for the same offense' Cowper sought to align his argument with other contemporary objections to the use of the appeal of felony as a trial *de novo*. Authorities like Coke or, significantly, Judge Holt, also cautioned against the threat of double jeopardy when they considered the question of retrial through appeal. For example, in a case heard two years earlier, Holt acknowledged that 'the statute of [1487] is severe in overthrowing a fundamental point in the law, in subjecting a man that is acquitted to another trial, which is putting his life in danger for the same crime; therefore the purview of [the statute] ought to be taken strictly.'[122] However, Holt did allow retrial when necessary; following that 'strict purview' of interpretation meant that the statute should be applied to allow retrial when the judges were convinced that the circumstances of guilt warranted it.[123] Spencer Cowper's case did not fall into that category, William Cowper insisted, because his brother's innocence had been proven in a 'long + full trial' and 'unfeigned + violent prosecution'.

Cowper underscored this identification between acquittal and innocence in another, even lengthier, set of notes he compiled in advance of presenting arguments at the Lord Keeper's chamber in the Inner Temple.[124] Given the fact of acquittal, Cowper reasoned, Mary Stout's actions were in danger of violating statutory provisions against bringing a false appeal.

> And tis <u>no obj[ection] to say the Def[enden]t was Indicted</u> & so ye Ap[peal] not in danger of ye Stat[ute] [W.2.c.12, penalty for bringing false appeal]
> That was law when ye Ind[ictmen]t is depending, because of ye P[re]sumpson of guilt; & this was usually ye ca[se] of p[er]sons Indicted, when ye Ind[ictment] stayed till ye ap[peal] determined
> But wth submission, <u>after acquittal, ye p[re]sumpson is stronger on side of ye Appellee</u> then if nev[er] Indicted
> … ye p[re]sumpson of Innocence being stronger after acquit[tal] then if nev[er] Indict[ed] …[125]

[122] *Armstrong v Lisle*, Kelyng, J, 93, 103, 84 *English Reports* 1096, 1101, cited by Ernst, 'Moribund Appeal of Death', 184–5.

[123] Ernst, 'Moribund Appeal of Death', 184–5, 187–8.

[124] Not only these notes but also the fact that he engaged in argument in the judges' chambers provides another indication of Cowper's participation in the legal community. 'Argument for my Bro Spenser at Ld Keeper Wrights Chamber in the Inner Temple May 27 1700 p[re]s[e]nt: Ld Keeper, M[aste]r of Rolls, Ld Ch. J. Treby, Ld. Ch. B. Ward, M[iste]r Just. Powell', HALS Panshanger D/EP F96, fol. 78.

[125] Ibid., fols 80–1.

Since Spencer Cowper had already been acquitted after indictment, it was argued, he should be presumed innocent, while Stout's pursuit of appeal should be regarded as suspect. In print, the Cowper defence enhanced these claims about Mary Stout's malicious intent and potential violation of statute and maxim by pointing out that she 'who would prosecute this appeal, was the principal prosecutor of the indictment'.[126] Through the indictment Stout already had ample opportunity to press her case, and the fairness of the process, Cowper concluded, should not be compromised by the use of the appeal. Giles Jacob reiterated the same point several years later in his *Laws of Appeals and Murder*, explaining that '[t]he Appellant in his Appeal seeks only revenge for the Death of his Ancestor, but the King by his Indictment prosecutes to have an example of Justice'.[127]

This question of appeal of felony after indictment was particularly important in cases of prior acquittal, but it was also a matter for debate in cases of prior conviction. An appeal might still be deemed necessary by a victim's family in cases where there was unreasonable delay in attainting the offender, or, as Cowper noted, where the attainted offender was going to be pardoned.[128] Would English law allow an appeal of felony in these circumstances, and for what reasons? Cowper's example of appeal in the case of pardon was likely a reference to an important recent case, *Wilson v Law* (1694), heard by Judge Holt, along with Giles Eyre and Samuel Eyre in the Kings Bench. Cowper was of counsel to Wilson in that appeal and a manuscript 'Report at large of ye Case of ye Appeal brought in Wilson v Law' can be found among William Cowper's papers relating to his brother's case.[129] It is not surprising that Cowper would point to this case, finding it necessary to acknowledge his own role in prior disputes, or to cite a significant recent precedent. But the reference to this earlier appeal was also a strategic move in which Cowper could signal his broad concurrence with the court's recognition of the right of appeal. This would make it all the more convincing when he claimed that his brother's case was an exception in which appeal was not warranted. An effective and experienced counsellor like Cowper

126 *Case of Spencer Cowper*, 1196, #3. Not only did Mary Stout pursue the indictment 'with all imaginable industry', the pamphlet alleged, but also with prejudice and partisanship.

127 Jacob, *Laws of Appeals and Murder*, 68.

128 'Reasons + auth. Agt a New Writ', HALS, Panshanger D/EP F96, fol. 84 (autrefois convict but not yet attainted). Note that according to Giles Jacob the surest bar to appeal – even safer for the accused than acquittal – was conviction and benefit of clergy. Jacob, *Laws of Appeals and Murder*, 68, 121; cf Ernst, 'Moribund Appeal of Death', 176, 178.

129 'A Report at large of ye Case of ye Appeale brought by Wilson v Law, Pasche 6th Gul. & Mar. B.R. Rot.', HALS, Panshanger D/EP F96, fol. 4, 1–4; 'Tuesday Nov. 6, A(nno) 6 W. & Mar', HALS, Panshanger D/EP F96, fols 50–1. *Wilson and Law*, Skinner 549, 90 *English Reports* 247, identifies Cooper (sic) as arguing for the plaintiff in this case.

would try to use the justices' own reasoning to persuade them to rule against the appellant this time.

In many ways, however, *Wilson v Law* was an ambiguous and risky precedent for the Cowpers, not so much because the plaintiff's appeal was allowed, but because many defects in form and deviations from procedure were allowed, and even affirmed, by the judges in that case. Some of the judges' statements could be used to undermine the Cowpers' later claims that Mary Stout's appeal violated procedural requirements. *Wilson v Law* was, in fact, a widely reported and significant case for debate over questions about procedure in which Holt and the others reflected on the value of traditional rules for ascertaining truth and achieving justice. The discussion of common law interpretation in that case helps to illuminate the context, and content, of William Cowper's legal thought.

Much like Sarah Stout's death, the death of Edward Wilson generated rumours about illicit affairs and lovers' quarrels. The victim, known as Beau Wilson, was notorious in 1690s London for his extravagant lifestyle and good looks. Numerous explanations were given for his conflict with another young man about town, John Law; gossip and speculation persisted into the early eighteenth century when Wilson, like Spencer Cowper, became the subject of scandals circulated by the commentator Delariviere Manley. According to the account in the records of the Old Bailey court, where Law was tried for murder in 1694, the dispute between the two men was 'concerning a Woman, one Mrs. Lawrence … upon which, on the 9th of April Instant, [Law and Wilson] met in Bloomsbury Square, and there fought a Duel, in which Mr. Wilson was killed'.[130] In this case, as in Spencer Cowper's, after indictment and trial the heir of the deceased sued out a writ of appeal:

> John Law, A Scot, gent. was indicted for the murder of Edward Wilson in a duel in Bloomsbury Square, upon which indictment he the said Law was tried at the Old-Baily, and convicted of murder, and had judgment of death, but was reprieved.
>
> Thereupon Robert Wilson, the brother of the person killed, and who was his heir, sued forth an original writ of appeal for murder directed to the Sheriff of Middlesex, in whose custody Mr. Law remained, (viz) in Newgate-Gaol, returnable in Easter-term ann. 6 W.&M. in B.R.[131]

The defence response to Robert Wilson's actions was to challenge his writ of appeal, as well as every subsequent motion and procedure, looking for mistakes in order to argue that this plaintiff's case was not 'sufficient in

130 Proceedings of the Old Bailey, oldbaileyonline.org, ref # t16940418–28. Philip Carter, 'Wilson, Edward (called Beau Wilson)', *ODNB*.

131 *Wilson versus Law*, Carthew 332, 90 *English Reports* 794.

law'.[132] Defence counsellors Serjeant Thompson, Serjeant Levinz and Mr Carthew, were vigorous and effective in seeking out these 'several exceptions ... two to the return of the writ, four to the count, and one to the joinder in demurrer'.[133] The specifics of these exceptions are discussed in consistent detail in the printed reports and in the manuscript case notes held, and likely written, by William Cowper;[134] Cowper's notes provide additional detail about the defendant's delaying tactics within the courtroom. The defence critique generally focused on the Latin forms employed at different stages in the appeal, arguing first that grammatical errors led to imprecise or mistaken meanings concerning, for example, the location of the court, or the nature of the command to the sheriff for return of the writ. But Holt and the other judges relied on context and common sense when they interpreted the Latin text, and allowed defects in form to be ignored where the meaning could be easily inferred.[135] The defence's second set of arguments, challenging the accuracy of Latin phrases used to denote 'the time and place where the fact [of murder] was committed' was similarly dismissed by the judges.[136] The judges deemed that 'the appellant had alledged [the hour and venue] with certainty enough', citing prior case law and established authorities that attested to the same pattern of usage for terms like *circa horam* and *parochia*.[137] Throughout these hearings the judges placed significant emphasis on precedent and common usage in their interpretation of these alleged defects in Wilson's appeal.

The focus of debate in *Wilson v Law* epitomises the kind of formalism that critics of the common law often pointed to. Yet the judges' response to such formalist defence arguments sheds light on the meaning understood to lie within common law procedure and prescription. In *Wilson v Law*, and numerous other cases of appeal, 'justices inconsistently enforced pleading requirements' to ensure that the parties accepted the verdict of the court

132 *Wilson against Law*, 4 Mod 290, 87 *English Reports* 401; *Wilson against Law*, 3 Ld Raym 72, 92 *English Reports* 570.

133 *Wilson vers Law*, 1 Ld Raym 21, 91 *English Reports* 910; cf *Wilson and Laws*, Skinner 552, 90 *English Reports* 248.

134 The concluding sentence of the manuscript 'A Report at large of ye Case of ye Appeale', HALS, Panshanger D/EP F96, fol. 51 states: 'In this cause I was for ye appellt fro ye beginning to ye end.'

135 *Wilson and Laws*, Skinner 552–554, 90 *English Reports* 248–9; *Wilson versus Law*, Carthew 332–3, 90 *English Reports* 795; *Wilson and Law*, Skinner 443–4, 90 *English Reports* 197; 'A Report at large of ye Case of ye Appeale', HALS, Panshanger D/EP F96, fol. 4, 3, D/EP F96, fols 50–1.

136 *Wilson versus Law*, Holt, K.B. 62, 90 *English Reports* 932; *Wilson against Law*, 4 Mod 291, 87 *English Reports* 402.

137 *Wilson and Laws*, Skinner 553, 90 *English Reports* 248; 'A Report at large of ye Case of ye Appeale', HALS, Panshanger D/EP F96, fols 50–1. The key authorities cited were Rolle, Dyer, Bulstrode and Coke's *Institutes* and *Entries*.

as 'just' and 'reasonable'.[138] Since the verdict had to be acceptable to the defendant as well as appellant in this, like other, cases, requirements were relaxed on both sides. For example, the court at first explained that Law's initial request for extra time to plead 'ought not to be granted … upon a general prayer for delay or to search out for mistakes in ye proceedings'. Yet when it became clear that defence counsel was not prepared to proceed without extra time, '… at last upon much importunity, & yt ye Appellee might have no colour of exception to ye justice of the Court, ye Appellee had two days time … given him to plead, so as he would stand by it'.[139] Similarly, the court seriously considered all of the defence claims purporting to show that Wilson's appeal was faulty in its written forms and in the actions taken.[140] Judge Holt was notably willing to take extra time in hearing the case so as to examine each claim thoroughly.[141] Holt here displayed that strong concern with adherence to formal rules of pleading that he would express, most famously, a few years later in the controversial prosecution of John Tutchin for libel. There Holt moved to quash the guilty verdict because of a technical error committed by a clerk.[142] At the end of *Wilson v Law*, however, all the judges, Holt included, overruled the defence exceptions and allowed Wilson's appeal to move forward. Indeed in rendering his verdict Holt was willing to offer a general pronouncement in favour of the appeal which emphasised proper interpretation of statute and process:

> [A]nd Holt Chief Justice said, though the law is nice in exceptions to appeals, because the life of a man is endangered, yet two statutes have been made in favour of appeals, scil. the Statute of Gloucester, cap. 9, and 3 Hen. 7, and it being a legal suit, it ought to be allowed in a reasonable manner.[143]

138 Ernst, 'Moribund Appeal of Death', 178–9.

139 'A Report at large of ye Case of ye Appeale', HALS, Panshanger D/EP F96, fol. 4, 1. Cf Holt later advising defence counsel to prepare for the appeal of felony trial ahead of time, and his willingness to adjust the timing of proceedings when they did not: 'he said there could be no Tryal at Barr this Term, unless upon ye last day; wch ought not to be, ye Deft in such case having not a reasonable time to move in arrest of Judgment & therefore he rebuked ye Attorny for not doing as he advised last Term when he told him he might prepare for a Tryal at Barr ye same day they should give Judgment in ye Dem:r …', HALS, Panshanger D/EP F96, fol. 4, 4.

140 Note that several reports emphasise the court's rejection of exceptions but a few, like *Wilson and Law*, Skinner 443–4, 90 *English Reports* 196–7, record more uncertainty, and point to the ways in which court allowed for more time for consideration.

141 'A Report at large of ye Case of ye Appeale', HALS, Panshanger D/EP F96 fol. 4, 4.

142 Lee Sonsteng Horsley, 'The Trial of John Tutchin, Author of the *Observator*', *The Yearbook of English Studies*, 3 (1973): 136–7. Compare this, however, to other cases where Holt was willing to relax pleading formalities, such as *Calvert v. Prior*, Holt 540, 90 *English Reports* 1197, or *Speak and Kent*, Holt 547, 90 *English Reports* 1201.

143 *Wilson and Laws*, Skinner 553–4, 90 *English Reports* 249.

In Cowper's notes, Judge Holt is recorded as concluding with an even stronger affirmation, adding right to reason in favour of the justice of the appeal, when he averred 'yt an Appeal is ye just right of ye Subject & not to be overthrown on too nice Excep~ions'.[144]

Robert Wilson was clearly successful, with William Cowper's help, in convincing the judges to grant his appeal. Despite his success in court, however, Wilson ultimately failed to secure just punishment for his brother's murder. John Law managed to escape from custody with 'ye connivance of the marshal', and fled back to Scotland, thus avoiding a second trial.[145] Law spent the next several years traveling throughout Europe, settling for a time in France. There he had his greatest triumph and greatest defeat: John Law was the financial advisor who famously pushed forward the schemes for a royal bank and for the Mississippi Company that were adopted by the French crown. Law was eventually pardoned for the crime of murdering Edward Wilson in 1719 shortly before the bursting of the Mississippi Bubble, and the collapse of his system, in 1720.[146]

Five years after *Wilson v Law*, when William Cowper made the claim that Mary Stout's writ of appeal should fail because it was improperly sued out, he couldn't be sure that the judges would accept this argument. For example, since John Law had been accorded extra time, perhaps Holt and the others would not be persuaded by the Cowpers' complaint that Mary Stout deliberately strained time restrictions in bringing her appeal.[147] Cowper needed to show that the alleged procedural defects undermined the reasonableness and justice of Stout's cause. So although the Cowpers introduced some exceptions to the writ based on formal requirements of timing and language, most of their arguments had to do with requirements regarding standing. If they could undermine the court's acceptance of Mary Stout as a legal agent, they could challenge the basic legitimacy of the process by which she had obtained the writ of appeal. Their central focus was on infancy and guardianship. The Cowpers asserted that Stout's writ was defective because Sarah's

144 Holt's full statement is recorded in Cowper's notes as follows: 'I am of ye same opinion, Appeal is a nice Action in Law, but yet 2 Stat. have been made in favour of Appeals, ye 1st ye Stat. of Gloc to prevent ye abating Appeals on too nice exception 2d Stat. 3 H. 7 – that conviction or acquittal on an Indictmt shall be no Barr in an Appeal, so yt an Appeal is ye just right of ye Subject & not to be overthrown on too nice Excep~ions.' 'A Report at large of ye Case of ye Appeale', HALS, Panshanger D/EP F96, fol. 50.

145 Ibid., fol. 51. *Wilson vers Law*, 1 Ld Raym 22, 91 *English Reports* 911.

146 Francois R. Velde, 'John Law's System', *The American Economic Review*, 97, 2 (May, 2007): 278–9; Earl J. Hamilton, 'John Law of Lauriston: Banker, Gamester, Merchant, Chief?', *The American Economic Review*, 57, 2 (May, 1967): 273–82; Richard Bonney, 'Law, John' *ODNB*; Antoin Murphy, *John Law, Economic Theorist and Policy Maker* (Oxford, 1997).

147 *Case of Spencer Cowper*, 1193; 'Argument for my Bro Spenser at Ld Keeper Wrights Chamber in the Inner Temple May 27 1700', HALS , Panshanger D/EP F96, fols 79, 81.

heir, the infant Henry Stout, had no guardian when the writ was sued out of Chancery.[148] They insisted further that only the appellant or his mother, his 'guardian by nurture', could have legally obtained such a writ.

> 1. Because the appellant infant, or his mother, guardian by nurture, had no notice that the writ was sued out, till above a month after the year and day past; and consequently the writ was never well sued out: it being in no body's power, by law, but the appellant's, to sue out such writ; and in case of infancy, as well as in the case of an appellant of full age, the writ is sued out in the person of the appellant, and should be done by the consent of his next friends; and no guardian assigned hath any thing to do therewith till the writ be pending.[149]

The defence was trying to show that these procedural defects indicated that the appeal was being brought without the appellant's consent. This lack of consent would mean that Stout's appeal was an unjust and unreasonable suit. Many of Cowper's defence claims thus promoted a view that recognised infants' ability to act outside the constraints of guardianship. In his notes, William Cowper composed a lengthy set of points on this topic of infants' agency, including further reflection on the intersection between case law and statute. William Cowper displayed a self-consciousness about the nature of legal interpretation, and a recognition of the tradition within which his own manuscript notes were composed. The prevalence of manuscript as well as print complicated the argument from precedent, Cowper admitted: since not all cases were 'known and reported', one was left to rely on those cases in print to reconstruct the legal roles of infants and guardians in earlier times.[150]

When the Cowpers focused on a strong assertion of infant agency they were challenging Mary Stout as guardian. But they were also seeking to justify their own actions when they had advised the infant in this case, Henry Stout, to thwart his guardian's pursuit of the appeal. Mary Stout objected to this Cowper interference, and to the delay of her appeal, by returning to the Kings Bench. Serjeant Levinz and Mr. Carthew, the same

148 *Stout against Towler*, 12 Mod 374, 88 *English Reports* 1388; 'Argument for my Bro Spenser at Ld Keeper Wrights Chamber in the Inner Temple May 27 1700', HALS, Panshanger D/EP F96, fol. 80.

149 *Case of Spencer Cowper*, 1195.

150 Note that statute of 3 Hen 7 was understood to enhance the role of guardians in appeal, but Cowper also explained that any precedents to the contrary (i.e. guardians earlier involved) were not 'known & reported … all ye cases in print before ye Stat[ute] being as before [viz:] ap[peal] by Inft in pson on ye writ.' 'Argument for my Bro Spenser at Ld Keeper Wrights Chamber in the Inner Temple May 27 1700', and 'Reasons + auth. Agt a New Writ', HALS, Panshanger D/EP F96 fols 80, 84. Cf also Jacob, *Laws of Appeals and Murder*, 4, which cites Edward Coke for the assertion that an infant heir is still required to 'commence his Appeal' and 'proceed in his Minority'; Jacob does not comment here on the issue of guardianship.

attorneys William Cowper had faced in *Wilson v Law*, were of counsel to Mary Stout. These men brought the motion to have her writ of appeal properly filed (or 'returned') by Hertford's under-sheriff Toler.[151] According to Toler's confession before the Kings Bench in this case, he 'upon Receipt of the Writ, had sent a copy of it to Cowper the Defendant's Brother, and likewise to Cowper the Defendant'. With such notice the Cowpers were able to compel the child and his family to retrieve and destroy the writ of appeal:

> After the writ was returnable, the mother of the appellant, at the instance and procurement of Cowper, came and demanded the writ of the sheriff, and the sheriff, without any assurance that the infant was the appellant, or the party who came with him was his mother, delivered the writ to them, who destroyed it.[152]

The Cowpers' defence of infant agency was designed to validate these steps that Henry Stout and his mother took, at the Cowpers' behest, to stop Mary Stout's appeal. But the Kings Bench judges were not persuaded by these justifications, and were in fact seriously troubled by the violation of writ process encouraged by the Cowpers and enacted by the sheriff. In their verdict the judges denied that an infant, or anyone else who was a 'stranger' to the writ, could recall it from the sheriff. Chief Justice Holt and Justice Gould judged that Sheriff Toler had committed 'an insufferable contempt' and the court punished him with imprisonment and a hefty fine. Justice Turton disagreed about the nature of this contempt by explaining that he 'relied upon the common practice of re-delivering writs to plaintiffs; and said much to induce the belief that the defendant did this ignorantly out of the simplicity of his heart'.[153] But the three judges were agreed in rejecting the Cowpers' arguments about infancy and guardianship.

The judges ruled against Cowper not only because of his misapplication of the laws regarding infancy but, even more, because of his willingness to tamper with common law due process. Holt especially viewed the Cowpers' collusion with the sheriff, and the sheriff's abuse of the Kings Bench writ, as a clear threat to the court's – and King's – ability to provide justice. Here the matters of integrity and knowledge, bias and fact, were once again at the centre of debate just as they had been during Spencer Cowper's trial at the Hertford assize. The focus on pleading process, on standing and entitlement to judicial writ, was tied to concerns about credibility, just as the focus on forensic science and expert medical witnessing had been. The Cowpers were clearly open to attacks on their integrity, but this did not deter them

151 *Rex vers Toler*, 1 Ld Raym 555, 91 *English Reports* 1271. See also *Case of Mary Stout*, 1197–8, for accusations about delaying tactics employed by Toler.

152 *Stout against Towler*, 12 Mod 374, 88 *English Reports* 1388. See also *Case of Mary Stout*, 1198, where it is alleged that the sheriff indicated that William and Spencer Cowper approached him first to ask if any writ had been delivered.

153 *Rex vers Toler*, 1 Ld Raym 557, 91 *English Reports* 1272.

from advancing charges of bias against Mary Stout. In arguing against the right of appeal, the Cowpers depicted Mary Stout as prejudiced and untrustworthy. William claimed that Mary manipulated the legal process by lying to Allerton and Elizabeth Stout about the nature of her suit in order to gain their cooperation. Mary Stout used their child Henry 'as [an] instrument of her revenge' Cowper argued, and the law should not countenance this twisting of the truth for the 'gratification of her malice'.[154] This depiction of Mary Stout as hysterical and vindictive in this appeal echoed the claims the Cowpers had made earlier about her daughter Sarah Stout. Testimony regarding mental states was an important part of the evidence produced in the Kings Bench and the Hertford courtrooms because the Cowpers pursued a consistent strategy of provoking debate about credibility and objectivity.[155]

Moreover, just as Spencer Cowper had tried to enhance his own credibility by grounding his defence in medical and scientific expertise, William Cowper now sought to defend his own objectivity by emphasising his commitment to legal-professional norms. In order to counter the charges of bias and collusion laid against them, William insisted that he had acted according to professional standards. All he, alone, had done was to provide Henry Stout with objective legal counsel:

> No friend or relation of ye appellee…were acquainted wth their design to fetch ye writt exc[ept] Mr W.C. Brother of S.C: to whose Chamber in ye Temple ye Infant his Mo[ther] Uncle + aunt Allerton + a friend of ye Uncles a Brewer in Southwark came … a few days before ye last Term, in order to advise about ye Re{covery?} of ye Estate (for it seems they had been told Mr W.C. being in probability exasperated by M.S. her usage toward his Bro[ther] would be likely to assist them agt her to the best of his Power) and he freely told them, he would be sure for his Bro sake to advise them to put an end to a malicious + groundless proceeding, wch yet would serve to make his Bro: ye talk of ye town for some time; but yt if he had been a stranger to ye Deft he should have advised ye same thing viz yt not to try their Pedigree in an appeal, if they designed to proceed at Law for ye Estate: wch they saying they did he said he would not undertake to be a manager but would fro[m] time to time give ye best advice he could, provided at ye same time they did not do him a disservice in proceeding agt … his Bro[ther] …without ground, … wch they heartily promised not to do: This Mr W.C. … owned in open Court + is no otherwise proved.[156]

154 'Argument for my Bro Spenser at Ld Keeper Wrights Chamber in the Inner Temple May 27 1700' and 'Reasons + auth. Agt a New Writ', HALS, Panshanger D/EP F96, fols 81, 84.

155 *Trial of Spencer Cowper*, 1165–71. A letter from Pennington Cowper to Judith Cowper, apparently not produced at the trial, also refers to Sarah Stout's melancholy and mental instability. HALS, Panshanger D/EP F81.

156 'Reasons + auth. Agt a New Writ', HALS, Panshanger D/EP F96, fol. 85. The ellipses here indicate where the text was changed, and words crossed out, by Cowper.

This was William Cowper's attempt to cloak his activities in the guise of professional respectability. Yet William Cowper's admission that he had been involved in the destruction of the writ of appeal in a professional, rather than personal, capacity was of real concern to the judges in this case. They clearly had good reason to suspect that biased evidence was being produced, and biased actions were taking place, on both sides. Having 'owned [his involvement] in open Court', William addressed the matter again when he spoke before the judges who now, finally, considered 'the petition [that] was preferred to Sir Nathan Wright, lately made Lord Keeper of the Great Seal of England, to have a new writ of appeal granted'.[157] The judges had also received a 'cross-petition preferred in the infant's name, praying that no new writ of appeal should be sued out in his name'.[158] Cowper addressed Lord Keeper Wright, Master of the Rolls John Trevor, Chief Baron Edward Ward, Chief Justice George Treby and his fellow judge of the Common Pleas John Powell when they conferred on this matter, 'hearing of counsel on both sides for six hours and more', in the Lord Keeper's chambers.[159] Using all of his notes about timing, infancy, guardianship and shrieval authority, and referring to the long lists of authorities he had compiled for this purpose, Cowper persuaded the judges to deny Mary Stout's request for a new writ of appeal.

The judges' decision to deny Mary Stout's appeal was based on a number of considerations. The first was procedural, in that the time limit for bringing an appeal of felony ('a Year and a Day after the Death of the Person') had elapsed.[160] Of course the judges had already countenanced other irregularities in this writ process, such as the defendant's collusion with the infant and the sheriff. But they explained away this apparent inconsistency by contrasting the defendant's involvement in the destruction of the writ in this case with a more notorious and egregious instance of interference and witness tampering committed by Sir John Jackson in the earlier case of *Rex v. Fenwick and Holt*.[161] The judges acknowledged, as they had in *Wilson v Law* and numerous other cases, that they had the responsibility to interpret and enforce pleading requirements so as to preserve both justice and

157 *Rex v Toler*, 1 Ld Raym 557, 91 *English Reports* 1272; 'Argument for my Bro Spenser at Ld Keeper Wrights Chamber in the Inner Temple May 27 1700' and 'Reasons + auth. Agt a New Writ', HALS, Panshanger D/EP F96, fols 79, 81, 85.

158 *Case of Mary Stout*, 1199.

159 *Rex v Toler*, 1 Ld Raym 557, 91 *English Reports* 1272.

160 Jacob, *Laws of Appeals and Murder*, 4; *Rex v Toler*, 1 Ld Raym 557, 91 *English Reports* 1272; *Stout against Toler*, 12 Mod 375, 88 *English Reports* 1389.

161 Statements recorded as made by Lord Keeper Wright and Chief Justice Treby in 'Argument for my Bro Spenser at Ld Keeper Wrights Chamber in the Inner Temple May 27 1700', HALS, Panshanger D/EP F96, fols 79, 81. On Sir John Jackson's case see Giles Dunscombe, *Tryals per Pais: Or, the Law of England Concerning Juries by Nisi Prius*, 3rd edn (London, 1695), 164; Nelson, *Law of Evidence*, 19; *Rex v. Fenwick and Holt*, 1 Sid. 153–5, 82 *English Reports* 1027–8.

the authority of the courts. Here they aimed to accomplish this goal by punishing the sheriff for his violation of procedure, and by adhering to procedure by respecting established time limits.

The second consideration fuelling the denial of a new writ had to do with the exercise of discretion and conscience particularly associated with the authority of a lord keeper (or lord chancellor). When Lord Keeper Wright consulted his fellow judges, they 'all agreed, it was discretionary to grant [a new writ] or no; but agreed it was not proper to do it'.[162] The judges relied on maxims like 'What is doubtful ought not to be proceeded on in such a case', or 'Life more precious than limb', to express the justice of following conscience and natural reason in this case.[163] Lord Keeper Wright followed the dictates of his conscience, and denied Mary Stout's appeal.

The admission of discretion, however, also introduced the possibility of judicial bias, and the danger that such bias would lead to arbitrary decisions rather than fair and reliable verdicts. Chief Justice Treby's strongly-worded denial of Mary Stout's petition could be understood as betraying this kind of bias in favour of Cowper: 'Treby ... alledging, for reason, that an appeal was a revengeful, odious prosecution, and therefore deserved no encouragement.'[164] It was Treby's attack on the appeal – and on Stout – that prompted Chief Justice Holt to articulate his ringing defence of the appeal as emblematic of common law justice:

> Upon which occasion Holt Chief Justice said, he wondered that it should be said that an appeal is an odious prosecution. He said, he esteemed it a noble remedy, and a badge of the rights and liberties of an Englishman. The Statute of Gloucester, 6 Ed. 1, c. 9, has provided, that it shall not be abated so lightly as before it had been ; but if the appellant declares the fact, the year, the day, the hour, the time of the King, and with what weapon, the appeal shall be maintained. And 3 H1. 7, c. 1, which gives power to proceed at the suit of the King within the year, does yet save the appeal to the party after acquittal. And therefore since this remedy hath been favoured by Acts of Parliament, and tends to the support of families, and is of evident necessity in some cases (to say nothing of this present case, but only that a very odd method has been taken, and that too publicly avowed, for withdrawing of this appeal) the Judges ought to encourage appeals.[165]

162 *Stout against Toler*, 12 Mod 375, 88 *English Reports* 1389; *Rex v Toler*, 1 Ld Raym 557, 91 *English Reports* 1272 n (a).

163 Statements recorded as made by Lord Keeper Wright and Chief Justice Treby in 'Argument for my Bro Spenser at Ld Keeper Wrights Chamber in the Inner Temple May 27 1700', HALS, Panshanger D/EP F96, fols 79, 81. Recall Cowper's reference to the maxim against double jeopardy.

164 *Stout against Toler*, 12 Mod 375, 88 *English Reports* 1389.

165 *Rex v Toler*, 1 Ld Raym 557, 91 *English Reports* 1272.

Treby's statement and Holt's equally strong response, have become the lasting legacy of this case, preserved in contemporary reports and modern accounts, because they speak to the question of common law justice. In the same way as he defended the 'Appeal as the just right of the Subject' in the case of *Wilson v Law*, here too Holt described it as one of an Englishman's 'rights and liberties'. The appeal was a common law remedy, reinforced by statute, that stood for Holt as a vital safeguard against the fraud, deception and arbitrary justice that threatened in this case.

Chief Justice Holt's vehemence may also be an indication of his discomfort with the final verdicts in Spencer Cowper's trial and Mary Stout's appeal. In later years, it seems, Holt confided to an acquaintance that he thought Spencer Cowper was guilty and had simply gotten away with murder. This rumour was recorded in a notebook of case reports compiled by the Inner Temple barrister Herbert Jacob, and it may have circulated more widely:

> My Uncle Herbert told me that the CJ believed SC was guilty of the Murder. & used one argumt of his belief, because the murder being committed in the Assize time at Hertford, where ye CJ was Judge of Assize, and SC being brought before him the next morning after ye fact, he thought he discovered upon his examination evident tokens of Guilt.[166]

Chief Justice Holt was assigned to the Home Circuit in the winter of 1698/9, and thus he was likely to have been present at the Hertford assizes when Sarah Stout's dead body was discovered.[167] His examination of Spencer Cowper, if it took place, was not recorded or used as testimony in this case. But those questions about testimony and witnessing, and concerns about the legal truth and justice produced in this adversarial contest, remained troubling to Holt. These concerns were only exacerbated by the continued

166 FLP, Carson, LC 14. 66, fol. 161. These reports were composed by Herbert Jacob when he was a student, and later copied by his law clerks c.1715, so as to be passed on to his nephew. In this passage Jacob added that he was not convinced by this evidence of guilt, and found Cowper by his own acquaintance to be 'mild' 'sweet' 'well-tempered' and 'incapable of committing so villainous an action'. Herbert Jacob was called to the bar of the Inner Temple in 1699; thereafter he was a practicing barrister acquainted with men like Cowper, and Attorney General Philip Yorke. Jacob owned numerous properties, and collected a sizable library of legal books and manuscripts. Many of these books were bequeathed to the Inner Temple Library after his death in 1725; a portrait of his Uncle Herbert by Carlo Muratto was also given to the Inner Temple. Herbert Jacob Will, NA, Prob 11/605; J.H. Baker, *English Legal Manuscripts in the United States of America, Part II:1558–1902* (London, 1999), 315.

167 J.S. Cockburn, Appendix I, Judges in Commission 1559–1714, *A History of English Assizes* (Cambridge, 1972), 280. Cockburn notes, p. 263, that '[w]hen assizes conflicted with a parliamentary session the senior judge on each circuit normally remained in London to attend Parliament.' Since there was a parliamentary session between 6 December 1698 and 4 May 1699, it is possible that Holt remained in London.

insinuations of bias, partisanship and corruption, pointedly noted by the chief justice in his reference to the 'very odd method' used to withdraw Stout's writ of appeal. All Holt could do in the end, however, was to return to a reliance on common law procedures and precedents in order to defend the integrity of the law. Since the withdrawal of Stout's writ had been 'too publicly avowed' any decision that relaxed requirements might foster questions about the verdict, and so threatened to undermine the reputation of the courts.[168] In concurring with the verdict, and making this final statement, Holt sought to convince himself, as well as his fellow judges and the public, that the courts and the common law system they upheld were the surest guard of truth and justice because they were rooted in tradition, authority and accepted past practice.

168 Holt further expressed this worry in his statements and actions against Sheriff Toler: 'The Court of King's Bench, to shew their resentment, committed Toler to the prison of the King's Bench for his fine, though the clerk in Court would have undertaken to pay it. And Holt, Chief Justice said to Toler, that he had not been in prison long enough before; and that he might now, if he pleased, go to Hertford, and make his boast that he had got the better of the King's Bench.' *Rex v Toler*, 1 Ld Raym 557, 91 *English Reports* 1272.

4

Common Law, Credit, and the Growth of Commerce

English common law jurisprudence developed in the context of changes in eighteenth-century evidentiary practices and the growth of the adversary criminal trial. As the trial of Spencer Cowper, and appeal by Mary Stout, demonstrated, there were important connections made between contemporary ideas about objectivity, truth and fact, and contemporary conceptions of authority and justice. The judges' ruling on the matter of Stout's appeal also points to a second important arena for the development of common law jurisprudence in the eighteenth century: jurisdictional controversy between common law and equity. One indication of this controversy is given in the heated exchange between Justices Treby and Holt – and especially in Justice Holt's insistence that the lord keeper's, or lord chancellor's, discretion in granting a new writ of appeal must be informed by a deference to common law remedies, and by an appreciation for stability in common law judgments.

This kind of claim about the benefits of adherence to common law emphasised the justice of procedure and precedent but, as we know, Holt and others also recognised that injustice could sometimes result from too rigid an application of formal rules. In order to address such instances of potential injustice the king's chancellor had begun to exercise a judicial authority in his court of Chancery as early as the fourteenth century. Chancellors were meant to look to conscience, to principles of natural law and universal justice in order to fulfill the spirit of the law, and to rule on what was 'right'. Over time a body of equity law developed in the English Chancery, providing new kinds of remedies where the rigidity of common law – with its closed system of Latin writs and formalised pleading in law French – meant either that new problems could not be dealt with at common law, or that the common law would produce an unjust result. But jurisdictional controversies with common law authorities also developed over time, and lawyers, judges and litigants frequently debated how far the authority exercised by an equity court like Chancery, and by an equitable judge like the chancellor, should extend. These debates, in turn, stimulated discussion about what kind of law provided stronger protections and surer justice. Such contests between Chancery and the common law courts continued into the eighteenth century, and they demonstrate especially well the significance of contemporary legal-philosophical reflection on the nature of law and of justice.[1]

One important reason why these jurisdictional disputes persisted in eighteenth-century England was that new problems arose for the courts to address as a result of broad and rapid economic change. Such change was, of course, related to longer-term economic trends: the expansion of long-distance trade, the growth of international and domestic markets, and the employment of financial techniques like bills of exchange, mortgages or annuities had been evolving since the sixteenth century.[2] But the late 1680s and early 1690s saw the beginning of a period of a dramatically increased rate of growth in public finance. After 1689 the creation of a national debt, the Bank of England, and means of state funding through new kinds of long-term and short-term loans, presented new challenges for the common law. These changes had serious implications for the courts' role in maintaining established protections for the security of property.[3] This was also the beginning of a period of advances in private finance, a period in which there was greater popular awareness of, and greater diffusion of popular participa-

1 Scholars often describe this jurisdictional controversy as the 'fusion debate', using terminology later applied to the nineteenth-century movement towards rationalisation and the merger of common law and equity courts. On the history of this 'fusion debate' see Michael Macnair, 'Lord King & Lord Talbot: An Eighteenth-Century Attempt to Reduce Delay in Chancery and its General Lessons', in C.H. van Rhee ed., *The Law's Delay: Essays on Undue Delay in Civil Litigation* (Antwerp, 2004), 252–68; essays by Michael Lobban, James Oldham, and Joshua Getzler in a forum on chancery reform in *Law and History Review*, 22, 2 & 3 (Summer & Fall, 2004). Henry Horwitz, *A Guide to Chancery Equity Records and Proceedings, 1600–1800* (London, 1998), 40, asserts that there was not significant competition, but rather 'overlap' and 'comity' between Chancery and other courts in this period; my argument is about jurisdictional controversy which was stimulated by such overlap. See also Horwitz's emphasis on jurisdictional complexity in his 'Chancery's "Younger Sister": The Court of Exchequer and its Equity Jurisdiction, 1649–1841', *Historical Research*, 72, 178 (June, 1999): 168–9.

2 On connections to longer term growth see Larry Neal, *The Rise of Financial Capitalism: International Capital Markets in the Age of Reason* (Cambridge, 1990); Craig Muldrew, *The Economy of Obligation: The Culture of Credit and Social Relations in Early Modern England* (London, 1998).

3 Scholars' debates about the mechanisms for establishing security of property after 1689 were much stimulated by Douglas C. North and Barry R. Weingast, 'Constitutions and Commitment: The Evolution of Institutions Governing Public Choice in Seventeenth-Century England', *Journal of Economic History*, 49, 4 (December, 1989): 803–32. For interpretations about the role of the common law courts see also, for example, Ron Harris, 'Government and the Economy 1688–1850', in Roderick Floud and Paul Johnson eds, *The Cambridge Economic History of Britain since 1700, Volume 1, 1700–1850* (Cambridge, 2004), 208–11, 225–30; Rogers, *Early History of the Law of Bills and Notes*; Stuart Banner, *Anglo-American Securities Regulation: Cultural and Political Roots, 1690–1860* (Cambridge, 1998). The seminal work on financial revolution and the public debt was, of course, P.G.M. Dickson, *The Financial Revolution in England: A Study of the Development of Public Credit 1688–1756* (London, 1967).

tion in, financial practices.[4] The expansion of the stock market and private investment were significant in stimulating the growth of new kinds of financial instruments, for example, or new kinds of contractual expectations that also had a real impact on the way in which English law negotiated the experience of change. As new issues came before the courts, and new remedies developed in common law and equity, jurisdictional conflicts sometimes emerged.

The nature of credit and the problem of debt were clearly fundamental questions for legal dispute, and these issues were also debated broadly by a society in which borrowing was a main engine of economic growth.[5] Anxieties were expressed about the uncertainty, volatility and inefficiency of markets, and critics voiced suspicions about the potential for fraud in speculators' manipulation of risks and returns. Of course, there were also many who justified public credit as necessary for a successful national defence, and those who praised corporate and private credit for creating new industries, new jobs, and for generating overall wealth. There were still others who pursued a slightly more detached focus on data collection, compiling practical information on interest rates and the means of calculating the value of bills of exchange, bank notes or lottery tickets. Whether practical, positive or negative this wide-ranging public discussion was fundamentally engaged in investigating the ephemeral nature of the new wealth, and through such investigation contemporaries confronted key epistemological questions.[6] Those concerns about truth, proof and fact that, as we've seen, were an important part of the development of enlightened scientific, legal and print cultures, were also fuelled by debates about this market-oriented culture. And since law was one of the most crucial mechanisms for assimilating the changes wrought by the growth of public and private finance, contemporary debates about economic change also shaped contemporary definitions of justice.

4 Neal, *Rise of Financial Capitalism*, 10; Anne L. Murphy, *The Origins of English Financial Markets: Investment and Speculation before the South Sea Bubble* (Cambridge, 2009); Ron Harris, *Industrializing English Law: Entrepreneurship and Business Organization 1720–1844* (Cambridge, 2000), 53–9; Natasha Glaisyer, *The Culture of Commerce in England 1660–1720* (Woodbridge, 2006); Julian Hoppit, 'Attitudes to Credit in Britain 1680–1790', *The Historical Journal*, 33, 2 (June, 1990): 305–22.

5 Hoppit, 'Attitudes to Credit', 306–7; Hoppit, *Risk and Failure in English Business 1700–1800* (Cambridge, 1987), chs 2–3; Craig Muldrew, 'Credit and the Courts: Debt Litigation in a Seventeenth-Century Urban Community', *Economic History Review*, New Series, 46, 1 (February, 1993): 23–38; Muldrew, *Economy of Obligation*, chs 8–9.

6 Natasha Glaisyer, 'Calculating Credibility: Print Culture, Trust and Economic Figures in Early Eighteenth-Century England', *Economic History Review*, 60, 4 (November, 2007): 685–711; Pocock, *Machiavellian Moment*, ch. 13; Pocock, *Virtue, Commerce, and History*, ch. 6; Hoppit, 'Attitudes to Credit', 685–711; Mary Poovey, *Genres of the Credit Economy: Mediating Value in Eighteenth and Nineteenth-Century Britain* (Chicago, 2008).

Early eighteenth-century judges and lawyers grappled with the consequences of the new market practices. In the process many of them made arguments on behalf of common law stability and the authority of tradition. Yet these were not a simple, blinkered rehashing of old 'ancient constitutionalist' ideas. Their conception of common law justice developed in conjunction with contemporary ideological debate about commercial and financial innovation. And these economic and jurisprudential debates were part of broader enlightened philosophical trends, affected by contemporary investigation into the moral-philosophical implications of economic change. The question of jurisdiction, for example, was understood in terms of new ideas about human desires, about the morality of 'getting and spending'. Moral-philosophical reflection on the nature of human passions informed discussion of the place of equity in relation to common law, first regarding the question of whether Chancery encouraged novelty and expansion in commercial law; and, second, regarding questions about the extent of the chancellor's authority as it was founded in natural law and universal morality. Moreover, there was a specifically gendered aspect of these discussions, since concerns about women's engagement in commercial society as consumers, investors and property-owners was a significant part of contemporary debate. New areas of protection for women's property interests developed in Chancery and conflict over such developments, within the courtroom and without, is one important indication of the ways in which problems of jurisdiction, doctrine, economy, morality and jurisprudence were understood to converge.

As the next three chapters will show, there is ample evidence in both the legal literature and in legal practice that this matter of jurisdictional controversy was an especially important locus for the development of common law jurisprudence. This first chapter begins with a close study of one of the authors of the legal literature, Sir Robert Atkyns, because he was an important early contributor to these controversies in print and in the courtroom. We begin here, too, because the commercial context and changing content of Atkyns' jurisprudence have generally been misunderstood, and this misunderstanding has led scholars to regard Sir Robert Atkyns simply as representative of a static 'ancient constitutionalism' that endured into the early eighteenth century. The fact is that Atkyns engaged in new debates after 1689, and his ideas developed in new enlightened contexts, signifying, I will argue, that his jurisprudence should not be interpreted as a recapitulation of seventeenth-century arguments for custom and immemoriality.

This misinterpretation of Atkyns' later jurisprudence stemmed from scholars' awareness that Atkyns, as one of the architects of the Revolution Settlement in 1689, clearly defended history and tradition as essential to political legitimacy. He frequently underscored the continuity of the constitution and of the common law: 'We ourselves of the present Age, chose our Common Law, and consented to the most ancient Acts of Parliament,' Atkyns characteristically claimed, 'for we lived in our Ancestors a

Thousand Years ago, and those Ancestors are still living in us.'[7] Atkyns had defended a view of fundamental law and consent against perceived Stuart tyranny throughout the later seventeenth century, and he is easily associated with that era's ancient constitutionalism. A distinguished and unwavering Whig politician of the first generation, Atkyns rose to the rank of serjeant-at-law during the Restoration, served as a reader of Lincoln's Inn, and attained a place on the bench of the Common Pleas. By 1680 however Atkyns was purged from that court because of his connections with Exclusionists, like Lord Russell, who tried to circumscribe Stuart claims to the throne. During his 'forced retirement' Atkyns continued to act, and write, in defence of common law and ancient constitution as part of the Whig cause throughout the 1680s.[8] And after the Revolution he was rewarded with judicial appointment as chief baron of the Exchequer, now taking the place of his own nonjuring younger brother Edward.[9]

Indeed, Sir Robert came from an even more accomplished legal family than William and Spencer Cowper: Robert and his brother perpetuated the legacy of their father, grandfather and great-grandfather, all of whom had been readers of Lincoln's Inn and all of whom had held judicial office. Like his sons, father Edward Atkyns was a judge of the Common Pleas and baron of the Exchequer, serving under both Stuart and Cromwellian regimes.[10] The Atkyns were also important in the world of legal publishing. Sir Robert's brother Edward, and their first cousin Richard Atkyns, held the royal patent to publish law books for forty years from the restoration of Charles II. Many legal abridgments, manuals, collections and reports were 'printed by the assigns of Richard and Edward Atkyns, Esquires' until the second decade of the eighteenth century.[11]

7 Robert Atkyns, *Enquiry into the Power of Dispensing with Penal Statutes*, in Atkyns, *Parliamentary and Political Tracts* (London, 1734), 190. This evocative phrase of common law traditionalism has been noted by scholars like Greenberg and Lieberman.

8 Julia Rudolph, *Revolution by Degrees: James Tyrrell and Whig Political Thought in the Late Seventeenth Century* (Basingstoke, 2002), 102, 195 n. 43; Janelle Greenberg, 'Atkyns, Robert', *ODNB*. Atkyns later published his letters to the Russell family, along with his arguments condemning the verdict against Russell, in *A Defence of the Late Lord Russel's Innoccency ... Together with an Argument in the Great Case Concerning Election of Members to Parliament* (London, 1689), and *The Lord Russel's Innocency Further Defended* (London, 1689).

9 'Atkyns, Robert', *ODNB*; Foss, *Judges of England*, vol. 7, 306–10; Rudolph, *Revolution By Degrees*, 195 n. 43.

10 Robert Atkyns, *An Enquiry into the Jurisdiction of Chancery in Causes of Equity* (London, 1695), epistle dedicatory. Foss, *Judges of England*, vol. 7, 53–5; James S. Hart, Jr. 'Atkyns, Edward', *ODNB*. Note also that Robert's grandson continued this legacy: John Tracy Atkyns was a law reporter under Lord Chancellor Hardwicke, and a cursitor baron of the Exchequer 1755–73. Foss, *Judges in England*, vol. 8, 238–9; N.G. Jones, 'Atkyns, John Tracy', *ODNB*.

11 Cousin Richard Atkyns attained fame as a tenacious controversialist, opposing the power of the Stationers' Company, defending the royal prerogative, and promoting a

Judge Atkyns 'earned a reputation as "a very learned man" who was second only to Sir Matthew Hale in legal erudition,' and like Hale he is still remembered as a significant theorist and historian of the common law.[12] Because of this prominence before 1689 scholars assumed that even after the Revolution Atkyns continued to repeat his defence of common law against any 'encroachments' by prerogative power. So, W.S. Holdsworth credited Atkyns' *Enquiry into the Jurisdiction of the Chancery in Causes of Equity* (1695) with offering 'the last protest made by a common lawyer' against such potential abuses by the court of Chancery.[13] Atkyns' modern biographer, Janelle Greenberg, agreed that this defence of the common law courts was his 'last public act'; and Michael Macnair concluded that Atkyns' arguments were among a number of persistent 'common law constitutionalist objections to the equity jurisdiction' rehearsed in the early eighteenth century as 'part of wider efforts to restore the "ancient constitution"'.[14]

It has not been recognised, however, that Atkyns' post-Revolution writings on common law and constitution were written in a different context: the context of litigation concerning changing commercial and financial practices. Atkyns' *Enquiry into the Jurisdiction of Chancery* and his very last publication, the *Treatise of the True and Ancient Jurisdiction of the House of Peers* (1699), were aimed to support Atkyns' own cause in a dispute that had made its way through the courts of Exchequer and Chancery and ended in appeals to the House of Lords.[15] The dispute centred on questions about credit, debt and fraud in mortgage and trust. In *The Case of the said Sir*

partisan history of printing. Pierre Bayle, *A General Dictionary Historical and Critical*, trans. Rev. John Peter Bernard, Thomas Birch, John Lockman et al., vol. 2 (London, 1735), 409–10; Johns, *Nature of the Book*, 304–23; David Stoker, 'Atkyns, Richard', *ODNB*. Richard Atkyns' own polemical publications on the development of print included *The Original and Growth of Printing* (London?, 1660?) and *The Kings Grant of Privilege for Sole Printing Common Law Books Defended* (London, 1669). An important focus in the controversy with the Stationers was publication of an edition of *Rolle's Abridgment* with Matthew Hale's preface. On royal patents and law books see also H.S. Bennett, *English Books and Readers 1558–1603* (Cambridge, 1965).

12 'Atkyns, Robert', *ODNB*, quoting, in part, H.C. Foxcroft ed., *A Supplement to Burnet's History of My Own Time* (Oxford, 1902), 122.

13 W.S. Holdsworth, *A History of English Law*, vol. 1 (London, 1927), 465.

14 'Atkyns, Robert', *ODNB*; Macnair, 'Common Law and Statutory Imitations of Equitable Relief', 117–18; see also Horwitz, *Guide to Chancery Equity Records*, 2 n. 6.

15 Note that Atkyns himself made a connection between these texts and his earlier publications in order to claim that he wasn't just making a personal argument, but was still motivated by 'love to my Countrey, and Gratitude to mines, and my Ancestors Profession'. Atkyns, *Enquiry into Jurisdction Chancery*, 21–2. The only commentator on Atkyns' treatises to notice the connection between these later texts and the dispute with the Tooks was the late eighteenth-century legal scholar Francis Hargrave. Hargrave cautioned that this personal interest may 'somewhat detract[] from the authority of these pieces' but he also confirmed Atkyns' own claim that the ideas expressed were consistent with Atkyns' other distinguished publications on law and constitution. Francis Hargrave,

Robert Atkyns upon his Appeal against a Decree obtained by Mrs Elizabeth Took and others, Plaintiffs in Chancery – a text that was appended to the *Enquiry* – Atkyns portrayed himself as the victim of an attempt by Thomas and Elizabeth Took to evade a debt, and perpetuate a fraud, by proclaiming the property in question to be held in trust. Atkyns viewed this trust as a novel and nefarious way to erode the common law of property, and as an invention wrongly upheld by Chancery.

Sir Robert Atkyns' later ideas about trusts and Chancery should not be read primarily in terms of the earlier problem of prerogative power. Rather they must be understood in the context of internal legal changes such as doctrinal developments in mortgage and trust law. His ideas must also be analysed in terms of the broader external context of enlightened discourses about credit and credibility. This case offers an interesting example of debate over the question of protection for creditors that was especially pressing after 1689. Indeed Atkyns' litigation took place during a first intense period of dislocation, which led to reflection on the nature of economic change and the rule of law. In the 1690s 'England was racked by political instability, war, financial innovation at the public and corporate levels, speculative manias, a massive recoinage and a financial crisis of some magnitude,' Julian Hoppit reminds us. 'It was in this unique environment that the first concerted discussion of credit took place.'[16]

Like other jurists, Atkyns defended common law as a means for preserving the security of property against those fraudulent practices that stemmed from the expansion of credit, and were fuelled by commercial innovation. He and others also regarded common law as a way to provide certainty against the volatile and arbitrary justice sure to result from over-expansion of the chancellor's jurisdiction – an expansion that was also a consequence of economic and cultural change. This early eighteenth-century reaffirmation of the justice of common law tradition and prescription was not evidence of rigidity, nor a simple rejection of commercial practices. It was, rather, indicative of an interest in preserving the stability and civility of the post-Revolution state and society. Indeed, contests over the economic implications of Revolution Principles, continued disputes about the jurisdiction of Chancery, and continued changes in commercial law were interconnected and significantly affected the development of common law jurisprudence. Exploration of the nature of the authority of common law took place in cases and treatises like Atkyns' and, as subsequent chapters will show, in a legal literature on equity and natural law, and in public trials of judicial and financial corruption. In these other venues the definition of common law justice as honest, credible and sociable developed in conjunction with contemporary trends in natural

preface, *The Jurisdiction of the Lords House, or Parliament … by Lord Chief Justice Hale*, (London, 1796), clxxxix–cxciv.

16 Hoppit, 'Attitudes towards Credit', 308.

jurisprudence, moral-philosophical debate, and cultural practices of civility and politeness that were also part of British, and European, Enlightenments.

Marriage and mortgage

The dispute that generated jurisdictional conflict, and inspired Sir Robert Atkyns' late legal philosophy, was centred on a debt contracted in 1689. In the spring of that year Atkyns lent a man named Thomas Took L820. In return Atkyns was granted a conveyance of nineteen houses in Holborn as security for the loan.[17] Took's willingness to mortgage nineteen properties as security reflects the size of this loan, but it also hints at the problem of Took's prior indebtedness. Thomas Took had to offer substantial security because he required this loan in order to free himself from imprisonment for debt.[18] Given Took's proven inability to meet his obligations, to be creditworthy, Atkyns' loan appears to be an act of generosity, and his negotiation of a mortgage simple prudence. But Thomas Took later contended that he was *forced* to borrow such a large sum by Atkyns, and that his own indebtedness was caused, in part, by the complicated history of promises and disappointments that existed between the two men. Took explained that he had been awarded a Chancery judgment against Atkyns in an earlier dispute. Now, Took complained, Atkyns was simply trying to free himself from that judgment by unfairly constructing this loan and mortgage.[19] The problem of debt, and matters of reputation and credibility, were at stake for both sides.

The earlier dispute occurred in 1687 and concerned the marriage portion provided for Thomas' wife, Elizabeth Took (nee Atkyns). Elizabeth's father Richard Atkyns was the son of Robert's first cousin Henry Atkyns. Six years younger than Robert, Richard Atkyns followed in his cousin's footsteps: he was educated at the same school in Hertford, matriculated at the same Cambridge college (Sidney Sussex) and, following in a long line of Atkyns men, was admitted at Lincoln's Inn.[20] The two men shared the educational, professional and social status associated with the Atkyns lineage. These family bonds exerted a varied influence when Robert was involved

17 NA, C111/220, fols i, iiii; Robert Atkyns, *The Case of Sir Robert Atkyns … Upon his Appeal Against a Decree* (London, 1695), 3. The question of the nature of this possession – whether Sir Robert was granted possession in fee simple or in reversion only – will become an issue of dispute (see for example, *Case of Robert Atkyns*, 11). Note that there are variant spellings of both names, Atkyns/Atkins and Took/Tooke in the records; I will quote the names as they appear in the records, but will adhere to a consistent spelling of Atkyns and Took in my own text.

18 Atkyns, *Case of Robert Atkyns*, 3.

19 NA, C111/220, fol. iiii.

20 John Venn and J.A. Venn, comp., *Alumnae Cantabrigienses* (Cambridge, 1922–54); see also the Atkyns genealogy set out in FSL, G.c.1.

in arrangements for the marriage of his cousin's daughter Elizabeth. In time, economic interests, familial reputation and competing claims about credibility led to conflict.

During the initial negotiations between the Atkyns and Took families Robert used inducements of money and feeling to help persuade Thomas' mother to agree to her son's marriage to Elizabeth Atkyns. Thomas' father Ralph Took had died several months before his son was born in 1662, and his wife Elizabeth married Carew Reynell, a Tory writer on economy and philosophy, in the following year. She served as guardian – sometimes sole, sometimes joint with her new husband – of the properties her son Thomas inherited from his father and grandfather. [21] When Thomas reached the age of fourteen these marriage negotiations took place, and Elizabeth Reynell was persuaded to consent to his match not only because she was to receive L2000, paid by the bride's father Sir Richard Atkyns, for her own 'use and benefit,' but also because she was 'very intimate with the defendant Sir Robert Atkins.'[22] The intimacy between Elizabeth Reynell and Robert Atkyns stemmed from the fact that Robert and his brother Edward Atkyns were executors of the estate of Elizabeth Reynell's late father-in-law (and her son's namesake) Thomas Took. The connection was likely strengthened by the bond both families had with another prominent family, the Dacres.[23] Sir Robert served as trustee of the L2000 agreed upon in the Took-Atkyns marriage settlement and by the time of this initial Chancery suit had already seen L1800 of the portion either handed over to, or used on behalf of, Elizabeth Reynell.[24]

All of the considerations that shaped Elizabeth Atkyns' and Thomas Took's marriage plans are a good example of the 'tangled webs of economic and social dependency' described by Craig Muldrew, 'which linked...households to others within communities and beyond, through the numerous reciprocal bonds of trust in all of the millions of bargains they transacted'. Moreover the agreements reached as part of the relationship between the

21 *Charles Reynell, Esq., Administrator de Bonis non ... appellant, John Atkins, Esq., late John Tracy, Administrator de Bonis non ... respondent, The Respondent's Case* (London, 1739), 1. V.E. Chancellor, 'Reynell, Carew', *ODNB*.

22 *Tooke versus Sir Robert Atkins & Al*', 1 Vern 451, 23 *English Reports* 579. Apparently these monies were used to buy out a portion of Thomas' estate inherited from his grandfather, which was then put in trust for Elizabeth Reynell, and administered by trustees Robert Atkyns and Michael Brighouse. *The Respondent's Case*, 1.

23 *The Respondent's Case*, 1. Sir Robert Atkyns' mother Ursula was the daughter of Sir Thomas Dacre of St Andrew le Mott, and his second wife Anne was the daughter of Sir Thomas Dacre, and great-niece of his mother. See Foss, *Judges of England*, vol. 7, 55, 310; Henry Summerson, 'Dacre family (per 1542–1716)', *ODNB*; also *Doe Ex Dim Atkyns v Horde et al.*, 2 Cowp 689–90, 98 *English Reports* 1310. Sir Henry Dacre served as one of Thomas Took's guardians, and was involved in the management of properties while Thomas was under-age. NA, C111/220, fol. ii.

24 *Tooke Versus Sir Robert Atkins & Al*', 1 Vern 451, 23 *English Reports* 579.

Atkyns and the Tooks provide a clear indication of the ways in which 'economic trust was interpreted in terms as emotive as other forms of human interaction such as neighbourliness, friendship and marriage'.[25] Thus the fact that Thomas Took's mother was economically and emotionally invested in these marriage negotiations was not unusual, nor was the amount of the portion paid by the bride's father. The more atypical claim that the payment was made to benefit Elizabeth Reynell was an indication of an agreed-upon bargain, by which the mother 'designed to make an advantage' when marrying off her son 'who was heir to a good estate'.[26] But once that son reached the age of majority he brought a complaint about this arrangement to the Chancery, in April 1687.

Thomas Took pursued a conventional legal strategy by disputing his marriage settlement, and seeking to recover his wife's portion in Chancery.[27] In this suit the credibility of Elizabeth Reynell and her trustee Robert Atkyns came into question. Written documents brought by their defence counsel seemed to confirm 'that this money was intended for the use and benefit of the mother', and precedent affirmed that the mother's promised consent was 'sufficient consideration' for this agreement to stand. But the validity of these defence claims was undermined when the other party to this agreement, Elizabeth's father Richard Atkyns, offered contradictory testimony. Richard testified against his cousin Robert, and enhanced the credibility of his son-in-law's complaint:

> Sir Richard Atkins being examined in the cause, and in effect deposing that the money was intended as a portion with his daughter, the Lord Chancellor decreed for the plaintiff, and that in the first place the mother should pay as far as she was responsible, and Sir Robert Atkins the residue; but both to be liable to satisfy the moneys to the plaintiff.[28]

In the face of the father's statement, Elizabeth Reynell's and Sir Robert Atkyns' testimonies were considered to be misleading and, equally important, their motives in negotiating the marriage settlement were suspected to be untrustworthy. Questions were raised regarding Elizabeth Reynell's administration of her sons' properties, and ultimately the Chancery decreed in his favour 'declaring, that as they would not see the Heir defrauded, so

[25] Muldrew, *Economy of Obligation*, 97, 125. And cf Amy Erickson on the particular complexity of issues, and interested parties, in marriage settlement cases, Amy Louise Erickson, *Women and Property in Early Modern England* (London, 1993), 117.

[26] *Tooke Versus Sir Robert Atkins & Al'*, 1 Vern 451, 23 *English Reports* 579.

[27] Erickson, *Women and Property*, ch. 7; Tim Stretton, *Women Waging Law in Elizabethan England* (Cambridge, 1998); Stretton, 'Women, Property and Law', in Anita Pacheco ed., *A Companion to Early Modern Women's Writing* (Blackwell, 2002), 40–57; Nancy E. Wright, Margaret Ferguson and A.R. Buck eds, *Women, Property and the Letters of the Law in Early Modern England* (Toronto, 2004).

[28] *Tooke Versus Sir Robert Atkins & Al'*, 1 Vern 451, 23 *English Reports* 579.

they who had received the 1800 *l.* and the Plaintiff's Rents, should answer the same to him'.[29] There is ample evidence of ongoing conflict between Thomas and his mother over his inheritance and her dower rights; such competition between the interests of sons and widows was a familiar feature of family settlement disputes, and the quarrel between Thomas and his mother continued well after this case.[30] It is not clear that Robert Atkyns encouraged such conflict, and there is no proof that he had enriched himself at the expense of the Tooks. Regardless of whether he had benefited financially, however, Atkyns as trustee was responsible for the monies due. The amount of the 'residue' owed by Sir Robert is made clear in Thomas Took's later reference to the 'six hundred pounds parte of the intended portion of one thousand eight hundred pounds' awarded by Lord Commissioner Sir William Rawlinson.[31]

Anxieties about fraud, concerns about truth, and the social and emotional forces shaping the experience of credit and debt are all obvious in this initial dispute. These and other aspects of a broader enlightened debate about credit and credibility will continue to be an important context for understanding the subsequent litigation which shaped Robert Atkyns' ideas about common law justice. Indeed contemporary market practices, and critics' concerns about those practices, will become increasingly relevant to the relations between the creditors and debtors in this case, causing the web of motive, reputation and interest to become even more tangled. First, the troubling persistence of debt and lack of ready money are apparent in both Atkyns' and Took's actions. The Chancery award remained unpaid, despite the court's initial decree of 19 April 1688 and further Chancery orders of 26 May 1688, 26 November 1688, and 8 May 1689.[32] During this period Thomas Took did not receive the monies owed and at the same time he faced legal process, and ultimately imprisonment, for his own unpaid debts.

Now Took's imprisonment was not unusual: creditors often used the wide discretion afforded by law to detain recalcitrant debtors like Took, and force repayment from them. Creditors relied on the hope that the threat of imprisonment, or the desire for freedom from imprisonment, would 'drive [debtors] to strenuous efforts to pay off the debt'.[33] This recourse to imprisonment was inefficient – it did not ensure creditors' satisfaction and was mainly, in Joanna Innes's words, a form of 'legalized bullying'. Yet, as Innes also notes, the 'legal procedures governing indebtedness were of consider-

29 *The Respondent's Case*, 1.

30 Ibid., 2.

31 NA, C111/220, fol. iiii.

32 Ibid.; *Tooke Versus Sir Robert Atkins & Al'*, 1 Vern 451, 23 *English Reports* 579.

33 Joanna Innes, 'The King's Bench Prison in the Later Eighteenth Century: Law, Authority and Order in a London Debtor's Prison', in John Brewer and John Styles eds, *An Ungovernable People: The English and their Law in the Seventeenth and Eighteenth Centuries* (New Brunswick, 1980), 255.

able importance inasmuch as they were supposed to sustain confidence in the system of credit which underlay the English economy'.[34] In order for credit to be extended there had to be credible expectation of repayment enforced by law. Moreover, as the example of Atkyns and Took reminds us, debtors were also creditors themselves – and creditors, debtors – so that there was a certain equality of vulnerability to, as well as widespread awareness of, the force of the law.

Inhabitants of debtors' prisons often manipulated that awareness of law to their own advantage, using their confinement as a way to resist their prosecutors, and to avoid repayment. The main force of the law was in fact directed against the debtor's person, in physical restraint, rather than against their property. Legal process was hedged with restrictions that protected land and monies, and so imprisoned debtors could continue to transact business, to engage in money-making activities both within and outside of the prison, and to negotiate with their creditors as well as other people with whom they had financial dealings. As part of a community of debtors in prison Thomas Took even had access to useful legal and financial advice from popular 'debtors handbooks' that circulated, from other inmates experienced in law and business, and from 'gaol lawyers' who 'provided instruction in techniques of manipulating the law to the creditor's loss'.[35] While in prison Took was part of 'an increasingly conspicuous population of unreformed, unrepentant and largely unrestrained insolvent debtors in English gaols' that continued to expand, Margot Finn has shown, in the eighteenth and nineteenth centuries.[36]

This kind of lack of repentance, and unrestrained willingness to manipulate the law, may be evident in Thomas Took's appeal, from debtors' prison, to Robert Atkyns for a loan. But of course we have to remember that Took's negotiating partner was a man who, in Took's eyes, was himself untrustworthy, tied to the suspect actions and outstanding debts incurred by Thomas' mother. Indeed, in the later dispute over this loan negotiated in 1689, Took alleged that it was Robert Atkyns who engaged in unfair manipulation. When Took came to him for a loan of L220, Atkyns did not grant the request and simply deduct this amount from the L600, that portion of the Chancery award he was responsible to pay. Rather Atkyns 'took advantage of the defendant being a prisoner and of his great want of money', Took complained, and 'refused to lend him two hundred and twenty pounds unlesse he might be secured the six hundred pounds alsoe'.[37] Took would receive the needed money on the condition that Atkyns would be released from his liability for monies already spent by Thomas' mother

34 Ibid., 253; Margot Finn, *The Character of Credit: Personal Debt in English Culture 1740–1914* (Cambridge, 2003), 110–12.

35 Innes, 'King's Bench Prison', 256–7.

36 Finn, *Character of Credit*, 109.

37 NA, C111/220, fol. iiii.

Elizabeth Reynell. In effect, Atkyns was willing to provide a new loan, and to pay a portion of the Chancery award as a kind of loan against Elizabeth Reynell's debt to her son, but he wanted to have some recompense for his efforts, and some hope of future repayment.

Thomas Took agreed to this deal. It is possible that he agreed to the loss of part of the Chancery award out of desperation bred of his desire to get out of prison; or out of resignation, once he became aware that Sir Robert did not fully accept liability for the spent marriage portion.[38] Or perhaps Took agreed because he thought the deal was to his own advantage. Trained in debtors' prison in the art of manipulation, perhaps Thomas Took hatched a plan to trick Sir Robert Atkyns into parting with his money by offering a security that, Took believed, was irredeemable. As the following passage from the loan dispute indicates, the mortgaged properties were already part of a trust established by Thomas Took for his wife Elizabeth:

> Thomas Tooke becomeing indebted to the plaintiff Sir Robert Atkyns in eight hundred and twenty pounds principall money to him paid in or about Aprill one thousand six hundred eighty nine by deed of lease and release conveyed the reversion or remainder in fee of the Rose Taverne and the rest of the houses and the rents to the plaintiffe and his heires for secureing the said eight hundred and twenty pounds and interest and for further security the defendt Thomas Tooke assigned to the plaintiffe the overplus of the said rents made payable to himselfe upon or out of the said trust.[39]

By the terms of the loan agreement Robert Atkyns gained a right to the monies left over after rent payments made up Elizabeth's separate maintenance, and he and his heirs were granted the reversion of these properties, becoming the remaindermen in a resettlement of this portion of Took's estate.[40] By the terms of the trust noted here, the trustees Richard Atkyns and John Bennett had title to these nineteen houses in trust to pay Elizabeth Took L200 per annum as her separate maintenance (increasing to L300

38 The later account of these events in *The Respondent's Case* suggests that Robert and Thomas both considered Elizabeth Reynell culpable, and that they joined together to try to force her to pay the 1800L due. *The Respondent's Case*, 2.

39 NA, C111/220, fol. i.

40 For similar examples of the use, or manipulation, of lands held in trust see Samuel Carter, *Lex Vadiorum, The Law of Mortgages* (London, 1706); *Treatise of Feme Coverts or the Lady's Law: Containing all the Laws and Statutes Relating to Women under Several Heads* (London, 1732), 77, 153–4; Philip Hamburger, 'The Conveyancing Purposes of the Statute of Frauds', *The American Journal of Legal History*, 27, 4 (October, 1983): 364. On inheritance practices and strict settlement, Lloyd Bonfield, *Marriage Settlements 1601–1740: The Adoption of the Strict Settlement* (Cambridge, 1983); Baker, *Introduction to English Legal History*, 293–4.

per annum if she were widowed). Robert's cousin Richard Atkyns died in 1689, leaving Bennett sole trustee of these mortgaged properties.[41]

Robert Atkyns was an experienced judge and lawyer, and he must have considered this undertaking to be an acceptable risk – and a fortunate opportunity to cancel the Chancery judgment in Took's favour. Perhaps Atkyns made this loan and negotiated this mortgage in order to take advantage of a young, indebted, incompetent heir, and to obtain a lucrative security by fraudulent means. Or, now enmeshed in the financial troubles of an unsuccessful and unsavoury relative, perhaps he was trying to protect himself from suffering further losses.[42] Both men had experience in financial transactions, and there were certainly mixed motives, and uncertainties, on both sides. Their dispute encompasses multiple features of the new economy: the vagaries of business cycles, the consequences of insolvency, the ubiquity of risk. The concerns about trust and reliability that fuelled their transactions were typical of the concerns raised by contemporaries as they confronted questions about fairness and legal protection newly exposed by the credit economy.

Three years after the L820 loan was granted to Thomas Took, Robert Atkyns still had not received any interest payments, nor had the mortgage been redeemed. So in 1691 Atkyns commenced a suit as plaintiff in his own court of Exchequer against John Bennett, Thomas and Elizabeth Took and Thomas and Elizabeth Collins.[43] The barons of the Exchequer often heard mortgage cases like this on the 'equity side' of their court. Although Chancery was the older equity court, the Exchequer's equity jurisdiction had grown in tandem with Chancery equity in the sixteenth and seventeenth centuries, and the two courts generally followed each others' decisions.[44] As chief baron, Sir Robert Atkyns was surely familiar with these kinds of cases and would know what to expect when bringing suit in his own court.

His case was 'heard at Serjeants Inn Hall in Fleet Street upon Tuesday the seventh of July...before the right honorable Sir Edward Nevill Knight, Sir Nicholas Lechmere Knight, and Sir John Turton Knight, three of the

41 NA, C111/220, fol. i; also Venn and Venn, *Alumnae Canatbrigienses*, and FSL, G.c. 1, confirm the death of Richard in 1689.

42 Atkyns, *Case of Robert Atkyns*, 6; NA, C111/220, fol. ii. See also the concerns about the dangers of mortgages for improvident heirs in A *Precaution to Young Gentlemen and Others who Mortgage Estates* (London, 1741); and the discussion of the significance of the remedy of the equity of redemption to protect these heirs in David Sugarman and Ronnie Warrington, 'Land Law, Citizenship and the Invention of "Englishness": The Strange World of the Equity of Redemption', in John Brewer and Susan Staves eds, *Early Modern Conceptions of Property* (London, 1995), 120–4.

43 NA, C111/220, fol. i.

44 W.H. Bryson, *The Equity Side of the Exchequer: Its Jurisdiction, Administration, Procedures and Records* (Cambridge, 1975), 5, 11–13; Horwitz, 'Chancery's "Younger Sister"', 161–9. NA, C111/220, fols v–vi.

then Barons of this court'.[45] The suit was first aimed to recover overdue rent payments on one of the mortgaged properties, the Rose Tavern. This valuable property, apparently forgotten by the Tooks and neglected by the holders of its sub-lease, Thomas and Elizabeth Collins, 'hath for some time been forgotten and stood empty and the goodes the particulers thereof unknowne to the plaintiffe are imbesled and the said house left mizrably out of repaire and the custom and credit of the said house utterly lost'.[46] Robert Atkyns asserted that he was 'intituled to the said whole rent of eighty pounds per annum reserved upon this said lease of one and twenty years of the Rose Tavern'.[47] Further, Atkyns claimed a right to the 'overplus' from the rents on the other properties signalling his recognition, at this time, of the trust established by Thomas Took for his wife Elizabeth. The rents on these properties should have totaled L360 leaving a sizable 'overplus' for Sir Robert.[48]

This demand for rents and profits spoke to the second, and main, aim of Sir Robert's Exchequer suit: to compel Thomas Took to redeem his mortgage or to forfeit these properties.[49] Indeed, the central matter barons Nevill, Turton and Lechmere discussed was whether the mortgage held by Atkyns was security for a L220 or L820 debt and, additionally, what was the penalty for default on this debt? In addressing the question of penalty, and grappling with the broader question of protections for creditors, much of this Exchequer case focused on the calculation of rent arrears to be paid by the tenants of the Rose Tavern because this was seen as a way to generate income for the plaintiff and defendants. This is an important indication of the court's creativity in negotiating this credit relationship, and a refutation of Innes' claim that 'the courts played no more than a passive and procedural role, never attempting to ascertain the debtor's resources nor to impose any kind of settlement'.[50] Here the Exchequer was active in trying

45 NA, C111/220, fol. iiii.

46 Ibid., fol. ii; Atkyns, *Case of Robert Atkyns*, 8. On the typicality of overdue rent payments in late seventeenth-century England see Muldrew, *Economy of Obligation*, 107–8.

47 NA, C111/220, fol. ii.

48 Atkyns, *Case of Robert Atkyns*, 10.

49 Atkyns later explained: 'That his Bill in the Exchequer was designed merely to state the Debt owing to him by Mr. Took, and to compel him to a Redemption of the Mortgage, or to be barr'd of his Redemption; and all Parties, (as was propos'd to Sir Robert on the behalf of Mr. Took,) were inclin'd to get an Act of Parliament pass'd for the sale of Mr. Took's Estate; and to have the Debt due to Sir Robert upon the Mortgage, and the Debts to his other Creditors paid off, and a provision afterwards made for Mrs. Took, which Sir Robert offer'd to further: So that it was not so seasonable nor proper at that time to question their Title, nor to object Fraud against it.' Atkyns, *Case of Robert Atkyns*, 10. The Exchequer decree also indicates that Atkyns' primary focus was on mortgage and equity of redemption.

50 Innes, 'King's Bench Prison', 253.

to broker a settlement. It is also worth noting Atkyns' flexibility in response to the court's persuasions: if he were to receive monies from the property, as outlined, the agreement with Took would be redefined as a living gage (*vivum vadium*), and would reflect Atkyns' willingness to apply these profits to a reduction of the L820 loan – a willingness that was unusual for a creditor at the time.[51]

The verdict of the court, based on such negotiations and flexibility, provided firm protection for the creditor Atkyns. In October 1691 the barons of the Exchequer determined that the mortgaged premises should be considered as security for the entire amount of L820. Took was ordered to pay his debt which amounted, with interest and costs, to L908 15s 10p. Payment was due by the first day of the next Easter term (1692), and if Took defaulted the penalty would be foreclosure, defined at the time as loss of the 'equity of redemption' of the properties.[52] This meant that Took would be denied the ability to redeem or regain his property – an ability, and persistent right, generally recognised by equity law at the time. In response to the Exchequer ruling Thomas Took now appealed to the House of Lords. Although this right of appeal was still a matter of contention, it had been partly resolved some twenty years earlier, and Took was able to exploit the opportunity to have the verdict reviewed.[53] After consideration, the Lords sent the case back to the Exchequer for rehearing, where attorneys argued before the same barons Lechmere, Turton and Nevill. The barons affirmed their first judgment and ordered Thomas Took to pay his debt by the first day of Michelmas term.[54]

The barons were dealing with principles of mortgage and debt but they were also confronting the nature of credit, and the challenge of determining who was the most credible actor in this case. Sir Robert Atkyns was clearly benefited by his weighty social status, as well as his official status and long-standing professional reputation. He must have had a reasonable hope of getting a favourable hearing from his colleagues, and the possibility of undue influence is a factor here: the significance of patronage and connections might have encouraged dishonesty, or at least partiality towards

[51] NA, C111/220, fol. ii; Baker, *Introduction to English Legal History*, 311.

[52] NA C111/220, fols iiii–v. The matter was referred to deputy remembrancer Tobias Eden, and was to be continued in 'paper of causes'. Eden made his report, 12 October, that L908, 15s, 10p was due to Robert Atkyns by 26 October. Three barons read this report, heard Atkyns' lawyer Newport (Took did not present any exceptions to the report, nor attend with a lawyer), and then ratified the report and called for payment by Easter 1692. If payment was not made, Took would be said to default.

[53] Bryson, *Equity Side of the Exchequer*, 31.

[54] 'House of Lords Journal, Volume 15: 22 January 1692', *Journal of the House of Lords: Volume 15: 1691–1696*, British History Online, http://www.british-history.ac.uk/report.asp?compid=11800&strquery=tooke. From 21 to 28 April 1692 attorneys Newport, Ward, Dodd argued on behalf of Atkyns; attorneys Slone (?), Williams, Finch appeared on behalf of Took. NA C111/220, fol. vi.

the chief baron. Yet it is also important to remember that contemporaries regarded these same factors – family, profession, community – as the essential means by which to establish a reputation for reliability and trustworthiness.[55] Moreover it is likely that Atkyns was actually expected to bring this cause to his own court because he was a member of its community. In its original jurisdiction the Exchequer heard suits involving officers of the court; by the mid-seventeenth century its jurisdiction had expanded, and Exchequer equity was in practice open to 'all comers', but there may still have been some presumption that as an official of the court Atkyns would have his suit heard there. As an elite plaintiff Atkyns was typical of the kind of suitor who dominated the Exchequer, and his 'land-related dispute' was also standard for the court. Finally, given Atkyns' Whig politics, and his earlier critiques of Chancery, it is also not surprising that he brought suit in an equity court that had seen its jurisdiction expand during the seventeenth century partly as a result of anti-Chancery sentiment and suspicions.[56]

These sociopolitical and sociocultural factors were at play as the barons considered the evidence and reached a verdict. The clearest result of their legal reasoning was a ruling that abrogated the principle of a mortgagor's equity of redemption. This principle that the mortgagor had an enduring right to regain his property rested on an understanding that when a mortgage was made the mortgaged property was understood to stand merely as security for the loan, and the lender obtained no 'collateral advantage' to whittle away that property by postponing repayment or applying penalties thereafter. Since mortgaged property was conceived of as security only, the lender's interest was 'mere personalty', that is a right to the money. The mortgagor's equity of redemption was, by contrast, coming to be seen as a form of real property.[57] According to this principle Robert Atkyns should be able to insist on repayment but not on possession of the property.

These mortgage rules had become entrenched by the last decades of the seventeenth century. Historians point especially to the significance of Lord Chancellor Nottingham's decisions in the two decades just before Atkyns' case was heard; Nottingham is also credited with the maxim 'once a mortgage always a mortgage' that was so crucial to the defence of a mortgagor's right to redeem. 'Like the trust', Baker avers, the equity of redemption 'had become an equitable estate' and the courts generally upheld this principle, safeguarding owners from loss of property.[58] These developments in mort-

55 Muldrew, *Economy of Obligation*, ch. 6.

56 Bryson, *Equity Side of the Exchequer*, 13–15, 24–7, 165; Horwitz, 'Chancery's "Younger Sister"', 161–2, 167–173.

57 Sugarman and Warrington, 'Land Law, Citizenship, and the Invention of "Englishness"', 114–17. Cf Carter, *Lex Vadiorum*, 175, citing Hardres 469, on the distinction of mortgage from trust; Lord Chancellor Hardwicke offers another clear statement in *Casburne v Scarfe*, 2 Jac. & W. 194, 37 *English Reports* 600.

58 Baker, *Introduction to English Legal History*, 314; Sugarman and Warrington, 'Land

gage law in Chancery and Exchequer were an important part of commercial change in this period because they allowed for the growth of the culture of borrowing, but also allowed for reliable expectations between parties. This was particularly significant, some historians have argued, for preserving the security of landed property. David Sugarman and Ronnie Warrington assert, for example, that the development of mortgage principles made credit possible, and encouraged loans, but crucially did so while maintaining the protection of landed interests.[59]

If equity of redemption afforded this balance of innovation and stability, and thus could assuage some of those contemporary fears about the volatility or insubstantiality of credit, why were the Exchequer barons willing to deny this legal principle? The ruling in *Atkyns v Tooke* was, of course, not the sole exception to the principle of enduring mortgage. Numerous cases could be cited which demonstrated constraints on a mortgagor's equity of redemption. Some of these cases indicated that a mortgagor 'must come in time', and that an unreasonable lapse of more than two decades would generally result in forfeiture.[60] Other cases suggested that attempts by a mortgagor to use the same property as security for other debts would also result in the loss of the equity of redemption; the key factor here was that the mortgagor must have acted without giving notice to his creditors, and so might be suspected of an attempt to defraud them.[61] A statute of 1692, aimed to supplement the Statute of Frauds of 1677, specifically 'denied the benefit of equitable rules' in those cases where lands were mortgaged without 'notice of prior encumbrance'.[62] The legislature and equity courts clearly did recognise limits on the equity of redemption and this recognition seems to have been based upon an evaluation of the status of the security, tied to broader concerns about 'sharp practice' in financial transactions. This concern about fraud and false dealing was especially pressing at this moment because of the

Law, Citizenship, and the Invention of "Englishness"', 114–15; D.E.C. Yale, 'An Essay on Mortgages and Trusts and Allied Topics in Equity', in Yale ed., *Lord Nottingham's Chancery Cases*, Selden Society vol. 79 (London, 1961), 7–207; Yale, Introduction, in Yale ed., *Manual of Chancery Practice and Prolegomena of Chancery and Equity* (Cambridge, 1965). Cf R.W. Turner, *The Equity of Redemption: Its Nature, History and Connection with Equitable Estates Generally* (Cambridge, 1931).

59 Sugarman and Warrington, 'Land Law, Citizenship, and the Invention of "Englishness"', 112, 124.

60 Carter, *Lex Vadiorum*, 172–4; the thirteenth and fourteenth chapters of this text are focused on the principle of equity of redemption. But see the example of a mortgage redeemed after 50 years, *Grubb v. Woodhouse*, 2 Freeman 187, 22 *English Reports* 1151.

61 Carter, *Lex Vadiorum*, 184–5. Cf examples of bills to foreclose the equity of redemption where a mortgagor engages in fraudulent activities, William Brown, *Praxis Almae Curiae Cancellariae*, 296.

62 Hamburger, 'Conveyancing Purposes Statute Frauds', 380; Yale, 'Essay on Mortgages and Trusts', 66.

patent boom that had begun to take shape in October 1691.[63] With regard to credit obtained through mortgage, if the mortgagee appeared to have little chance of getting repaid – whether because of length of time elapsed, or because of further debts and encumbrances incurred – the mortgagor's equity of redemption could be extinguished.

And yet these kinds of objections or exceptions did not exert a clear influence on the barons' decision in the case of *Atkyns v Tooke*. The barons did not deny Thomas Took his equity of redemption because decades had elapsed without repayment and, although Robert Atkyns will later make this accusation, there is no mention in the 1692 Exchequer decree of suspicion of further encumbrances and attempted fraud. Took's personal history of incurring debt may have been regarded as an indication that Sir Robert's L820 loan was far from secure; other creditors had already pursued legal process, and sent Took to debtors' prison, in the hopes of being repaid. On the other hand, Thomas Took does not seem unusually indebted given contemporary norms, and he may even have used his 'custodial confinement' as a way to evade his creditors. In fact, Took appears to be a good example of the economic progress that some legal historians claim resulted from equity's encouragement of credit and commerce: he negotiated loans, converted real estate into capital, and employed other forms of property transfer through trusts and jointures.

The barons of the Exchequer reached their decision because they confronted a jurisprudential problem that was highlighted in the claims of the two men. Just what was the nature of equitable justice? Which principles and precedents should be followed and why? The ruling in the case of *Atkyns v Tooke* demonstrates that the barons were influenced by some conceptual and jurisdictional objections to an expansive definition of the equity of redemption. When the barons had to balance recognition of the equitable principle of enduring mortgage with adherence to the principle of stability in common law conveyancing they opted for the value of common law stability. In Atkyns' case the barons of the Exchequer upheld the deed of lease and release by which Thomas Took conveyed his property to Atkyns and so affirmed an interest in land that had gained protection within the common law over and above the defendant's equity of redemption.[64] Chief Baron Atkyns and Baron Turton had similarly emphasised the significance of 'the sealing of the conveyance of the freehold' and the payment of purchase money, to their ruling in another contemporary case of foreclosure (*Bowater*

63 Hoppit, 'Attitudes to Credit', 308.

64 NA C111/220, fols iv–vi. As Baker points out, the practice of lease and release emerged as one of the modes of legal conveyance that developed in association with the Statute of Uses, and was itself an important example of the modification of common law by legislation and equity. By the 1620s this conveyancing device was 'in general use' and '[d]uring the seventeenth century it became the common form'. Baker, *Introduction to English Legal History*, 305–6.

v. Hartley 1692), which upheld the surrender of mortgaged properties.[65] The kind of broad concern about stability and the jurisdiction of common law over property that was expressed in these decisions had been voiced two decades earlier by the respected jurist Matthew Hale. In *Roscarrick v Barton* (1672), a case where the central issue was one of time limits on the equity of redemption, Chief Justice Hale warned: 'By the Growth of Equity upon Equity, the Heart of the Common Law is eaten out, and legal settlements are destroyed.'[66] Although Hale's complaint is sometimes depicted as the last such statement about the ways in which equity of redemption threatened the stability of property under common law, clearly these kinds of concerns persisted, especially at a time of renewed debate about the relationship between equity and common law, and between commerce and common law. Indeed, well into the eighteenth century judges in equity took pains to deny that they had any intention of invading the property jurisdiction of the common law courts.[67] The barons of the Exchequer were sensitive to this jurisdictional question, and its jurisprudential implications. Their jurisprudence, which was shared by Sir Robert Atkyns, associated common law stability not simply with the preservation of landed interests but with an even broader sense that common law would afford certainty and preserve justice in the face of ephemeral, potentially meaningless, credit practices.

The meanings of trust

The conveyance of the Rose Tavern and other houses to Sir Robert Atkyns was successfully upheld and, with Thomas Took twice-defeated in the Exchequer, Atkyns' property interest seemed secure. But now the Tooks sought another venue for their dispute, returning to the equity court to find justice. Elizabeth Took brought a bill in Chancery in an attempt to assert her own legal interest in her husband's mortgaged properties. This was an effective strategy since it subjected Atkyns to a prior settlement claim that he had been able to avoid in his Exchequer suit. In Chancery 'secured creditors seeking to seize land that had been pledged as security had to contend with the claims of family members in all preexisting family settlement agree-

65 *Bowater v Hartley* (Ex. 1692), W.H. Bryson ed., *Equity Cases in the Court of Exchequer 1660 to 1714*, Medieval and Renaissance Texts and Studies vol. 313 (Tempe, Arizona, 2007), 332–3.

66 *Roscarrick v Barton*, 1 Chan. Cas. 219, 22 *English Reports* 770.

67 Sugarman and Warrington, 'Land Law, Citizenship, and the Invention of "Englishness"', 115, depict Hale's as the 'last' objection. This particular caution regarding property law is affirmed by Baker: 'It has … been a constant tendency for judges to treat rules of property law – including in due course the principles of equity relating to property – as standing in greater need of certainty than matters of contract and tort.' Baker, *Introduction to English Legal History*, 200; cf Lieberman, *Province of Legislation Determined*, 72, 78.

ments', Claire Priest explains, and this was the 'costliest component' of mortgage foreclosure.[68] Elizabeth Took brought this kind of claim before the court in Trinity Term 1694:

> The plaintiff Mrs. Took by her Bill in Chancery sets forth a Title to John Bennet, Esq (as her Trustee) to a Lease for Lives in Nineteen Houses in Castle-Yard in Holbourn, in Trust to pay her 200 l. per Ann. Clear above all Charges and Payments, for her Life, as a Separate Maintenance while her Husband Lives. This was by a Deed made by her Husband, Mr. Took, in April 1686.
>
> And by the same Deed she claims further 300 l. per Ann. Clear in like manner for her Jointure, if she outlive her Husband.[69]

With the move to Chancery, not only were the parties to the suit and the venue changed, but the legal issue was also changed. Whereas the Exchequer suit had been focused on mortgage law and the mortgagor's equitable estate, the Chancery suit was concerned with trust and the equitable estate of beneficial ownership. Women's property in the trust was characteristically protected by the chancellor in equity. And in the course of this stage of the conflict between Atkyns and Took the meaning of a defence of common law stability came to be gendered in important ways.

Upon the creation of a trust, like Elizabeth Took's, the agreement between trustor (Thomas Took) and trustee (John Bennett) was understood to vest legal ownership in the trustee. Ownership of the trust property was transferred at common law. However, since that ownership was meant to be exercised for the good of the beneficiary of the trust, English law slowly came to recognise that the beneficiary had an equitable estate, or beneficial ownership, in the trust. While common law could only recognise the fact of property transfer and trustee ownership, the trustee's obligations and the beneficiary's ownership came to be protected by the law of equity in Chancery.[70] In her case against Atkyns, Elizabeth Took laid claim to this kind of beneficial ownership of the leases for life of these several houses in Holborn through her trustee, John Bennett. Such leases were 'classified as "chattels real", halfway between real and personal property', and were those properties put in trust in order to provide for Elizabeth as part of a resettlement of Took's estate.[71]

The development of the law of trusts is usually understood within the context of the history of inheritance practices, and important changes in

68 Claire Priest, 'Creating an American Property Law: Alienability and its Limits in American History', *Harvard Law Review*, 120, 2 (December, 2006): 405.

69 Atkyns, *Case of Robert Atkyns*, 3.

70 Baker, *Introduction to English Legal History*, 250–7.

71 Erickson, *Women and Property*, 24, Baker, *Introduction to English Legal History*, 294; Neil Jones, 'Uses, Trusts and a Path to Privity', *Cambridge Law Journal*, 56, 1 (March, 1997): 176–7.

feudal property relations in the sixteenth century.[72] As the Took trust indicates, the development of different forms of women's separate property, and the emergence of the strict settlement in the seventeenth century, were especially significant features of inheritance practices that affected the development of the trust. Jointure and separate maintenance were two important examples of these forms of female property ownership that modified common law coverture restrictions, and were prevalent in the seventeenth century. Both were said to be established in Elizabeth Took's trust. Jointure, long utilised as a substitute for dower, was the means by which a wife and husband jointly owned land to be used for their mutual benefit during the marriage, and then to support the survivor of the marriage. Such lands were usually purchased with the wife's portion, and by the sixteenth century the jointure was typically generated in this form of an annuity derived from rents. Separate maintenance, by contrast, was a payment made only to a wife, and was not based on the portion she brought to a marriage. Rather it was, as Robert Atkyns acknowledged, 'the same thing with Alimony', whereby a wife would be afforded an allowance during a period of separation from her husband.[73]

'The necessity of ameliorating the effects of coverture led to an early and widespread use of a variety of complex forms of property transfer: legal instruments which were often also financial instruments,' Amy Erickson has asserted. These legal instruments 'helped to establish a climate in which the concept of legal security for notional concepts of property became commonplace'.[74] Elizabeth Took's beneficial ownership of her trust was this kind of notional property, and the security of that property was defensible in equity. In this period more and more women like Elizabeth turned to equity to protect such property claims. Scholars estimate that the number of female plaintiffs in Chancery rose from seventeen percent in the mid-

72 It is narrated as a history of the effects of the Statute of Uses. See for ex.: Baker, *Introduction to English Legal History*, 250–7, but 291; Baker, *The Oxford History of the Laws of England, Volume 6, 1483–1558* (Oxford, 2003), ch. 35, esp. 683–6; A.W.B. Simpson, *An Introduction to the History of the Land Law* (Oxford, 1961), 199–207; Jones 'Uses Trusts and Privity', 177–82; Jones, 'The Use Upon a Use in Equity Revisited', *Cambrian Law Review*, 33 (2002): 67–80.

73 Atkyns, *Case of Robert Atkyns*, 6; Erickson, *Women and Property*, 25, 112–13; Baker, *Introduction to English Legal History*, 270.

74 Amy L. Erickson, 'Coverture and Capitalism', *History Workshop Journal*, 59 (Spring, 2005): 5; and Erickson, *Women and Property*, 106–7. Horwitz's comparison of Chancery and Exchequer equity confirms this 'relative high (and rising) percentages of estate and trust suits in Chancery.' Horwitz, 'Chancery's "Younger Sister"', 170. See also Joanne Bailey, 'Favoured or Oppressed? Married Women, Property and "Coverture" in England 1660–1800', *Continuity and Change*, 17, 3 (December, 2002): 351–71; Lloyd Bonfield ed., *Marriage, Property and Succession* (Berlin, 1992); Eileen Spring, *Law, Land and Family: Aristocratic Inheritance in England 1300–1800* (Chapel Hill, 1993).

sixteenth century to twenty-six percent in the early eighteenth century.[75] The broader trend of increased female participation, and indeed frequent initiation, of suits in the equity courts is a key context not only for understanding Elizabeth's actions, but also for thinking about the nature of this whole series of disputes between Robert Atkyns and the Tooks. Questions about 'women's law' implicated a wide range of people, the cases litigated usually involved a complex set of issues that had persisted over several years, or even generations, and these issues entailed jurisdictional complexity, if not conflict.[76] For these reasons, matters of 'women's law' were important for stimulating reflection on the nature of justice and authority. The tangled web of people involved in such matters meant that the scope of participation in such reflection was varied and extensive. Equally important, many judges like Robert Atkyns had personal as well as professional experience with cases concerning trusts, jointure or separate maintenance and this was surely a factor in the transformation of such disputes into venues for the articulation of contemporary ideas about common law justice.[77]

For Robert Atkyns the dispute about Elizabeth Took's trust claim in Chancery revolved first around the question of contract as he insisted that her trust lacked the necessary consideration, or reciprocity, between parties to the agreement. Atkyns was strategic in focusing on contract. It is true that when this case took place, in the 1690s, trusts were generally defined in proprietary more than contractual terms, indicating adherence to that notion of a beneficiary's property right in the trust. And yet trust law remained fundamentally concerned with contractual questions, specifically regarding the relationship between the trust agreement and this common law doctrine of consideration.[78] Robert Atkyns pressed this issue of consideration in his

75 Erickson, *Women and Property*, 114–16. Henry Horwitz finds a 'sizeable increase in the proportion of women plaintiffs' from 14.4% in 1627 to 21.2% in 1818–19, Horwitz, *Guide to Chancery Records and Proceedings*, 42. And note the general abundance of trust, jointure and mortgage quarrels reported in published collections of Chancery cases like Thomas Vernon, *Cases Argued and Adjudged in the High Court of Chancery* (Dublin, 1726), or Robert Lucas, *Cases in Law and Equity, Chiefly During the Time the Late Earl of Macclesfield Presided in the Courts of King's-Bench and Chancery* (London, 1736).

76 Erickson, *Women and Property*, 117; Margaret R. Hunt, 'Wives and Marital "Rights" in the Court of Exchequer in the Early Eighteenth Century', in Paul Griffiths and Mark C.R. Jenner eds, *Londonopolis: Essays in the Cultural and Social History of Early Modern London* (Manchester, 2000), 111.

77 Sir Robert Atkyns engaged in the creation of various trusts for Elizabeth Reynell, for his own wife Anne, and for his own daughter and granddaughter. Will of Sir Robert Atkyns, NA Prob/11/5/14. Atkyns' heirs continued to be embroiled in litigation over these family properties: see *The Respondent's Case*, and *Doe Ex Dim Atkyns v Horde et al.* For other judges' experience see for example the comments of Master of the Rolls, Joseph Jekyll, concerning the dispute between the heirs of Lord Chancellor Cowper and Judge Spencer Cowper, *Cowper v Cowper*, 2 P. Wms. 735–7, 24 *English Reports*, 935–6.

78 Atkyns, *Case of Robert Atkyns*, 5–6. Ibbetson, *Historical Introduction Obligations*, 206; John H. Langbein, 'The Contractarian Basis of the Law of Trusts', *Yale Law Journal*, 105,

dispute because it was central to whether Chancery would enforce Elizabeth Took's trust. 'The Chancery would not enforce the declaration of trust unless there was some consideration for it,' David Ibbetson explains, 'but "consideration" here was wider than at Common law: it included not only something given in exchange but also the "natural love and affection" presumed to exist between kin, and was therefore of particular use in giving effect to intra-family settlements of property.'[79] Until the end of the eighteenth century there was a persistent recognition of consideration in a valid declaration of trust, but the content of consideration, and the meaning of 'nature' and 'blood' (or kinship) remained open to interpretation.[80]

This openness or contestability underscores the fact that the doctrine of consideration was itself in flux. Although the premise that reciprocity was the central factor in a valid agreement between parties remained at the heart of the model of contract, developments in commercial practices and new kinds of contracts increasingly presented challenges to this common law doctrine.[81] By the late seventeenth and early eighteenth centuries, common law had begun to reflect the ideology of a speculative society, allowing for some looser conceptions of what constituted a valid contract. At the same time, the progressively widespread culture of credit mediated against too strict an enforcement of traditional limits on contract. For much of this period jurists and judges like Atkyns were working out what kinds of promises should be enforced and where the boundaries of common law lay, in this way shaping English commercial law as it developed within the common law system.[82] Robert Atkyns' challenge to the Tooks' trust agreement took advantage of the fact that jurisdiction in many areas remained unset-

3 (December, 1995): 634; Simpson, *History of Common Law of Contract*, 327–74, on the early development of the doctrine of consideration in the law of uses.

79 Ibbetson, *Historical Introduction Obligations*, 206–7.

80 Ibid., 207. For cases providing examples of this interpretation of 'consideration of nature and blood' see *A Treatise of Fraud, Covins and Collusions. Wherein is Treated of Fraudulent Conveyances to Defraud Cerditors and Purchasers by Fraudulent Mortgages, Marriage Agreements, Last Wills…* (London, 1710), 54–5; Thomas Blount, *The Resolution of the Judges upon Several Statutes of Bankrupts: As Also the Like Resolution Upon 13 Eliz. And 27 Eliz. Touching Fraudulent Conveyances* (London, 1670), 184, 192–3; and FSL, MS ADD 1025.

81 Ibbetson, *Historical Introduction Obligations*, 142–6, 203–13; Simpson, *History of Common Law of Contract*, especially pt. II chs 4, 7; Kevin M. Teeven, *A History of the Anglo-American Law of Contract* (Westport, CT, 1990), chs 3–4.

82 Rogers, *Early History of the Law of Bills and Notes*, 2, 148, 167; Ibbetson, *Historical Introduction Obligations*, 204–8; Baker, *Introduction to English Legal History*, 354; Muldrew, *Culture of Obligation*, 173–4, Muldrew, 'Interpreting the Market: The Ethics of Credit and Community Relations in Early Modern England', *Social History*, 18, 2 (May, 1993):173, 177. On the 'rise of assumpsit' and earlier 'extension of promissory liability' see Ibbestson, *Historical Introduction Obligations*, ch. 7, Simpson, *History of Common Law of Contract*, pt. II, chs 1–3. There is some debate among legal historians – such as Macnair, Ibbetson, Baker and Oldham, for example – about the timing of these changes

tled, and he clearly engaged with contemporary debate about the changes in English law that were catalysed by economic development. When he questioned Chancery's authority over this trust agreement Atkyns latched onto an especially significant area of uncertainty by focusing on changes in contract law. Moreover, he cleverly associated the worrisome new trends in contract law with complaint against the emergence of Chancery's authority regarding uses and trusts.[83]

Two areas of economic development were especially important for generating these questions about the boundaries of contract enforcement. First, the growth of the stock market meant that there were new financial practices, new professional opportunities and new venues for information-gathering and social interaction. Just as with the emergence of other areas of enlightened development in organisation, communication or conversation, contemporaries expressed a range of concerns about the changes taking place, and many of these concerns were relevant to thinking about contract. For example, questions about control and availability of information, or about professional responsibility, were pertinent to defining consideration in a valid contract. Indeed these issues were a particularly important part of the discussion over agreements for future sale of stock, known as executory contracts, that were becoming a focus for controversy at this time. The Kings Bench had its first hearing of this kind of dispute in 1693, just before Took's case was brought to the Chancery; many other cases concerning 'stockjobbers' were heard in the first decades of the eighteenth century. In 1693, and subsequent disputes, the courts confronted these new issues and sought a balanced approach. The judges did promote the new securities market, and allowed for many different kinds of contracts that were becoming available with the growth of the market in stocks 'by enforcing even the most speculative transactions and narrowly construing would-be statutory limits on trading', Stuart Banner explains. At the same time the judges checked potential abuses generated by these new kinds of agreements by relying on 'traditional common law categories' regarding agency, for example, or fraud.[84]

Other commercial activities were also relevant to changes in contract law. The increasing use of bills of exchange, for example, was especially important in furthering a newly-expansive definition of contract, and weakening the doctrine of consideration. By the mid-seventeenth century bills of exchange were legally defined less in terms of a transaction that had taken place between two parties, and more as instruments that created obligations. This approach

in contract law, and about related questions regarding Lord Mansfield's reputation for novelty and significance.

83 Atkyns, *Enquiry into Jurisdiction Chancery*, 8–9, 15–16, 20–1. Cf also Atkyns' earlier judicial rulings such as *Smith v. Smith* in Bryson ed., *Equity Cases in the Court of Exchequer*, 322–3.

84 Banner, *Anglo-American Securities Regulation*, 111–12, 117.

accorded with the widespread use of bills at the time as a form of currency, and also helped to further the law's expanding conception of liability.[85] This extension of liability for bills of exchange encouraged the development of credit and markets but again the courts looked to common law categories, and especially to established rules of pleading, in order to forestall abuses and protect creditors. The judges elaborated a law of bills, and other elements of commercial law, 'within the common law system itself', James Rogers has shown, 'in response to developments in commercial and financial practice'.[86]

Chief Justice Holt was an influential actor in these developments and he has become known for his views on commercial law as much, or perhaps even more than, for his views on the criminal appeal. Holt's rulings in important cases concerning bills of exchange and other financial instruments are well recorded, and specific instances where he expressed worries about the negative implications of change have gotten special attention. In *Clerke v. Martin* (1702), for example, Holt famously ruled against the negotiability of another kind of financial instrument, promissory notes, insisting that a suit for debt based on such an instrument would undermine the common law:

> Holt Chief Justice was totis viribus against the action; and said, that this [promissory] note could not be a bill of exchange. That the maintaining of these actions upon such notes, were innovations upon the rules of the common law; and that it amounted to the setting up of a new sort of specialty, unknown to the common law, and invented in Lombard-Street, which attempted in these matters of bills of exchange to give laws to Westminster Hall.[87]

Holt recognised that the extension of liability for bills of exchange had affected the usual common law action of *indebitus assumpsit*, expanding the possibility for recovery of a contractual debt.[88] Although he appreciated the commercial benefits that stemmed particularly from the use of bills of exchange, Holt was reluctant to further this legal expansion through a simple conflation of commercial and non-commercial instruments. Holt's ruling in 1702, like his 1699 defence of the appeal, is another example of the chief justice's strong desire to maintain the protections afforded by common law.

The example of Holt, and these broader contexts of legal, economic and cultural change are vital for understanding Judge Atkyns' arguments against Chancery in his case, and for appreciating the development of his common law jurisprudence. Atkyns' rejection of the authority of Chancery,

85 Baker, *Introduction to English Legal History*, 369–70; Rogers, *Early History of Law of Bills and Notes*, 94, 127, 149.

86 Rogers, *Early History of Law of Bills and Notes*, 2, 144–8.

87 *Clerke v Martin*, 2 Ld Raym. 757, 92 *English Reports* 6. 'Specialty' signifies being under seal but without consideration. Erickson, 'Coverture and Capitalism', 2.

88 Baker, *Introduction to English Legal History*, 368–9.

and defence of common law, were clearly bound up with his disquiet about the new, more capacious definition of contract that was being introduced. Like Holt, Robert Atkyns was apprehensive about what changes in contract law might bring, but his objections to these trends were not based on a rigid insistence that contract must include a narrow and traditional kind of consideration. What Atkyns objected to was the increased potential for fraudulent agreements that could be encompassed by this broader definition of contract, and upheld if the courts became more lax.[89] Here it is useful to remember that this anxiety about fraud, and related interest in matters of proof and trust, were characteristic not simply of legal debate but also of contemporary enlightened debate about the moral implications of economic change. When Robert Atkyns defended the authority of common law against equity in the 1690s he defined common law justice in the terms of these newer fears: no longer was he engaged in the defence of common law as immemorial, consensual and anti-tyrannical, but rather conveyed an understanding of common law as honest, credible, moral and sociable.

According to Atkyns, Elizabeth Took's trust exemplified the kind of fraudulent dealings that were being encouraged by the development of commercial law in equity. There were various reasons why Atkyns suspected that Took's trust was an illicit agreement between husband, wife and trustee aimed to hide monies from valid creditors. First, he explained, there was no reason, or consideration, to motivate Elizabeth and Thomas to move towards the creation of a trust in 1686. A separate maintenance had, Atkyns charged, already been settled in 1684, when Elizabeth agreed to the 'barring of her Thirds', or relinquishing of her prospective dower rights, so that her husband could borrow money to repay his debts.[90] It was in this earlier exchange that Elizabeth gained a separate maintenance of L100. Since the 'barring of her Thirds' and creation of a separate maintenance had already occurred in 1684, why was this trust allegedly established to provide her maintenance in 1686? Atkyns not only demonstrated that there was no consideration for the agreement of 1686, but now he also raised the concern that the timing for creation of trust and separate maintenance was suspicious. This trust was not related to any marriage arrangement, as

89 Atkyns' sense that judges must be cognizant of the wider implications of their rulings stemmed from his involvement in some of the major cases of the 1670s and 1680s. Indeed, in one of his defences of parliament, revolution and rule of law published in 1689, Atkyns clearly affirmed the ideal that 'Judges ought to have good Consideration in all Cases depending before them, not only of the present Cases, but also of the *Consequences*, What general Prejudice may ensue upon them either to the King or Subject.' Atkyns, *The Power, Jurisdiction and Privilege of Parliament, and the Antiquity of the House of Commons Asserted* (London, 1689), 14; also reprinted in Atkyns, *Parliamentary and Political Tracts*, 23.

90 Atkyns, *Case of Robert Atkyns*, 5–6. Stretton, 'Women, Property and Law', 49–51; Erickson, 'Coverture and Capitalism', 3–4 on typicality of this relinquishing of dower rights; cf also examples in *Treatise of Feme Coverts*, preface, 77.

was more common, but was rather made late in the marriage as way to deal with financial problems, enabling Elizabeth 'secretly' to support her bankrupt husband. Clearly, Atkyns explained, 'the Estate for Life, made by the Husband, Thomas Took, to Mr. Bennet in Trust for a Separate Maintenance for the Wife is Fraudulent', simply created, as Gardiner's authoritative conveyancing manual explained, 'with intent and purpose to deceive and defeat Creditors of their just Debts and Duties'.[91]

The 1686 trust was likely another tactic that the couple used, much like the 1687 suit against Reynell and Atkyns concerning Elizabeth's marriage portion, in an attempt to raise needed funds. By the agreement of 1686 Elizabeth gained an increased maintenance of L200, Atkyns explained, and 'She has 300l per. An. besides, clear above all Payments settled upon her for her Jointure, in Lieu of her Thirds (if she survive;) which is far greater in proportion too, than the whole Estate would have born, had she been left to her Thirds. And this is a more suitable Recompence too for her Thirds, being in case she survive, (as the Thirds would have been,) but she must hook in a Separate Maintenance too in the mean time, while the Husband is alive.'[92] Not only had Elizabeth acquired a jointure in 1686, although she had already secured financial support when she earlier relinquished her dower rights, but she also obtained this greater separate maintenance.[93] There was clear immorality in Elizabeth's collusion with her husband, Robert Atkyns asserted. Here Atkyns insinuated that the Tooks found ways both to defraud their creditors and to enrich Elizabeth, entitling her to maintenance and jointure far beyond the couple's means.[94] Although he had been privy to the marriage arrangements of Elizabeth and Thomas, Sir Robert claimed that he was not aware of their property agreements since then, and at the time of his Exchequer bill he had simply accepted the validity of the 1686 deed of trust. Since he 'had not so fully discovered the Fraud of the Separate Maintenance, as he has done since, [he] believd; (as the Deed for the Separate Maintenance does alledge, see her Deed,) that the Rents were sufficient to answer her the 200l. per. An. and that 160l. per. An. over, would have been left for Sir Robert'.[95]

From Atkyns' account, and other information conveyed by the Exchequer and Chancery suits, it is clear that Elizabeth's property was frequently reassessed, and this demonstrates one way in which she, as a wife, operated as an object of exchange in the family economy. These reassessments further indi-

91 *Case of Robert Atkyns*, 5. Robert Gardiner *Ars Clericalis: the Art of Conveyancing explain'd*, 2nd edn (London, 1692), 30. On the usual timing for the creation of trusts along with marriage agreements see Erickson, *Women and Property*, ch. 6; Baker, *Introduction to English Legal History*, 270.

92 Atkyns, *Case of Robert Atkyns*, 6.

93 Ibid.

94 Ibid., 6, 8.

95 Ibid., 10.

cate the potential insecurity and fluctuating value of her property – obvious here, for example, in the notional future value of her jointure.[96] However Elizabeth Took's assets and actions also point to the ways in which she, as a wife, was an agent of exchange. Although coverture gave her husband certain benefits and powers over her, it did not enable him to alienate joint property, nor to dispose of his wife's separate property brought to the marriage, without her consent. This consent was necessary but it was also constrained. As an agent, Elizabeth had a moral as well as legal obligation to assist her husband and family. Indeed in marital disputes, Margaret Hunt has shown, participants recognised this ethical factor. A characteristic contemporary question, Hunt claims, was posed in these terms: 'But what if a husband was in danger of being imprisoned for debt or would suffer a serious blow to his credit unless his wife agreed to liquidate their joint real-estate assets? As his wife and helpmeet was she not morally obligated to consent to the sale?'[97] The dispute between Atkyns and Took clearly involved this kind of question about the fairness or morality of using Elizabeth's property for Thomas' good. Their dispute raised related principles such as a wife's duty to her own preservation, and her consequent right to maintenance. Also relevant was the husband's moral obligation to honour his agreements, not only to his creditors but also to his wife and family.[98]

Robert Atkyns acknowledged this male responsibility to provide for wife and family, and repeated an offer of compromise he made earlier in the Exchequer suit, suggesting that he would be satisfied with possession of only the Rose Tavern out of tenderness and respect for Elizabeth Took.[99] Atkyns also advanced several more legal claims against the Took trust, engaging in detailed argument about the enforcement of written agreements under seal, for example, or the applicability of prior knowledge and the doctrine of notice to his case.[100] Fundamentally, however, Atkyns sought to redefine

96 Erickson, *Women and Property*, 119; Spring, *Land Law and Family*.

97 Hunt, 'Wives and Marital "Rights"', 116.

98 Ibid., 118–19. See also Bernard Capp, 'Gender, Conscience and Casuistry: Women and Conflicting Obligations in Early Modern England', and David M. Turner '"Secret and Immodest Curiosities?" Sex, Marriage and Conscience in Early Modern England', in Harald Braun and Edward Vallance eds, *Contexts of Conscience in Early Modern Europe, 1500–1700* (Basingstoke, 2004), 116–50.

99 Atkyns, *Case of Robert Atkyns*, 8, 10; NA C111/220, fols i-ii.

100 NA C111/220, fol. iiii: both Elizabeth Took 'and the defendant John Bennett Esquire by himselfe in their answers sett forth the deede of settlement made upon them but know not of the deede made to the plaintiffe' Atkyns. On sealed documents see Ibbetson, *Historical Introduction Obligations*, 203 n. 3, Baker, *Introduction to English Legal History*, 351–2. Clearly Atkyns admitted the existence of the deed and since this was, presumably, a sealed document there was no need for recourse in his argument to clauses in the Statute of Frauds and Perjuries (1677) requiring 'written evidence of important legal transactions as a prerequisite to their enforcement'. Simpson, *History of Common Law of Contract*, 599, 617–19; Atkyns, *Case of Robert Atkyns*, 10–11. On the doctrine

what was at issue in this dispute with Thomas and Elizabeth Took: the case was really about fraud in the trust agreement, and had little to do with his own mortgage agreement with Thomas Took. The matter of freehold and the facts of a fraudulent conveyance, as defined by Elizabethan statute, Atkyns explained, 'ought to be tried by a Jury, and determined at the Common Law'.[101] Atkyns insisted upon the principle of stability in conveyancing and the jurisdiction of common law, rather than Chancery, over fraud in this instance. He proposed a solution, frequently employed in the Exchequer, of recourse to common law jury trial to decide such issues of fact and freehold.[102] Indeed during the Chancery hearing Atkyns apparently called for reflection and clarification on the question of 'Jurisdiction of Courts of Law and a Court of Equity', and he urged the judges to voice their opinions on this fundamental procedural, and jurisprudential, issue. Atkyns returned to this theme even after the Chancery ruled against him in this case, seeking an appeal to the Lords who ought to reconsider his proposal, and to remedy the 'Encroachments of the Courts of Equity'.[103]

Judge Atkyns was not simply resisting or misunderstanding legal and commercial change in his challenge to equity's jurisdiction. Seen first in the context of the commercial and financial innovations of the early eighteenth century, Atkyns' defence of common law can be usefully compared to other kinds of arguments made for the protection of property, stability and certainty against corruption and fraud. Second, his claims about the justice of common law clearly must be understood in the context of changes in English law allowing for female property ownership. The centrality of conflicts over separate maintenance, trust and jointure in the set of cases between Atkyns and the Tooks provides a good indication of the ways in which issues of 'women's law' were perceived as challenges to common law. Robert Atkyns was indignant at the prospect that Elizabeth Took's separate maintenance, or alimony, might be preferred to his fee in reversion. 'Separate maintenances are but of late Invention, and bring many mischievous consequences after them,' he protested, '[a]nd not one Precedent of the *Chancery* (as 'tis believ'd) can be produc'd, where ever,

of notice, and exceptions to the liability of a recipient of trust property, see Macnair, 'Conceptual Basis of Trusts', 227–9; Atkyns, *Case of Robert Atkyns*, 3–7; Atkyns, *Enquiry into Jurisdiction Chancery*, 38–40.

101 Atkyns, *Case of Robert Atkyns*, 5. Cf Atkyns, *Enquiry into Jurisdiction Chancery*, 37–8 on jury trial as proper venue for trial of fact.

102 Horwitz, 'Chancery's "Younger Sister"', 176–7. On the scope of equity's jurisdiction over fraud see Ibbetson, *Historical Introduction Obligations*, 208–11; Michael Lobban, 'Contractual Fraud in Law and Equity, c.1750–c.1850', *Oxford Journal of Legal Studies*, 17, 3 (Autumn, 1997): 446–9, 457–65.

103 Atkyns, *Case of Robert Atkyns*, 6–7, 12. And compare Atkyns, *Enquiry into Jurisdiction Chancery*, 38–40 where he expands this discussion of encroachment, and threat to settled estates. In 1739, when the Atkyns and Reynell descendants are quarrelling, the House of Lords reconsiders this recourse to common law jury trial. *The Respondent's Case*, 3.

(before this Decree) a Separate Maintenance hath been Countenanc'd against a Purchaser.'[104] Atkyns warned that equitable protections for women were being expanded by the Chancery, and that they plainly had the potential to subvert common law. This line of argument is an important part of those fears about the subversion of the common law that inspired reflection on the nature of that law. Gendered norms regarding the priority of male property rights influenced legal thinking, but norms regarding male responsibility for the protection of women also shaped legal philosophy and practice.

All of Robert Atkyns' claims conveyed jurisprudential coherence and ideological persistence. His actions demonstrated financial persistence as well, since he was willing to pursue this costly suit well past the point at which most Chancery cases were dropped.[105] But in the end Sir Robert Atkyns' case was not compelling to the Chancery. The Chancery issued a decree for the plaintiff in this case in 1694, affirming Elizabeth Took's 'Separate Maintenance to be good in law against Sir Robert's Mortgage'.[106] The court also issued an injunction to stop Sir Robert from pursuing his challenge to the validity of Took's declaration of trust.

Why did Robert Atkyns lose this case in the Chancery? One reason he alleged was that his adversaries continued to have recourse to fraud and corruption throughout their Chancery suit. Atkyns complained to his colleague Lord Keeper Somers about abusive Chancery practices, like the multiplication of suitors and fees, that were being employed by the plaintiff's side. Not only did one Bedford, a Chancery clerk, 'needlessly thrust himself in to be a Plaintiff, and drew the Bill himself,' but the plaintiff's lawyers also padded their bill with 'scandals' against Atkyns. These scandalous charges asserted that Sir Robert was exploiting his own position and power, and even illegally bringing suit in another man's name, in order to ruin Elizabeth Took completely.[107] Atkyns insisted that these charges were detrimental to his case and to his career, and he appealed to the Lord Keeper, and subsequently to the Lords, for damages to be paid for the harm he suffered. This desire to restore his good reputation may have motivated Atkyns to pursue publication of his cause in his *Enquiry into the Jurisdiction of the Chancery in Causes of Equity* and *The Case of Sir Robert Artkyns … Upon his Appeal against a Decree*, both published in 1695. However, rehashing the details in print likely only added to the scandal and notoriety he wanted to avoid. And the recourse to print did not help his case: in 1696 the Lords affirmed Elizabeth Took's victory in Chancery, showing no indication of bias toward

104 Atkyns, *Case of Robert Atkyns*, 11.

105 Horwitz, *Chancery Equity Records and Proceedings*, 25; Hunt, 'Wives and Marital "Rights"', 112.

106 Atkyns, *Case of Robert Atkyns*, 3.

107 Ibid., 9.

Atkyns, a man they had named the speaker of their house just a few years before.[108]

What do the Lords' and Chancery's ruling against Atkyns tell us about the development, and the efficacy, of his common law jurisprudence? Was he, after all, simply a champion of an outdated reliance on common law prescription and proceduralism that were increasingly irrelevant in this new age? Evidence from other contemporary Chancery rulings confirm that Robert Atkyns was certainly not alone in being troubled by developments in trusts, nor was he unusual in his advocacy of the preservation of common law, especially regarding its jurisdiction over property. 'Trusts are to be governed by the same Law and are within the same Reason as legal Estates,' a case reported in the early eighteenth century declared, 'and this is a Maxim which has obtained universally.'[109] The scope of Chancery's protection of English wives' property held in trust remained unsettled in the eighteenth century, but a distinction did begin to develop between trusts created before and trusts created during a marriage. In later disputes this second kind of trust – one of the kinds that the Tooks laid claim to, and that Atkyns attacked – was, in time, deemed a 'voluntary settlement' that should be considered 'fraudulent' and void if it was in conflict with a claim to the same properties by a purchaser with a valid contract.[110] Atkyns' case may have contributed to this resolution. But since his was a hard case, involving multiple layers of property negotiation that had occurred both before and during the Tooks' marriage, the decision was made in favour of protecting Elizabeth's equitable interest.[111]

That decision, and the evolving distinction among types of trusts, are examples of the careful balance between common law and equity, between settled rules and justifiable exceptions, that was being worked out by judges and litigants in this period. In establishing the balance between common law and equity judges had to be cognizant of the ways in which participants in this emerging credit economy might employ new techniques so as to evade their settled agreements and valid debts. These disputes about trusts clearly indicate that contemporaries were aware of the potential for fraud. Robert Atkyns pointed to this greater threat of fraud and injustice when he

108 'House of Lords Journal Volume 15: 6 February 1693', *Journal of the House of Lords: Volume 15: 1691–1696*, British History Online, http://www.british-history.ac.uk/report.asp?compid=11904&strquery=atkyns%20robert.; 'House of Lords Journal Volume 15: 13 March 1696', *Journal of the House of Lords: Volume 15: 1691–1696*, British History Online, http://www.british-history.ac.uk/report.asp?compid=12282&strquery=tooke.

109 *Sutton v Sutton*, 2 Eq Ca Abr 738, 22 *English Reports* 626, citing Master of the Rolls Joseph Jekyll.

110 *Doyly v Persall*, 2 Freeman 138, 22 *English Reports* 1113, n. 4.

111 Atkyns' right of reversion was not extinguished when he lost this Chancery case, and his descendant John Tracy Atkyns did inherit the Holborn properties (along with continued legal challenges from the Reynells) in the early eighteenth century. NA Prob/11/514; *The Respondents Case*.

connected his specific arguments against the law of trusts to broader warnings about the danger of a spreading Chancery jurisdiction over mortgages and contract.[112] Was Chancery encouraging too much novelty and expansion in these and other areas of emerging commercial law? *An Enquiry into the Jurisdiction of the Chancery* was 'Humbly submitted to the Consideration of the House of Lords', exhorting them to settle the matter of jurisdiction since they had the authority 'to keep the Inferior Courts within their Bounds'.[113]

Robert Atkyns' last publications defended common law tradition in this new commercial context. His texts on jurisdiction include familiar lawyerly accounts of the history of common law and constitution, but they also articulate the contemporary sense of uncertainty about economic and legal change, and they command recognition of the important protections afforded by established tradition. One set of his arguments emphasised the benefits of common law because it guaranteed clearly delimited and disinterested standards against the fallibility and partiality of the chancellor, that 'One Man of great Power'.[114] Another related set of arguments in Atkyns' texts highlighted the value of common law knowledge and experience because it had been tested by a community of men. Finally, in contrasting the singular and self-interested judge in equity with the responsible and rule-bound judges of common law, Robert Atkyns suggested that the problem of deceit and fraud was endemic to the Chancery itself. Atkyns asserted that Chancery officials sought to enrich themselves at the expense of suitors, leading to the destruction of established estates.[115] Even more, he charged that 'since the Chancery hath been so exalted' the Inns of Court had been degraded and the very profession of common law had been subverted. The chancellor's use of patronage and preferment, he explained, had created new incentives for those men seeking advancement in the law. No longer were study, merit and honour encouraged, but now 'an inferior sort of Men oftentimes procure themselves to be admitted of the Inns of Court, and called to the Bar, and suddenly leap into mighty Practice and extraordinary Gain in the Court of Chancery'.[116]

In the course of his critique of Chancery's jurisdiction Robert Atkyns offered a powerful defence of the justice and authority of common law that spoke to the concerns of a new commercial age. All of his arguments underlined an association between common law and enlightened values of credibility, community, and certainty. Many of these same arguments and

112 Atkyns, *Enquiry into Jurisdiction Chancery*, 24, 38–9; and recall his arguments against novelty and fraud in contract in Atkyns, *Case of Robert Atkyns*, 5–6.

113 Atkyns, *Enquiry into Jurisdiction Chancery*, titlepage, 21, 48.

114 Ibid., 30, 5; see also Atkyns, *A Treatise of the True and Ancient Jurisdiction of the House of Peers* (London, 1699), 31.

115 Atkyns, *Enquiry into Jurisdiction Chancery*, 24, 38–9.

116 Ibid., 36.

concerns will be articulated and refined by treatise writers engaged with Enlightenment natural law jurisprudence, for example, or by later critics of the Chancery who embraced an enlightened vocabulary of virtue and corruption as they elaborated English common law jurisprudence in the early eighteenth century.

5

Common Law Jurisprudence and the Philosophy of Natural Law

In eighteenth-century England ideas about natural law also developed within the context of controversy over the jurisdiction of common law and equity. In the course of these controversies natural law jurisprudence and common law jurisprudence evolved in conjunction with other philosophical trends. English legal theorists drew upon a variety of philosophical positions – 'religious' as well as 'secular', 'social' as well as 'individualist' – providing further evidence for Frederick Beiser's claim that 'the natural law theory of the Enlightenment' encompassed 'different, even competing traditions'.[1] Moreover, the evidence derived from these debates about the jurisdiction of common law and equity demonstrates that arguments from natural law did not simply supplant or supersede common law arguments for the authority of prescription and precedent. If the previous chapters primarily argued against the image of common law jurisprudence as static in the eighteenth century, this chapter further challenges perceptions of the irrelevance of common law jurisprudence within this period of Enlightenment 'natural law fervour'.

Natural law jurisprudence was not the only jurisprudence. Nor was natural law simply a veneer, superimposed upon but not integrated with common law doctrines and ideas. Indeed David Ibbetson has shown that the attraction to natural law actually affected the formulation of substantive common law doctrines; he demonstrates the significant influence of natural law on the development of trusts, contracts, unjust enrichment and torts.[2] These four areas of English law are also, unsurprisingly, all areas of jurisdictional dispute between common law and equity in this period. In focusing on this doctrinal influence, however, (the way natural law affected 'the rules') Ibbetson consciously set aside the complex question of jurisprudential influence, and instead proposes a conventional, and progressive claim: beginning with Matthew Hale and culminating with William Blackstone's successors, Ibbetson asserts, superior natural law concepts gradually corrected and

1 Frederick C. Beiser, *The Sovereignty of Reason: The Defense of Rationality in the Early English Enlightenment* (Princeton, 1996), 281.

2 Ibbetson, 'Natural Law and Common Law', 6, 8–9, 13–18; and contrast Ibbetson, *Historical Introduction Obligations*, 219.

supplanted the 'medievalism' and 'antiquarianism' of common law.[3] Michael Lobban, the major contemporary historian of common law jurisprudence, also underscores the transformative influence of natural law and positivist theories on men like Hale, and similarly suggests that there was a hiatus in common law thinking until its 'reassertion' in the later eighteenth century during the 'age of Blackstone'.[4] Other scholars have made the case for the predominance of natural law jurisprudence in early eighteenth-century legal thought by focusing on the pronounced influence of one aspect of natural law philosophy: the voluntarism and contractualism of the works of Hugo Grotius and Samuel Pufendorf.

This accepted narrative of the growth of natural law philosophy rests on the false assumption of a necessary dichotomy in jurisprudence, and contributes to a general sense of inevitable movement towards a systematic and modern common law committed to 'analysis in terms of general legal categories'.[5] That assumption is also embedded in that conventional narrative, already encountered, which dismisses the literature of the common law and privileges a story of progress towards a coherent treatise literature in the late eighteenth and early nineteenth centuries. Such narratives fail to recognise the ways in which natural law theory developed along with common law jurisprudence. Too little attention has been paid to evidence of how eighteenth-century English writers on natural law and equity engaged with common law as well as Roman law; or were shaped by the early eighteenth-century Pyrrhonist controversy; or demonstrated interest in the philosophy of language and the advance of social theory.[6] Within the development of jurisprudence in the early eighteenth century ideas about prescription

3 Ibbetson, 'Natural Law and Common Law', 6–7.

4 Lobban, *History of Philosophy of Law in the Common Law World*, 95, and chs 3–4 more generally.

5 Ibbetson, 'Natural Law and Common Law', 7. One important example of the evidence against claims for a necessary dichotomy in jurisprudence appears in Donald R. Kelley, 'Law', in J.H. Burns with the assistance of Mark Goldie eds, *The Cambridge History of Political Thought 1450–1700* (Cambridge, 1991), 66–95, and Kelley, *The Human Measure: Social Thought in the Western Legal Tradition* (Cambridge, Mass., 1990), 209–19. While Kelley explores the contribution of ideas about custom in Roman and early modern natural jurisprudence, he does also rely on conventional ideas about the triumph of abstract and rationalist elements of the natural law tradition in the nineteenth century.

6 There has, of course, been a good deal of interest in the interconnected development of philosophical trends in eighteenth-century Scottish jurisprudence. Some important examples include, Forbes, *Hume's Philosophical Politics*; Forbes, 'Natural Law and the Scottish Enlightenment', in Campbell and Skinner eds, *Origins and Nature of Scottish Enlightenment*, 186–204: Haakonssen, *Science of a Legislator*; Haakonssen, *Natural Law and Moral Philosophy*; Haakonssen, 'Natural Jurisprudence and the Theory of Justice', in Alexander Broadie ed., *The Cambridge Companion to the Scottish Enlightenment* (Cambridge, 2003), 205–21; Hont and Ignatieff, *Wealth and Virtue*; Tatsuya Sakamoto and Hideo Tanaka eds, *The Rise of Political Economy in the Scottish Enlightenment* (London, 2003); James Moore, 'Natural Rights in the Scottish Enlightenment', in Mark Goldie and

and continuity, case law and common learning, were not simply dismissed; nor clearly subordinated to enlightened ideas about reason and nature; nor divorced from other trends, especially in moral philosophy.

In order to recover early eighteenth-century jurisprudential self-understanding it is necessary to appreciate this interplay between natural law and common law ideas, and the ways in which both were affected not only by philosophical but also by wider cultural and economic trends. Contemporaries believed that the foundations of justice lay in a mixture of universal principles and specific experience. Even more, they emphasised comparison and competition between legal authorities as the means by which a mutual transformation of natural law and common law occurred, and a higher justice was achieved. These were all vital elements of eighteenth-century English jurisprudence.

Natural law, common law jurisprudence, and print

While tracts like Robert Atkyns' have been dismissed as outdated, and other practical texts like the abridgments have been glossed over as incoherent, a select few early eighteenth-century texts have been distinguished by scholars as more serious works of jurisprudence. These are the texts associated with the genre of 'Institutional' writings: works that followed the simple and logical structure of Justinian's *Institutes*, and aimed to provide an explanation of the origins of law as well as a systematic account of legal principles and practices.[7] The *Institute of the Laws of England* (1720) and *New Institute of the Imperial or Civil Law* (1704), written by the scholar and cleric Thomas Wood, are two important examples. These early eighteenth-century legal texts deliberately worked within the forms and subject matter of Justinian's *Institutes*, while also expressing principles of natural law jurisprudence.[8] A *Treatise of Equity* (1737), written by the learned Exchequer official Henry Ballow, was similarly reliant upon Roman law concepts and categories, and demonstrates the clear influence of natural law jurisprudence. Thus, Ballow's treatise is accepted as a source of jurisprudence within the Roman and natural law traditions even though it is a focused monograph on certain areas of English law, rather than a comprehensive institute like

Robert Wolker eds, *The Cambridge History of Eighteenth-Century Philosophy* (Cambridge, 2006), 291–316.

7 Cairns, 'Blackstone, English Institutist', 324–7; Lobban, 'Blackstone and Science of Law', 316–17; K. Luig, 'The Institutes of National Law in the Seventeenth and Eighteenth Centuries', *Juridical Review*, 17 (1972): 193–226.

8 See for example Wood, *New Institute of Civil Law*, xiii–xv, for a claim to even improving the Justinian system by tinkering with the 'heads' he employed. See also Simpson, 'Rise and Fall of Legal Treatise', 656.

Wood's texts. All of these works adopted parts of the Institutional structure as well as the theoretical interest in the grounds and principles of law.

Many other early eighteenth-century commentators on law evinced knowledge of and interest in Roman law. There is also evidence of such familiarity in the references made by common law judges to Roman law principles and to the history of civil law.[9] This English turn to Roman law was part of a broader European trend in the seventeenth and eighteenth centuries which grew out of the legal humanism of the sixteenth century. Legal humanists in this earlier period mounted a critique of Roman law, but at the same time they strengthened its influence.[10] And as systems of national law developed, in seventeenth and eighteenth-century France and Spain for example, legal teaching and legal texts continued to be formulated within a Roman structure. Although European lawyers and theorists were anxious to delineate their own national law systems as distinct from the *ius commune* (which was understood to be derived from the *Corpus Juris Civilis* and the *Corpus Juris Canonici*), their conceptual approach still derived 'from the *Institutes* of Justinian [which], by reason of its systematic and comprehensive nature provided an excellent means of expressing a national law viewed as an organized whole'.[11] Similarly, while English common law and equity were understood to be distinct from Roman law and civil law, the Institutional structure was exceptionally useful. It is not surprising that when the civilian Thomas Wood set out to compose his survey of English common law he was influenced by Justinian's conceptual approach and divisions of persons, actions and things.[12]

Henry Ballow echoed this same conceptual structure in organising his *Treatise on Equity*. His first four books, on agreements (or contracts), uses

9 Lobban, *Common Law and English Jurisprudence*, 19–26. Among contemporary works on civil law, Jean Domat's *Les Lois Civiles dans Leur Ordre Naturel* was the most important of translated works. See also Kelley, 'Law', 67–70, on 'Romanist' and 'Romanoid' assumptions.

10 David J. Ibbetson, *Common Law and* Ius Commune (London, 2001), 4; Cairns, 'Blackstone English Institutist', 323.

11 Cairns, 'Blackstone English Institutist', 327, and see more generally 321–7. Also Alan Watson, *The Evolution of Western Private Law* (Baltimore, 2001), 251–2; Ibbeston, *Common Law and* Ius Commune, 12–13; Lobban, 'Blackstone and Science of Law', 312; Jean-Louis Halperin, 'French Legal Science in the 17th and 18th Centuries: To the Limits of the Theory of Law', in Damiano Canale, Paolo Grossi and Hasso Hoffman eds, *A History of the Philosophy of Law in the Civil Law World, 1600–1900*, vol. 9 of Enrico Pattaro ed., *A Treatise of Legal Philosophy and General Jurisprudence* (Dordrecht, 2009), 43–4. Examples of such Institutes would include James Dalrymple, Viscount Stair, *The Institutions of the Law of Scotland* (Edinburgh, 1681), or William Forbes *Institutes of the Laws of Scotland*, 2 vols (Edinburgh, 1722–1730), as well as the work of Jean Domat.

12 On this division, in Gaius' Institutes, into persons, things and actions see Peter Stein, *Roman Law in European History* (Cambridge, 1999), 19–20; on influence in England and Europe, Cairns, 'Blackstone English Institutist', 337, 343.

and trusts, mortgages and pledges, and last wills and testaments fit within the Institutional category of things incorporeal; books five and six, on damages and interest, and on evidence, are relevant to that part of the law concerned with actions. At times, English lawyers and theorists also turned to specific Roman legal concepts, such as *usufruct*, to make sense of new legal practices evolving in the eighteenth century.[13] In particular, it was believed that knowledge of laws enacted by the Romans to promote trade and manufacture, and to govern the colonies in their extensive empire, could be of use to English lawyers and policy-makers.[14] The interest in Roman law among early eighteenth-century English lawyers and theorists was uncontroversial and well-established.

This interest in Roman law was also, significantly, linked to a growing interest in natural law in the seventeenth and eighteenth centuries. In much the same way that Roman law provided a means of systematising national law, the categories and classifications of Justinian's *Institutes* also remained important in the exposition of natural law in the period. Moreover, the principles upon which Roman law was based were understood to be principles of natural law, essentially understood as the law of reason.[15] By the mid-seventeenth century European legal thinkers began to focus decisively on natural law, and the centre of legal studies moved from France and Italy toward the Netherlands. The influence of Arnold Vinnius, contemporary of Hugo Grotius and professor of law at Leyden, is one indication of this transition: Vinnius' 1642 commentary on Justinian's *Institutes* clearly articulated a Dutch jurisprudence that drew upon natural law and customary law as well as Roman law. Vinnius' text remained an important reference work throughout the eighteenth century.[16] Indeed it was cited by numerous English legal thinkers including, for example, Robert Atkyns in his texts on Chancery and on the jurisdiction of the House of Lords, Thomas Wood in his institute on civil law, Geoffrey Gilbert in his treatise on evidence law, and John Fonblanque in his edition of Ballow's equity treatise. Eighteenth-

13 Macnair, 'Conceptual Basis of Trusts'. But see also Alan Watson on some fundamental divergences between English law and Roman law, Watson, *Roman Law and Comparative Law* (Athens, GA, 1991), ch. 16; Watson, *Evolution of Western Private Law*, ch. 9.

14 William Strahan, 'Preface' and 'Dedication' to Jean Domat, *The Civil Law in Its Natural Order: Together with the Public Law. Written in French by Monsieur Domat...and translated into English by William Strahan LL.D* (London, 1722).

15 Lobban, 'Blackstone and Science of Law', 316–17; Watson, *Evolution of Western Private Law*, 255–6; Stein, *Roman Law in European History*, 107. See for example Wood, *New Institute of Civil Law*, 4, on Roman law compiled from law of nature and law of nations. In addition to the works discussed below see, for example, *A Dissertation on the Law of Nature, the Law of Nations, and the Civil Law in General. Together with Some Observations on the Roman Civil Law in Particular. To Which is Added, by Way of Appendix, a Curious Catalogue of Books, Very Useful to the Students of these Several Laws* (London, 1723).

16 Stein, *Roman Law in European History*, 99–100.

century English, like European, legal writers did participate in what David Ibbetson describes as 'a fervour of Natural Law thinking' during this 'heyday of Natural Law'.[17]

As has been noted, natural law already had a place in the definition of Roman law, and this Roman conception of law founded on natural reason was developed by later jurists.[18] The notion of underlying reason or rationality was an important part of seventeenth and eighteenth-century jurisprudence in a variety of ways. First it was essential to the drive towards systematisation and definition among continental jurists, like Jean Domat, providing a basis upon which they could conceive of a general definition of law and a regularised division of legal concepts.[19] Second, the idea of natural and foundational reason was part of the defence of the certainty of law against the conventionalist and relativist arguments of modern scepticism.[20] And, of course, questions about the operation of reason as a component of human nature, and the means by which humans come to know this natural law, were a central part of debate among theorists in the seventeenth and eighteenth centuries.

Major figures in the development of modern natural law jurisprudence included Hugo Grotius and Samuel Pufendorf, whom scholars regard as important representatives of European Enlightenment philosophy.[21] Their works, *De Iure Belli et Pacis Libri Tres* (1625) and *De Iure Naturae et Gentium Libri Octo* (1672), were well-known to English lawyers and legal theorists, and their commonly expressed conception of self-preservation as a universal principle, labeled as the 'first law of nature', was generally accepted by early modern thinkers.[22] Where debate flourished, however, was in considering problems regarding the ways in which humans recognise that natural law, and the reasons that motivate or oblige them to follow it. Grotius and Pufendorf themselves agreed that pure or 'right' reason (axiomatic, mathematical)

17 Ibbetson, 'Natural Law and Common Law', 4; Ibbetson, *Common Law and* Ius Commune, 27.

18 Kelley, 'Law', 69. See also the important texts Kelly cites, Otto von Gierke, *Natural Law and the Theory of Society 1500–1800*, trans. Ernst Troeltsch (Cambridge, 1934) and Richard Tuck, *Natural Rights Theories: Their Origin and Development* (Cambridge, 1979).

19 Kelley, 'Law', 87–8. On Domat's understanding of the relationship between faith and reason, Halperin, 'French Legal Science', 53.

20 Richard Tuck, 'The "Modern" Theory of Natural Law', in Anthony Pagden ed., *The Languages of Political Theory in Early Modern Europe* (Cambridge, 1987), 108–11, 114–15.

21 Israel, *Enlightenment Contested*, 194–200; Haakonssen, *Natural Law and Moral Philosophy*, 30, 43–6; T.J. Hochstrasser, *Natural Law Theories in the Early Enlightenment* (Cambridge, 2000).

22 Grotius' earlier natural law works included *De Iure Praedae* (mss 1605; one part published as his *Mare Liberum* 1609); Pufendorf previously published *Elementa Jurisprudentiae Universalis* (1660). See also Richard Tuck, 'Grotius and Selden', in Burns with Goldie eds, *Cambridge History of Political Thought*, 499–529.

was sufficient for the knowledge of this natural law, but they diverged on the question of obligation or will.[23]

Successors examined both knowledge of, and obligation to, the law. Philosophers like John Locke, Richard Cumberland or Ralph Cudworth proposed a variety of explanations for human knowledge of natural law, developing empirical and experiential as well as axiomatic conceptions of reason. Theorists placed a strong emphasis on the idea that this law of nature was essentially the law of reason, its content deducible from rational reflection on human nature, and not dependent on divine revelation.[24] Despite this rationalist emphasis, however, theorists remained interested in conceptualising God's role in creating humans with reason, and directed toward a goal of self-preservation. Further controversy developed over the problem of obligation, and here arguments not only about reason and revelation, but also about sentiment and sociability informed contemporary understanding of human behaviour and spurred the development of moral-philosophical debate.[25]

Reflection on natural law is obvious and important in the works of English legal thinkers like Wood and Ballow. It is essential to these authors' definition of justice, to their expressed conception of the origins and underlying authority of law. 'The *Original* or Primary Law of Nations, or the Law of natural Man, is that which unimprov'd Reason has planted amongst all Men, and is the true *Law of Nature*;' Thomas Wood explained. This natural law is 'a discerning Principle in Men of good and ill; or the dictate of right Reason, declaring from its conformity or disagreeableness every Action to be good or evil. Its *Object* is Natural good or evil, but the Will or Choice being determin'd, then it is a *Moral* good or evil.'[26] There are clear echoes here of the ideas of Grotius and Pufendorf; elsewhere Wood includes overt citations to the texts of these and other natural law theorists. As a doctor of civil law trained at Oxford, Wood was well versed in continental jurisprudence on natural law and jus gentium. Indeed, a translation of *Les Loix Civiles dans Leur Ordre Naturel*, the work of that renowned French philosopher of law Jean Domat, was one of Wood's many publications, and was included in some editions of Wood's *New Institute of Civil Law*.[27]

23 Kelley, 'Law', 89.

24 Watson, *Evolution of Western Private Law*, 252; Ibbetson, 'Natural Law and Common Law', 5; Beiser, *Sovereignty of Reason*, 270–1; Stein, *Roman Law in European History*, 107; Hochstrasser, *Natural Law Theories* and Haakonssen, *Natural Law and Moral Philosophy*.

25 Hochstrasser, *Natural Law Theories*, 2; Beiser, *Sovereignty of Reason*, 267, 275, 278–81; Darwall, *British Moralists and the Internal 'Ought'*; Haakonssen, *Natural Law and Moral Philosophy*; Michael B. Gill, *The British Moralists on Human Nature and the Birth of Secular Ethics* (Cambridge, 2006).

26 Wood, *New Institute of Civil Law*, 2.

27 Wood's translation of Domat was *A Treatise on the First Principles of Law in General: Of their Nature and Design, and of the Interpretation of Them* (London, 1705). Bound with Folger Shakespeare Library 1704 copy of Wood's *New Institute of Civil Law*, FSL

Henry Ballow, deputy chamberlain of the Exchequer, was another well-regarded English scholar who was engaged with natural law theory. The only extant text attributed to Ballow, a *Treatise on Equity*, was published early in his career, and it remained widely read even after the author's death. A revised version, with extensive notes added by the equity lawyer John Fonblanque, appeared in multiple editions in late eighteenth and early nineteenth-century England and America.[28] In this text Ballow, like Wood, turned to natural law in order to explain the foundations of legal authority. Moreover, at the very opening of the *Treatise* Ballow articulated a theory of natural law as part of his explicit defence of the jurisdiction of equity in relation to common law:

> Equity therefore, as it stands for the whole of natural Justice, is more excellent than any human Institution; neither are positive Laws, even in Matters seemingly indifferent, any further binding, than they are agreeable with the Law of God and Nature. But the Precepts of the natural Law, when enforced by the Laws of Man, are so far from losing any Thing of their former Excellence, that they receive an additional Strength and Sanction. Yet as the Rules of the municipal Law are finite, and the Subject of it infinite, there will often fall out Cases, which cannot be determin'd by them; for there can be no finite Rule of an infinite Matter, perfect. So that there will be a Necessity of having Recourse to the natural Principles; that what was wanting to the finite, may be supplied out of

171–441q. Robert B. Robinson, 'The Two Institutes of Thomas Wood: A Study in Eighteenth Century Legal Scholarship', *The American Journal of Legal History*, 35, 4 (October, 1991): 434 refers to publication of these together; Simpson, 'Rise and Fall of Legal Treatise', 656 and M.H. Hoeflich, 'Wood, Thomas', *ODNB*, assert that Domat was included in later editions of Wood's *Institute of the Laws of England.* Note also that the subtitle of Wood's *Institute of the Laws of England* – 'Laws of England in their Natural Order' – echoes Domat's title. On Domat's text see Halperin, 'French Legal Science', 48–61.

[28] N.G. Jones, 'Ballow [Bellewe], Henry', *ODNB*. [Henry Ballow] *A Treatise of Equity* (London, 1737); *A Treatise of Equity, With the Addition of Marginal References and Notes by John Fonblanque Esq.*, 2 vols (London, 1793–4). The Fonblanque revised version appeared in five editions in England, and four more in America in the late eighteenth and early nineteenth centuries. Simpson, 'Rise and Fall of Legal Treatise', 647. The attribution of the text to Ballow has been questioned since the eighteenth century; Michael Macnair repeats some of the early doubts especially regarding Ballow's lack of legal experience and knowledge of Roman law, Macnair, 'Conceptual Basis of Trusts', 210 n. 9. A.W.B. Simpson also raises questions by pointing to some contemporary attribution of this text to Geoffrey Gilbert, Simpson, 'Rise and Fall of Legal Treatise', 647 n. 91. However most modern scholars – including Holdsworth, Jones, and Ibbetson – generally accept evidence of Ballow's authorship; they especially note Francis Hargrave's confirmation of Ballow's authorship, as well as the fact that portions of a corrected manuscript of the text were passed to Ballow's literary executor after the author's death.

> that which is infinite. And this is what is properly called Equity in Opposition to strict Law ...[29]

Equity is said to fulfill the just intentions of the common law in those exceptional cases where common law provided no remedy, or where strict adherence to the common law would produce injustice.[30] As Ballow's statement demonstrates, the idea of equity as expressive of natural justice was tied to a broader understanding that the common law, like all law, was binding in so far as it was congruent with the law of nature, with 'that natural Justice and Equity, which ought to be the Ground-work and Foundation of all Laws'.[31]

Ballow's interpretation of equity as fulfilling or fixing common law – in Maitland's phrase, equity as 'a gloss on the law' – was conventional.[32] His use of the language of infinity, and emphasis upon the divine foundations of equity, called upon an older medieval interpretive tradition as well as contemporary natural law debates.[33] Ballow further integrated the ideas of influential modern jusnaturalists into his analysis of equity with his use of quotation from Grotius on the title page of the treatise and, even more, in his serious reliance on Samuel Pufendorf throughout the text. Ballow's late eighteenth-century editor, Fonblanque, sought to demonstrate Ballow's 'profound erudition' by noting this use of Pufendorf, Grotius, Pothier and

29 Ballow, *Treatise of Equity*, 2–3.

30 Cf Wood on exceptional cases where common law produces injustice: fraud, accident, trust. Wood, *New Institute of Civil Law*, 11–12; Wood, *Institute of the Laws of England*, 459ff. And see also Lord Chancellor Cowper's statement: 'For the Court of Chancery cannot controul the Maxims of Common Law, because of general Inconveniences; but only when the Observation of a Rule is attended with some unusual and particular circumstances that create a personal and particular Inconvenience'. Lucas, *Cases in Law and Equity* (London, 1736), 1.

31 Ballow, *Treatise of Equity*, 2; also 100: 'For by the Law of Nature, when two Duties happen to interfere at the same Point of Time, that which is the most honest and best is to be preferr'd. And so it shall be in Construction; for the Intendment of Law is agreeable to Nature, and on the better Side'. Cf Wood, *Institute Laws of England*, 10.

32 F.W. Maitland, *Equity: Also the Forms of Action at Common Law: Two Courses of Lectures*, A.H. Chaytor and W.J. Whitaker eds (Cambridge, 1910), 19; Lobban, *History of Philosophy of Law in Common Law World*, 20–22, 54. Further contemporary evidence of conventionality, in addition to Cowper and Wood cited above, may be found for example in Geoffrey Gilbert *Lex Praetoria*, in *Two Treatises on the Proceedings in Equity and the Jurisdiction of that Court* (Dublin, 1756), Richard Francis, *Maxims of Equity, Collected From, and Proved by Cases Out of the Books of the Best Authority, in the High Court of Chancery* (London, 1727), and William Strahan, Preface to *The Civil Law in its Natural Order*.

33 Harold Berman, 'Medieval English Equity', in Berman, *Faith and Order: the Reconciliation of Law and Religion* (Atlanta, 1993), 55–82; Mauro Bussani and Francesca Fiorentini, 'The Many Faces of Equity: A Comparative Survey of the European Civil Law Tradition', in Daniela Carpi ed., *The Concept of Equity* (Heidelberg, 2007), 101–35. See also Francis Oakley, *Natural Law, Law of Nature, Natural Rights* (New York, 2005).

other authorities.[34] A modern legal historian like David Ibbetson has also highlighted Ballow's intensive use of Pufendorf by showing that the first half of the *Treatise of Equity*, concerning contracts, 'for the most part... consists of brief paraphrases of or unattributed quotations from the English translation of Pufendorf's *De iure naturae et gentium*, followed by illustrative material from English case law'.[35] Here we can begin to see that dialogue or interaction between natural law and common law jurisprudence in the sources as well as topics of Ballow's work.

Ballow points to the work of the jusnaturalists, and situates contractualism at the heart of equity, from the very first sentences of this treatise. He opens with a familiar distinction between distributive and commutative justice first employed by ancient philosophers and jurists like Aristotle and Ulpian, and reaffirmed by later natural law theorists like Aquinas or Pufendorf.[36] In writing about equity, Ballow explained, he would focus upon the 'commutative, or that which governs contracts':

> For an Action or Suit, which is the Remedy the Law hath provided for the Obtaining Justice, is but a legal Demand of some Right, and all civil Rights must arise from Obligations, and these Obligations are founded on Compacts, it follows of Necessity, that the proper Subject of Law is Contracts, and that Justice the chief End of Law, which teaches the Performance of them.[37]

Ballow is clear that both law and equity must be understood as fundamentally concerned with contract. And this foundational premise determines the conceptual logic underlying the organisation of much of his text: Ballow's treatise on equity begins as a treatise on contract; it then moves to consider trusts as a form of contract, and elaborates the trustee's responsibilities and beneficiary's rights in the performance of the terms of the trust.

Ballow's interest in these topics is not, however, only an indication that he was affected by the contractualism of jusnaturalists like Pufendorf. As Ibbetson noted, Ballow combined reflection on natural law with an attention to numerous examples from proceedings in the English courts. This is an indication that Ballow was led to address principles of law through his confrontation with case law as well as natural law, and here clearly he

[34] *A Treatise of Equity* (London, 1799), ii–iii.

[35] Ibbetson, *Historical Introduction Obligations*, 218, and see 218–19 nn. 98–109 where Ibbetson also cites the specific passages in Ballow that are 'mirrored', 'copied' or 'derived' from Pufendorf. Also Ibbetson, 'Natural Law and Common Law', 15.

[36] Ballow, *Treatise of Equity*, 1; cf Wood, *New Institute of Civil Law*, 1–2. Beiser, *Sovereignty of Reason*, 271, 276; Stein, *Roman Law in European History*, 67. For a useful modern discussion of the distinction between distributive and commutative justice, tied to an analysis of this philosophical tradition, see James Gordley, 'Moral Foundations of Private Law', 2–4.

[37] Ballow, *Treatise of Equity*, 2.

too, like Atkyns, struggled with some of those contested areas of contemporary law regarding contract and commerce. Cases that highlighted jurisdictional disputes between common law and equity led, indeed required, him to think about the foundations and obligations of law; and cases having to do with disputes over women's property were again a focus of concern.[38] The development of law regarding trust presented a particular conundrum. As we have seen, common law recognised a trustee as the rightful owner of property held in trust. Yet that trustee was expected to utilise the property for the benefit of another, and equity was meant to protect that beneficiary's rights and ownership. Serious questions arose about the nature, and enforcement, of the trustee's obligation. If that obligation was founded in a conveyance of property at common law, and the trustee was recognised as a lawful owner, Ballow and others asked, what exactly was the authority of equity? What was the basis for that authority?[39] Could a rational or natural law basis simply override, and potentially erode, the legality and stability of a common law of property?

Many English lawyers and theorists like Ballow turned to analogous Roman law concepts in order to answer such difficult questions about the English trust. So for Ballow, the English trust was comparable to the Roman principle of *depositum*: a 'contract of deposit, where the owner of property put it in the hands of another person for safekeeping'.[40] Ballow defined trust as one of 'the particular Kinds of Agreements which occur most usually in Chancery' in the second book of his treatise, after an initial discussion 'of agreements in general'. Equity's enforcement of this contract of deposit, or trust, could then be seen simply as the realisation of the intention, and natural justice, underlying common law contracts.[41]

Ballow's analysis accorded with an idea of equity as the fulfillment of common law, while it also allowed for his persistent recognition of the authority of common law practice. Yet some scholars regard this assimilation of common law and equity as an indication of Ballow's failure to solve the logical and legal puzzle of the trust. Indeed this has even been seen as a sign of Ballow's deep confusion – a confusion fundamentally caused by his inclusion of ideas derived from Roman law, natural law and social contract theories. The implication underlying this criticism is that English thinkers wholly derived their legal principles from external sources, in order to supply English law with a theory that it would otherwise lack.[42] Ballow's adoption

38 Ibid., 5–6, 10, 16, 20–21, for examples Ballow cited concerning jointure and separate maintenance; and see 29, 34 for examples comparable to Sir Robert Atkyns' case.

39 Ibid., 54, 58–60, 62.

40 Ibbetson, 'Natural Law and Common Law', 13; Macnair, 'Conceptual Basis', 213–18.

41 Ballow, *Treatise of Equity*, 52; see also 72–6 on the office and duty of a trustee.

42 David Ibbetson suggests that Ballow was led to use the concept of *depositum* mainly because he was reading and incorporating Basil Kennet's translation of Pufendorf which 'used the language of trusts and trustees to render the Roman law contract known as

of these foreign concepts, scholars insist, led him to construct a theory at odds with the practice of English law he described. It did not, in the end, explain the fact of legal ownership vested in the trustee at common law, or compass the requirement of consideration in contract, both detailed in Ballow's explanation and examples.[43] This clash of practices and ideas is said to produce, in David Ibbetson's colourful description, 'the mangled remnants of a once-coherent theory, a skeleton glued together from a selection of bones picked from Pufendorf, with one or two added from elsewhere, on which the rules of Common law and Equity hung loosely and inelegantly'.[44]

But early eighteenth-century writers saw things differently. For men like Ballow, or Thomas Wood, the authority of English law lay in 'mingling' not 'mangling': common law and equity were understood to work together, in competition as much as harmony, both necessary to produce final justice. And the theoretical foundations, or 'backbone', of that justice lay in ideas and in examples that were derived from precedent and prescription as well as nature and reason. Just as judges like Atkyns or Holt looked to the framework of common law in order to interpret and integrate new elements of trust or contract law, writers like Wood and Ballow developed their legal theory by means of reflection on common law as well as natural law jurisprudence. And these eighteenth-century thinkers drew upon the work of English predecessors like William Lambarde, John Selden and Matthew Hale – authors who similarly emphasised that mixture of equity with common law, of natural reason with established precedents and rules, in their conceptions of justice.[45]

Ballow, Wood and other early eighteenth-century jurists also developed their jurisprudence through the mixed methods and structures of their texts.

depositum'. Ibbetson, 'Natural Law and Common Law', 13–14, and see Ibbetson, *Historical Introduction Obligations*, 218–19. Kennet's translation first appeared in 1703 and went through multiple editions in the first few decades of the eighteenth century. A related view is conveyed in the work of James Gordley: he argues that private law concepts like contract were derived from the ideas of early modern Spanish theologians and jurists who, in turn, influenced seventeenth-century jusnaturalists like Grotius and Pufendorf. Gordley, 'Moral Foundations of Private Law', and Gordley, *Philosophical Origins of Modern Contract Doctrine.*

43 On consideration see Ballow, *Treatise of Equity*, especially bk I, ch v; also 5, 8, 11, 55–6.

44 Ibbetson, *Historical Introduction Obligations*, 219; Ibbetson, 'Natural Law and Common Law', 14–15, offers a slightly more positive view by conceding that this 'skeleton' 'worked well enough in practice', and detailing the ways in which Ballow's work remained influential.

45 Lobban, *History of Philosophy of Law in Common Law World*; Burgess. *Politics of the Ancient Constitution*, 58–68; Whitman, 'Why did the Revolutionary Lawyers Confuse Custom and Reason?', 1321–68. In addition to the discussion of the works of Thomas Wood and John Selden below, see the prefaces to Edmund Wingate, *Maxims of Reason: Or the Reason of the Common Law of England* (London 1658), and Francis Bacon, *Elements of the Common Law of England* (London, 1630).

They emphasised the compilation of cases, forms of pleading and statutes, and called upon abridgment and encyclopedic as well as Institutional traditions. One artful representation of these mixed methods and mixed principles appears in the frontispiece image preceding the text of Wood's *Institute of the Laws of England*. There the author's portrait and coat of arms rest upon a bookcase which holds, on the left, copies of the *Biblia sacra*, the *Corpus Juris Civilis* and the *Corpus Juris Canonici*, and on the right, the printed law reports of Dyer, Coke and Croke. Wood's work is also an important demonstration of the ways in which a belief in the justice of precedent developed through the interaction between common law culture and Enlightenment print culture.

The text of Wood's other Institute, the *New Institute of the Imperial or Civil Law*, offers important evidence of a theory of mingled or mixed justice even in a text that, as we have seen, rests firmly upon an articulation of the authority of the law of nature. Wood first mounts an argument for the significance of civil law here by identifying it with reason and with natural law.[46] Yet he quickly turns to explain the relevance of civil law in England, as elsewhere in Europe, through a conception of mixture:

> But when I compare [the civil law], as it is receiv'd in other Nations, with the *Common* Law of *England*, it must be acknowledged that the Laws of this Nation (as they are now mixed and tempered) suit admirably to the genius of our People. For they have set prudent bounds to the Power of our Princes, and secured a proper Liberty for the Subject. They are very *particular* and *certain*. Presidents and adjudged Cases have been preserv'd for many Ages to direct in the determination of most Points; so that an Arbitrary Judge has less room to exert himself here, than in any other Law.[47]

Wood's explanation refers to the valuable restraint afforded by rules and precedents, and emphasises the principles of stability and reliability, as he elucidates the role of common law in the provision of justice. Where English common law was deficient however, Wood explained, the civil law could be relied upon to correct it. And so he points to civil law administered in military affairs, and canon law administered in the ecclesiastical courts, as recognised parts of English law.[48] Further, Wood reiterates the idea that English law did not simply resort to an external set of courts and practices, but rather that 'there is a mixture in the *Principles*, *Maxims* and *Reasons* of these two Laws [common law and civil law]; and indeed the Laws of all Countries are mixed with the Civil Law'.[49]

Such ideas about 'mixture', 'prudent bounds', and the possibility of bene-

46 Wood, *New Institute of Civil Law*, i.

47 Ibid., vi.

48 Ibid., vii–viii.

49 Ibid., xi.

ficial conflict in thwarting 'arbitrary' judges, were elaborated in another contemporary text on equity and natural law. Richard Francis, author of the popular *Maxims of Equity* published in the years between Wood's and Ballow's treatises (and similarly republished in several subsequent English and American editions), explained these mixed foundations of justice in the preface to his text.[50] Here Francis insisted that justice was the preserve of the common law judge who was 'bound…to observe the strict Rules of Law; and [to]…determine according to the known Customs and Statutes of the Realm' as much as it was the preserve of the equity judge who, directed by conscience, that 'infallible Monitor within his own Breast', was 'bound to determine according to the original and eternal Rules of Justice'.[51] Justice could only be produced from the juxtaposition of rigid tradition and unfettered conscience, Francis explained. While natural justice might be infallible, human nature was not, and tradition was vital to correct this deficiency.

> The narrow-minded Person, who labours under his great Affection for Form and Order cannot see the Beauty of this Contrivance, whereby Justice is produced from such jarring Jurisdictions; and what neither strict Form and Order, or absolute Latitude in judging can separately produce, is effected by the excellent Temperature of both together. This hath been judiciously compared to the mingling of two Herbs, which of themselves are Poison, but together make a wholsome Medicine.[52]

Francis does not simply insist that equity fulfills the just intention of common law. Rather he explains that it is through salutary conflict that the *mutual* transformation of common law and equity, of specific and universal justice, is achieved. The fact that Francis' explanation was based upon a comparison of the duties of common law and equity judges is another reminder that the use of natural law and Roman law concepts was still, in the eighteenth century, understood within the context of that jurisdictional debate between law and equity. Moreover, it is important to note that Francis calls upon the work of earlier theorists of the common law, repeating William Lambarde's image of mixed poisons producing good medicines, and echoing Matthew Hale's caution against partial judges.[53]

50 On the publishing history of Francis' *Maxims of Equity* see Simpson, 'Rise and Fall of Legal Treatise', 646; W.H. Bryson, 'Francis, Richard', *ODNB*.

51 Francis, *Maxims of Equity*, 2.

52 Ibid., 3. Here Francis emphasises that 'human Providence is too weak' and 'human nature is too Corrupt' to produce infallible laws and reliable conscience; this leads him to the solution of pitting one deficiency against another.

53 William Lambarde, *Archaeion: Or a Discourse upon the High Courts of Justice in England* (London, 1635), 71–2; Lobban, *History of Philosophy of Law in Common Law World*, 57, 88.

Thomas Wood also turned to the work of earlier theorists in his *New Institute of the Imperial or Civil Law* as he set out to describe England's mixed legal system through a series of influential natural images. The first reference Wood made was to an image of common law as a body of water:

> All this together make up our *Common* Law; and though it runs down thro' different Channels, yet every part of it (even that in the Spiritual Courts) may claim the name of the *Common* Law of *England*. For the whole is a composition of the *Feudal*, *Civil* and *Canon* Laws; and its *Definitions*, *Divisions* and *Maxims* are drawn out of one of those three Laws.[54]

The allusion to water is made more explicit in the text by the fact that Wood's image of channels follows directly upon his depiction of Admiralty law as that part of this mixed common law which dealt with 'Matters arising upon the Sea and relating to Sea Affairs'.[55] This depiction of flowing channels contributing to one common body of water was meant to resonate for readers with another familiar water image: an image of the river or the sea as a symbol of continuity within change. This analogy to a body of water as ever changing yet ever the same was used by Aristotle to describe the state, and by John Selden and Matthew Hale to describe the common law.[56]

Wood's affirmation of this kind of common law imagery is further indicated by the second of his natural images depicting a mixed and mingled English law. Here Wood begins with a botanical analogy: 'True it is,' he admits, 'that the Common and Civil Laws had not the same Root or Stock; yet by Inoculating and Grafting, the Body and Branches do seem at this day to be almost of a piece.'[57] Wood's reference to roots and branches was a fairly uncommon identification between grafting and mixture, and at first seems to convey an impression of civil law improving and ultimately usurping common law.[58] It was more likely, however, that Wood was consciously echoing the defence of common law offered by the seventeenth-century theorist, and Lord Chancellor, Francis Bacon. In his proposals for 'amending' and 'compiling' English law Bacon had insisted that he sought to preserve custom and common law even when he contemplated reform and rationalisation. 'I dare not advise to cast the law into a new mould,' Bacon explained. 'The work which I propound tendeth to pruning and grafting the law, and not to plow up and planting it again; for such a remove I should

54 Wood, *New Institute of Civil Law*, viii.

55 Ibid., vii-viii.

56 Rudolph, *Revolution by Degrees*, 57.

57 Wood, *New Institute of Civil Law*, xi–xii.

58 I owe this general point regarding mixture to conversation with Wolfram Schmidgen, based on his new work 'Exquisite Mixture: The Virtues of Impurity in Early Modern England' (Philadelphia, 2012).

hold indeed for a perilous innovation.'[59] Bacon also clearly connected that language of grafting to his praise of the mixed nature of common law:

> It is true [the laws of England] are as mixt as our language, compounded of *British*, *Roman*, *Saxon*, *Danish*, *Norman* customs. And surely as our language is thereby so much the richer, so our laws are likewise by that mixture the more complete. Neither does this attribute less to them, than those that would have them to have stood out the same in all mutations. For no tree is so good first set, as by transplanting and grafting.[60]

Thomas Wood's image of grafting and mixture was similarly tied to an emphasis upon antiquity and continuity within adaptation. Abandoning Bacon's analogy to language, however, Wood turned immediately from the 'Body and Branches' of his imagined tree to a final image of the planks of a wooden ship: 'For the *English* Law has received great alterations, and is very much unlike it self;' Wood concluded, 'or (as Mr. Selden expresses it) *In regard of its first Being it is like the Ship, that by often mending hath no piece of the first Materials*.'[61] This explicit reference to that classic common law image, derived from John Selden's *Notes on Fortescue* (a text later edited by Wood, in an edition of Selden's collected works) handily conveyed the idea that the authority of law resides in history, continuity and custom as well as reason and nature.[62]

It is significant that Wood openly turns to the legal antiquarian John Selden. It is another indication that early modern lawyers and legal theorists did not share the discomfort modern scholars experience when explanations from reason and from experience, or from natural law and common law, coexist, and sometimes clash. Much like earlier seventeenth-century

59 Francis Bacon, 'A Proposition for Compiling and Amendment of our Laws', in Bacon, *Law Tracts* (London, 1737), 9. Wood might have read this short tract in manuscript and, as indicated in the next passage footnoted below, Bacon used this same language of grafting and mixture in 'An Offer of a Digest of the Laws' which was available in print before Wood produced his text. See also David Lieberman on Robert Peel's deliberate use of Bacon's words on pruning and grafting in his 1826 parliamentary speech regarding law reform legislation. David Lieberman, 'Legislation in a Common Law Context', in Diethelm Klippel and Reiner Schulze eds, *Common Law und Europaische Rechtsgeschichte Zeitschrift fur Neuere Rechtsgeschichte*, 28, 1/2 (2006): 122–3.

60 Francis Bacon, 'An Offer to our late Sovereign King James, of a Digest to be made of the Laws of England', in Bacon, *Certain Miscellany Works of the Right Honourable Francis Lord Verulam, Viscount St Alban* (London, 1670), 52. This text appeared in an earlier 1629 edition of *Certain Miscellany Works*, as well as in the later *Law Tracts* (London, 1737) where the very same passage concerning language, mixture and grafting was also included in Bacon's 'Proposition for Compiling and Amendment of our Laws', 3.

61 Wood, *New Institute of Civil Law*, xii.

62 Lobban, *History of Philosophy of Law in Common Law World*, 61; Postema, 'Classical Common Law Jurisprudence (Part I)', 173–4; John Selden, *Opera Omnia*, vol. 3, ed. Thomas Wood (London, 1726).

theorists such as Selden or Hale, Wood had a complex understanding of the role of reason in the creation of law. This is apparent in his reliance on natural law and common law concepts and images. It is evident too in the fact that Wood similarly incorporated positivist ideas about the contribution of legislators and legislation in his explication of the development of civil and common law.[63]

This incorporation of positivist ideas is noticeable from the introductory chapter of the *New Institute of the Imperial or Civil Law*, where Wood moved from claims about the law of nature and universal justice, to a distinction between a primary and a secondary law of nations, to a delineation of civil law, 'that Law which every Commonwealth or City has established and appointed peculiarly for it self'.[64] This civil law, composed of edicts, codes and customs, written and unwritten, is said to be deduced from reason and nature, but also to emerge within specific circumstances in time. Wood further recognised custom as a valid source of law: custom has great authority, he averred, since it is the product of popular practice and continued consent. But the authority of this unwritten law, Wood explained, rests both in its rationality ('a Custom must be reasonable and not against a natural or divine Law') and in its conscious use and approval over time.[65] Here for Thomas Wood, like his predecessor Matthew Hale, the role of judges and legislators is vital to an affirmation of the rationality and realisation of the prescriptive force of law.[66]

Thomas Wood's contribution to English jurisprudence has been noted by several scholars who have usefully analysed the ways in which his ideas were informed by natural law and Roman law traditions, prior Institutional models, and by contemporary ideas about legal reform.[67] What has not been well understood, however, is Wood's reliance on the common law jurisprudence of predecessors like Selden and Hale. And what has been wholly ignored is the way in which Wood's jurisprudence was also informed by his engagement with questions about the selection, organisation and citation of sources – those characteristic concerns of Enlightenment print culture, and of eighteenth-century legal culture.

63 Burgess, *Politics of the Ancient Constitution*, ch. 2; Lobban, *History of Philosophy of Law in Common Law World*, 61–3; Postema, 'Classical Common Law Jurisprudence (Part I)', 174–5; Postema, 'Classical Common Law Jurisprudence (Part II)', 19–20. On Blackstone's similar 'major intellectual debt' to Selden and Hale, see Lieberman, *Province of Legislation Determined*, 44.

64 Wood, *New Institute of Civil Law*, 4.

65 Ibid., 4–5, 7, 9–10.

66 Cf also Wood, *Institute Laws of England*, 4–8, 10. Lobban, *History of Philosophy of Law in Common Law World*, 88–9.

67 Lobban, *Common Law and English Jurisprudence*, 23–6; Lobban, 'Blackstone and Science of the Law', 318–21; Cairns, 'Blackstone English Institutist', 337–8; Lieberman, *Province of Legislation Determined*, 38, 65.

Wood addressed these methodological questions, and evaluated different legal genres like reports, Institutes and commentaries, through reference to his own major sources, the works of John Cowell and Edward Coke. First Wood openly admitted that Cowell's *Institutiones Juris Anglicani* (1605) was a model for his own *New Institute of the Imperial or Civil Law*: 'I follow Cowell,' Wood, explained, 'when I maintain that the Laws of *England* are a composition of the *Civil*, *Canon* and *Feudal* Laws, and that there is a greater Affinity or Union between them than the Professors of the Civil and Common Laws do generally apprehend.'[68] Second, Wood expressly demonstrated Cowell's impact in that same civil law Institute where he claimed to surpass what he saw as Cowell's simplistic application of the 'method of the *Imperial* Institutes'. And finally, in his common law Institute Wood, like Cowell, attempted to impose some Institutional structure on common law, roughly organising his material around the categories of persons, things and actions.[69] Yet Wood was also drawn to Coke's *Institutes*, and openly acknowledged the influence of Coke rather than Cowell in this *Institute of the Laws of England*. Wood certainly criticised Coke's *Institutes*, deriding it as a mere commentary that failed to provide the 'methodical organization' and 'instruction' that were the hallmarks of Institutional texts. But he also praised Coke '*as the Firmest and Surest Foundation to Build on*', and '*the most Methodical, Clearest, most Judicious and most Authentick Reporter*'.[70]

Wood looked to Coke as well as Cowell in order to convey a deeper understanding of the law. He employed both the methodical Roman structure and the abridgment approach in his two Institutes. Wood self-consciously followed the categories, and logical organisation of topics and sub-topics, typical of the Institutional genre. Wood also conceived of the categories and topics of his texts in terms familiar from the commonplace tradition and contemporary common law abridgment literature, as 'titles' or 'heads' useful for 'young Scholars'.[71] The material within each topic or head in Wood's texts was composed of definitions and specific illustrations, with additional citation of statutes and other authorities added in the common law Institute. Moreover the very layout of Wood's Institutes resembled the abridgments. In the *New Institute of Imperial or Civil Law* each point is enumerated, using both Roman and Arabic numerals; secondary or additional material, included just below a major point, is differentiated by its

68 Wood, *New Institute of Civil Law*, xvi; Cairns, 'Blackstone English Institutist', 333. See also 'Fulbeck, *Parallele of Civil, Cannon and Common Law* (1601)', listed among the texts on 'Law Canon Civil & Feudal' in the library catalogue of Judge Martin Wright, IT, Barrington 63.

69 Wood's text is organised into books devoted to persons, estates, pleas of the crown, and courts. Wood, *Institute Laws of England*, table of contents, 10.

70 Cairns, 'Blackstone English Institutist', 337; see Wood, *Institute Laws of England*, v.

71 Wood, *New Institute of Civil Law*, xiii–xiv.

appearance in a smaller font; and sources are cited in the margins.[72] Wood's *Institute of the Laws of England* is even more like a topical abridgment: each chapter opens with definition of terms and concepts, and demonstrates a further tendency towards classification. Consider, for example, the classification of types of corporations in Book I, chapter 8, or the delineation of the geographical scope of English law in the British Isles and the list of those six grounds of law in the introduction to the text, as instances of this classificatory impulse.[73]

Wood combined this logic of definition and classification with an emphasis on detail, and he enumerated particular examples drawn from a lengthy list of standard common law sources. Wood not only cited Bracton, Fortescue and Coke, but also Hale's *Pleas of the Crown*, Dalton's *Compleat Justice*, West's *Symboleography*, Fitzherbert's *Natura Brevium*, the abridgments of D'Anvers, Rolle and Staunford, Bacon's *Elements of the Law*, Noy's *Grounds and Maxims*, numerous nominative reports, law dictionaries, and many other familiar authorities.[74] His work was aimed at a student and professional audience that valued the practical legal literature as much as it was written for a scholarly audience interested in natural law. Indeed, both of Wood's Institutes of civil and common law, like his essay on legal education, were widely-read texts published in multiple editions throughout the century, and cited by generations of students at the Inns of Court as well as Oxford and Cambridge.[75]

Richard Francis' *Maxims of Equity* also looked like a typical common law abridgment, and was largely composed of exemplary case law. Henry Ballow's approach was even closer to Wood's since he employed the same kind of mixed structure in his *Treatise of Equity*. Ballow relied on some typical Institutional categories and, as Macnair and Ibbetson rightly note, he also used an analytic framework derived from a theory of contract.[76] But Ballow's text is not only logical and systematic. It is also inductive, building layer upon layer of enumerated examples. The structure of Ballow's text reflects a familiarity and compatibility with contemporary abridgments and encyclopedias. It also indicates that the author endorsed common law ideas about the authority of law residing in precedent and prescription. The

72 See chapter 2 above. Compare the use of different fonts, and distinctions made to highlight new or additional materials, in D'Anvers' *General Abridgment of the Common Law*.

73 Wood, *Institute Laws of England*, 1–9, 109ff. Compare also the formats of Francis, *Maxims of Equity*, and Geoffrey Gilbert, *The Law of Uses and Trusts* (London, 1734).

74 Other familiar citations include: Finch, St German, Perkins, Kitchin, and law reporters Ventris, Hobart, Shower, Dyer, Croke, Levinz, Siderfin, Bulstrode, Modern Reports.

75 'Wood', *ODNB*; Simpson, 'Rise and Fall of Legal Treatise', 656 nn. 161–2; Robinson, 'Two *Institutes* of Wood', 432–3.

76 Macnair, 'Conceptual Bases of Trust', 220.

evidence of marginal citations added to the text by one contemporary reader confirms that Ballow's treatise should be read in this way: this reader wrote in references to Rolle's *Abridgement*, or to printed case reports like Croke's, frequently and throughout the text.[77]

It is essential to understand works of early eighteenth-century jurisprudence, like Ballow's or Wood's, within this wider contemporary context of Enlightenment print culture. An appreciation of this abridgment context, as well as the Institutional context, allows us to understand the authors' strategies and intentions in new ways, and to challenge the old conclusion that Thomas Wood, and others, failed 'to use the deductive structure coherently'.[78] It enables us to see that these writers contributed to eighteenth-century common law thought through the structures as well as the content of their texts, and thus validated the idea that legal authority was founded in accepted past practice and exemplary tradition.

Finally, an awareness of this broader cultural context leads particularly to a new understanding of important legal-constitutional intentions in Thomas Wood's texts. As we've seen, Wood confronted problems in organising and conveying great amounts of information. Like the authors of eighteenth-century abridgments and encyclopedias, Wood too generated insights and expressed the essential unity of his work through the use of comparison, juxtaposition and cross-reference. The *New Institute of the Imperial or Civil Law* provides ongoing comparisons between civil, canon and common law, while the *Institute of the Laws of England* frequently points the reader from one section to another in the text.[79] This strategy was, in fact, highlighted by the author of a 1729 abridgment of Wood's Institute, *The Laws of England Delineated*. The text presented Wood's *Institute of the Laws of England* in the form of a detailed outline with occasional cross-referencing, the author explained, for '*the Use of such as love a Method in their Reading, and are desirous to have not only a partial and piece-meal Insight into, but a general and comprehensive View of the* Laws of England'.[80] Wood himself explained that his *New Institute of the Imperial or Civil Law* was largely premised on the use of comparative examples.

> By the way I have added *Notes*, and therein observ'd the chief difference of the Laws of *England*, as also the *Principal* differences in the Laws and Practice of other *Nations* from it, and what Conformity or Disagreement there is in the Law *Divine*; what alterations have been made in the *Canon* Law, &c. that our young

[77] Ballow, *Treatise of Equity* (1737), FLP, Carson LC7 93.

[78] Lobban, 'Blackstone Science of Law', 318.

[79] Characteristic examples in Wood, *Institute Laws of England*, 42, 63, 116, 138.

[80] *The Laws of England Delineated* (London, 1729). This text is laid out to be read horizontally, with the text flowing over two pages without interruption.

> Gentlemen may be led to compare the Equity and *Polity* of each, and be able hereafter to judge what ought amongst our selves to be Confirm'd or Reform'd.[81]

It is this comparative approach, and Wood's interest in reaching a broad audience of civil lawyers, common lawyers, and interested gentlemen, that makes this text 'a milestone in English juristic writing', M.H. Hoeflich agrees.[82] Like John Selden before him, Thomas Wood developed an understanding of English law as one example of a broader European pattern.[83] This emphasis on comparison is another part of Wood's conception of mixed and mingled law, and is tied to his assertion that there is 'Affinity or Union' between civil and other kinds of law.

In addition, it is likely that when Wood published these examples of comparative law in 1704 he was contributing to contemporary discourse about Union between England and Scotland. Scholars have identified such interests and motivations in John Cowell's *Institutiones*, published soon after the union of crowns in 1603, but they have neglected to recognise Wood's similar intentions in publishing this *New Institute of the Imperial or Civil Law* in 1704, or his *Some Thoughts Concerning the Study of the Laws of England Particularly in the Two Universities* in 1708.[84] It is true, as Cairns and others have noted, that both of Wood's Institutes were probably aimed to fulfill his goal, articulated in 1708, to make legal study more accessible to students and young gentlemen outside the Inns of Court.[85] The primary impetus for this educational project, however, may not have been Wood's recognition of the need to prepare men for the responsibilities of authority, nor simply his desire to promote civil law. Rather in the context of proposed, and then realised, Scottish Union, the methodological value of comparative law had a peculiar significance. Although Scots law and English common law remained separate after the Treaty of 1707, contemporaries surely understood Wood's reference to 'Affinity or Union' and his exhortation to comparison, judgment and reform, as commentary on the potential benefits of progress towards incorporating union.

A new awareness of these multiple political, cultural and intellectual contexts allows for a better understanding of Wood's influential texts, and

81 Wood, *New Institute Civil Law*, xiv.

82 'Wood', *ODNB*.

83 John Selden's *Notes on Fortescue* – one of the works that Wood edited – was a project in comparative history; Selden's comparative approach to law and legal history also influenced Matthew Hale. D.E.C. Yale, *Hale as A Legal Historian* (London, 1976), 7.

84 Cairns, 'Blackstone English Institutist', 338; Brian P. Levack, *The Formation of the British State: England, Scotland and the Union 1603–1707* (Oxford, 1987).Wood's *Some Thoughts Concerning the Study of Law* was also published in a second edition in 1727.

85 Cairns, 'Blackstone English Institutist', 338; Lieberman, *Province of Legislation Determined*, 65. It is also likely that Wood was contributing to debates over law reform legislation that were taking place 1705–6.

their contribution to the development of common law and natural law jurisprudence in the eighteenth century. This deeper understanding of Wood's contribution also has significant implications for the analysis of William Blackstone's even more famous *Commentaries on the Laws of England*. As Wilfrid Prest and others have noted, Blackstone studied Wood's *Institute of the Laws of England*. Indeed Blackstone, like other readers, annotated at least one of his copies of Wood's text with copious marginal notes. Blackstone's lectures were in part a fulfillment of Wood's call for the addition of common law to the university curriculum, and the *Commentaries* that grew out of these lectures, like Wood's Institutes, an attempt to offer students a useful introduction to the law. [86] Prest is surely right to pay tribute to the '... magnitude of [Blackstone's] achievement as the last and most successful in a long line of writers who had struggled to develop a methodical and systematic exposition of the common law'. Yet we must take care to recognise the range of meanings contemporaries attributed to these values of 'method' and 'system'.[87] Contemporaries believed that Blackstone's accomplishment lay in his talent for historical, theoretical and analytical exposition, but they also recognised that commonplacing, abridgment, collection and comparison were valued modes of legal analysis for Blackstone, as they had been for Wood and Ballow.

Collection and abridgment remained important values even for critics of the 'obscurity' of eighteenth-century common law. So, for example, when a later eighteenth-century commentator, Joseph Simpson, decried the 'number, bulk and obscurity' of English law contained in the reports and statute books, the language he used in his proposal for amendment was the language of commonplace and abridgment – of 'reducing' and 'digesting' cases and acts to their 'proper heads' – as much as it was the language of science and reform.[88] Moreover, when Simpson depicted the 'wilderness' of the law, or his contemporaries praised Blackstone for a work that brought the knowledge of law 'from Darkness to Light', they deliberately echoed the same claims made for the abridgments and reports of Jacob, Bacon and Coke. This evidence, too, encourages us to understand Blackstone's engagement with print culture, like his engagement in a variety of other literary, aesthetic and commercial enlightened pursuits, as a continuation of legal-cultural trends that had developed in the earlier part of the eighteenth century.[89]

86 Prest, *William Blackstone*, 68, 109.

87 Ibid., 12; Lobban, *Common Law and English Jurisprudence*, 25–6.

88 Joseph Simpson, *Reflections on the Natural and Acquired Endowments Requisite for the Study of the Law*, 4th edn (London, 1765), vii–viii, and separate chapters on note-taking and commonplacing; see especially 39–40 for his discussion of the benefits and drawbacks of the abridgment literature. Cf Lemmings, *Professors of the Law*, 138.

89 Prest concludes his biography with a depiction of Blackstone as a British Enlightenment figure: Prest, *William Blackstone*, 308–11.

Moral philosophies and jurisprudence: Shaftesbury, Ballow and Somers

Scholars' previous emphasis on apparent incoherence in texts like Wood's or Ballow's, and on common lawyers' failure fully to adopt natural law principles, has masked the significance of ongoing traditions of common law jurisprudence. Such emphasis has also led scholars to neglect relevant contemporary political and cultural contexts, like the engagement with questions about data organisation and the proliferation of print, or the concern with the legal-constitutional implications of Union, or the attention to the expansion of commercial law and controversies about the enforcement of contracts and trusts, that are crucial to the analysis of these texts. Similarly, scholars' narrow focus on one aspect of natural law theory has obscured the relevance of different kinds of philosophical contexts to our understanding of the evolution of English jurisprudence. Attention should especially be directed to the ways in which jurists and lawyers responded to what were perceived as the central moral challenges of the eighteenth century associated with economic development: that is, questions regarding commercialisation and corruption.

At the same time that early eighteenth-century moral-philosophical debates flourished, controversies erupted over official corruption, and legal and political reform.[90] Public political debates about the effects of commercial prosperity frequently led to a critique of monied interests, national debt and big government. Controversy also, at times, centred specifically on Chancery procedures, personnel and jurisdiction as part of contemporary reflection on the jurisprudence and jurisdiction of equity.[91] Moral philosophers and social theorists articulated classical republican ideas about the dangers of corruption and an obligation to a civic good. They also explored new ideas about the nature of appetite and sentiment, and about the effect of human passions on the social order. Early eighteenth-century legal thinkers like Thomas Wood and Henry Ballow, John Somers and Giles Jacob, were deeply interested in such questions about sociability and sentiment, and took part in contemporary debates about the grounds of moral obligation.

90 Istvan Hont, 'The Early Enlightenment Debate on Commerce and Luxury', in Goldie and Wolker eds, *Cambridge History of Eighteenth-Century Political Thought*, 379–418; David Fate Norton and Manfred Kuehn, 'The Foundations of Morality', in Haakonssen ed., *Cambridge History of Eighteenth-Century Philosophy*, vol. 2, especially 942–3; Gill, *British Moralists on Human Nature*, 128; Maxine Berg and Elizabeth Eger eds, *Luxury in the Eighteenth Century: Debates, Desires and Delectable Goods* (Basingstoke, 2003), especially chs 1–2.

91 *Reasons Humbly Offered…for Preventing Delays and Expences in Suits in Law and Equity*, 3, 13–15, 17–18, 21–2; *Proposals Humbly Offer'd … for Remedying the Great Charge and Delay of Suits at Law and Equity* (London, 1707), 8–12 (London, 1724), 16, 41–7; *The Tryal of Thomas Earl of Macclesfield in the House of Peers, for High Crimes and Misdemeanors, upon an Impeachment* (London, 1725).

These moral-philosophical discussions about luxury and commerce, civility and sociability, are important contexts for understanding these men's jurisprudence.[92]

As we have seen, Wood, Ballow and others were clearly influenced by a theory of natural law understood as a law of reason, but a related theory of natural law that 'centered on human sociability' was equally important to these legal thinkers in the eighteenth century.[93] At issue was that question about how and why humans were obliged to follow natural law. The 'sociality principle' expressed in Samuel Pufendorf's natural jurisprudence was a significant part of this debate. Pufendorf insisted that an impulse towards self-preservation, that first law of nature, was not incompatible with human sociability. He explained that man was obliged to natural law because that 'law could only have originated in a combination of man's instinct for sociability and his calculation of the rationality of a social life as the best means to self-preservation'.[94] Evidence of these social origins lay more in historical kinds of argument than in the geometric or axiomatic methods Pufendorf and other jusnaturalists often favoured. But Pufendorf used a variety of arguments and methods and this eclecticism made him persuasive.[95]

Henry Ballow adopted the emphasis on sociability in his *Treatise on Equity*, and specifically followed one line of Pufendorf's argument by drawing connections between sociality and language. Language acquisition was, in fact, at the heart of Pufendorf's account of human social development. For Pufendorf, human speech was the key to mutual aid; as an 'instrument of greatest usefulness for the life of man', speech was proof that humans are naturally social. Since speech was vital to that end of self-preservation, Pufendorf concluded, it was controlled by natural law: the 'law of nature is understood to command that *no man shall deceive another by the use of signs which have been instituted to express his thoughts*.'[96] It is not surprising that Henry Ballow picked up on this 'contractual character of language' in Pufendorf's account, and similarly insisted that men must adhere to the agreement made by following conventional language use.[97] Ballow repeated the command against deception through speech, and affirmed the conven-

[92] David Lieberman has analysed the reactions and contributions of later eighteenth-century legal thinkers, like Mansfield and Blackstone, to these philosophical discourses. But Lieberman has ignored the response of an earlier generation of jurists. David Lieberman, 'Property, Commerce and the Common Law: Attitudes to Legal Change in the Eighteenth Century', in John Brewer and Susan Staves eds, *Early Modern Conceptions of Property* (London, 1995), 145–6.

[93] Hochstrasser, *Natural Law Theories*, 2; see also Beiser, *Sovereignty of Reason*.

[94] Hochstrasser, *Natural Law Theories*, 40.

[95] Ibid., 41, 60–5.

[96] Samuel Pufendorf, *De Jure Naturae et Gentium, Libri Octo*, trans. C.H. and W.A. Oldfather (Oxford, 1934), bk iv, ch. 1, 458.

[97] On Pufendorf's conception of language agreement see Hannah Dawson, *Locke, Language and Early Modern Philosophy* (Cambridge, 2007), 151–2.

tional and sociable foundation for what he terms the signification of words in several places in his text. For example, in a lengthy discussion of equity's proper role in the execution of wills and the enforcement of marriage articles, Ballow adds the following general observation:

> ... that Interpretation is a Collection of the Meaning out of Signs most probable: And these are Words, and other Conjectures. As for Words; the Rules are well express'd in the ancient Form of making Leagues, which appointed, that the Words should be expounded fairly, in the common Sense that the Words bore in that Place at that Time.[98]

Like his model, Samuel Pufendorf, Ballow turned to recorded history as well as conjectural history to elucidate the obliging force of law.

Pufendorf was, many scholars have shown, a recognised source for Ballow's treatise. Yet there may also be evidence here of the impact of another theorist, Anthony Ashley Cooper, Third Earl of Shaftesbury, who was an important contributor to philosophical debate in Britain at this time. Ballow might have encountered Shaftesbury's discussion of the evolution of language as an essential component of human sociability in the *Soliloquy, or Advice to an Author*, an essay included in Shaftesbury's popular *Characteristics of Men, Manners, Opinions, Times* (1711). Here Shaftesbury offered a history of linguistic development which traced a change from the simple expression of needs among 'the weakest and more imperfect societies of mankind, such as those composed of federate tribes or mixed colonies,' to the flourishing of the arts, such as poetry, rhetoric and music, in modern 'free nations'.[99] It is possible that Ballow was impressed by this narrative of social development. It is even more likely that Ballow was affected by Shaftesbury's related and commanding definition of virtue, with its emphasis on order and harmony.

Shaftesbury's philosophy rested upon the assumption that in each person lay a natural 'social feeling or sense of partnership with human kind'.[100] From this foundation he defined virtuous action as the pursuit of a social or public good. 'When in general all the affections or passions are suited to the public good or good of the species,' Shaftesbury explained, '... then is the natural temper entirely good.'[101] This is a teleological account of virtue

98 Ballow, *Treatise of Equity*, 47. See also 48, sect. 13, and compare 50, sect. 18 where Ballow allows that it may sometimes be necessary 'to deviate from the receiv'd Sense' of words if a too literal definition results in an absurd meaning that would contradict the intention of the parties to an agreement.

99 Anthony Ashley Cooper, Third Earl of Shaftesbury, *Soliloquy or Advice to an Author*, in Lawrence Klein ed., *Characteristics of Men, Manners, Opinions, Times* (Cambridge, 1999), 106–7. This essay was, as Klein notes, also published separately sometime between 1708 and 1710, before the collected work of the *Characteristics* appeared.

100 Shaftesbury, *Sensus Communis*, in Klein ed., *Characteristics*, 50.

101 Shaftesbury, *Inquiry Concerning Virtue or Merit*, in Klein ed., *Characteristics*, 172.

in which an innate moral sense guides each person towards a proper end, that is, the ultimate good of the system of which he is a part. Shaftesbury is well known for these sentimentalist elements of his philosophy – for his notion of 'moral sense' and his attention to passion, affection, feeling. Yet Shaftesbury also linked virtue to conscious decision-making. Reflective and intentional contribution to the public good is essential to Shaftesbury's definition of virtuous action and, again, it is part of his explication of an innate human moral sense. For Shaftesbury '[p]eople are virtuous if and only if their actions flow from properly functioning moral sentiments', Michael Gill asserts, '[a]nd reason tells us that moral sentiments are functioning properly if and only if they promote the well-being of the species as a whole'.[102]

This idea of the pattern of nature and universal order was not unique to Shaftesbury. It was also articulated by a jusnaturalist like Richard Cumberland, whose ideas were incorporated, in part, in Pufendorf's treatise on natural law. Henry Ballow likely encountered these ideas in Pufendorf's work, or directly in Cumberland's work; Cumberland's emphasis on universal system and reliance on classical sources were an important contribution to the philosophy of the Cambridge Platonists, and presumably attractive to a scholar of the Greek language, and the 'old philosophy', like Ballow.[103] Yet Ballow also indicated his familiarity with Shaftesbury's particular version of such ideas. He echoed Shaftesbury's precise language of virtue, for example, in his own opening definition of justice. Ballow asserts:

> And this is the golden Rule of Equality, that God himself observes, in the Distribution of the several Parts of the World, dealing to every one according to his Deserts: As in Musick, the best Instruments are given to those who play best. And the same Order ought to be observ'd in States, if they would be truly happy, taking God and Nature for their Pattern; that they may be of a Piece and consistent with the rest of the Universe.[104]

Ballow's allusion to harmony, and reference to musical aptitude in his image of distributive justice, was similar to Shaftesbury's repetition of Stoic ideas about the connection between a delight in aesthetic harmony – partic-

102 Gill, *British Moralists on Human Nature*, 94; cf also Norton and Kuehn, 'Foundations of Morality', 948–9.

103 'Ballow', *ODNB*. Richard Cumberland's influential text was *A Treatise of the Laws of Nature*, trans. John Maxwell (London, 1727). On Cambridge Platonists see Darwall, *British Moralists and Internal Ought*, chs 4–5; Beiser, *Sovereignty of Reason*, chs 4, 7; J.B. Schneewind, *The Invention of Autonomy: A History of Modern Moral Philosophy* (Cambridge, 1998), ch. 10. Although Cumberland was influential, it is not likely that Ballow turned to him for those ideas about speech and signification: a brief section on speech in Cumberland's treatise was concerned with sacred history and climate theories of regional and national difference rather than with signification and civil history.

104 Ballow, *Treatise of Equity*, 2; Norton and Kuehn, 'Foundations of Morality', 947.

ularly notable in the musician's elevated perception – and a capacity for virtue.[105]

Indeed, a general association between virtue and aesthetics was a significant theme in Shaftesbury's philosophy. Shaftesbury expressed such ideas in similar terms in another influential part of his *Characteristics*, the *Inquiry Concerning Virtue or Merit*:

> This too is certain, that the admiration and love of order, harmony and proportion, in whatever kind, is naturally improving to the temper, advantageous to social affection, and highly assistant to virtue, which is itself no other than the love of order and beauty in society ... if the order of the world itself appears just and beautiful, the admiration and esteem of order must run higher and the elegant passion or love of beauty, which is so advantageous to virtue, must be the more improved by its exercise in so simple and magnificent a subject. For it is impossible that such a divine order should be contemplated without ecstasy and rapture since, in the common subjects of science and the liberal arts, whatever is according to just harmony and proportion is so transporting to those who have any knowledge or practice in the kind.[106]

Shaftesbury's association with what Lawrence Klein terms a 'culture of politeness' is apparent in this passage. Like Joseph Addison and Richard Steele, Shaftesbury was a proponent of 'polite moralism', an advocate of literary endeavour and conversation as a forum for moral development.[107]

English legal culture has traditionally been regarded as the antithesis of this culture of politeness, the law's focus on the procedural, technical and adversarial seen as necessarily opposed to the refined and enlightened culture of the club and coffeehouse. And yet it is possible to demonstrate a wider concern among English legal thinkers with these terms of contemporary moral debate. Ballow's treatise is one kind of example, evidence of the influence of various trends in natural jurisprudence with regard to the question of moral obligation.[108] In addition to the ideas expressed in the *Treatise* we have evidence of citation: we know that Ballow read and quoted the works

105 Virtue linked to 'moral doctrine of decorum' or love of an ordered life. Monroe C. Beardsley, *Aesthetics from Classical Greece to the Present*, (Tuscaloosa, 1975), 70; text on music by Diogenes of Babylon. For analysis of Shaftesbury's views on aesthetics see, for example, Jerome Stolnitz, 'On the Significance of Lord Shaftesbury in Modern Aesthetic Theory', *Philosophical Quarterly*, 11, 43 (April, 1961): 97–113; Dabney Townshend, 'From Shaftesbury to Kant: The Development of the Concept of Aesthetic Experience', *Journal of the History of Ideas*, 48, 2 (April–June, 1987): 287–306; Preben Mortensen, 'Shaftesbury and the Morality of Art Appreciation', *Journal of the History of Ideas*, 55, 4 (October, 1994): 631–50.

106 Shaftesbury, *Inquiry Concerning Virtue or Merit*, in Klein ed., *Characteristics*, 191.

107 Lawrence Klein, *Shaftesbury and the Culture of Politeness: Moral Discourse and Cultural Politics in Early Eighteenth-Century England* (Cambridge, 1994).

108 See also, for example, Ballow's concern with civility and morality in his discussion

of Grotius and Pufendorf, among other philosophers. Similar indications of engagement with contemporary philosophy can be found by considering the kinds of books that other jurists purchased and studied. The libraries of Lord Chancellors Somers, Cowper, and Macclesfield, and of Judge Martin Wright, for example, included relevant contemporary works like Grotius' *De Jure Belli et Pacis*, Pufendorf's *De Jure Naturae et Gentium*, collected volumes of the *Tatler* and *Spectator*, or of the philosophical works of Fenelon. There are also examples of surviving copies of specific philosophical texts owned by lawyers, such as the copy of an abridgment of John Locke's *Essay Concerning Human Understanding* owned by the reporter and judge John Strange.[109] Finally it is notable that great numbers of lawyers appear in subscription lists appended to texts like the 1727 edition of Cumberland's treatise on natural law.

Lawyers' personal notes and letters provide another indication of this attraction to contemporary definitions of civility, passion and refinement. In a letter to a friend the lawyer and scholar Roger North, for example, turned to the language of passion and politeness when he lamented the immorality of his own time. His was an age of 'daily confirmation that knavery hath contracted a firme allegiance with Impudence', North noted, a time when morals were so reversed that wicked behaviour 'is openly professed as a virtue, and Nothing [considered] so despicable as Integrity of Mind, and manners; the barriere of shame is utterly lost, and at every Instance observable [men] doe but sneer or (as they say) laugh in their sleeves'.[110] Lawyers like North also wrote essays on philosophical topics themselves, which they circulated in manuscript as well as print.[111] Giles Jacob, for example, published a set of *Essays Relating to the Conduct of Life* (1717) which included 'Philosophical Notions, some Thoughts of Divinity, many of Morality', and employed the vocabulary of 'sociability', 'manners' and 'passion'. In these essays on topics like self-government, marriage, honesty and beauty, Jacob defined an exemplary life largely within the terms of contemporary moral-philosophical debate about the dangers of economic corruption.[112]

of the enforcement of penalties against immoral acts, like gambling, prostitution, not countenanced by law. Ballow, *Treatise of Equity*, 23ff.

109 IT, Barrington 63; HALS, Panshanger D/EP 214; FSL, 175–076q; William L. Sachse, *Lord Somers, A Political Portrait* (Manchester, 1975), 192–6; Sotheby's, *The Library of the Earls of Macclesfield Removed from Shirburn Castle*, 12 vols (London, 2004–2008).

110 FSL, V.b. 268, in *Bishop Burnet's History of his Own Time*, vol. 4 (London, 1809), letter following 208; cf also, for example, the entries on topics like friendship, virtue, music, business, charity, flattery, gratitude in Commonplace Book c.1690–1705, HALS, Panshanger D/EP F82.

111 Jamie C. Kassler, *The Honourable Roger North 1651–1734: On Life, Morality, Law and Tradition* (Farnham, 2009). And note that North, too, was particularly interested in the connections to be made between music and moral character.

112 Giles Jacob, *Essays Relating to the Conduct of Life* (London, 1717), esp. essays 7–8, 12–15; see also Jacob, *Memoirs of the Life of the Right Honourable Joseph Addison Esq.*, *Late*

Similar ideas about proper conduct, and admonitions against the contemporary erosion of moral character, surface in the discussion of covenants for gambling or for prostitution in Henry Ballow's treatise.[113] These kinds of reflections on the dangerous influence of prosperity and luxury can also be found in the preface to the popular *Legal Provisions for the Poor: Or, A Treatise of the Common and Statute Laws Concerning the Poor* (1710) a text that reached its fifth edition in 1725. Here the barrister and 'library keeper' of the Inner Temple, Samuel Carter, offered a history of charity and morality, from ancient Rome to seventeenth-century England, in a short philosophical essay that introduced his ensuing 'methodical guide for justices of peace, church-wardens, and overseers'.[114]

A final, important example is *A Discourse Concerning Generosity*, another text composed by a legal thinker who was fully engaged with contemporary moral-philosophical trends. The likely author was the prominent judge John Somers. Somers was accomplished as a man of letters, and man of law and politics, by the time this treatise first appeared in print in 1693. More than a decade earlier he had written two important Exclusion tracts, *A Brief History of the Succession to the Crown of England* (1680) and *The Security of Englishmen's Lives, or, The Trust, Power, and Duty of the Grand Juries of England* (1681), and had a hand in the composition of a third, *A Just and Modest Vindication of the Proceedings of the Two Last Parliaments* (1681). In those early years of his political career Somers also pursued literary endeavours, contributing translations of ancient prose and verse to new editions of Plutarch's *Lives* (1683–86) and Ovid's *Epistles* (1680).[115] At the Revolution Somers was active in the Convention, helping to draft the Declaration of

One of his Majesty's Principal Secretaries of State. With a Particular Account of his Writings (London, 1719).

113 Ballow, *Treatise of Equity*, 24–26. On contemporary expressions of suspicions about gambling see Hoppit, 'Attitudes to Credit', 309, 313.

114 Samuel Carter, *Legal Provisions for the Poor: Or, a Treatise of the Common and Statute Laws Concerning the Poor either as to Relief, Settlement, or Punishment* (London, 1710), preface. Carter published other works on mortgage and conveyancing, and a volume of reports from the reign of Charles II. Stuart Handley, 'Carter, Samuel', *ODNB*. He may also have been the translator of Jacques Cassagnes' *A Moral Treatise upon Valour* published in 1695: the title of a copy FSL C 1215.2, records that the text was 'Done into English by Mr. Carter, of the Inner-Temple. Licensed, Aug. 15. 1694. Edw. Cooke', but another edition dated 1694, Wing 133:10 (and with differences in the dedication, title page and text pagination) is attributed to Samuel Compton.

115 Campbell, *Lives of the Lord Chancellors*, vol. 5, 65–8; Sachse, *Lord Somers*, 15–19. One of Somers' verse translations was of Ovid's *Dido to Aeneas*, that lament later used to characterise, and critique, Spencer Cowper's relationship with Sarah Stout. Somers' Exclusion tracts were subsequently reprinted in numerous editions throughout the eighteenth century: the *Brief History of the Succession* was published again in 1689 and 1714 (and also appeared in a Dutch translation in 1689), while the *Security of Englishmen's Lives* saw at least six new English editions, as well as some North American editions, from the 1680s to the early 1770s.

Rights; a subsequent defence of the Revolution Settlement, *A Vindication of the Proceedings of the Late Parliament of England* (1690), has been attributed to him as well.[116] And Somers continued to write, and to engage with philosophical and literary as well as political affairs, even as he took on increased governing responsibility after 1689 as a central member of the Whig Junto. One indication of these commitments is the fact that Somers was a member of the Kit Cat Club and became a fellow of the Royal Society in 1698, serving as president of that body 1698–1703.

In addition to *A Discourse Concerning Generosity*, Somers is suspected to have authored several texts on domestic politics and foreign affairs published in the 1690s and early 1700s.[117] John Somers 'wrote many things which are not published in his Name', Joseph Addison later explained when eulogising his friend. This tendency towards anonymity was, according to Addison, an indication that Somers was more interested in advancing the public good, and avoiding 'vainglory', than in garnering fame for himself.[118] Even though 'it is to be lamented, that this extraordinary Person, … wrote several Pieces, as well as performed several Actions, which he did not assume the Honour of,' Addison insisted, '…no Author of the greatest Eminence would deny my Lord *Somers* to have been the best writer of the Age in which he lived.'[119] Of course Addison's claims for his friend's (and patron's) literary skills, do not stand as sufficient proof that *A Discourse Concerning Generosity* can be counted as part of Somers' wider output. A better indication of Somers' authorship of this text is to be found, first, in a manuscript notation on a copy of the second, 1695, edition held by the British Library. The phrase 'Lord Somers, some say', is written in the same hand as that likely noting the book's owner in 1705, 'Kath: Blount'. Perhaps this Katherine Blount was a relation of Elizabeth Fanshawe Blount, a married woman who lived in Somers' Hertfordshire household and served, many suspected, as his mistress.[120] If this Katherine Blount did enjoy some closer connection

116 Sachse, *Lord Somers*, 29–37; Rudolph, *Revolution by Degrees*, 103, 195 n. 47.

117 *Jus Regium; Or the King's Right to Grant Forfeitures and other Revenues of the Crown* (London, 1701), *Jura Populi Anglicani; Or the Subjects Right of Petitioning Set Forth* (London, 1701), *Anguis in Herba: Or, the Fatal Consequences of a Treaty with France* (London, 1702) and *A Letter Balancing the Necessity of Keeping a Land Force in Times of Peace, With the Dangers that may Follow on it* (London, 1697) are said to be Somers'. Somers' biographer admits only the first two attributions: Sachse, *Lord Somers*, 160, 180. See also Lois Schwoerer, *No Standing Armies! The Antiarmy Ideology in Seventeenth-Century England* (Baltimore, 1974).

118 Joseph Addison, *Prodesse Quam Conspice*, No. 39, Friday May 4, 1716, in *The Freeholder, Or Political Essays* (London, 1716), 229. Addison uses Somers' own motto as the title for this essay.

119 Ibid., 228.

120 Sachse, *Lord Somers*, 68. Not only did Delariviere Manley's *New Atlantis* and Swift's *Examiner* spread this rumour, but an anonymous broadside *Fathers Nown Child* referred to it as early as 1694, verses 17–18. The identification of this Katherine Blount, and attribu-

to Somers' household, she might have had sound reasons for acknowledging his authorship. Yet as Somers' biographer William Sachse notes, the British Library catalogue does not credit this work to Somers, although the Wing Catalogue does; Sachse follows Peter Laslett in remaining uncertain about authorship but other scholars like John Marshall and David M. Turner attribute the text to Somers, and most library catalogues similarly follow Wing's attribution.[121]

Second, and equally important, the *Discourse Concerning Generosity* fits with John Somers' intellectual and political engagements in these years. Somers had become lord keeper in 1693 (as we know he heard the cause concerning Elizabeth Took and Sir Robert Atkyns in this capacity in 1695), and would be elevated to the position of lord chancellor in 1697. As foremost equity judge Somers would have been preoccupied with questions regarding natural law and moral obligation which are the central issues of this text. The *Discourse Concerning Generosity* aims to 'engage Men to the sincere Love and Practice of Vertue and Goodness' by exploring principles of nature through the little-studied concept of generosity.[122]

It must be granted, Somers explains in his preface, that in leading men to virtue one should work with man's natural sense of ambition and self-esteem, honour and shame, hope and fear, since such passions can be harnessed for good, producing in men 'good and forcible Motives to Virtue'.[123] Somers adds that the diversity of men's 'dispositions' justifies this approach: 'if the Arguments or Motives of the one sort do not take fast hold of Men, those of the other sort peradventure may'.[124] Yet Somers is aware that in playing upon the passions, and offering calculations of hope and fear, he might be laying himself open to criticism, and perhaps to charges of Hobbism. It was Descartes however, Somers explains, who served as the major inspiration for this treatise: Descartes' 'lively tho' short Description … of Generosity' in his *Passions of the Soul* (Paris 1649, London 1650) provides the starting point for Somers' treatise.[125] The significance of Somers' reference to, and reliance on,

tion of the *Discourse* to Somers, is uncertain because of other, later materials on the front boards of this copy.

121 The notation of Somers' authorship can be clearly viewed in the reproduction of the British Library copy available through *Early English Books Online*. Compare John Harrison and Peter Laslett, *The Library of John Locke* (Oxford, 1965), 141, 236; John Marshall, *John Locke: Religion, Resistance, Responsibility* (Cambridge, 1994), 159; David M. Turner, *Fashioning Adultery: Gender, Sex and Civility in England 1660–1740* (Cambridge, 2002), 64.

122 John Somers, A *Discourse Concerning Generosity* (London, 1695), A2r. Campbell's assessment of Somers' lord chancellorship emphasises Somers' contribution in establishing civil law principles and doctrines especially with regard to legacies, trusts and charities. Campbell, *Lives of the Lord Chancellors*, vol. 5, 97.

123 Somers, *Discourse Concerning Generosity*, preface, A3v.

124 Ibid., A4v.

125 Ibid., A5r.

Descartes is threefold. First, it signals his agreement with Descartes' claim that generosity is key to the question of morality since it 'is of so very extensive a Nature that it does in a sort pervade the whole Body of Morality'.[126] Second, the open appeal to Descartes demonstrates that Somers expressed some interest in what scholars often define as typically enlightened ideas about human progress and perfectability.[127] And finally, it fits with Somers' preoccupation throughout the text with the question of the proper balance between passion and reason – a preoccupation, again, that scholars regard not only as typical of seventeenth-century moral philosophy, but also as a crucial factor that 'paved the way for the transformations in moral and psychological thinking known as the Enlightenment'.[128]

Much of Somers' discussion reinforces the idea that human actions are founded upon a divinely-given law of nature, known to humans through reason. Religion itself is defined as 'the Law of the rational Nature, or the complex of these Laws which are given by God Almighty unto Mankind for the Government of their Lives and Actions'.[129] Man's exercise of the virtue of generosity must also be acknowledged to have its roots in an 'intellectual power of the soul', Somers avers. The operation of generosity entailed the passions, to be sure, but in its best or 'more large and comprehensive' sense generosity should be understood as 'a general principle of the rational nature and the fruitful parent of many particular virtues'.[130] Similarly justice, one of these particular virtues, is defined as 'a constant and uniform purpose of giving to everyone his due' and understood to be a universal principle, here associated with the Aristotelian concept of distributive justice developed by jusnaturalists like Cumberland, Pufendorf and, later, Ballow.[131]

While such natural and universal principles may be known to all rational men, however, they must be practised, Somers insisted. Here as elsewhere Somers points to the importance of conceiving of virtuous actions in their social context. Further, he alludes to the significance of experience or past practice to the definition of a moral good. And he relies upon contemporary

126 Descartes' claim is quoted by Amy M. Schmitter, '17th and 18th Century Theories of Emotions', Edward N. Zalta ed., *The Stanford Encyclopedia of Philosophy (Fall 2008 Edition)*, http://plato.stanford.edu/archives/fall2008/entries/emotions-17th18th/.

127 See, for example, Peter A. Schouls, *Descartes and the Enlightenment* (Kingston, Ont., 1989).

128 Susan James, 'Reason, the Passions and the Good Life', in Garber and Ayers eds, *Cambridge History of Seventeenth-Century Philosophy*, vol. 2, 1391.

129 Somers, *Discourse Concerning Generosity*, 6, part of an association made between definitions of honour and religion; see his further discussion of honour and divine/natural law, 44–6.

130 Ibid., 18–19; also 12.

131 Ibid., 80. In addition to Somers' interest in and study of ancient authors (evident for example in his work on editions of Plutarch and Ovid), Somers read widely in civil law. Sachse notes that his library catalogue 'lists nearly 300 printed works under the heading "Jus civilis"'. Sachse, *Lord Somers*, 13.

understanding of man's instinct for sociability, as well as instinct for self-preservation, in order to explicate the nature of justice and generosity.[132] For Somers, like other moralists of the time, David Turner notes, '[g]enerosity was central to the principle of benevolent sociability that was at the core of emerging notions of politeness'.[133] Somers even articulates that idea of a connection between reason, love of virtue and aesthetic appreciation that, we have seen, became such an important part of Shaftesbury's philosophy of moral sense.

> But further: because it is found that Men are naturally bent to desire and prosecute those things which appear to be lovely and amiable; It seemeth proper, that we should likewise take all fit Occasions to contemplate and represent to our selves the amiable nature of this Vertue of Generosity; that as it is very beautiful in it self, so it may appear, in a lively manner such to our Minds.... Nor will Generosity appear to us Lovely, as it is, unless we turn the Eyes of our Minds towards it. It is necessary therefore ... to observe, how beautiful it appears to be in such as exercise it in a just manner; what a Charm and Engagement it carries with it; how Decent, how Venerable, how Agreeable to our best Thoughts, it is. By this means we shall be inspired with the Love and Admiration of it, and consequently be engaged to pursue it with Vigour.[134]

The *Discourse Concerning Generosity* as a whole is suffused with these languages of reason and passion, sociability and civility.[135]

This philosophy of politeness and emphasis on sociability clearly informed Somers' understanding of justice as distributive, as a universal principle of 'giving to everyone his due'. For the generous man, Somers explains, 'is not content to do strict Justice to other men; But chuseth to render them more than what is in strictness due, rather than less'. Here the principle of justice expands with the identification between equity and generosity. The generous man, Somers continues, is equitable: he 'relaxes and qualifies, as far as he lawfully may, what is rigorous and extreme; and exerciseth Justice with that Moderation and Equity which is indeed the Flower and perfection of it'.[136] Somers articulates that conventional idea of equity perfecting or fulfilling the common law, and depicts the equitable judge, in the guise of the generous man, balancing rigid tradition with individual mercy. As we have seen, these ideas and images will be repeated by later authors like Ballow and Francis as part of a mixed conception of justice. It is worth

132 See also the sections on self-preservation, procreation, happiness, self-esteem, and on the habits and performance of virtues, Somers, *Discourse Concerning Generosity*, 35–7, 49–50, 136–40.

133 Turner, *Fashioning Adultery*, 64.

134 Somers, *Discourse Concerning Generosity*, 141–2.

135 Ibid., 16, 69, 62–5, 129–30 for sections on 'civility' in particular.

136 Ibid., 81; cf 88–89.

noting, too, that Somers points to the particular merits of fidelity in trusts, and gratitude towards creditors or benefactors, as other aspects of this equitable justice.[137]

Broadly speaking, ideas about natural law, and the articulation of a theory of a social contract underpinning legal government, permeate Somers' other, political, treatises. There are exceptions of course: for example, Somers depicts justice simply as the preservation of custom and common law, and denies that salutary mixture of rigid tradition and individual conscience, in the *Vindication of the Proceedings of the Late Parliament of England*, a polemical defence of just resistance to illegitimate authority.[138] However, given his general political-theoretical commitments, and given his responsibilities as chief officer of the state's highest equity court, it is not surprising that Somers was interested in further reflection on natural law, that 'sociality principle', and contemporary discussion about the grounds of moral obligation.

In addition to the works he composed, certain holdings in John Somers' vast library also signal interest in these areas of moral-philosophical debate, and point to his familiarity with contemporary languages of passion and reason. Somers amassed a collection of over nine thousand printed texts, hundreds of manuscripts, and thousands of drawings and prints.[139] Books on English law, British history, and civil law accounted for a sizable portion of the collection, but works of literature, philosophy, philology, geography, ancient and modern history, natural history, medicine and mathematics were all well-represented. The greatest number of books, Somers' biographer William Sachse notes with some surprise, were those classified as 'theological, where we have upwards of 1300 entries'.[140] These 'theological' books, much like those classified as works of philosophy and literature, included texts that engaged with contemporary questions about morality, sociability and civility. One interesting example is Somers' ownership of the *Essays*

137 Ibid., 82.

138 John Somers, A *Vindication of the Proceedings of the Late Parliament of England* (London, 1690), 13–14. The full passage reads as follows: 'Our happiness then consists in this, that our Princes are tied up to the Law, as well as we, and upon an especial account obliged to keep it up in its full force; because if they destroyed the Law, they destroy at the same time themselves, by overthrowing the very Foundation of their Kingly Grandeur, and Regal Power: So that, our Government not being Arbitrary, but Legal, not Absolute, but Political, our Princes can never become Arbitrary, Absolute, or Tyrants, without forfeiting at the same time their Royal Character, by the breach of the essential Conditions of their Regal Power, which are to act according to the ancient Customs and standing Laws of this Nation.'

139 Sachse, *Lord Somers*, 192, 196.

140 Ibid., 193, and 207 n. 22 where Sachse points out that the first thirty-eight folios of the 142 which listed entries under theologia are missing from Somers' catalogue. Sachse's recounting of the contents of the library also indicates that the holdings in English law, British history, and civil law together totaled something like 900 texts.

upon Several Moral Subjects (1698) written by the controversial nonjuror Jeremy Collier.[141] These essays dealt with subjects like pride, covetousness, pleasure and reason. Here Somers would have encountered a contribution to contemporary discourse about passion, desire and corruption, incorporated within a critique of a post-1689 Whig economy and politics. Two other men who became influential equity judges also had access to these works and these debates: Joseph Jekyll, Somers' brother-in-law, and master of the rolls 1717–1738, and Philip Yorke, later Earl of Hardwicke, husband of Somers' niece, and lord chancellor 1737–1756, jointly inherited the bulk of Somers' library.[142]

Finally, Lord Chancellor Somers engaged with contemporary moral-philosophical debate as an active participant in London's literary and club culture. As a principal member of the Whig Kit Cat Club, Somers spent much time in conversation with other members, such as the literary lights Joseph Addison and William Congreve, the influential London bookseller Jacob Tonson, and Whig party leaders like Thomas Wharton and Robert Walpole.[143] These men were political and cultural figures who pursued wit and politeness at the same time as they argued over military policies or impeachment proceedings. The club was another venue where legal arguments and legal theories were entertained, and a place where judges like Somers encountered new ideas and cultural trends. Recognition of the importance of patronage relationships in the club is even more important in understanding the nature of these encounters, or this influence. The Kit Cat Club was 'a place – perhaps *the* place in London, and hence in the nation, where patron, collector and writer…could meet on something like an equal footing', Sachse asserts. John Somers was a valued patron for many influential eighteenth-century writers, as well as a collector of their works, and an author himself. The list of men who thus acknowledged Somers' patronage is long and includes poets and essayists, like Joseph Addison and Jonathan

141 John Somers' copy of Jeremy Collier, *Essays upon Several Moral Subjects: In Two Parts*, 3rd edn (London, 1698) is held by the Folger Shakespeare Library, FSL 259–731q. The appearance on the front boards of Somers' armorial bookplate indicates his ownership; there are no manuscript notes in the text. This was the third edition of Collier's essays; further corrected editions continued to be published in the first decades of the eighteenth century.

142 Sachse, *Lord Somers*, 196. See also Richard Cooksey, *Essay Upon the Life and Character of John Lord Somers, Baron of Evesham: Also Sketches of an Essay on the Life and Character of Philip Earl of Hardwicke. Proposed to be inserted in a Compendious History of Worcestershire* (London, 1791). This late eighteenth-century assessment of Somers and Hardwicke gives some indication of the ways in which the reputation of the common law, and its assimilation into ideas about 'Enlightenment liberty and constitution', was effected.

143 Sachse, *Lord Somers*, 189–91; Brewer, *The Pleasures of the Imagination*, 40–4; Abigail Williams, *Poetry and the Creation of a Whig Literary Culture, 1681–1714* (Oxford, 2005), ch. 6.

Swift, and historians, poets and philosophers, like Thomas Madox, John Dennis and Anthony Ashley Cowper, Third Earl of Shaftesbury.[144]

Somers' relationship with Shaftesbury is particularly interesting because it sheds light on some of those different ways – professional, political, personal – that Lord Somers engaged with contemporary ideas about morality and law. Somers was, first, a patron for the philosopher, and their correspondence is taken up with news about Shaftesbury's works in draft and reactions to his works in print. These surviving letters are evidence of Somers' continued interest in literature and philosophy, but at the same time they bear witness to contemporary doubt about the proper relationship between philosophy and politics. So, for example, Shaftesbury praised Somers by contrasting his actions with those of a younger generation of prominent men who were addicted to 'gallantry and pleasure', and who neglected philosophy and the higher pursuit of true happiness.[145] Yet this admiration for Somers was tinged with uneasiness since, as Shaftesbury later admitted, a dedication to philosophy, willingness to stake out a position in current moral-philosophical debates, or open affiliation with a philosopher, could be controversial for a statesman.[146]

Shaftesbury and Somers were well aware of the potential for controversy, and the relevance of moral-philosophical debate to public life, because a concern with morals and manners had played a role in Lord Somers' impeachment in 1701. The articles of impeachment against Lord Chancellor Somers had detailed charges that were strongly political in nature and he was clearly held accountable, along with other government ministers, for the perceived failures of Williamite foreign policy. Yet there was also a marked emphasis in these impeachment proceedings on the moral danger of economic and religious corruption. Somers and others were vilified for the benefits they received through the perquisites of office and through additional monetary expressions of royal favour. Moreover, this critique of corruption was linked to a defence of common law tradition and practice: Somers was attacked, for example, by critics who said his rulings in Chancery encroached upon the Exchequer's jurisdiction, undermined security of property, and unjustly enriched Somers and his associates.[147] Contemporary

144 Sachse, *Lord Somers*, 198.

145 Shaftesbury, Letter to Lord Somers, 20 October 1705, in Benjamin Rand ed., *The Life, Unpublished Letters and Philosophical Regimen of Anthony, Earl of Shaftesbury*, (London, 1992), 337.

146 Ibid., 386–7, 394–5, 400–2, 420–1, 430–2, letters of 12 July 1708, 10 December 1708, 2 June 1709, 26 May 1710, 30 March 1711.

147 *Proceedings in Parliament against William Earl of Portland, John Lord Sommers, Edward Earl of Orford and Charles Lord Halifax upon an Impeachment for High Crimes and Misdemeanors*, in Sollom Emlyn ed., *A Complete Collection of State Trials and Proceedings for High Treason and other Crimes and Misdemeanors*, vol. 5 (London, 1730), 339–83, see especially 350–6. Among the charges was also one for aiding and abetting the actions of Captain Kidd, to the 'detriment' of trade and 'prejudice' of merchants.

criticism of Somers also called upon moral-philosophical debate when it focused upon his alleged adultery, sexual libertinism and religious heterodoxy.[148]

Although these impeachment proceedings ended in acquittal, Somers was removed from the bench and remained out of office for several years. Throughout this period of political and professional adversity the philosopher and the judge maintained their friendship. Shaftesbury employed the languages of civility and morality in letters that denounced the trial and removal of Somers from the bench as an 'ungrateful service' suffered. And Shaftesbury continued to praise Somers for maintaining his commitment to virtue and public service even after 1701. He urged Somers to enjoy the 'liberty of mind' and 'command of passion' characteristic of true fame and philosophical good.[149] In these letters, and in his publications, Shaftesbury expressed central tenets of his philosophy of moral sense, especially ideas about the quality and control of the human passions, that remained influential in the development of moral-philosophical debate in the first few decades of the eighteenth century.

It is not surprising, then, that when another lord chancellor was impeached in 1725 Shaftesbury's philosophy was deemed particularly relevant. This lord chancellor, Thomas Parker, Earl of Macclesfield, was, like his predecessor John Somers, a man of letters and a friend of philosophers. Macclesfield was, in fact, particularly close to an outspoken *critic* of the Earl of Shaftesbury: the controversial physician-philosopher, Bernard Mandeville. As the following chapter will demonstrate, contemporary characterisations of the relationship between Lord Chancellor Macclesfield and Dr Mandeville and, more broadly, the contemporary critique of Macclesfield's actions, provide a compelling example of the ways in which Enlightenment debates regarding luxury and eighteenth-century debates about common law justice were wholly intertwined.

148 Sachse, *Lord Somers*, 67–8.

149 Shaftesbury, Letters of 20 October 1705 and 2 June 1709, in Rand ed., *Life, Unpublished Letters*, 336–341, 400–2.

6

Common Law and the Morality of Markets

Among the numerous volumes on law in the Macclesfield library at Shirburn Castle – a library that, by 1750, housed tens of thousands of books and manuscripts, in multiple languages, on topics such as economics, science, mathematics, theology, music and architecture as well as law – there was a bound collection of three texts on Chancery and equity.[1] Robert Atkyns' *Enquiry into the Jurisdiction of Chancery in Causes of Equity … and The Case of the said Sir Robert Atkyns upon his Appeal*, Richard Francis' *Maxims of Equity*, and Henry Ballow's *A Treatise of Equity* were gathered together in a folio volume encased in a handsome nineteenth-century binding.[2] This was likely a rebinding of tracts originally collected by the first Earl of Macclesfield, Thomas Parker, chief justice of the Kings Bench (1710–1718) and lord chancellor (1718–1725), and his son George Parker, second Earl of Macclesfield, noted politician and astronomer. As we have seen, these tracts differed in terms of genre and style, and they presented varied perspectives on the jurisdiction of equity, and the nature of law in general. Not only do they provide further evidence of continued debate over common law and equity, and of the conjoined development of common law and natural law theory in the eighteenth century, but their juxtaposition in Macclesfield's library may also be said to indicate the vitality of jurisprudential reflection on law and morality.[3]

1 'Tracts on the Chancery 1695–1737', lot #3038, *Library of the Earls of Macclesfield, Part Eight: Theology, Philosophy, Law and Economics*, 354. On the Macclesfield library and sale see Quarrie, 'Scientific Library of the Earls of Macclesfield'; Quarrie, Introduction, *Library of the Earls of Macclesfield, Part One: Natural History*, 8–21; Carol Vogel, 'Inside Art', *New York Times*, 20 February 2004; Marcus Binney, 'Future Unknown for Castle with Secret Past', *The Times*, 17 January 2005.

2 'Binding: nineteenth century half calf, red morocco label'; possibly bound by the third earl of Macclesfield. *Library of the Earls of Macclesfield, Part One*, 19, 21, *Part Eight*, 354. The catalogue also indicates that the Atkyns text includes some manuscript notes. While Atkyns' (1695) and Francis' (1727) texts were published in the lord chancellor's lifetime, Ballow's (1737) text was published five years after the lord chancellor's death.

3 Compare also lot # 2755, 'Law, works in English', *Library of the Earls of Macclesfield, Part Eight*, 182, which combined Claude-Joseph de Ferriere, *The History of the Roman or Civil Law … Translated into English* (1724), Robert Gardiner, *Ars Clericialis: the Art of Conveyancing explain'd* (1698), John Herne, *The Law of Conveyances* (1658), Giles Jacob,

Indeed, in his reading habits and intellectual interests, and in his personal and professional fortunes, Macclesfield exemplifies the interplay between legal thought, moral philosophy and the movement for moral reform that is a primary focus of this chapter, as well as the last. There is evidence of responsiveness to philosophical and theological debate, for example, in Macclesfield's engagement with contemporary ideas about the nature of reason. His attraction to both empirical and axiomatic demonstration is indicated by his friendship with, and patronage of, men like Edmond Halley, Isaac Newton and William Jones; by his election to the Royal Society; and by his impressive collection of books on mathematics, science and natural history.[4] The implications of rationalism and empiricism for theology were also of interest to Macclesfield and he was apparently sympathetic to the defenders of rational, as opposed to revealed, religion. His patronage of 'freethinking controversialists', like John Toland and Pierre Desmaizeaux, further encouraged the impression that Macclesfield was somewhat radical in his views, tending towards deism or even atheism.[5] Macclesfield also exemplifies English legal culture's engagement with questions about passions and pleasures, virtue and vice. His close familiarity with men like Bernard Mandeville is one indication of his involvement in such contemporary discussion. And his impeachment for corruption and venality in 1725 provides another, especially interesting, example of legal and political debate over 'private vices and public benefits' that stood at the centre of eighteenth-century moral-philosophical discourse. Here Macclesfield provides an important example of the practical impact of legal conflicts and philosophical concerns.

Macclesfield's experiences and intellectual commitments serve further as a valuable reminder of the many different facets of eighteenth-century philosophy. First, they remind us of the variety of arguments – among them rationalist, empiricist, sentimental – made in the course of reflection on questions about natural law and moral obligation in this period. Macclesfield's association with rational religion, and his role in debates over luxury, self-interest and civility, highlight the philosophical, theological and political implications of these debates. These debates about moral behaviour and

A Treatise of Laws: or, a General Introduction to the Common, Civil and Canon Law (1721), and John Rastell, *Les Terms de la Ley* (1685).

4 A.A. Hanham, 'Parker, Thomas, first earl of Macclesfield', *ODNB*; Quarrie, 'Scientific Library of the Earls of Macclesfield', 8–9, 11–16.

5 'Parker, Thomas', *ODNB*; Wilfrid Prest, 'Law, Lawyers and Rational Dissent', in Haakonssen ed., *Enlightenment and Religion*, 173–82. Quarrie, Introduction, *Library of the Earls of Macclesfield, Part Eight*, 8–13, focuses particularly on the Earl's ownership of works on toleration – for example, the works of Giordano Bruno and Michael Servetus. For political and philosophical aspects of the 'atheism' charge similarly made against Bernard Mandeville, John Trenchard and Thomas Gordon, see Annie Mitchell, 'Character of an Independent Whig – "Cato" and Bernard Mandeville', *History of European Ideas*, 29, 3 (September, 2003), 296.

obligation were also, of course, of concern to the broad-based movement for moral reform, and emerged in the activities and ideas of members of such societies as much as in the pages of philosophical discourse. Macclesfield's role as an emblem of moral decay and corruption thus points to the sociolegal implications of these debates: the Religious Societies, Societies for the Reformation of Manners, Society for the Propagation of the Gospel in Foreign Parts and the Society for the Promotion of Christian Knowledge are another facet of eighteenth-century sociability, and Enlightenment practices, that are relevant for understanding the development of moral philosophy and jurisprudence.[6] Finally, Macclesfield reminds us that in England ideas about morality and justice were expressed within those contexts of jurisdictional controversy and the critique of equity; and that in the course of such controversies legal philosophy developed in conjunction with other philosophical trends. Lord Chancellor Macclesfield is an important figure because he was clearly engaged, both practically and philosophically, in many of these debates. As we have seen, other judges and legal writers, like John Somers, Giles Jacob or Henry Ballow also provide evidence of such engagement. But as Macclesfield's library suggests, and his impeachment demonstrates, the lord chancellor especially confounds and challenges any simple definitions of law, Enlightenment, or of the relationship between them. He gives new meaning to the motto he employed – the one later adopted by Immanuel Kant – *Sapere Aude*!

Charges, common law and crime

In the spring of 1725, Lord Chancellor Macclesfield was publicly accused of financial misconduct that was motivated, it was said, by a rapacious greed. The details of this misconduct were elaborated in the twenty-one articles of impeachment exhibited before the House of Lords concerning the disgraced lord chancellor.[7] Prominent among the details were the main charges of extortion, abuse of trust, encouragement of risky investment with court funds by his subordinates, and orchestration of a cover-up when such investment led to embezzlement, culminating in a programme of perjury and deceit. Macclesfield had already resigned his office on 4 January 1724/5, in the face of mounting criticism and in the aftermath of an investigation undertaken

6 Margaret Hunt, *The Middling Sort: Commerce, Gender and the Family in England 1680–1780* (Berkeley, 1996), 103–4, on moral reform and 'club culture'.

7 'House of Lords Journal Volume 22: May 1725, 1–10', *Journal of the House of Lords: Volume 22: 1722–1726*, British History Online, http://www.british-history.ac.uk/report.aspx?compid=113815. All twenty-one articles of impeachment were laid out on the opening day of trial, and are recorded in *The Trial of Thomas Earl of Macclesfield, Lord High Chancellor of Great Britain, before the House of Lords, for High Crimes and Misdemeanors in the Execution of his Office, State Trials*, vol. 16, 768–84.

by a committee of the Privy Council (and prompted by Walpole), into his Chancery masters' accounts. Upon Macclefield's resignation, Master of the Rolls Joseph Jekyll became first commissioner of the great seal, taking on this responsibility along with fellow commissioners Geoffrey Gilbert and Robert Raymond, until a new chancellor could be appointed.[8] From February to May the nature of proceeding was debated by Lords and Commons, Chancery masters were interrogated by special committee, and the articles of impeachment drawn up. Over the course of the month of May the House of Lords sat for thirteen full days, presided over by their Speaker Peter King, in order to try the case for impeachment brought before them by the Managers of the House of Commons. The trial ended on Thursday 27 May with a unanimous vote: Macclesfield was found guilty of 'taking of several of the Masters in *Chancery* very great and exorbitant Sums of Money, for their Admission into their respective Offices'.[9] Moreover, it was found that not only did Macclesfield frequently sell the office of Chancery master, but he also allowed unfit men – men who could not afford the price of office – to pay for their places out of suitors' assets held by their predecessors in office. It was the revelation that some of these masters had speculated with suitors' monies in the hopes of making up the difference in their suitors' accounts (as well as enriching themselves) that led to the initial investigations. When these masters' accounts suffered losses because of failed investments, caused especially by the bursting of South Sea Bubble, Lord Chancellor Macclesfield tried to conceal the problem. He sought to make up the missing monies out of other masters' funds as a way to prevent an enquiry.[10]

The underlying fraud consisted in this scheme that depended upon a steady stream of deposits, here suitors' fees and assets, in order to pay for those offices. Had subsequent investment of these assets been successful the

[8] Edmund Heward, 'The Early History of the Court Funds Office', *The Journal of Legal History*, 4, 1 (1983): 50; Holdsworth, *History of English Law*, vol. 12, 204–5; Foss, *Judges of England*, vol. 8, 32, 130–1, 157. The commissioners served from 7 January to 1 June, when Peter King was appointed lord chancellor. Reports of Macclesfield's resignation, and of the placing of the seal in the hands of Commissioners Jekyll, Raymond and Gilbert, appeared in a number of contemporary periodicals, including the *Daily Post*, *Daily Journal*, *Weekly Journal*, and *Dublin Gazette*.

[9] 'The Trial of Thomas Earl of Macclesfield', in Thomas Salmon ed., *A New Abridgement and Critical Review of the State Trials*, vol. 1 (Dublin, 1737), 874. A L30,000 fine was imposed, which Macclesfield apparently had paid in full by 11 August 1725. G.E. Aylmer, 'From Office-Holding to Civil Service: The Genesis of Modern Bureaucracy', *Transactions of the Royal Historical Society*, fifth series, 30 (1980): 99 n. 24, citing the notes of Lord Chancellor King, in Peter, First Lord King, 'Notes of Domestic and Foreign Affairs during the last years of the reign of George I and the early part of George II', appended to the second volume of Peter, Seventh Lord King, *The Life of John Locke* (London, 1830). See also Holdsworth, *History of English Law*, vol. 12, 205.

[10] Heward, 'Early History Court Funds Office', 46–48; Holdsworth, *History of English Law*, vol. 12, 206; *Trial of Thomas Earl of Macclesfield*, 778–9, 1070, 1074–80.

scheme might have worked, but the fraud was exposed when more suitors sought to reclaim their monies than could be accommodated by the existing assets in the masters' accounts.[11] The general economic and political crisis caused by losses suffered in the South Sea Bubble is clearly an important context for this particular crisis in Chancery. In the aftermath of the market crash there were calls for vengeance against corrupt ministers, duplicitous company directors, and other well-placed men who had profited from speculating in the market before the bubble burst. Macclesfield was not accused of illicit speculation himself. He had purchased South Sea stocks in the third subscription of June 1720 at the peak of the bubble, and authorised the sale of his stock in August 1723 when prices had already fallen, so it is not clear that he aimed to 'ride the bubble'.[12] But Macclesfield became an emblem of such greed, gambling and deceit. Since he had already resigned from the chancellorship, impeachment was seized upon as a way for opponents to embarrass Whig ministers, but it was also a way for those ministers to preserve their own power by offering up a scapegoat.

Scholars generally characterise Macclesfield's fall from power, then, as an episode in Whig politics, part of ministerial rivalries and reshuffling in the period of Robert Walpole's ascent to power.[13] The actions of Serjeant Thomas Pengelly, one of the principal prosecution managers of this impeachment, can be regarded as an example of some of these party interests at work. Pengelly was likely motivated to oust Macclesfield out of a sense of both professional and political rivalry. First, Pengelly was excluded from the centre of Walpolean power because of his close association with the independent Whig Somerset, and so may have been looking for some measure of political advantage. In addition, earlier in his career Pengelly

[11] Note that soon after Lord Chancellor Macclesfield resigned this kind of complaint about a deficiency in the accounts was made in a petition to the House of Commons by 'the Earl of Oxford and Lord Morpeth, as guardians of the person and estate of Elizabeth Duchess Dowager of Montagu, a lunatic'. Heward, 'Early History Court Funds Office', 50. Morpeth acted as one of the prosecutors in the trial, opening the nineteenth article of impeachment during the fourth day of the trial. *Trial of Thomas Earl of Macclesfield*, 1025–32. Calculations regarding these deficiencies, and payments directed to make up the funds, continued after the trial. CUL, Cholmondeley (Houghton), 65 29 fol. 3.

[12] John Carswell, *The South Sea Bubble* (Stanford, 1960), 161; FSL, Carson Collection Letters, Form for the Sale or Transfer of Stock, D.S. August 27 1723.

[13] Wilfred Prest, 'Judicial Corruption in Early Modern England', *Past & Present*, 133 (November, 1991): 89 describing this as a 'party-political' case; Aylmer, 'From Office-Holding to Civil Service', 98 n. 19; Shimon Shetreet, *Judges on Trial: A Study of the Appointment and Accountability of the English Judiciary* (Amsterdam, 1976), 128. Walpole had initially supported Macclesfield's promotion to the office of lord chancellor, to replace William Cowper; Joseph Jekyll was similarly 'cultivated' by Walpole. David Lemmings, 'Lord Chancellor Cowper and the Whigs, 1714–16', *Parliamentary History*, 9, 1 (May, 1990): 165–8. On Walpolean politics and the Bubble see also Patrick Kelly, '"Industry and Virtue versus Luxury and Corruption": Berkeley, Walpole and the South Sea Crisis', *Eighteenth-Century Ireland*, 7 (1992): 57–74.

had unsuccessfully jostled for preferment and place with Macclesfield's favourite Philip Yorke, and lingering resentment against Macclesfield would have added to the sweetness of revenge in orchestrating this impeachment. Indeed Yorke, who was attorney general in 1725, also acted according to the dictates of preference as much as legal principle when he refused to participate in the impeachment of Macclesfield, his friend and mentor.[14] Finally, in mounting this prosecution, Pengelly acted upon other motives as well as he sought to respond to the real challenges presented by the economic crisis of 1720. Pengelly was engaged as counsel to the Bank of England, and to trustees who were charged with managing the estates of delinquent South Sea Company directors. He was also conspicuously involved in committees of inquiry and in drafting legislation aimed at protecting investors and punishing unethical speculators. Of course here too such principled reprisals that Pengelly advocated sometimes conveniently coincided with his own professional interests in serving his clients. For example, Pengelly's anti-corruption efforts to expel the swindling businessman and MP John Ward from the Commons were part of his work on behalf of one of Ward's legal adversaries, the dowager duchess of Buckingham.[15]

Pengelly's legislative and prosecutorial activities, including the impeachment trial of Lord Chancellor Macclesfield, tell us about politics, patronage and corruption in government and law. His activities also point to a longer process of law reform, to legal adaptability in the face of commercial change, and in response to the emergence of new financial instruments and institutions in early eighteenth-century England.[16] For example, one important outcome of Macclesfield's impeachment was the implementation of new procedures, and the creation of an enhanced role for the Bank of England in its relationship with Chancery. Henceforth, when masters deposited suitors' monies and securities at the Bank of England the records of these transactions were to be held at the Bank as well as the Chancery Report Office. Most important, all interest on these securities was also deposited at the Bank, and recorded in the masters' books there. 'From that moment the masters ceased to have control over the suitors' funds,' Edmund Heward explains. 'The Bank in effect acted as a custodian trustee while the masters

[14] Romney Sedgwick, *History of Parliament, House of Commons 1715–1754* (London, 1970), vol. 2, 569–70; Foss, *Judges of England*, vol. 8, 148; Lemmings, *Gentlemen and Barristers*, 121–2. Another of Macclesfield's defence counsel, John Strange, was also personally and professionally connected to the Earl, having trained in the same law office (of Charles Salkeld) as both Philip Yorke and Macclesfield's nephew, Thomas Parker. 'Strange, John', *ODNB*.

[15] Lemmings, *Gentlemen and Barristers*, 181; Sedgwick, *History of Parliament*, vol. 2, 519–20.

[16] See above, chapter 4.

remained the administrative trustees.'[17] The crisis and its aftermath must be understood here as another arena in which the conception and regulation of trusts was central to broader legal developments, and in which innovation was tied to an insistence upon procedural regularity and effective administration. Subsequent legislation established a new financial-judicial office, the Accountant-General of the Court of Chancery, in whose name all cash and securities were to be held; this put even greater distance between the masters and their suitors' funds.[18] The crisis in Chancery is part of a broader history of legal reform, of institutional change, and of the development of a civil service in eighteenth-century England. These changes, along with the machinations of party politics linked to the spread of corruption in government, law and finance, are among the socio-economic and sociopolitical aspects of commercialisation that are crucial to understanding Macclesfield's impeachment.[19]

And yet there are other cultural and philosophical aspects of commercialisation that are equally relevant to the analysis of this trial. The crisis in Chancery was also a jurisdictional conflict between common law and equity, and it stimulated jurisprudential debate about what kind of law provided stronger protections and surer justice. This legal-philosophical debate was embedded in contemporary philosophical and ideological debate about commercial and financial innovation. The impeachment proceedings indicate that English lawyers were involved in active reflection on the moral-philosophical implications of economic change. Some like Macclesfield were deeply engaged with philosophical and theological discourse. Others like Speaker Peter King – who was also chief justice of the Common Pleas at this time – and Master of the Rolls Joseph Jekyll, were notably active in the eighteenth-century movement for moral reform.[20] Indeed it was Jekyll, a prominent advocate for the Society for Promoting Christian Knowledge and the Society for the Propagation of the Gospel, who pushed for the investigation of ministerial corruption after the collapse of the South Sea

17 Heward, 'Early History Court Funds Office', 52. On enhanced role of the Bank see Ann M. Carlos and Larry Neal, 'The Micro-Foundations of the Early London Capital Market: Bank of England Shareholders during and after the South Sea Bubble, 1720–25', *Economic History Review*, 59, 3 (August, 2006): 503. A description of the administrative tasks of Chancery masters appears in *Trial of Thomas Earl of Macclesfield*, 836–9.

18 Heward, 'Early History Court Funds Office', 52–3.

19 Aylmer, 'From Office-Holding to Civil Service', 91–108; Brewer, *Sinews of Power*, esp. ch. 3; and cf Bruce G. Carruthers, 'Politics, Popery and Property: A Comment on North and Weingast', *The Journal of Economic History*, 50, 3 (September, 1990): 693–8.

20 David W. Hayton, 'Moral Reform and Country Politics in the Late Seventeenth-Century House of Commons', *Past & Present*, 128 (August, 1990): 55, 61, 66, 72, 81; Foss, *Judges of England*, vol. 8, 32, 130–1, 157; Peter Clark, 'The Mother Gin Controversy in the Early Eighteenth Century', *Transactions of the Royal Historical Society*, Fifth Series, 38 (1988): 75–7; Jonathan White, '"The Slow but Sure Poyson": The Representation of Gin and its Drinkers 1736–1751', *Journal of British Studies*, 42, 1 (January, 2003): 40.

Bubble. Jekyll was a man of principle as well as party and profession. He was certainly motivated by a desire to preserve the well-functioning of his own court of Chancery, and by the prospect of his own advancement; rumours were circulating soon after Macclesfield's resignation that Jekyll 'will be the person nominated for Lord Chancellor'.[21] But Jekyll was also motivated by an antipathy to wickedness and vice, and by a growing sympathy for Country critiques of the corrupt financial and political practices of court Whigs.[22] In his and others' arguments against Macclesfield some of the concerns of the campaigns for moral reform became intertwined with strands of public debate over financial innovation concerning, for example, the dangerous volatility of markets, or the ephemeral nature of credit and trust.

These impeachment proceedings also reveal the operation of a set of contemporary cultural concerns regarding gender and commercialisation. Macclesfield's guilt was construed not just as a failure of character, but as a failure of male honour; his corruption was seen as a kind of venality equal to the violation of women's bodies. And here the case for impeachment advanced gendered concerns in another, related, set of arguments. Anger was particularly directed at the lord chancellor for his failure to protect *female* suitors' interests: those women who came to Chancery for protection where common law failed them, critics complained, were left violated and exposed. The case for impeachment came to be framed as the case for protecting women from the dangers posed by a rich, powerful and unscrupulous man. Finally, this gendered perception of danger and corruption helped to foster an ongoing scepticism about legal doctrine regarding the equitable law of trusts, and this contributed to the reaffirmation of the authority, stability and justice of common law. In this impeachment episode, as in the trials of Judge Atkyns, conceptions of common law justice developed as part of a debate about financial innovation which was itself part of broader enlightened philosophical reflection on the implications of economic change. The critique of Macclesfield was also a critique of equity, and of Chancery's *authority*, and in the course of this trial the benefits of common law tradition and stability came to be aligned with morality and the public good.

Much of the dispute over the lord chancellor's guilt centred on the charge of extortion or selling offices, and it is here that we first find elements of common law jurisprudence articulated by both prosecution and defence. The prosecution construed the sale of office as 'an Offence at the Common Law, and punishable by Fine and Imprisonment'.[23] Evidence of this common

21 Newsletter 29 February 1724/5, NLW, Longueville 1187, fol. 14.

22 Walpole maintained that Jekyll's increasing animosity towards his ministry stemmed from his disappointment at not being named lord chancellor when Macclesfield resigned; and among his contemporaries, Jekyll acquired a reputation for inconsistency and shifting loyalties. Sedgwick, *History of Parliament*, vol. 2, 174–5.

23 *New Abridgement and Critical Review*, vol. 1, 880.

law offence could be found in several ways. First, it was shown to be rooted in general custom and prescriptive example: accepted practice showed that it was illegal to appoint 'subordinate Officers for Gift or Brocage' and, more broadly, illegal to accept gifts or payment for performing other official functions. 'The ancient Law of *England*,' the Commons' managers insisted, 'was that none having any Office concerning the Administration of Justice, should take any Fee or reward of any Subject for the doing of his Office, to the End he might be free, and at Liberty to do Justice.'[24] Second, charters and statutes of former kings – the two most important examples being 12 Richard II c.2 (1388) and 5&6 Edward VI c.16 (1552) – were adduced as confirmation of this custom, providing an 'additional Constraint or Obligation upon the superior Officer, by an oath not to commit the Offence'.[25] A good deal of legal debate revolved around the interpretation of these statutes even though the prosecution maintained that Macclesfield's actions constituted a violation of common law whether or not he took the oath 'against buying and selling of offices' that was prescribed in such legislation.[26]

One important point at issue here was the proper status of Chancery personnel, since the definition of Chancery masterships as judicial rather than ministerial office was at the heart of the charge of corruption. Thomas Lutwyche, an MP with some reputation for legal learning, and one of only two Tory prosecutors in this trial, explained:

> The words of the statute of R.2, are general, and in point of reason it should extend to this case above others; because the offices of Masters in Chancery do not only concern the administration of justice, but are in some measure judicial; they transact a great part of the business of the Court, and have usually been in commission together with the Master of the Rolls, and the judges, for hearing of causes.[27]

24 Ibid., 879.

25 Ibid., 880.

26 '... and it still remains an Offence at the Common Law, and does not depend on that Statute, but is a great Offence, although the Oath be not taken'. *New Abridgement and Critical Review*, vol. 1, 880. Macclesfield's defence argued that these statutes were either obsolete and/or only applied to lesser officers like sheriffs. *Trial of Thomas Earl of Macclesfield*, 1107–8. See also the depiction of Macclesfield's denials about oath-taking as 'undignified' in George Wilson, *The Trial of the Earl of Macclesfield Faithfully Abridg'd. With Remarks Thereon* (London, 1727), 11; and the frequent recourse to discussion of statutes and oaths in Britannicus (i.e. Thomas Gordon), *The Justice of Parliaments on Corrupt Ministers, in Impeachments and Bills of Attainder, Consider'd*, (London, 1725), 3–4, 9–10, 20.

27 *Trial of Thomas Earl of Macclesfield*, 1361. For Lutwyche's parliamentary career and reputation see Sedgwick, *History of Parliament*, vol. 2, 231–2; Lemmings, *Gentlemen and Barristers*, 208. On statute and sale of office see also David I. Levine, 'Calculating Fees of Special Masters', *Hastings Law Journal*, 37 (September, 1985): 145–6; R.B. Ball, 'The Chancery Master', *Law Quarterly Review*, 77 (1961): 331.

This ambiguity in the definition and practice of office has a lengthy history, traced by Linda Peck in her study of early Stuart patronage and corruption. As examples from Anglo-Saxon governance demonstrate, early officials acted as judges as well as administrators, fulfilling both roles in the implementation of the king's justice. This blurring between ministerial and judicial office persisted for centuries, Peck explains, and was further complicated by the identification between office and property, and the association between office and gift. Gifts proffered to officials, long an acknowledgement of the recipient's power and status, continued to be an essential part of patronage and place in the eighteenth century. The development of increasingly sophisticated markets, and abundance of commodities to be exchanged, did not preclude the continued development of gift-giving practices.[28] But the 'equivocal meaning' of such gifts, and their ready connotation of partiality, or corruption, remained important as well. Equally problematic was the tradition that office was a species of property held by the officeholder.[29] This was a tradition rooted in medieval law, and called upon by Macclefield's defenders, but it also raised questions about undue interest and venality, and might easily be harnessed to polemical images of suspect French-style judicial practices.

Participants in Macclesfield's impeachment trial were aware of these traditions and examples and exploited their useful ambiguities. For instance, defence counsel defined the Earl's right to nominate men to office as a species of property, and strongly endorsed each man's 'natural right to dispose of his own estate or interest, his own friendship or favour, upon what consideration he pleases: it is his own and therefore he has a right to make any just and legal advantage of it'.[30] Such arguments were aimed to associate Macclesfield's actions with principles of natural justice and, even more, with the defence of property interests and stability which was key a common law theme. Macclesfield's adherence to custom and common law was further underscored by another of his advocates, the civilian lawyer Exton Sayer, in an explication of the distinction between custom and nature. Sayer reminded the Lords that the chancellor was not accused of selling favourable verdicts (alluding here to those infamous charges against Lord Chancellor Bacon) but simply of selling offices or places:

> My Lords, the writers upon the law of nature have properly distinguished between selling justice, and offices concerning the administration of justice…. With them the selling justice is absolutely forbid, is absolutely corrupt and immoral. The

[28] Finn, *Character of Credit*, 7–9.

[29] Linda Levy Peck, *Court Patronage and Corruption in Early Stuart England* (Boston, 1990), 162–7.

[30] See Probyn's vigorous defence of the right of nomination to office as a species of property. Probyn insists that Macclesfield's actions indicate no 'crime', no 'injustice', no 'immorality'. *Trial of Thomas Earl of Macclesfield*, 1087–8.

> selling offices is matter of mere policy, varied in different governments, prohibited in some, allowed in others.[31]

Examples of such policies from different nations and different times were given to demonstrate the variability, and historicity, of custom. There was evidence from ancient Rome and from modern France and, presumably most effective, evidence of this practice in England. So, for example, defence counsel referred to ancient instances of the purchase of the office of justicier included in Thomas Madox, *The History and Antiquities of the Exchequer of the Kings of England* (1711), as an indication of accepted practice in England.[32] The justice of Macclesfield's actions was a justice of common law, founded in prescription, reason and legislation; the sale of masterships was prescriptive practice, illuminated by exemplary cases and consonant with natural justice.

Here, as elsewhere, Lord Chancellor Macclesfield's defence counsel argued from precedent and ancient usage, and denied that the sale of office was a violation of common law. Indeed, both Sayer and the principal counsellor for the defence, Serjeant Probyn, depicted the lord chancellor as unfairly singled out, since all Macclesfield had done was to follow the practice of 'the many great and learned persons who executed this high office before him'.[33] Probyn and Sayer then introduced testimony regarding the purchase of masterships under Macclefield's immediate predecessors, Lord Chancellors Harcourt and Cowper. It was true, these advocates admitted, that Cowper had broken with tradition when he refused the usual New Year's gifts, and eschewed an obvious patronage appointment for his brother, so as to avoid an appearance of bribery or impropriety (and perhaps to avoid revisiting association with his brother's scandal). And yet, the defence showed, there was evidence that masters had paid L500 to the sitting chancellor, and another L3000 to the retiring master, for admission to their offices in Cowper's time. Further evidence demonstrated that Harcourt too had received sums of L700 and L800 upon admission of masters, with L2000 paid to retirees. This testimony elicited some pointed questions about these payments, and defensive comments about the continued security of suitors' funds, from Lord Harcourt himself who was sitting among the Lords during the trial.[34]

Contemporaries might also have recalled the practices of Cowper's predecessor Lord Keeper Nathan Wright, or of the earlier renowned judge, Lord Keeper Francis North, both of whom clearly benefited from their control over

31 Ibid., 1109.

32 Ibid., 1088, 1364. Such arguments, and these specific references to and interpretation of Madox's history, were countered by the prosecution in a discussion of both the content and nature of such precedents.

33 Ibid., 1090, cf 1131.

34 Ibid., 1152–4.

appointment to, and sale of, offices.[35] Indeed Serjeant Probyn insisted that the practice of selling offices was sanctioned, in the language of the common law, by reference to 'time immemorial': 'The precedent is too ancient for us to discover when it was first made;' he explained, 'and I humbly submit it to your lordships, that the immemorial, constant usage and practice of it in all ages since, will sufficiently establish the reasonableness and justice of the precedent.'[36] Defence counsel John Strange asserted that any interpretation of relevant statutes regarding office-holding must also take into account this matter of ancient and constant usage.[37] And Sayer added in his statement that witnesses could testify to that constant 'opinion and practice of the Earl's predecessors'. Such common opinion based on prescriptive practice, he explained, must be acknowledged as more authoritative than statute, and as constitutive of justice:

> Usage (if ancient) has so great authority, that it makes the common law of England; and though with us it cannot repeal a statute, or destroy its force, which it does in other countries, yet, my lords, there is an equity to be observed; and reason as well as humanity must inform your lordships, that no man ought to be treated with the utmost severity which an old statute may direct; when great examples may have led him to the action, and a long connivance of his predecessors promised him security from censure.[38]

In this argument for precedent and common law made on behalf of the highest judge of the highest equity court – and by an advocate of Doctors Commons – equity was construed as that fair recognition of the power of precedent. It would be equitable, Sayer argued with exquisite logic, to make an exception based on the idea that following prior examples was right; and it would be equitable, he claimed, to recognise prescription here more than legislation. The critique of the chancellor, and of the operations of the Chancery, led the defence to make claims about the justice of adhering to established procedures and stable traditions.

The lord chancellor was here depicted as an adherent of custom more than conscience. The conventional image of the chancellor as guardian

35 Prest, 'Judicial Corruption', 86–7; Aylmer, 'From Office Holding to Civil Service', 98–9; Foss, *Judges of England*, vol. 7, 411; Shetreet, *Judges on Trial*, 127; John Hatsell, *Precedents of Proceedings in the House of Commons … Vol. 4. Relating to Conference and Impeachment* (London, 1796), 115.

36 *Trial of Thomas Earl of Macclesfield*, 1090; also *New Abridgement and Critical Review*, 875, 879; Holdsworth, *History of English Law*, vol. 12, 206.

37 *Trial of Thomas Earl of Macclesfield*, 1133–4. Strange's version of statutory interpretation was advocacy of deference to both original intent ('contemporary usage') and continual usage.

38 *Trial of Thomas Earl of Macclesfield*, 1108. On legal knowledge and transition from 'common erudition' to 'common opinion' see Baker, *Law's Two Bodies*, 86–7, and chapter 2 above.

of natural law, concerned with universal justice that would 'fix' or 'fulfill' common law, was noticeably absent from both defence and prosecution claims about justice and right. For example, this emphasis on prescription and precedent also informed arguments meant to justify Macclesfield's failure to respond to contemporary crises in economy and law. Participants acknowledged that procedural reforms were long overdue in the court of Chancery. The business of the court had grown, and the sums of money administered by Chancery masters had also increased, so that past practice was now insufficient for current circumstances. Yet defence counsel insisted that it would have been imprudent, if not impossible, for Macclesfield as a single chancellor to effect such reforms since, in Serjeant Probyn's words, 'the ancient practice of every court is the law of that court; and it would be a dangerous experiment for any one presiding judge to vary it'. Probyn added the dictum that 'He that acts without a precedent, acts upon the peril of his own judgment' – another clear contrast to the usual image of the independent judgment of a lord chancellor.[39] The idea of precedent was of course not unknown in Chancery, and the sense of equitable doctrine and reference to prior decisions was well-established by this time. But what is notable about this defence emphasis on custom and precedent is that it was tied to a claim about common law, and about right and authority as grounded in tradition and prescription.

Although the usual image of the chancellor as 'unfettered conscience' is largely absent from this trial, the prosecution did articulate conventional complaints against an 'arbitrary chancellor'. Here is another indication that particular disputes about office and corruption in this trial were part of a wider discourse developing in the legal literature of the time concerning the nature of equity, the role of the lord chancellor, and the definition of justice. However, while contemporary thinkers like Henry Ballow, Thomas Wood or Richard Francis insisted that it was the 'mixture' of rigid tradition in common law and unfettered conscience in equity that produced justice, lawyers in Macclesfield's trial underscored the contrast between common law and equity. In particular, the prosecution drew upon some notorious images and inflammatory arguments in order to reanimate an old association between a powerful lord chancellor and the dangers of arbitrary rule. For example, the twenty-first article of impeachment, charging that Macclesfield 'suspended' and 'dispensed' with law, clearly employed the language of Stuart tyranny.[40] This language and these kinds of associations were also apparent in the prosecution's suggestion that the lord chancellor aimed at reviving the court of wards, and finally in the insinuations made about

39 *Trial of Thomas Earl of Macclesfield*, 1093.

40 Ibid., 782.

Macclesfield's suspected Jacobitism (and here, some did add, the sale of judicial offices must be seen as a French-absolutist practice too).[41]

Such arguments are an indication that this trial served as another venue for the contest over claims to Revolution Principles between opposition and court Whigs. Prosecution managers used these kinds of Whiggish arguments against the Whig lord chancellor in order to call to mind both the principles of 1688 and the principles articulated in an important earlier episode in Whig history. This was the conflict between Sir Edward Coke and James I's Lord Chancellor Thomas Egerton, Baron Ellesmere, over the scope of equity and the protections offered by common law against the encroachments of an arbitrary chancellor, and king.[42] Framing this impeachment trial as an episode in the longer history of jurisdictional conflict between Chancery and the common law courts, and between tyranny and the demands of 'National Justice', had a clear resonance, and jurisprudential value.[43]

Again, much of Macclesfield's defence against this critique of equity lay in associating the lord chancellor with the defence of common law principles. Macclesfield highlighted his own part in the preservation of common law during the years he spent at King's Bench, as successor to the respected Chief Justice John Holt. Many would remember his early successes too, in defence of the Whig printer John Tutchin and in impeaching the Tory minister Henry Sacheverell, in those celebrated Whig trials.[44] During his impeachment trial Macclesfield demonstrated professional integrity, and adherence to common law, by criticising the procedural irregularities allowed by his opponents. He pointedly, and repeatedly, attacked prosecution managers for coaching the Chancery masters who served as witnesses against him. In this way Macclesfield also reinforced contemporary unease about the credibility of these masters who had to be indemnified before they would testify, and some of whom remained insolvent and subject to imprisonment for debt.[45]

41 Ibid., 782–3; Wilson, *Trial of Macclesfield Faithfully Abridg'd*, 57, 62. Wilson also made comparisons between Macclesfield's counsel John Strange and Sir Robert Filmer, 50–1.

42 Mark Fortier, 'Equity and Ideas: Coke, Ellesmere and James I', *Renaissance Quarterly*, 51, 4 (Winter, 1991): 1255–81; G.W. Thomas, 'James I, Equity and Lord Keeper Williams', *The English Historical Review*, 91, 360 (July, 1976): 506–28.

43 Newsletter 16 February 1724/5, NLW, Longueville 1187, fols 7–8. Cf Julian Hoppit, 'The Myths of the South Sea Bubble', *Transactions of the Royal Historical Society*, Sixth Series, 12 (2002): 159–60 on the political reaction and rhetoric of 1720–21.

44 *Trial of Thomas Earl of Macclesfield*, 1086, 1322; *New Abridgement and Critical Review*, 577. Horsely, 'Trial of John Tutchin, Author of the Observator'. The example of Sacheverell was a more ambiguous one, and could be used to underline Macclesfield's 'fall', Newsletter 6 May 1725, NLW, Longueville 1187, fol. 50.

45 *Trial of Thomas Earl of Macclesfield*, 849–57, 1146–51; Heward, 'Early History Court Funds Office', 51; Newsletter 16 February 1724/5, and 20 February 1724/5, NLW, Longueville 1187, fols 7–8, 11–12; CUL, Cholmondely (Houghton) 65 29 fols 4–12 includes a handwritten transcript of this portion only of the courtroom debate.

Defence counsel Sayer furthered this line of argument when he urged the Lords to make their judgment in adherence to common law tradition, and the stability of established practice. He pleaded with the Lords to exercise their judicial power according to that 'sacred rule' and 'peculiar blessing of our nation, to have certain known laws to be the guide of our actions, and the measure of our punishment'.[46] These appeals were expressive of a Whiggish defence of stability and civility, and of contemporary discourse concerning credibility and reputation, both characteristic of a moderate, commercial Enlightenment.

Mandeville and moral discourse

The fact that prosecution and defence laid claim to Revolution Principles, to the traditions of ancient constitution and the continuity of English liberties, is an indication that this trial was particularly, and unsurprisingly, bound up with debate over that key result of 1688, the financial revolution. The pursuit of a modern, commercial, market-driven and debt-ridden society was at the heart of domestic and foreign policy under Whig government in the early eighteenth century. And as we have seen, contemporary moral and social theorists began to develop new ideas about the nature and role of human passions in social development, as well as new critiques of the corrupting effects of prosperity. This was a moment when moral-philosophical debate intensified and multiplied; a time of republican and sociological discourse when the ideas of men like Fenelon, Mandeville, Shaftesbury and Hutcheson circulated widely. Macclesfield's trial was filled with this contemporary discourse about credit, avarice and luxury. His impeachment must be understood within the context of arguments about human appetites, sentiment and sociability, and about private vices and public good, that stood at the centre of enlightened moral-philosophical debate.

Attention to the work of Bernard Mandeville within these debates about luxury and public virtue is particularly important to the analysis of Macclesfield's impeachment, first because of the close association between the two men. The lord chancellor was a friend and patron of the physician-philosopher: Macclesfield owned at least one of Mandeville's books and likely read others; Mandeville was a frequent and witty companion at the Earl's dinner table; and the two men enjoyed intimate conversation and correspondence.[47] Their relationship should not simply be seen as a result of

[46] *Trial of Thomas Earl of Macclesfield*, 1111–12.

[47] F.B. Kaye, Introduction, Bernard Mandeville, *The Fable of the Bees Or Private Vices, Publick Benefits*, vol. 1 (Oxford, 1924), xxvi–vii. Mandeville's *Pensees Libres sur la Religion, L'eglise et le Bonheur de la Nation: traduites de l'anglois* (The Hague, 1723) is listed in the catalogue of the Macclesfield library; this was a French translation of Mandeville's *Free Thoughts on Religion, the Church and National Happiness* (London, 1720). Berkeley's

the lord chancellor's acquaintance with Mandeville while the philosopher was employed as a Whig propagandist in the early 1720s but rather should be viewed as another indication of Macclefield's engagement with contemporary philosophical discussion.[48] Suspect philosophical commitments and controversial associations or friendships were at issue in the trial. And Mandeville is especially relevant, second, because *The Fable of the Bees*, his notorious defence of vice as conducive to the public good, was published in its extended and most provocative version in 1723, shortly before Macclesfield's troubles began.[49]

Mandeville's *Fable* was a statement made in defence of financial revolution. First published as *The Grumbling Hive* in 1705 to support Whig foreign policy, and to counter Tory-Jacobite attacks on 'the corrupt regime of debt and luxury', Mandeville's essay was republished and extended as *The Fable of the Bees* in 1714, and again in 1723 in the aftermath of the South Sea Bubble. It was Mandeville's elaboration on an 'already-established discourse on the volatile moral relations between public virtue and the demands of commerce' – a particularly heightened discourse in this period of recrimination against stockjobbers and speculators, and a discourse that was fundamental to the charges against Macclesfield.[50] Moreover, this discourse about virtue and commerce was not only conducted in these terms of English politics, between new and old whigs and in the language of civic humanism, but it was also a broadly European debate that notably engaged French and Scottish, as well English, thinkers at this time. Clearly one important target for Mandeville was Archbishop Fenelon's *The Bees* (1689), a text aimed to criticise the economic policies, and despotic tendencies, of Louis XIV. While Fenelon opposed the 'social contagion' of luxury and consumption, expressing, among other things, a fundamental mistrust of human nature, Mandeville defended self-interest and commercial wealth as the keys to

and Hutcheson's texts are also listed, among other philosophical works, providing some confirmation that the Earl must have been acquainted with Mandeville's contributions to philosophical debate. See *The Library of the Earl of Macclesfield removed from Shirburn Castle, Part Eight*, 262, 344.

48 Hundert, *Enlightenment's Fable*, 6.

49 First published 1705 as a satirical pamphlet *The Grumbling Hive*; republished with added commentary as *Fable of the Bees* 1714; and republished and extended again in 1723, with an attack on Shaftesbury, entitled *A Search into the Nature of Society*, appended along with his 'viciously satirical' *Essay on Charity and the Charity Schools*. Hont, 'Early Enlightenment Debate on Commerce and Luxury', 387, 395; Thomas A. Horne, *The Social Thought of Bernard Mandeville: Virtue and Commerce in Early Eighteenth-Century England* (London, 1978), 33.

50 Hundert, *Enlightenment's Fable*, 24; Pocock, *Machiavellian Moment*, ch. 14; M.M. Goldsmith, *Private Vices, Public Benefits: Bernard Mandeville's Social and Political Thought* (Cambridge, 1985); Goldsmith, 'Liberty, Luxury and the Pursuit of Happiness', in Pagden ed., *The Languages of Political Theory in Early Modern Europe*, 238–51; Hoppit, 'Attitudes to Credit', 309–11.

economic growth, national strength and security. Mandeville was also influenced here by French Jansenist ideas about the operation of human appetites and passions. La Fontaine's fables, which explored many of the 'dominant themes of Jansenism,' were an important inspiration for both Mandeville and Fenelon.[51]

Finally Mandeville's defence of the self-interested pursuit of wealth, his embrace of luxury, and his identification of self-love as the engine of society, were a clear challenge to the Earl of Shaftesbury's philosophy of moral sense, with its claims about sociable moral development aimed at the public good. Mandeville's essay entitled 'A Search into the Nature of Society', which was appended to the 1723 edition of the *Fable of the Bees*, was a first attempt to position his work as a response to Shaftesbury; subsequent dialogues published in 1729 and 1732 'restated Mandeville's *oeuvre* as a debate with Shaftesbury'.[52] Mandeville tied the critique of Shaftesbury's philosophy of moral sense to a critique of the movement for moral reform in 1723, when he added an *Essay on Charity and Charity Schools* to the new edition of his *Fable*. This controversial essay offered a sharp attack on the moral reformers.

Contemporary concern with commercial development, and the terminologies of moral sense and moral reform, were essential elements in the debate over Macclesfield's guilt. Participants took the measure of the lord chancellor's animating passions, and made allusions to the ideas of Shaftesbury and Mandeville in courtroom argument over Macclesfield's motives. For example, prosecutors asserted that destructive passions overcame Macclesfield's rational interests and derailed his moral sense. These passions – the avaricious desire for wealth, an insatiable greed – clearly diminished the chancellor's care for the public welfare, they argued, and ultimately undermined his professional actions.[53] In his own courtroom speech Macclesfield insisted that the whole case against him rested upon false interpretation of his motives for acting. The prosecution focused on his alleged avarice and greed, yet that 'charge of [his] desire of gain' was misdirected, Macclesfield explained, because it entailed a fundamental misinterpretation of his feelings and intentions. In response to such misinterpretation the challenge for his defence was to demonstrate that 'amassing a great estate was never [Macclesfield's] view; and that rapacious and base ways of getting money are not consistent with [his] way of laying it out'. If the defence successfully

[51] Hont, 'Early Enlightenment Debate on Commerce and Luxury', 382–92; Horne, *Social Thought of Bernard Mandeville*, 21–5, 31; Hundert, *Enlightenment's Fable*, 23–35. For relevance of Dutch political and intellectual contexts see Hundert, and Mitchell, 'Character of an Independent Whig', 291–311.

[52] Hont, 'Early Enlightenment Debate on Commerce and Luxury', 395, 399; Horne, *Social Thought of Bernard Mandeville*, 32–50; Hundert, *Enlightenment's Fable*, 118–26.

[53] Examples of reference to Macclesfield's passions: *Trial of Thomas Earl of Macclesfield*, 807–8, 1167, 1248, 1330, 1352; note also the frequent discussion of the matter of 'compassion' throughout the proceedings.

confuted the charge of avaricious motives, Macclesfield concluded, then the 'sting of this impeachment is taken out':

> without this, though there should have been imprudence, indolence, too great confidence, perhaps credulity, irresolution, or any other defect or weakness, there has been nothing wicked.[54]

Macclesfield underscored the link between emotion, intentionality and criminality, betraying that influence of philosophical discourse on legal concepts when he explained that '[i]t is such a corrupt heart only can change actions that in themselves are innocent, and some of them perhaps commendable, into so many crimes'.[55]

In signalling his conformity to moral sense and reason Macclesfield did not go so far as to claim that when he took part in the customary practice of selling masters' offices his actions were fundamentally aimed at securing the public good. But he did suggest that his actions indicated some feeling and regard for public welfare since he did not knowingly, or even carelessly, advance incompetent men to office. That kind of an act that 'prejudiced the public' would clearly be immoral and criminal, he conceded; any benefit accrued would simply be an aggravation of the crime. Macclesfield deliberately added, to these lords who were steeped in the traditions of patronage and place, that such an act would be criminal whether linked to monetary gain, or done 'for the sake of kindred, or friendship, or for recommendation', these other aggravating factors.[56]

Finally Macclesfield turned to an obviously Mandevillian argument about public benefits and private vices as justification for his actions. The lord chancellor maintained that he had fulfilled his duty by placing well-qualified men into office, and that he had simply benefited, as his predecessors had done, by collecting monies for the appointment to Chancery masterships. 'If the public have all the benefit it can have, where is the immorality?' Macclesfield asked. 'Where is the crime, if I have an advantage too?'[57] Indeed, the individual pursuit of gain was, as Mandeville had shown in his *Fable*, the engine of common wealth, and the foundation of common good. Against this 'dangerous position' the prosecution's Thomas Lutwyche returned to the themes of universal morality in order to connect the sale of office with the sale of justice. Would anyone agree, Lutwyche asked, that the public should not be concerned if a judge accepts money for a judgment in a cause – that is, for dispensing justice – even if the ruling is good? The end result was not the only consideration, Lutwyche explained; virtue is a constant, moral principles are founded in nature, and acceptance

54 Ibid., 1329; *New Abridgement and Critical Review*, 879.

55 *Trial of Thomas Earl of Macclesfield*, 1328; *New Abridgement and Critical Review*, 879.

56 *Trial of Thomas Earl of Macclesfield*, 1274; *New Abridgement and Critical Review*, 878.

57 *Trial of Thomas Earl of Macclesfield*, 1274; *New Abridgement and Critical Review*, 878.

of Macclefield's arguments 'would tend to universal corruption' rather than public good.[58]

Participants in this trial thus articulated familiar terms of debate over the relationship between commerce and social welfare, and regarding the place of the passions in human nature. This enlightened moral-philosophical discourse was central to the expression of ideas about judging and about justice, and helped to determine the outcome of Macclesfield's trial. References to the specific arguments of important authors, like Mandeville or Shaftesbury, were also made in commentaries on Macclesfield's particular case, and on other impeachments, circulated by opponents and supporters soon after the Earl's conviction. Published texts included George Wilson's 1726 *Bribes no Perquisites, Or the Case of the Earl of Macclesfield, Being Impartial Observations Upon his Lordship's Tryal,* Thomas Gordon's 1725 *The Justice of Parliaments on Corrupt Ministers, in Impeachments and Bills of Attainder, Consider'd,* and several anonymous texts such as *A Vindication of the Lord Chancellor Bacon from the Aspersion of Injustice Cast upon him by Mr Wraynham* 1725, and *An Enquiry into the Origin of Parliamentary Impeachment: with a History of the Most Remarkable.*[59] These texts point to that close interrelationship between legal culture and print culture, first because they are another manifestation of the genre of 'notorious trials' that was becoming increasing popular, especially in London's periodical press, in the early eighteenth century. Second these texts also engaged with questions about commerce and credibility, and were relevant to the concerns of readers of popular texts on investment, interest and other aspects of trade that were also being printed in greater numbers in the early eighteenth century.[60] Indeed these commentaries on Macclesfield's case sought to publicise generally critical analyses of the lord chancellor, and to use them to enhance the credibility of attacks mounted by proponents of moral reform who viewed the South Sea Bubble as one more indication of dangerous trends in contemporary political and religious affairs.

George Wilson, for example, countered Mandeville's defence of private vice by effecting a satirical reversal of terms. In attacking positive depictions of Macclesfield's character Wilson mocked the defence emphasis

58 *Trial of Thomas Earl of Macclesfield,* 1363; *New Abridgement and Critical Review,* 880–1.

59 George Wilson's *Bribes no Perquisites, Or the Case of the Earl of Macclesfield, Being Impartial Observations Upon his Lordship's Tryal* (London, 1726) appeared in a second edition which was entitled *The Trial of the Earl of Macclesfield, Faithfully Abridg'd. With Remarks Thereon* (London, 1727).

60 Michael Harris, 'Trials and Criminal Biographies: A Case Study in Distribution', in R. Myers and M. Harris eds, *Sale and Distribution of Books from 1700* (Oxford, 1982), 1–36; David Lemmings, 'The Dark Side of Enlightenment: *The London Journal,* Moral Panics, and the Law in the Eighteenth Century', in David Lemmings and Claire Walker eds, *Moral Panics, the Media and the Law in Early Modern England* (Basingstoke, 2009), 139–56; Glaisyer, 'Calculating Credibility'; Glaisyer, *Culture of Commerce in England,* chs 3–4; Mary Poovey, *Genres of the Credit Economy,* 30–85.

on the lord chancellor's charitable works as their disingenuous attempt to produce '*Private Virtues*' as '*significant* Apologies for *Publick Vices*;' he added that 'doing *Evil* that *Good* may come of it is but the arguing of a very weak Casuist.'[61] Like Mandeville and Fenelon, Wilson also turned to the recounting of fable – Aesop's 'Story of Two Travellers' which he found in one of the popular editions by Roger L'Estrange – in order to oppose Macclesfield's casuistry. If the moral of Mandeville's fable, and Macclesfield's actions, was that 'Fraud, Luxury and Pride' are acceptable, even necessary, for the production of public wealth, the moral of Wilson's chosen fable was that the thief who used some of his ill-gotten gains to help the poor performed no true charitable public work.[62]

Wilson's focus on charity was here aimed as a response to that other controversial facet of Mandeville's ideology: the critique of moral reformers who promoted the new charity schools. Mandeville's 1723 *Essay on Charity and Charity Schools* was purposefully dedicated to the Societies for the Reformation of Manners, and it further implicated members of the SPCK and other elite supporters of the schools (and critics of Macclesfield) like Joseph Jekyll or Peter King, in its arguments against their paternalistic and hypocritical motives. Wilson's fable not only defined Macclesfield's charity as hypocritical but it also underscored the association between the lord chancellor and Mandeville's most notorious work. This *Essay on Charity* was likely what led to an attempted prosecution of Mandeville's publisher when the Grand Jury of Middlesex brought charges of 'Blasphemy', and the 'Subversion of all Religion and Civil Government' against this edition of the *Fable*.[63]

Thomas Gordon and John Trenchard, writing under the pseudonym 'Cato', also offered reflections on the charity schools in the *British Journal*, and their work was presented by the same Middlesex Grand Jury in July 1723.[64] Indeed, although Cato's reputation for promoting classical virtue, and Gordon's endorsement of impeachment in 1725 seem to indicate a sharp divergence between the ideas of Gordon and Trenchard and those of Mandeville, their work was not wholly dissimilar. Gordon, Trenchard and Mandeville all shared an antipathy to the charity schools, and to the

61 Wilson, *Trial of Macclesfield Faithfully Abridg'd*, 44, 49, and see also 52, 67.

62 Ibid., 45–6. Bernard Mandeville, 'The Moral', *The Fable of the Bees*, vol. 1, 37. Debate about charity took place in the trial as well: *Trial of Thomas Earl of Macclesfield*, 1081, 1087, 1101, 1118, 1174, 1240–63, 1374.

63 Bernard Mandeville, 'A Vindication of the Book &c', *The Fable of the Bees*, vol. 1, 443–6; Hundert, *Enlightenment's Fable*, 122, 192–7; Irwin Primer, *Bernard Mandeville's 'A Modest Defence of the Public Stews': Prostitution and its Discontents in Early Georgian England* (New York, 2006), 4–5; M.M. Goldsmith, 'Mandeville, Bernard', *ODNB*.

64 The Grand Jury singled out the *British Journal*, nn. 26, 35, 36, 39 in their presentment. Mandeville, 'A Vindication of the Book &c', 446; Primer, *Bernard Mandeville's 'A Modest Defence'*, 4.

Societies for the Reformation of Manners more generally. Moreover, all three authors shared a broader anti-clericalism, especially directed against High Church Tory intolerance, and all faced accusations of deism.[65] Finally, Trenchard and Gordon had recourse, at times, to those ideas about private vices and public benefits that are usually associated with Mandeville's thought rather than with Cato's civic republican ideals. 'For all its invocation of ancient virtue,' Mark Goldie reminds us, 'the anti-government paper, *Cato's Letters*, embraced commerce.'[66]

Yet despite these similarities with Mandeville, and Macclesfield, Gordon articulated support for the lord chancellor's impeachment in the *Justice of Parliaments*.[67] This endorsement of impeachment was expressive of certain ideas about the proper operation, and role, of government and law, and is further evidence of the connections contemporaries made between morality and common law. First, Gordon's text took part in a printed debate stemming from Macclesfield's trial over the history of parliamentary impeachments, which was itself part of that longer-running discourse about the judicial authority of the House of Lords. The Lords contributed to this discourse in the weeks before Macclesfield's trial when they debated the proper venue for impeachment, the scope of their jurisdiction, and the weight of past prec-

[65] Mitchell, 'Character of an Independent Whig', 293–6, 301–3. For the complex meanings of such accusations of religious heterodoxy, and the broader relationship between Enlightenment and enthusiasm, see: Young, 'Newtonianism and the Enthusiasm of Enlightenment', and the essays collected in Lawrence E. Klein and Anthony LaVopa eds, *Enthusiasm and Enlightenment in Europe 1650–1850* (San Marino, 1998).

[66] Mark Goldie 'The English System of Liberty', in Goldie and Wolker eds, *Cambridge History of Eighteenth-Century Political Thought*, 66; Mitchell, 'Character of an Independent Whig', 303–4; M.M. Goldsmith, 'Liberty, Luxury and Pursuit of Happiness', 235–6.

[67] It is worth noting that Gordon's text on impeachments was published not only in the context of Macclesfield's impeachment, but also in the context of debate over the question of reversing Viscount Bolingbroke's attainder which was now before the Lords. The petition to restore Bolingbroke's properties enjoyed the support of Solicitor General Sir Clement Wearg who, at the same time, was pressing ahead with Macclesfield's impeachment. 'Debate on a Bill to enable the late Lord Bolingbroke to enjoy certain Estates, notwithstanding his Attainder' May 22, 24, *The History and Proceedings of the House of Lords From the Restoration in 1660 to the Present Time*, vol. 3 (London, 1742), 431–6, House of Commons Parliamentary Papers: Eighteenth-Century Parliamentary Papers Collection 1688–1834, http://gateway.umi.bhowell.com/openurl?url_ver=Z39.88–2004&res_dat=xri:hcpp&rft_dat=xri:hcpp:rec:hp_lords-000011; Henry St John, Viscount Bolingbroke, *Political Writings*, David Armitage ed., xxvi–vii. Bolingbroke's *Craftsmen* essays would soon articulate important arguments against the Whig ministry and monied interest, and against corruption and patronage. On the development of such arguments, and the relationship between 'old whig' and 'Country' ideas, see the classic accounts of Caroline Robbins, *The Eighteenth-Century Commonwealthmen: Studies in the Transmission, Development and Circumstance of English Liberal Thought from the Restoration of Charles II until the War with the Thirteen Colonies* (Cambridge, Mass., 1959); Pocock, *Machiavellian Moment*; Pocock, *Virtue, Commerce, and History*.

edents.[68] Similar questions were aired in the anonymous *Vindication of the Lord Chancellor Bacon* which appeared at this time, as well as in *An Enquiry into the Origin of Parliamentary Impeachment: with a History of the Most Remarkable.*[69] In response especially to *An Enquiry into the Origin of Parliamentary Impeachments*, Gordon provided a strong defence of the Commons' power to initiate a prosecution, and he traced the origins of parliamentary impeachments, including the particular judicial power of the Lords, back to the ancient Saxons and Romans. Gordon's argument was here aimed against the *Enquiry*'s admission of Norman Conquest, and offered instead a common law ideology that found the legitimacy of law and government in antiquity and prescription.[70]

Gordon's defence of the justice of prosecution and impeachment was based upon an argument about rule of law.[71] He lauded the tradition of common law and constitution as a tradition of impartiality and a defence against corrupt, arbitrary and ultimately tyrannical power. Macclesfield's crimes were certainly understood to be another result of the corrupting influence of money, and the text does rehearse civic humanist kinds of arguments about ancient virtue and the public good. Yet the solution to the corruptions of avarice, luxury and passion was not viewed simply as a recourse to ancient republican virtue. Gordon had long been aware that England was no pure republic: the unequal distribution of property meant, he thought, that the best form of government possible was a limited monarchy in which an elite, made up of nobles and clergy, vied for patronage and place as they exercised power. This limited or mixed constitution provided necessary constraints on

68 *History and Proceedings of the House of Lords*, vol. 3, 426–8, House of Commons Parliamentary Papers: Eighteenth-Century Parliamentary Papers Collection 1688–1834, http://gateway.umi.bhowell.com/openurl?url_ver=Z39.88–2004&res_dat=xri:hcpp&rft_dat=xri:hcpp:rec:hp_lords-000011; 'House of Lords Journal Volume 22: April 1725, 21–30', *Journal of the House of Lords: Volume 22: 1722–1726*, British History Online, http://www.british-history.ac.uk/report.aspx?compid=113814. Newsletter 29 April – 6 May 1725, NLW, Longueville 1187, fols 43–50.

69 Thomas Gordon published his own reflections on Bacon's impeachment just after the bursting of the Bubble in *Francis, Lord Bacon, or the Case of Private and National Corruption and Bribery* (London, 1721).

70 Gordon, *Justice of Parliaments*, 14–15. And compare *An Enquiry Into the Origin of Parliamentary Impeachments: With a History of the Most Remarkable … From the Beginning to Our Time* (London, 1745?), 5–9, which rehearses those arguments about conquest, the composition of early parliaments, the meaning of baron, burgess, comites etc. Gordon's deliberate reply to *An Enquiry Into the Origin of Parliamentary Impeachments* offers proof that that text was available in 1725. Although the title page of *An Enquiry* offered no date, and most library catalogues date the text tentatively as 1745, evidence from Gordon's text, as well as archivist's notes at the Folger Shakespeare Library, confirm rather a publication date of 1725. FSL, DA30 O5 G8.

71 Gordon, *Justice of Parliaments*, esp. 2–3, 8, 15–16, 22, 29, 31, 35.

absolute power, and preserved rights and liberties.[72] But, as Whig government showed, this constitution also allowed for the pursuit of power and wealth, affording ample scope for the exercise of human passions. The role of law was to check the excesses of such passions. The suggestion made by Trenchard and Gordon (and by Mandeville) Annie Mitchell concurs, was that '[l]aws and constitutional mechanisms were there to restrain men, and their governors, when those passions threatened to become detrimental to the nation'.[73] Gordon's defence of impeachment was part of an insistence upon liberty and law against uncontrolled passion, and against Walpolean abuse of power. The justice of Macclesfield's impeachment was defined as the justice of a common law that provided security of property against boundless commercial change, and as the justice of a common law that provided certainty against arbitrary power.

Another particularly telling element of Gordon's defence of impeachment was that his arguments were marshalled in support of claims about the continued relevance of class, honour and reputation within this commercial society. The very opening of *The Justice of Parliaments* called upon the authority of Sallust and Juvenal to make the case that when men of a high social status perform criminal acts they were, justly, more prone to publicity and censure than 'Men of an obscure Class' might be.

> The Nature of their Crime alters, and takes a fresh Gloss, and Degrees of Heinousness, from the Character and Circumstances of the Persons by whom committed; and as the *Satyrist* justly remarks,
> – *Still more publick Scandal Vice extends,*
> *As He is Great, and Noble, who offends.*
>
> We make Allowances to *poor* Rogues and *undignified* Delinquents, from Poverty and Necessities driving them to unwarrantable Shifts for a Subsistence; but we have not the same Room to excuse Criminals, who are paid largely and have ample Perquisites for doing Justice, yet cannot perswade themselves to act with Conscience and Integrity.[74]

Honour and reputation, which were critical for the amassing of wealth, should be indicative of trustworthy character rather than a cover for fraud. In highlighting this comparison between the 'great and noble' and 'poor

72 Pocock, *Machiavellian Moment*, 473–4; Mitchell, 'Character of an Independent Whig', 296.

73 Mitchell, 'Character of an Independent Whig', 310. Cf Lemmings, 'Dark Side of Enlightenment', 152–3, on Cato's invocation of a 'law and order' vocabulary and advocacy of legislative solutions.

74 Gordon, *Justice of Parliaments*, 1–2; he returns to this theme 16–17, 27, 59; and finally underscores the particular honour associated with the Lords as judges, using the language of credit and debt to describe the dignity of nobility, 19–20, 22, 24, 27. On the influence of the Roman tradition see John Sekora, *Luxury: The Concept in Western Thought, Eden to Smollett* (Baltimore, 1977).

rogues and undignified delinquents', Gordon alluded to contemporary complaint that, in fact, wealthy offenders were usually left alone while the poor were subject to frequent fines and punishment. This was the thrust of Daniel Defoe's earlier critique of the Societies for the Reformation of Manners' campaign against prostitutes, bawds and drunks. '[T]he punishing vices in the poor, which are daily practiced by the rich,' Defoe explained, 'seems to me to be setting our constitution with the wrong men upward, and making men criminals because they want money.'[75] Gordon's defence of punishing the crimes of the lord chancellor was not only this kind of critique of the hypocrisy of the moral reformers, nor even simply an attack on Macclesfield, but must also be understood as a critique of an offender like Walpole who was left unscathed after 1720.[76] Such failure of legal restraints was more troubling for Gordon than the passions that led men, wealthy or poor, to crime.

Others who endorsed Macclesfield's impeachment also used the language of status and honour, but did so as part of a straightforward attack on the negative connotations of the lord chancellor's avarice. This discourse was typical of a cultural ideology of politeness, taste and civility associated with the Spectator project of Addison and Steele and, even more in the 1720s, with the philosophical works of the Earl of Shaftesbury. 'No single work was more important than the *Characteristics* in articulating the moral foundations for what has been called "the social theory of elite hegemony" in eighteenth-century Britain,' Mandeville's modern interpreter E.J. Hundert insists, 'or for naturalizing those modes of mannered display through which the governing classes publicly dramatized their right to rule.'[77] A construction of the problem of avarice within this 'polite' discourse appears in the trial records and in associated texts like Wilson's commentary. One set of arguments defined Macclesfield's true guilt as valuing money above good breeding. Critics of the Earl pointed to evidence of an ignoble reverence for money in Macclesfield's willingness to demean himself for as little as one hundred guineas, and in his propensity to advance 'mean men' – men of little fortune and less ability – to Chancery masterships.[78] The eleventh article of impeachment detailed this charge that Macclesfield 'did admit

75 [Daniel Defoe], *A Review of the Affairs of France*, I, no. 85 (26 Dec. 1704), quoted in Robert Shoemaker, *Prosecution and Punishment: Petty Crime and the Law in London and Rural Middlesex c.1660–1720* (Cambridge, 1991), 250.

76 Gordon includes a telling statement on the psychology of guilt, and the mortification suffered by a peer who is impeached, *Justice of Parliaments*, 16–17.

77 Hundert, *Enlightenment's Fable*, 124.

78 *Trial of Thomas Earl of Macclesfield*, 898–99; *New Abridgement and Critical Review*, 875, 875b. The language of class and credit is associated with an anti-Irish discourse in Wilson: one of the belittling criticisms he offers against John Strange is that Strange used a 'Hibernian Style' of questioning in the courtroom. Wilson, *Trial of Macclesfield … Abridg'd. With Remarks*, 11.

several persons to the said offices of Masters of the said Court of Chancery, who, at the time of such their admission, were of small substance and ability, very unfit to be trusted with the great sums of money and other effects of the suitors of the said Court, lodged in their hands by the orders of the said Court'.[79] A false sense of value underlay the crime: rather than calculating an applicant's immediate worth, and willingness to pay the chancellor's fee, Macclesfield should have considered the potential master's entire wealth and social worth.[80]

From the perspective of those governing classes, including his fellow lords and ministers, Macclesfield had subverted their common interests and reputation when he admitted inferior men to the masterships. These inferior men represented the sordid side of commercial development and prosperity: 'for men of small fortunes,' Commons manager Arthur Onslow reminded the lords, '… as they have more temptations, so they run less hazard than others in preying upon money that is entrusted with them; and it is this, my lords,' Onslow concluded, 'that encourages such men to give exorbitant rates for employments which afford them those opportunities.'[81] Such men, focused solely on material gain and unaffected by the civilising and moralising effects of polite society, were the very opponents of an urbane and sociable milieu. Onslow here tapped into contemporary opposition to the stock market as a venue that afforded opportunity for social mobility. He also extended another version of contemporary outrage as it was directed against the great impact of the burst bubble on 'high politics, high finance and high society'.[82] Had the lord chancellor been properly concerned with the social status of the masters, prosecutors explained, he would have been aware of their illicit motives, and he would have foreseen their perilous behaviour. Macclesfield's endorsement of such men instead, and his own wholesale pursuit of luxury and pleasure, were construed as a total abandonment of gentlemanly and enlightened culture.

Macclesfield's opponents not only advanced these kinds of arguments about nobility but their depictions of Macclesfield's guilt advanced a number of gendered concerns. First, in characterising his actions as a kind of moral degeneracy critics used sexual imagery long used by proponents of moral reform who depicted government ministers as 'pimps and panderers' and officeholders as 'common prostitutes'.[83] To Macclesfield belongs 'guilt without measure,' Arthur Onslow insisted for example, because the Earl 'brought a disgrace upon his country, by prostituting one of its highest courts of justice to his own avarice and corruption, to the rapine and corruption of

[79] *Trial of Thomas Earl of Macclesfield*, 775.

[80] Wilson, *Trial of Macclesfield…Abridg'd. With Remarks*, 64–5.

[81] *Trial of Thomas Earl of Macclesfield*, 899.

[82] Hoppit, 'Myths of the Bubble', 158. Murphy, *Origins of English Financial Markets*; Banner, *Anglo-American Securities Regulation*, 65–72.

[83] Hayton, 'Moral Reform and Country Politics', 84–5.

his inferior officers, and to the undoing of those, who, by the constitution of the kingdom, have been forced into his power'.[84] Most signally, those who were 'forced' and 'undone' by his 'prostitution' of justice were the large numbers of female suitors in Chancery. This kind of language called upon the familiar association between arbitrary power and rape.[85] It also echoed the legal and physical attacks on prostitution, sodomy and other 'lewd' and 'debauched' practices carried out by the Societies for the Reformation of Manners as they advanced prosecutions of brothels and bawdy houses in these years. The reference was deliberate since at this very moment in 1725 the prosecution of prostitutes and other 'lewd and disorderly persons' was a matter of legal controversy.[86] The association of Macclesfield with prostitution would have aligned the case against him with the cause of the reformers in this set of other contemporary cases.

This species of argument against Macclesfield's 'prostitution of justice' was also here aligned with argument against Mandeville, since the physician-philosopher had very recently published an argument against the prosecutions of brothels, and in favour of legalised prostitution, as part of his reevaluation of virtue and social good. Mandeville's *A Modest Defence of Publick Stews: Or, An Essay upon Whoring* first appeared in 1724 and was republished in 1725 with an 'Answer' appended in defence of the work of moral reform.[87] This 'Answer' to Mandeville advertised the progress made by the societies in combating 'the Prevalency of the most scandalous Vices, and', the author added, 'in many Instances, a visible Reformation has ensued'.[88] When Macclesfield's crimes were viewed as another form of prostitution his impeachment could easily be identified with the good work of moral reform, and with the refutation of Mandeville's claims. And yet even

84 *Trial of Thomas Earl of Macclesfield*, 899–900; further use of the language of prostitution 1061, 1075.

85 Julia Rudolph, 'Rape and Resistance: Women and Consent in Seventeenth-Century English Legal and Political Thought', *Journal of British Studies*, 39, 2 (April, 2000): 157–84.

86 Shoemaker, *Prosecution and Punishment*, ch. 9; Hunt, *Middling Sort*, 112–13, 115; Jennine Hurl-Eamon, 'Policing Male Heterosexuality: The Reformation of Manners Societies' Campaign Against the Brothels in Westminster, 1690–1720', *Journal of Social History*, 37, 4 (Summer, 2004): 1017–35; Faramerz Dabhoiwala, 'Sex and the Societies for Moral Reform, 1688–1800', *Journal of British Studies*, 46, 2 (April, 2007): 290–319; Randolph Trumbach, 'Sex, Gender and Sexual Identity in Modern Culture: Male Sodomy and Female Prostitution in Enlightenment London', *Journal of the History of Sexuality*, 2, 2 (October, 1991): 186–203.

87 Bernard Mandeville, *A Modest Defence of Publick Stews: Or, an Essay upon Whoring. As it is Now Practis'd in these Kingdoms* (London, 1724), and *A Modest Defence of Publick Stews: Or, an Essay upon Whoring ... Answer'd* (London, 1725). For Shaftesbury's views on sexual vice as part of moral-philosophical debate see, for example, Brian Cowan, 'Reasonable Ecstasies: Shaftesbury and the Languages of Libertinism', *Journal of British Studies*, 37, 2 (April, 1998): 111–38.

88 *Modest Defence of Publick Stews Answer'd*, 61.

here Mandeville's recognition of the power of self-interest and vice as the engine of commercial society was not so easily countered. The author of the 'Answer' found himself also obliged to offer a defence of the societies against the accusation that members prosecuted prostitution simply out of a mercenary design to enrich themselves. [89]

The example of prostitution as a money-making activity was, generally, at the centre of debate about commercial activity and corruption. 'For the reformers ... and Mandeville himself,' Laura Rosenthal avers, 'prostitution became an emblematic vice of excessive desire that commercial society had to confront.'[90] Of course, prostitution was conventionally understood as a female money-making activity, and the connection made between Macclesfield's 'excessive desire' and prostitution, and the crackdown on prostitution itself, were also expressive of contemporary fears about female sexuality and female agency. Such fears, extended further into conceptions of female depravity, were also articulated in the contemporary campaign against the gin trade, another special concern of Master of the Rolls Joseph Jekyll.[91] These anxieties, and related ideas about women's proper roles as agents and objects of exchange within marriage, appear in other elements of the charges against Macclesfield. For example, prosecutors launched a powerful and sustained complaint against the lord chancellor's refusal to protect the property of female suitors in Chancery. Those women who rightly looked to him for protection and support of settlements, they said, were now left penniless and powerless. Counsel made the case for impeachment, in part, by providing evidence of women whose fortunes were lost in Master Dormer's risky investment scheme. [92]

The masters' and chancellor's responsibility for their suitors' monies was defined as a trusteeship, and this made it easier to advance the charge of betrayal of widows and orphans which was another repeated discourse in the courtroom and in wider public discourse about the trial.[93] Indeed, trusteeship

89 Ibid., 64–5.

90 Laura J. Rosenthal, *Infamous Commerce: Prostitution in Eighteenth-Century British Literature and Culture* (Ithaca, 2006), 57; cf also Shelly Burtt, 'The Societies for the Reformation of Manners: Between John Locke and the Devil in Augustan England', in Roger D. Lund ed., *The Margins of Orthodoxy: Heterodox Writing and Cultural Response 1660–1750* (Cambridge, 1995), 149–69.

91 Hunt, *Middling Sort*, 112–13; Clark, 'Mother Gin Controversy', 70–1; White, 'Slow but Sure Poyson', 37, 47. See also Ingrid Tague, *Women of Quality: Accepting and Contesting Ideals of Femininity in England, 1690–1760* (Woodbridge, 2002).

92 One central example, introduced in Article XVI of the charges, *Trial of Thomas Earl of Macclesfield*, 778, was of Mrs Elizabeth Chitty whose monies were lost in Dormer's deficiencies; Macclesfield made up part of the losses himself, in an attempt to conceal the problem, but warned that no more of her money would be forthcoming. For other examples adduced of widows' monies lost see *Trial of Thomas Earl of Macclesfield*, 995–1001; Wilson, *Tryal of the Earl of Macclesfield...Abridg'd. With Remarks*, 22.

93 *Trial of Thomas Earl of Macclesfield*, 784, 809, 811, 899, 1030, 1059, 1073, 1375;

was seen as the essential factor that allowed for corruption. This focus on trusteeship provides another indication of contemporary uncertainty about Chancery's development of trusts as a means for female property ownership in equity. If trusts were prone to abuse even by those in Chancery who upheld them, it could be argued, then trusts were inherently unstable and ultimately unjust. Here was another facet of that jurisdictional and jurisprudential dispute between common law and equity in Macclesfield's trial, and another endorsement of common law authority and stability.

The rage expressed against the lord chancellor's failure to protect female property must, finally, be seen as an expression of concern about women's involvement in speculation. This was a concern that was tied to specific anger about the burst South Sea Bubble, as well as wider anxiety about 'new money' and the financial revolution. When prosecutors and commentators relied upon sentimental images of female suitors as weak, dependent and ruined they actually aligned the case for impeachment with contemporary hostility towards women's commercial activities.[94] In this sense, the anger against the lord chancellor was not so much expressive of disquiet about the exploitation of powerless women. It was, rather, the manifestation of a fear that commercialisation was undermining conventional gender roles.

Early eighteenth-century women were fully engaged in the contemporary economy and were, in fact, active investors, just as likely as men to buy and sell securities, and just as able to realise capital gains. Moreover, what has been described as the 'financial acumen' and 'financial independence' of women was evident both in their investment strategies and in their broader participation in business.[95] The activities of single women were especially

Macclesfield's defence not only rejected these arguments but also employed this same appeal to the image of defenceless widows and orphans, *Trial of Thomas Earl of Macclesfield*, 1106, 1118, 1166–7, 1251, 1257; *New Abridgement and Critical Review*, 881, 887; Wilson, *Trial of Macclesfield…Abridg'd. With Remarks*, 14, 17, 20–1; Newsletters 13 February 1724/5, 16 February 1724/5, 18 February 1724/5, NLW, Longueville 1187, fols 5–10. The newsletter of 18 February referred to a contemporary pamphlet entitled *Remarks on the Widdows and Orphans* which was answered by a pamphlet entitled *The Advocate*.

94 Margaret Hunt has cogently described the moral reform societies as male associations, and as expressive of a fear 'about female influence within spheres men preferred as far as possible to monopolize.' Hunt, *Middling Sort*, 112, 122.

95 Anne Laurence, 'Women Investors, "That Nasty South Sea Affair" and the Rage to Speculate in Early Eighteenth-Century England', *Accounting Business and Financial History*, 16, 2 (July, 2006): 245–64; Laurence, 'The Emergence of a Private Clientele for Banks in the Early Eighteenth Century: Hoare's Bank and Some Women Customers', *Economic History Review*, 61, 3 (2008): 565–86; Ann M. Carlos and Larry Neal, 'Women Investors in Early Capital Markets 1720–1725', *Financial History Review*, 11, 2 (October, 2004): 197–224; Ann M. Carlos, Karen Maguire and Larry Neal, 'Financial Acumen, Women Speculators, and the Royal African Company during the South Sea Bubble', *Accounting Business and Financial History*, 16, 2 (July, 2006): 219–43; Nicola Phillips, *Women in Business 1700–1850* (Woodbridge, 2006); Amy M. Froide, *Never Married:*

important here although, as we have seen, the financial independence and potential for property ownership by married women through the equitable modifications of coverture, were also significant. Contemporaries articulated ambivalence about, and at times overt hostility to women's financial independence and engagement in commercial activities in a variety of ways; these concerns were often tied to contemporary discourses about luxury, nation and class. Not surprisingly, the language of politeness, with its heightened attention to gendered definitions of civility, credit and honour, was an important part of public debate, for example, over appropriate female trades.[96] The outcry about the losses suffered by female suitors in Chancery was part of this broader ambivalence regarding women as property holders, and is another example of the relevance of gender concerns to contemporary arguments about financial innovation and commercial change. In this period of South Sea Crisis, of course, the evils of commerce were underscored and the dangers of gambling on the stock market were seen as equal for both men and women.[97] But the attack on Macclesfield's Chancery masters as investors was also part of a pointed critique of *women* as investors.

This gendered critique was part of a larger critique taking shape in which an unfettered and unmediated market culture was characterised as the antithesis of refinement, sociability, judgment and morality. Legal culture, by contrast, was valued as sociable, moral and masculine, and common law was associated, by both prosecution and defence, with public utility and the protection of property. Adhering to established procedures and allowing for gradual, incremental change were not understood in opposition to enlightened reason and public utility but were rather seen as the best ways to ensure justice. Moreover, this reaffirmation of common law tradition and prescription was understood to be the best way to negotiate financial innovation and commercial change, and to provide a legitimating ideology that could preserve the stability and ensure the civility of the post-Revolution state and society. In fact, for many of Macclesfield's critics the lord chancellor's actions and attitudes were especially offensive because they endorsed those controversial ideas, advanced by his friend Bernard Mandeville, that threatened to undermine both settlement and change. From this perspective, the most dangerous aspect of Mandeville's ideas, and of Macclefield's actions, was their potential to unmask the hypocrisies and contradictions underlying *both* law and economy. Mandeville characteristically expressed this very kind of open challenge to hypocrisy and 'moral self-delusion' in his 1723 essay *A Search into the Nature of Society*:

Singlewomen in Early Modern England (Oxford, 2005); Amy Louise Erickson, 'Coverture and Capitalism'.

96 Phillips, *Women in Business*, chs 8–9.

97 Laurence, 'Women Investors', 259–60.

> In all Civil Societies Men are taught insensibly to be Hypocrites from their Cradle, no body dares to own that he gets by Publick Calamities, or even by the Loss of Private Persons. The Sexton would be stoned should he wish openly for the Death of the Parishioners, tho' every body knew that he had nothing else to live upon[98]

Mandeville's arresting image was echoed by Thomas Gordon in *The Humourist* (1725) where Gordon remarked that '… if the *Reformation of Manners* should so far prevail as to abolish Fornication, Multitudes of Surgeons would be ruined.'[99]

In his defence against impeachment Macclesfield did not 'dare own' (lest he be stoned – or fined more heavily) that he had profited from others' miseries. But Macclesfield did surely reproduce Mandeville's and Gordon's charge against elitist hypocrisy when he claimed that his actions conformed to the pattern set by other chancellors and, further, when he insisted that advancing men to office for financial consideration was no different from advancing them 'for the sake of kindred, or friendship or recommendation'.[100] Lord Chancellor Macclesfield tried to expose the hypocrisy of his impeachment in other ways as well. His defence sought to unmask the mercenary motives of his prosecutors, like Lord Morpeth, who brought charges in the interest of their own financial gain more than in the interest of justice. Here counsellors tried to point out the ways in which those sentimental images of women and orphans were being used to manipulate an audience, and they challenged the Lords to see not only the political motives but also the tensions in economic thought that underlay this trial.[101] But the Lords refused to see, they did not 'dare to know', and they did not accept Macclesfield's defence. The only area of agreement between prosecution and defence in this episode was in the endorsement of common law justice. Both sides valued the adherence to past practice and the authority of tradition.

98 Mandeville, *A Search into the Nature of Society, Fable of the Bees*, vol. 1, 349. See also Hundert, *Enlightenment's Fable*, 124–5.

99 Thomas Gordon, *The Humourist* (London, 1725), 114–15, quoted in Mitchell, 'Character of an Independent Whig', 304.

100 *Trial of Thomas Earl of Macclesfield*, 1274. Macclesfield's defence did at times also endorse the argument from class interest by insisting, for example, that the lord chancellor had been deceived by some masters about their wealth and status. *Trial of Thomas Earl of Macclesfield*, 1174.

101 *Trial of Thomas Earl of Macclesfield*, 1166–7; *New Abridgement and Critical Review*, 877; on Morpeth see n. 11 above.

7

Legal Histories and Enlightened Historiography

The crisis in Chancery, and impeachment of Lord Chancellor Macclesfield in 1725, was a broadly significant moment in enlightened debate about the effects of economic change. Its significance is underscored by the fact that the contemporary response to revelations of corruption in law and government was not only moral-philosophical, concerned with sociability, civility or utility. The response was also historical, and was concerned with erudite evidence underpinning socio-economic explanation. In the aftermath of the impeachment histories of the Chancery were written by Samuel Burroughs and Philip Yorke as part of a continuing discussion about the justice of equity and the jurisdiction of that court.

These authors were prompted to write in response to the scandal and associated economic dislocation that fuelled ongoing controversies in the court. Yet their histories were not focused on the same questions about the sale and abuse of office that had animated the impeachment hearings. Indeed just after Macclesfield's conviction the sale of masterships was openly recognised as a traditional perquisite of the chancellor's office. His successor, Lord Chancellor King, was granted a pension increased by L1200 in order to compensate for the money he lost now that the practice was discredited and discontinued.[1] If Burroughs' and Yorke's histories of Chancery did not review this particular issue of the sale of office, however, they did focus on the matter of procedural regularity in the functioning of the court. Macclesfield's violation, or at least manipulation, of Chancery procedures was viewed as a key part of his guilt, and contemporaries were convinced that the development of regular process was necessary for the achievement of justice. A specific debate about process began when Peter King took up the office of lord chancellor and made new efforts towards greater accountability and transparency in his court. For example, King instituted strict oversight procedures regarding the administration of funds, and the methods of recording decrees. But fellow Chancery official Joseph Jekyll objected to these procedures which he viewed as intrusions into areas of his own jurisdiction as the master of the rolls. Conflict over the nature and scope of Chancery jurisdiction was reignited, and the two men turned to history,

1 Foss, *Judges of England*, vol. 8, 136; Holdsworth, *History of English Law*, vol. 12, 206.

written by proxies Burroughs and Yorke, in order to justify their own claims to authority.[2]

These histories of Chancery are among the many legal histories written and published in the early eighteenth century, all of which form an important part of an enlightened historiography developing in this period. Like other historians, authors of legal history were interested in charting the course of socio-economic, institutional and even, for some, cultural change in England. While the texts produced in debate between Burroughs and Yorke retained characteristics of earlier polemical histories of English law and government their work should not be dismissed, as scholars have tended to do, as a repetition of those seventeenth-century partisan controversies over equity, or over the antiquity of the commons. Nor should we simply regard their disagreement as a sign of unease about the inefficiency of the Chancery, which necessarily led towards a legislative resolution affirming the judicial authority of the master of the rolls.[3] Rather, we must recognise that participants in this debate were still grappling with the broad and varied consequences of economic and commercial change; and that in this instance contemporary analysis was articulated in historical more than moral-philosophical terms. Yorke's and Burroughs' concentration on institutional history and, more generally, eighteenth-century legal writers' focus on the historical development of English property and constitution, should be understood within the context of eighteenth-century historiography. Historians of English law were interested in social and economic as well as political and institutional development. Several legal histories were especially engaged with the contemporary definition and analysis of the impact of feudalism. These histories took part in an emerging Enlightenment historiography newly concerned with explanation for change over time.

Analysis of this legal historical writing is an important but neglected part of scholarly interpretation of enlightened historical writing. An historian like Adam Smith, for example, clearly turned to the work of the early eight-

2 Giles Jacob, *The Compleat Chancery Practiser: Or, The Whole Proceedings and Practice of the High Court of Chancery in a Perfect New Manner* (London, 1730), 45–9; Philip Yorke, *A Discourse of the Judicial Authority Belonging to the Office of Master of the Rolls in the High Court of Chancery* (London, 2nd edn., 1728), i–iv. Holdsworth notes that some of Peter King's other attempts at reform were also thwarted by Jekyll; both Holdsworth and Lemmings suggest that King may have been involved in drafting legislation to reform legal fees, and to change the language of legal proceedings, in 1731–33. Holdsworth, *History of English Law*, vol. 12, 213–14; David Lemmings, 'King, Peter', *ODNB*; cf Michael Lobban, '"Old Wine in New Bottles": The Concept and Practice of Law Reform c.1780–1830', in Arthur R. Burns and Joanna Innes eds, *Rethinking the Age of Reform, Britain 1780–1850* (Cambridge, 2003), 114–17.

3 These are the explanations offered by Holdsworth, *History of English Law*, vol. 12, 185, vol. 1, 215 and Michael Lobban, 'Preparing for Fusion: Reforming the Nineteenth-Century Court of Chancery, Part 1', *Law and History Review*, 22, 2 (Summer, 2004): 392 n. 7.

eenth-century judge and historian Geoffrey Gilbert in thinking through his economic history of Europe, but modern scholars have not. We must consider how legal historians like Gilbert or Samuel Burroughs contributed to a macro-narrative of progress from the fall of Rome to a modern, enlightened, society and economy.[4] Moreover, since collection, compilation and abridgment structures were essential to the legal histories, just as they were to other law books and history books published at this time, we must also consider the relevance of contemporary print culture and the ways in which these histories took part in that Enlightenment of communication, organisation and conversation.[5] Attention to the role of print will illuminate similarities in the development of legal and historical writing in this period and contribute to our further understanding of eighteenth-century common law jurisprudence. The value common lawyers attached to prescriptive example, or to antiquity, was not simply disputatious or a form of erudition, but was also part of contemporary knowledge production. The values of prescription and collection shaped both enlightened historiography and jurisprudence.

Geoffrey Gilbert is a crucial figure in this history of enlightened legal historical writing for several reasons. First, he was the author of major histories of the English courts, legal procedure and doctrine, such as *The History and Practice of the High Court of Chancery* (1758), *An Historical Account of the Original and Nature as well as the Law of Devises and Revocations* (1739), and *The History and Practice of Civil Actions in the Court of Common Pleas* (1737). Reports of Gilbert's judgments in the Irish Exchequer are also indicative of the judge's historical interests, revealing a tendency, as Michael Macnair explains, 'to go into the legal history of the topic at considerable length before coming to a rather brief...treatment of the issues in the case and the currently applicable authority'.[6] Macnair and other scholars have noted that Gilbert's historical texts were parts of a larger treatise on English law that the judge drafted in the first decade of the eighteenth century. Gilbert himself pointed to the overall plan of his work in several of his texts, and his stated goal was confirmed by one of his earliest editors, of the posthumously published *A Treatise on the Court of Exchequer*. This editor suggested that if the judge had fulfilled his intention 'to write a general History of the Courts of *Justice*...his Work would have been of great Utility to those who

4 Pocock, *Barbarism and Religion, Volume 2: Narratives of Civil Government* (Cambridge, 1999), 24. Pocock mentions Geoffrey Gilbert, *Ancient Constitution and the Feudal Law*, 243–4, as does R.J. Smith, *The Gothic Bequest: Medieval Institutions in British Thought 1688–1863* (Cambridge, 1987), 47 n. 13, but neither author offers analysis of Gilbert's work.

5 Philip Hicks, *Neoclassical History and English Culture: From Clarendon to Hume* (Basingstoke, 1996), ch. 6; Daniel R. Woolf, *Reading History in Early Modern England* (Cambridge, 2000), chs. 5–7.

6 Macnair, 'Gilbert and his Treatises', 254–5.

may have Occasion to study the *English* law on fundamental Principles'.[7] The different parts of Gilbert's treatise were published separately and, with the exception of his *Abstract of the Essay on Human Understanding*, all of his work was published posthumously, but his legal texts had an earlier influence through circulation in manuscript.

Thus another reason why Gilbert is a key figure in the analysis of eighteenth-century historiography is that the composition and circulation of his texts illuminate the relationship between scribal and print cultures in this period, and demonstrate the use of enlightened techniques of compilation in knowledge production. As we've seen, for example, Matthew Bacon likely had access to Gilbert's manuscripts in Ireland in the 1720s, and may have incorporated portions of Gilbert's work into his *New Abridgment of the Law* (1736–66). Here we should understand the uses of Gilbert's work as another part of those legal commonplace and abridgment traditions, and of the developments in compilation, organisation, circulation and retrieval of information that shaped early eighteenth-century ideas about the nature and authority of common law. Gilbert composed his texts within these traditions, as an amalgamation of narrative and example. This was not simply a flawed or weak approach in which, as Macnair suggests, 'analysis and historical beginnings drift into lists and commonplacing'.[8] Gilbert's methods were, rather, characteristic of an eighteenth-century culture of 'information overload' within which both common law and historical thinking developed.

A third, compelling, reason why Geoffrey Gilbert is a key figure in the development of legal history and common law jurisprudence is that as a judge and an historian he was engaged with both constitutional and institutional histories of law. More than one of his histories featured a separate essay, *On the Constitution of England*, to serve as a foundation for his project. Many of Gilbert's other treatises included reflection on changes in the established institutions, and social foundations, of the English constitution from the Saxon to Stuart eras. And as a judge on both the English and Irish benches Gilbert was involved in the investigation and resolution of major cases of constitutional significance. One of these major cases was Macclesfield's impeachment. Gilbert was appointed as one of the commissioners of the Great Seal upon Lord Chancellor Macclesfield's resignation in 1725, and soon after the trial he was elevated to the position of chief baron of the English Exchequer. Gilbert had been a puisne justice of that court since 1722, and before that he had served as chief baron of the Irish Exchequer. In fact it was his involvement as chief baron in an earlier Irish case of major constitutional significance, *Annesley v Sherlock* (1717–19), that led to Gilbert's first promotion to the English Exchequer. In the course of

7 Geoffrey Gilbert, *A Treatise on the Court of Exchequer* (London, 1758), iv. This work was first published in 1738 in a slightly different form, and entitled *An Historical View of the Court of Exchequer, and of the King's Revenues there Answered* (London, 1738).

8 Macnair, 'Gilbert and his Treatises', 260.

this dispute Gilbert offered a defence of the jurisdiction of the British House of Lords and, more generally, of the authority of the British over the Irish parliament. Not surprisingly his arguments in this case were well-received at Westminster and ultimately endorsed by the passage of the Declaratory Act (1720) asserting British legislative supremacy over Ireland.

Annesley v Sherlock was significant because of this ensuing legislation, and because the case fostered debate about the scope of equity jurisdiction, particularly regarding the matter of appeals from equity courts. Controversy surrounding this case led contemporaries to pose questions about the nature of justice, and to reflect on the ways in which legitimate authority had developed. These debates about the origins and authority of law were tied to contemporary questions about the constitution of empire in the British Isles. And such questions were understood in terms of the interpretation of history: controversy over the barons' ruling in *Annesley v Sherlock* contributed to a growing interest in the constitutional histories of Ireland, and of England, in the early eighteenth century.

This chapter begins with these early eighteenth-century imperial and constitutional histories in order to explore the role of history writing in the 1719 constitutional crisis between Ireland and Britain. An important part of understanding that role lies in analysing such histories within the context of broader historiographical trends in England and Ireland between 1689 and 1725. Like many other histories written at this time, for example by James Tyrrell, White Kennett, or Richard Cox, these legal histories were polemical works, engaged with contemporary partisan struggle over the nature of the ancient constitution. The Irish, or imperial, question is another reason why such party-political histories persist in the first two decades of the eighteenth century. A similar kind of partisanship affected the institutional histories written by Burroughs and Yorke after 1725, but so too did other concerns about historical explanation. As I turn to the analysis of their histories of Chancery, and to Geoffrey Gilbert's histories of the courts and other areas of English law, I intend to restore these examples of legal historical writing to their enlightened historiographical context. The fact that eighteenth-century legal history has generally been excluded from scholarship focused on the development of Enlightenment historiography is another reminder of that exclusion of common law from Enlightenment that this book has sought to challenge.

Ireland's legal past

The litigation between Maurice Annesley and Hester Sherlock that ignited the 1719–20 constitutional crisis between Ireland and Britain revolved around a dispute over property and trusteeship. This dispute began when Maurice Annesley, who served as trustee of the Sherlock family estates, laid claim to a portion of that estate. Annesley based his demand partly on an argument for his right to some recompense for the services he provided as trustee. Members of the Sherlock family contested Annesley's assertion of entitlement in a suit brought before the Irish Exchequer in the early years of the eighteenth century. In this original case Annesley's possession of part of the Sherlock estate was upheld by the Irish Exchequer judges, but their judgment was challenged several years later when the widow Hester Sherlock appealed to the Irish House of Lords. The Irish Lords reversed the first Exchequer decree, and restored the properties to Sherlock in June 1716. During the following spring and summer of 1717 a series of appeals and counter-petitions between the two parties ensued, all of which emphasised the underlying conflict over jurisdiction. First, Maurice Annesley petitioned the British House of Lords to reverse his dispossession and based his plea, in part, on the argument that the Irish Lords lacked jurisdiction to hear appeals from the Exchequer court. Hester Sherlock, in turn, neatly rejected the authority of the British Lords when she refused to provide an answer to Annesley's petition there. She further challenged their jurisdiction by petitioning the Irish Lords, once again, to uphold her property claims.[9]

These Sherlock properties included 'the town and lands of Little Rath, Bodingstown, Dar and Mullenasooky, lying in the county of Kildare'.[10] The sheriff of Kildare, Alexander Burrowes, also became caught up in the conflict over jurisdiction in the course of continued struggle over the Sherlock estate. Burrowes was accused of interfering with legal process because he refused to comply with the Exchequer barons' order to restore Maurice Annesley to possession – an order which these barons issued in compliance with a directive from the British Lords.

> The High Sheriff having refused to execute the said injunction, conceiving it to be a breach of the order, and of the rights and privileges of the *Irish* house of Peers, had several fines set upon him by the Barons of the *exchequer*; and on the other hand, the house of Peers of *Great-Britain*, upon report from the Lords Committees, appointed to enquire into the reason of the delay, in not obeying the orders of this house, relating to the appeal of *Maurice Annesley*, Esq; and how the same might more properly be enforced: Ordered, *January* the 23d, 1718/19, that the Barons of the court of *exchequer*, in *Ireland*, be directed to proceed by the most speedy and effectual methods, to cause possession of the estate of the said *Maurice Annesley*, as required by order of this house of the 6*th* of *February* last, to be restored to him.[11]

9 *A Collection of the Parliamentary Debates in England from the year MDCLVIII to the Present Time* (London, 1739), 268–70; Isolde Victory, 'The Making of the 1720 Declaratory Act', in Gerard O'Brien ed., *Parliament, Politics and People: Essays in Eighteenth-Century Irish Society* (Dublin, 1989), 14–16; David W. Hayton, 'The Stanhope/Sunderland Ministry and the Repudiation of Irish Parliamentary Independence', *The English Historical Review*, 113, 452 (June, 1998): 612.

10 *Collection of Parliamentary Debates*, 270.

11 Ibid., 269; see also *Proceedings of the House of Lords in Ireland against … Barons of the*

Chief Baron Gilbert, and the other barons Pocklington and St Leger, regarded Sheriff Burrowes' violation of established process as a threat to the Exchequer's capacity to provide justice. In response to Burrowes' actions they took steps similar to those taken by Chief Justice Holt in his conflict with Hertford's Sheriff Toler. First the Irish Exchequer barons fined and ultimately imprisoned Burrowes. Next they followed the British Lords' command to dispossess the female property holder, Hester Sherlock, in defiance of the Irish Lords' decree.[12]

The barons clearly insisted upon strict enforcement of procedure, and assertion of jurisdiction. Indeed Chief Baron Gilbert was especially willing to address the question of jurisdiction at issue between the Irish and British House of Lords when he defended the actions taken by his court. Gilbert asserted, 'I am not answerable to the Lords of Ireland for any proceedings on the orders of the Lords of Great Britain.' In return for his open acknowledgment of a superior authority in the British Lords Gilbert and his fellow barons were arrested, by order of the Irish House of Lords.[13] The anger at Baron Gilbert was especially fierce, partly because he had been held in high esteem by the Irish, and was even recently awarded an honorary degree by the University of Dublin. Now in response to what looked to the Irish like betrayal, Gilbert 'was left to the mercy of a mob, who broke the windows of his house, and [he] was told by Archbishop King that he had acted with such disregard of his oath as to deserve not only imprisonment, but even death itself, and the curses of all honest men'.[14]

Much like the English disputes involving Lord Chancellor Macclesfield, or even Chief Baron Atkyns, this Irish controversy about women's property led to expressions of public anger and to intense jurisdictional and jurisprudential debate. Moreover, contemporaries expanded the scope of debate by associating controversy over the Sherlock property with a whole series of recent conflicts over title to land in Ireland. These conflicts turned on the question of Irish parliamentary independence that was a matter of wider political interest especially after 1689. Two important prior cases, *The Irish Society v the Bishop of Derry* (1698) and *Lord Ward v the Earl of Meath* (1703), entailed similar deliberation on the nature and location of appellate jurisdiction to review cases. In these earlier instances when appeals were brought from the

Exchequer there for issuing Process in the Cause of Annesley and Sherlock, in Opposition to an Order of that House, in Thomas Salmon ed., *State Trials and Proceedings upon High Treason, and Other Crimes and Misdemeanors* (London, 1731), vol. 8, 351–61.

12 *Collection of Parliamentary Debates*, 269–70, *Proceedings of the House of Lords in Ireland*, 358–60. The orders from the British Lords to the Exchequer barons were signed by the clerk of the Parliament William Cowper, and conveyed in a separate letter to Chief Baron Gilbert from Lord Chancellor Macclesfield.

13 Hayton, 'Stanhope/Sunderland Ministry', 612; Victory, 'Making Declaratory Act', 17; *Collection of Parliamentary Debates*, 272–3.

14 F.E. Ball, *The Judges in Ireland*, vol. 2 (London, 1926), 89.

Irish Chancery to the Irish House of Lords, defenders of both the Irish and English Houses of Lords tied their assertions of ultimate appellate authority to a broader 'constitutional argument about relative powers between the two parliaments'.[15] These were also the years when controversial Irish legislation, such as the Woolen Act (1698/9) and the Act of Resumption (1700) regarding forfeited lands, was passed at Westminster. Since these policies were clear statements about British parliamentary authority, and clear challenges to Ireland's economic survival, they provoked vigorous response in Ireland, most famously in William Molyneux's *The Case of Ireland's being bound by Acts of Parliament in England, Stated* (1698). In the course of all of these cases and controversies Irishmen and women who rejected British claims to superior jurisdiction turned to history and precedent, as they had earlier in the seventeenth century, in order to demonstrate that Ireland was a separate kingdom, with a separate common law system and independent parliament that emanated from a shared crown.[16]

Thus in 1719, when the Irish Lords sought to explicate their decision regarding the Sherlock properties, defend the actions of Sheriff Burrowes and, most emphatically, justify their arrest and imprisonment of the barons of the Exchequer, they relied on many familiar arguments about common law and kingdom. The Resolutions of the Irish House of Lords, 28 July 1719, asserted that the barons 'in their proceedings in the cause between *Sherlock* and *Annesley*, and against *Alexander Burrowes*, Esq, late Sheriff of the county of *Kildare*, have acted contrary to law, and to the established practice of the King's courts'.[17] The Resolutions further tied this accusation to a warning that the barons' actions posed a dangerous challenge to the crown because they were 'in manifest derogation to, and diminution of, the King's prerogative'. A loaded language of 'betrayal' and 'pretended' authority was used to depict the chief baron as a threat:

> Jeffrey Gilbert, Esq. Lord Chief Baron of the court of Exchequer, having taken upon him to put in execution a pretended order from another court, contrary to the final judgment of this court of Parliament, in the cause between Sherlock and Annesley, is a betrayer of his Majesty's prerogative, and the undoubted ancient rights and privileges of this house, and of the rights and liberties of the subjects of this kingdom.[18]

15 Victory, 'Making Declaratory Act', 10.

16 Ibid., 10–14; Hayton, 'Stanhope/Sunderland Ministry', 610–11; Patrick Kelly, 'Conquest *versus* Consent as the Basis of the English Title to Ireland in William Molyneux's *Case of Ireland … Stated* (1698)', in Ciaran Brady and Jane Ohlmeyer eds, *British Interventions in Early Modern Ireland* (Cambridge, 2005), 339–40; Jim Smyth, '"Like Amphibious Animals": Irish Protestants, Ancient Britons, 1691–1707', *The Historical Journal*, 36, 4 (December, 1993): 792.

17 *Collection of Parliamentary Debates*, 272.

18 Ibid., 273.

This same charge was laid against barons Pocklington and St Leger. Such connected assertions about law and established court practice, and about prerogative, rights and liberties, were clearly reliant on statements about the origins and ancient practice of common law in Ireland. This history of law was further canvassed in a number of publications that appeared in 1719 and 1720, including *The Humble Representation made to the King's Majesty by the Lords Spiritual and Temporal in Parliament Assembled* (1719), *A Letter from a Member of the House of Commons in Ireland to a Gentleman of the Long Robe in England* (1720), *A Second Letter to a Gentleman of the Long Robe... Wherein some of the Late Illegal Proceedings of the Barons of the Exchequer in the Kingdom of Ireland are Plainly and Impartially Set Forth* (1720), and John Toland's *Reasons Most Humbly Offer'd to the Honorable House of Commons* (1720).[19] Molyneux's *Case of Ireland* was also republished at this time.

All of these texts reiterated the claim that in 1172 King Henry II had applied common law in Ireland at the request of the Irish, and had instituted a parliamentary constitution with the agreement or 'compact' of these ancient inhabitants. Sir Edward Coke's *Fourth Institute* was specifically cited, for example by the *Humble Representation to the King's Majesty* and *A Letter from a Member of the House of Commons in Ireland*, as unassailable authority for such an assertion:

> For there he [Coke] assures us that *not only King* John *as all Men agree; but* Henry *the Second also – did ordain and command, at the Instance of the* Irish, *that such Laws as he had in* England, *should be of force and observed in* Ireland. *And then he adds, hereby* Ireland *being of itself a DISTINCT DOMINION, and NO PART of the Kingdoms of* England, *was to have Parliaments held there as* England.[20]

The citation of Coke's *Institute* here was likely meant as an effective counterargument to the citation of Coke's judgment in *Calvin's Case*, which was often used by the English as a 'crucial precedent for establishing Ireland's status as a conquered territory in English law'.[21] The reference to Coke, and to other authorities like Matthew Paris or an Irish *Modus Tenendi Parliamenta*, was more generally aimed to underscore the ancient constitutionalist character of the history these texts presented. With these citations the texts of 1719–20 repeated the claims for original consent against conquest,

19 The full title of Toland's work was *Reasons Most Humbly Offer'd to the Honorable House of Commons why the Bill sent down to them from the Honorable House of Lords Entitul'd*, An Act for Better Securing the Dependency of the Kingdom of Ireland upon the Crown of Great Britain *shou'd not Pass into a Law.*

20 *A Letter from a Member of the House of Commons in Ireland to a Gentleman of the Long Robe in England* (London, 1720), 15; *The Humble Representation made to the King's Majesty by the Lords Spiritual and Temporal in Parliament Assembled* (Dublin, 1719), reprinted in *Collection of Parliamentary Debate*, 274, which cites both Coke and Matthew Paris.

21 Kelly, 'Conquest *versus* Consent', 338.

for precedent and rule of law, and for the antiquity of Ireland's parliament earlier and most effectively broadcast by Molyneux's 1698 *Case of Ireland*.[22]

This early eighteenth-century defence of an ancient Irish common law and constitution advanced a Protestant as well as a parliamentary history. And here the emphasis on original consent was significant. While an admission of conquest had earlier been useful to Irish Protestant polemicists who sought to justify the subordination of the Irish Catholic population in 1689, this had changed by the later 1690s.[23] Once the Revolution Settlement was more assured, and British legislation and judicature increasingly threatened their authority and security of property, the Irish Protestant ruling elite found the admission of conquest to be problematic. Conquest might easily be identified with a more absolute, and potentially arbitrary, power that the British parliament seemed eager to exercise.[24] This Irish elite now turned to arguments from common law and continuity in order to assert the antiquity of their presence in Ireland, and to insist that the basis of their rightful authority lay in consent and law. At the same time, however, they emphasised the loyalism and patriotism felt towards British rule by Irish Protestants whose consent was informed by ardour as well as interest. These themes were presented in a text like John Toland's *Reasons Most Humbly Offer'd* which insisted that all Irish Protestants respected the 'indissoluble knot' binding Ireland and Great Britain, happily recognised 'the dependence of Ireland upon the Crown of Great Britain', and were unanimously zealous for the security of Hanoverian succession.[25] It is not surprising that Toland would make such statements since he was well-connected in London political circles, an outspoken advocate of civil liberty, and staunch defender of Protestant succession. But the insistence upon consent in the constitu-

22 In addition to *Humble Representation to the King's Majesty* and *Letter from a Member of Commons in Ireland*, see Toland, *Reasons Most Humbly Offer'd*, 19; Kelly, 'Conquest versus Consent', 341–4; Victory, 'Declaratory Act', 28.

23 Kelly, 'Conquest *versus* Consent', 339; Smyth, '"Like Amphibious Animals"', 790, 795; see for example Richard Cox, *Hibernia Anglicana: Or, The History of Ireland from the Conquest thereof by the English to this Present Time*, vol. 1 (London, 1689). On Toland, Justin Champion, *Republican Learning: John Toland and the Crisis of Christian Culture 1696–1722* (Manchester, 2003).

24 Toland, *Reasons Most Humbly Offer'd*, 25–6.

25 Ibid., 8–10, 21–2. And cf John Toland's discussion of the Whig constitution in his *The State Anatomy of Great Britain. Containing a Particular Account of its Several Interests and Parties, their Bent and Genius, and what Each of Them, with the Rest of Europe, May Hope or Fear, from the Reign and Family of King George*, 4th edn (London, 1717). For a useful analysis of the self-understanding of early eighteenth-century Irish Protestants – and the problem of terminology for the historian – see Smyth, '"Like Amphibious Animals"', and David W. Hayton, 'Anglo-Irish Attitudes: Changing Perceptions of National Identity Among the Protestant Ascendancy in Ireland, ca. 1690–1750', *Studies in Eighteenth-Century Culture*, 17 (1987): 145–57.

tion was actually more widespread by this time, and effectively tied to the defence of Irish common law and constitution.

As they turned towards an insistence upon this historical, parliamentary Irish constitution, the texts published in the aftermath of *Annesley v Sherlock* mirrored a historiography that was developing, especially in England, in the late seventeenth and early eighteenth centuries. First, these Irish histories displayed a characteristic polemical and partisan thrust. In a text like the *Second Letter* the author moved from an extensive discussion of established legal practice and court procedure, to an attack on Chief Baron Gilbert for allowing his political interests to overcome his judicial responsibility; the text concluded with a critique of Gilbert, and the other judges, for not being 'Better acquainted with the Constitution of this Kingdom'.[26] Similar attacks appeared in the charged debates over English history between Robert Brady and James Tyrrell for example, or between Roger North and White Kennett, where the authors aired suspicions about the political motives clouding their opponents' historical understanding. English historians' strong political affiliations had been obvious in the Exclusion and Revolution periods, and continued to be relevant in the first decades of the eighteenth century.[27] For example an English Whig historian and barrister like Roger Acherley openly positioned his work as a vindication of Revolution Principles and Hanoverian succession. He aimed his *Britannic Constitution* (1727) against certain 'ecclesiastical gentlemen' who, he charged, composed apologies for absolute monarchy, and compiled histories that encouraged popular disaffection and promoted Jacobitism.[28]

26 A *Second Letter to a Gentleman of the Long Robe in Great Britain: Wherein some of the Late Illegal Proceedings of the Barons of the Exchequer in the Kingdom of Ireland are Plainly and Impartially Set Forth* (Dublin, 1720), 11–13, 29, 31–2. Toland similarly charged that the British Lords were aiming to monopolise power and destabilise the constitution. Toland, *Reasons Most Humbly Offer'd*, 20–1.

27 Hicks, *Neoclassical History*, ch. 5; Mark Knights, 'The Tory Interpretation of History in the Rage of Party', *Huntington Library Quarterly*, 68, 1–2, (March, 2005): 353–73. A Whig theorist and historian like James Tyrrell, for example, tried to deflect the charges of partisanship that might well be aimed at him by offering extensive accounts of his historical methods, and numerous references to the verifiable sources he used. But Tyrrell also used this discussion of method to couch his own partisan evaluations of other historians like Robert Brady or William Nicolson. James Tyrrell, *The General History of England, Both Ecclesiastical and Civil*, vol. 2 (London, 1704), i–ii, xv, xviii–xix.

28 Roger Acherley, *The Britannic Constitution: Or, The Fundamental Form of Government in Britain* (London, 1727), 5, 17. James Tyrrell pursued these same themes in his *Bibliotheca Politica: Or, An Enquiry into the Ancient Constitution of the English Government … in Fourteen Dialogues* which was published in collected editions in 1718 and 1727. These kinds of Whig themes also persist in the histories of England by Burnet, Clarendon and Oldmixon. Hicks, *Neoclassical History*, Karen O'Brien, 'The History Market in Eighteenth-Century England', in Isabel Rivers ed., *Books and their Readers in Eighteenth-Century England: New Essays* (London, 2001), 110–12.

In Ireland too, after 1720, the history of Irish law and government was understood to have continuing political repercussions, and this was true not only with regard to controversy over British claims to jurisdiction. Authors used the history of Irish law and government in order to advance understanding of a native Gaelic constitution. Of special importance here was the history of Ireland written by the Catholic historian Geoffrey Keating, first composed in the early seventeenth century but published, and translated into English, in multiple editions in the 1720s and 30s. Keating defended ancient Gaelic culture against what he saw as the biased attacks of English historians and, significantly, posited the existence of a parliament founded in pre-Christian times by the pagan Irish king Ollamh Fodhla.[29] Geoffrey Keating's 'ancient Irish constitution' was relevant to the matter of jurisdiction and appeal debated in the early eighteenth century but it also had other ramifications. As Colin Kidd has shown, Keating's work had an even more enduring political and cultural impact since such claims for Gaelic heritage were employed in a 'campaign for liberalisation of the anti-popish penal laws' during the longer course of eighteenth-century Catholic Enlightenment.[30]

In their advocacy of parliament's antiquity, and in their emphasis on consent in the constitution, many eighteenth-century Irish histories demonstrate key features of an older Whig historiography.[31] Some of the Irish texts of 1719–20 specifically connected these arguments about history of parliament to the matter of judicature and appellate procedure that was debated in the aftermath of *Annesley v Sherlock*. Here they echoed ideas about jurisdiction, and the protection of common law and constitution, articulated by Whig jurists such as Robert Atkyns and John Holt in England several years earlier. The *Letter from a Member*, for example, set out a familiar account of the historical evolution of parliament. Like Atkyns' *Treatise of the True and Ancient Jurisdiction of the House of Peers* (1699), this later narrative traced the growth of legislative and judicial power as it was exercised first by original assemblies and later by bicameral bodies in Ireland as well as England.[32] In the course of such accounts contemporaries communicated those familiar concerns about continuity and stability that were so impor-

29 Geoffrey Keating, *The General History of Ireland* (London, 1723), i–ii, 10, 222. Kidd, 'Gaelic Antiquity and National Identity', 1199–1200. An abridged and translated version of Keating's history was published with a Dublin imprint in 1713; the editions of the 1720s and 1730s have a London or Westminster imprint.

30 Kidd, 'Gaelic Antiquity and National Identity', 1200.

31 *Letter from a Member of Commons in Ireland*, 12–18; *Humble Representation to the King's Majesty*, 275, 284–5. Tyrrell, *General History*, vol. 2, xvii–xix; Acherley, *Britannic Constitution*, vi; Hicks, *Neoclassical History*, 98; D.W. Earl, 'Procrustean Feudalism: An Interpretive Dilemma in English Historical Narration, 1700–1725', *The Historical Journal*, 19, 1 (March, 1976): 38; Rudolph, *Revolution by Degrees*, ch. 3.

32 *Letter from a Member of Commons in Ireland*, 9–13; Atkyns, *Treatise of the True and Ancient Jurisdiction of the Peers*, 4, 6–7, 23–4.

tant to an understanding of the legitimacy of tradition in the early eighteenth century. These authors warned that the Irish Exchequer barons' and the British Lords' violation of 'rules of practice', established by 'ancient law and custom', would undermine liberty and property, introduce arbitrary authority, and destroy the established constitution.[33] John Toland went further when he composed his polemic against the proposed Declaratory Act. Toland not only underlined the significance of Ireland's and England's balanced constitution, but he also drew a deliberate analogy between the current Irish question and the problem of 'the encroachment in Judicature' by the British House of Lords aired by Justice Holt in the well-known case of *Ashby v White* (1704). Questions about the proper authority, social status and composition of the British House of Lords had been asked even more recently in debate over the proposed Peerage Bill in 1719.[34]

In these ways early eighteenth-century Irish legal histories confirmed certain trends in historiography, especially regarding claims for the antiquity of parliament and of common law. The affirmation of the authority of tradition, and the value accorded to prescriptive practice in the Irish debates of 1719–20, contributed to the persistence of ideas about common law justice. But these Irish histories also posed important challenges to an English, and traditionally Whig, version of the past, and these challenges too had implications for the development of historiography and common law jurisprudence. Clearly the main Irish arguments for the origins of common law and parliament in the reign of Henry II opened up a space for questioning early Whig ideas about the continuity of an ancient Gothic constitution. The assertion that Ireland's ancient constitution originated in royal grant and Irish native consent in 1172 stood in contrast to an English polemical history that had emphasised the uninterrupted continuity of their own common law and constitution since Saxon or even earlier times. That English emphasis on continuity and the slow evolution of prescriptive custom was articulated in the seventeenth century in order to undermine Stuart declarations about the centrality of royal authority in the formation of law.[35] When the Irish acknowledged the foundational role of Norman kingship in the origins of common law their history contested such English historical claims.[36] Ideas about the nature of Norman change, and informa-

[33] *Humble Representation to the King's Majesty*, 280–3, 286; *Second Letter* passim; Toland, *Reasons Most Humbly Offer'd*, 5–6, 13–14.

[34] Toland, *Reasons Most Humbly Offer'd*, 28–32; Hayton, 'Stanhope/Sunderland Ministry', 623; Clyve Jones, '"Venice Preserv'd or a Plot Discover'd": The Political and Social Context of the Peerage Bill of 1719', in Clyve Jones ed., *A Pillar of the Constitution: The House of Lords in British Politics 1640–1784* (London, 1989), 79–112.

[35] Rudolph, *Revolution by Degrees*, 69–87; Burgess, *Politics of the Ancient Constitution*; Smith, *Gothic Bequest*, ch. 1; Knights, 'Tory Interpretation of History', 357–8.

[36] William Molyneux's *The Case of Ireland's being Bound by Acts of Parliament in England, Stated* (Dublin, 1698), republished and still relevant in 1719, had earlier been attacked by

tion about the activities of monarchs like Henry I and II, stimulated developments in historical understanding. Indeed the narrative of Irish history composed in the early eighteenth century was produced during a key transitional period in contemporary historiography. At the same time as Irish legal history participated in the continued circulation of histories directed, and distorted, towards partisan ends, it also contributed to an understanding of the feudal past, and an interest in broader and newly narrative histories, that were developing between 1689 and 1725.[37]

Since Ireland's common law and constitution could only be traced back roughly five hundred years, historians focused on that moment of origin and the nature of change that occurred with the coming of Norman kingship. This led, in turn, to a greater appreciation of the ways in which law and parliament emerged from a set of socio-economic and military relationships with the crown. Irish histories here contributed to that historical inquiry ongoing since the later seventeenth century, when heightened interest in the history of monarchy led to insights into specifically feudal, and wider socio-economic, histories.[38] Moreover, in 1719 this Irish legal history pursued the further constitutional implications regarding royal prerogative that stemmed from the adoption of feudal history. These implications were made explicit in the declaration by the Irish that they had a separate, enduring relationship with the British crown. The conclusion of the Irish Lords' *Humble Representation to the King's Majesty* made such a claim, and in so doing not only enhanced royal prerogative but also raised the troubling spectre of renewed, unstable, multiple monarchy in Britain.

An Irish description of their 'immediate dependence' on the crown threatened the British constitution of king-in-parliament that had been enshrined in the Revolution Settlement, and recently reaffirmed in the Treaty of Union:

> And having thus, with all humility, laid before your Majesty your undoubted power and prerogative within this your kingdom of *Ireland*, the immediate dependence of the same upon your Majesty's crown, the right your Majesty has to hold Parliaments here as in *Great Britain*, and of finally determining therein all matters that wholly relate to this realm; together with the great encroachments that of late have been made upon your Majesty's prerogative.... With all

a Whig historian like William Atwood who decried Molyneux as 'another Brady' because his work endorsed royal absolutism. See Kelly, 'Conquest *Versus* Consent', 345–6.

37 Laird Okie, *Augustan Historical Writing: Histories of England in the English Enlightenment* (Lanham, 1991), 32–57; Hicks, *Neoclassical History*, 147–9; O'Brien, *Narratives of Enlightenment*, 13–18; Pocock, *Barbarism and Religion, Volume 2*, 170–4. While scholars have written extensively about Whig historiography they have generally overlooked this Irish dimension.

38 Pocock, *Ancient Constitution and Feudal Law*, 362–75; Pocock, *Virtue, Commerce, and History*, 215–310; Smith, *Gothic Bequest*, chs 1–2.

> humility assuring your Majesty, that no difficulties, which we may be laid under, shall hinder us from giving the utmost dispatch to all your Majesty's affairs; or from most cheerfully demonstrating that loyalty and affection to your Majesty's person, and attachment to your interest, which becomes your Majesty's dutiful and obedient subjects; wherof we again from our hearts make an humble tender to your most sacred Majesty.[39]

Here was an unambiguous statement defining Ireland's separate and equal constitution. The British parliament countered such Irish assertions of independent legislative and judicial power by passing the Declaratory Act. This legislation unequivocally 'declared that the Irish parliament was "subordinate unto and dependent upon" the King and parliament of Great Britain'. It decreed that the Irish House of Lords enjoyed no authority to hear appeals, and that the British parliament exercised direct legislative authority over Ireland.[40] Clearly the conflict that raged in the aftermath of *Annesley v Sherlock* was about broad parliamentary powers as much as it was specifically about appellate jurisdiction. Irish parliamentary authority was stated in stark imperial as well as historical terms, as the matters of British sovereignty and Irish dependence were addressed.[41]

This kind of imperial emphasis was essential to the 1719 controversy. The historical emphasis and feudal analysis were also important because they situated the Irish question at the heart of contemporary concerns. Similar kinds of insights into conquest and change were a key part of the interpretation of law and constitution formulated by English Whig and Tory theorists and historians for several decades after 1689. Starting in 1699, for example, when Robert Atkyns took up the question of the appellate authority of the English House of Lords he too considered evidence for the impact of Norman Conquest, and the role of feudal tenures in the evolution of the English parliament.[42] Atkyns rejected the idea that Norman monarchs were advised by assemblies made up solely of their tenants-in-chief, and he reaffirmed old Whig arguments for an ancient assembly, continuous since Saxon or even earlier times, that included freeholders as well as new feudal barons. Atkyns employed such arguments specifically to counter the idea of an ancient noble judicative power, and so to undermine the authority of the Lords' recent ruling against him in his appeal of the Took trust case.[43]

39 *Humble Representation to the King's Majesty*, 288.

40 Victory, 'Making of Declaratory Act', 9, 25.

41 Hayton, 'Stanhope/Sunderland Ministry', 615–19; Kelly, 'Conquest *versus* Consent', 340; Martin S. Flaherty, 'The Empire Strikes Back: *Annesley v. Sherlock* and the Triumph of Imperial Parliamentary Supremacy', *Columbia Law Review*, 87 (1987): 593–622. Flaherty also emphasises the significance of royal assent, and Hanoverian succession, to this resolution of the conflict.

42 Atkyns, *Treatise of Peers*, 15–17.

43 Ibid., 4–8, 11, 20–3, 26–9.

Yet Atkyns married such arguments about the continuity of parliament, and of prescriptive pre-Norman law, to an admission of change brought on after the Conquest. Here he manipulated Tory historians' claims about the origins of the constitution: Atkyns agreed with evidence demonstrating that the modern English parliament, made up of Lords and Commons, had only emerged in the thirteenth century. But what occurred at that time, Atkyns insisted, was the creation of a newly-formed House of Lords and not, as other historians argued, the first admission of the Commons. Citing recognised authorities like Spelman and Camden, he described the transformation that took place during the reign of Henry III:

> If this may be credited, then we have the *Epoche*, and the Date of our present Constitution, and the Original of the Division of that very ancient, great and numerous Assembly; and it made a mighty *Metamorphosis* and Change. The Freeholders parted with that great Power and Interest which they had both in Legislature and Judicature, from the very Foundation of the Government, and the Nation it self ... And thus they brake in two, and became two Houses both at one time, and were Twins in their Birth. Here was no *Primogeniture*, yet the one went away with a double portion upon the parting.[44]

Atkyns simultaneously reinforced the argument for an ancient commons, acknowledged the fact of historical change, and focused attention on the problem of balance within the English constitution. These were all elements of a more complex view of prescription and continuity emerging in the eighteenth century.

With this semi-revised history of the constitution Atkyns' *Treatise of the True and Ancient Jurisdiction of the House of Peers* offers the first hints of a transition in English historiography that developed more fully in the early decades of the eighteenth century.[45] Now Brady's and Spelman's evidence for Norman Conquest was taken up by Whig polemicists who began to trace out ensuing changes in feudal law and society. High church and Tory critics of Whig government, on the other hand, reaffirmed the old Whig ideal of an enduring ancient constitution in contests over the history of Convocation, for example, or in polemics against Walpolean politics. Ideas about the growth and corruption of a balanced constitution became a key feature of Hanoverian historical narrative and political argument.[46] While

44 Ibid., 24.

45 For discussion of the ways in which James Tyrrell's *Bibliotheca Politica* also shows some faint signs of this transition see Smith, *Gothic Bequest*, 27, and Rudolph, *Revolution by Degrees*, 74–5, 83, 88–91.

46 In addition to the scholarly literature on this Country ideology and opposition to Walpole cited in chapter 6 above, see also Isaac Kramnick 'Augustan Politics in English Historiography: The Debate on the English Past, 1730–35', *History and Theory*, 6, 1 (1967): 33–56. Cf Atkyns, *Treatise of Peers*, 23–5.

these critics bemoaned the corruption of the ancient constitution, however, they also began to identify different phases in its evolution. The delineation of stages in the feudal past was then expanded in important new ways by later eighteenth-century historians who narrated the interconnected development of European (and sometimes global) economies, societies and states.[47] This historiographical development was lengthy and complicated, and it involved historians of law like Samuel Burroughs, Philip Yorke, and Geoffrey Gilbert, as well as the historians of Ireland's constitution. If, as R.J. Smith has argued, early eighteenth-century historians like Thomas Madox or Lord Bolingbroke should not 'be forgotten, for they in a measure made the historical writing of the British Enlightenment possible', the same is true of early eighteenth-century legal historians.[48] Their work provides evidence of the historiographical complexity of this period, and brings to light the ways in which continued attention to the power of tradition and prescription formed part of an emerging enlightened historical understanding.

Legal histories in transition: Yorke, Burroughs and Gilbert

Philip Yorke became lord chancellor of England in 1737, ten years after he wrote his tract on Chancery. Yorke had already taken up the position of chief justice of the Kings Bench, along with a peerage as Baron Hardwicke, a few years earlier in 1733. When he wrote his *Discourse of the Judicial Authority Belonging to the Office of Master of the Rolls in the High Court of Chancery* (1727) however, he was still in the early years of his career, newly appointed to the post of attorney general. Yorke's appointment, like his involvement in the controversy over Chancery history, was largely due to the fact that he was well-connected and enjoyed the patronage of men like Lord Chancellor Macclesfield, and Lord Chamberlain Thomas Pelham-Holles, Duke of Newcastle. Yorke came to be active in most of the leading political issues of the day, beginning with his first major speech in parliament commenting on the Declaratory Bill. This speech carefully delineated the perilous implications of Irish constitutional and historical claims: Yorke forcefully argued that British legislation regarding Ireland was necessary because 'it deprived the Lords of Ireland from the exercise of a power to which they had no right, and which, if granted them, would of consequence make that kingdom independent of Great Britain, it being certain that, wherever the last resort lies,

47 J.P. Kenyon, *The History Men: The Historical Profession in England Since the Renaissance* (Pittsburgh, 1984), 39–40; O'Brien, *Narratives of Enlightenment*, 1–20; O'Brien, 'History Market', 106–23; Pocock, *Barbarism and Religion, Volume 2*, 12–21; Smith, *Gothic Bequest*, 27, 34–5.

48 Smith, *Gothic Bequest*, 46. See also Deborah Stephan, 'Laurence Echard – Whig Historian', *The Historical Journal*, 32, 4 (December, 1989): 843–66, on Echard's role in this historiographical transition.

there must be independency and the supreme power.'[49] It is not surprising that Yorke spoke in support of the ministry's proposed legislation since his election to parliament in 1719 resulted from the patronage of Newcastle, who was soon to be secretary of state. There were also other professional and personal interests informing Yorke's advocacy of the bill. On this issue Yorke joined forces with the Master of the Rolls Joseph Jekyll, who was not only his senior legal colleague but also, as his wife's uncle, a close and influential relative.[50] Jekyll and his nephew Yorke fought together for this legislation but they did not agree on everything – they diverged, for example, over support for Macclesfield's impeachment in 1725. However the two men were soon allied again in the historical controversy over Chancery procedure that emerged in the aftermath of impeachment.

The histories of Chancery produced between 1726 and 1728 were institutional histories mainly concerned with the roles and responsibilities of Chancery personnel as they evolved over time. Burroughs' and Yorke's histories thus continued a line of debate from the impeachment hearings by concentrating on evidence regarding the judicial status of Chancery officials. During the impeachment advocates had questioned whether it was more proper to characterise Chancery masters as ministerial or as judicial officers. Now, however, the question of judicial status was tied to a dispute about the balance of power shared by the lord chancellor and the master of the rolls. The specific issue that catalysed this dispute was a procedural matter, 'relating to [the Masters in Chancery] signing his Honour's Decrees which [the Master of the Rolls] had omitted to have done', Giles Jacob later explained in his tract on Chancery practice. When Jekyll failed to obtain these signatures the decrees 'were stopt or suspended by the Lord Chancellor; whereupon a warm Controversy arose between the Chancellor and Master of the Rolls'.[51] This controversy was expansive as well as warm, moving quickly from a disagreement over the method for recording decrees to a set of wide-ranging assertions about the royal, statutory and prescriptive bases of Chancery authority. This was a controversy that betrayed the jockeying for power between two great men, in which each side 'quot[ed] the like Ancient Records, Precedents and Authorities' in order to support their assertions.[52]

Clearly these early eighteenth-century histories of law and legal institu-

49 Hayton, 'Stanhope/Sunderland Ministry', 617–18; Victory, 'Declaratory Act', 27. Just two years after the Chancery controversy Yorke, still attorney general, would make a quite different, but even more influential statement about imperial law in the so-called Yorke-Talbot opinion regarding the legal status of slaves in Britain.

50 Foss, *Judges of England*, vol. 8, 185–8; Lemmings, *Professors of the Law*, 283–5; Sedgwick, *History of Parliament*, vol. 2 (London, 1970), 569. *Collection of Parliamentary Debates*, 268; Cobbett, *Parliamentary History of England*, vol. 4, 642–3.

51 Jacob, *Compleat Chancery Practiser*, 46.

52 Ibid., 47.

tions were still fuelled by partisanship. The direct link to political controversy gave these institutional histories a particular sense of urgency and this, W.S. Holdsworth commented, led to a familiar and misguided manipulation of antiquarian research:

> The controversy concerned but a small point of legal history. But the arguments used on either side remind us of the larger political controversies of the seventeenth century. Both were argued as questions of legal history. In both each side tried to elicit, from the uncertain precedents and forms of an earlier age, the answer to a question of which the makers of those precedents and forms had never dreamed.[53]

Holdsworth rightly identified the polemical and partisan quality of these legal histories, but he was mistaken in seeing this episode as a simple repetition of earlier controversies. Even more, Holdsworth was mistaken when he concluded that these 'old controversies' about the scope of equity and common law jurisdiction were unproductive and 'dead' by the eighteenth century.[54] This 1726–8 dispute about Chancery contributed to enlightened historiographical development. In these and other early eighteenth-century histories of legal institutions there is certainly evidence of attention to antiquity and prescription, and a recourse to precedent in the service of contemporary argument. At the same time, however, there is evidence of that growing interest in the analysis of socio-economic development, and attention to the potential for corruption to undermine culture and constitution. These were both key features of historiographical transition. Moreover these early eighteenth-century legal historians also contributed to developments in common law jurisprudence when they attended to historical change, offered ideas about causation, and expanded on the values of certainty and tradition against fraud and corruption.

One of these historians was Samuel Burroughs, who wrote *The History of the Chancery; Relating to the Judicial Power of that Court and the Rights of the Masters* (1726), the text that initiated printed debate over the balance of power between Lord Chancellor King and Master of the Rolls Jekyll. Burroughs was a minor scholar who was supported by influential men from legal and clerical circles; such patronage and partisanship are apparent in the composition of his history. For example it is likely that at least the second, expanded edition of this work, now titled *The Legal Judicature in Chancery Stated* (1727), was partly written by the Whig churchman and controversialist William Warburton. It has also been alleged that Burroughs composed his history in exchange for a rich reward, gained when Lord Chancellor King later appointed him to a mastership in Chancery.[55] The fact that Burroughs

53 Holdsworth, *History of English Law*, vol. 1, 215.

54 Ibid., vol. 12, 185.

55 B.W Young, 'Warburton, William', *ODNB*; Foss, *Judges of England*, vol. 8, 188.

was also well-connected, and well-regarded, in scholarly circles is indicated by his appointment to the committee charged with inspecting the Cottonian Library after fire destroyed some of its contents in October 1731. The Speaker of the House of Commons, Arthur Onslow, was personally involved in the immediate response to the fire, and he speedily appointed several men like Burroughs, 'some of whom are concerned in Offices, where Records as well of Paper as Parchment are lodged, ... to consider what was proper to be done for preserving and recovering, as much as possible, the Manuscripts which had so suffered'.[56] Burroughs had likely consulted the records of the Cottonian Library for his texts on the history of Chancery, and for his later text, *An Enquiry into the Customary-Estates and Tenant-Rights of those who hold Lands of Church and other Foundations* (1731). Here Burroughs' research into clerical property and power contributed to ongoing controversy over ecclesiastical history.

In advocating for the new lord chancellor in 1726, and claiming that Chancellor King exercised sole judicial authority in his court, Burroughs stressed the fact that the chancellor was authorised by royal commission, indicated by the delivery of the king's seal. This assertion that the lord chancellor was endowed with authority because he was keeper of the seal, was based on the generally accepted opinion that the Chancery originated as the king's secretariat where royal writs and other official documents were drawn up.[57] As Burroughs traced the evolution of the chancellor's authority from secretary and administrator, to judge of ordinary common law causes, to judge of equity and causes of conscience, his history betrayed that familiar emphasis on continuity with a Saxon past; Burroughs even occasionally had recourse to argument from evidence 'time out of mind'.[58] From the courts and assemblies of the county or the hundred, Burroughs explained, appeals and petitions were directed to the king, 'from the time of King Alfred till after the Conquest'. By the reign of Henry I, he concluded, the court of Chancery, like the other Westminster courts, had emerged in order to dispense royal justice as a court of record administering the royal common law.[59]

Burroughs' history of the Westminster courts relied on an assertion of Saxon preconditions, and the relevance of Saxon bureaucracy, but it also acknowledged the importance of conquest and change. Here, as elsewhere,

56 *A Report from the Committee Appointed to View the Cottonian Library* (London, 1732), 12.

57 Samuel Burroughs, *The History of the Chancery; Relating to the Judicial Power of that Court and the Rights of the Masters* (London, 1726), 3–4, 6–8, 67–8. Cf Pietro Giannone, *The Civil History of the Kingdom of Naples*, trans. Captain James Ogilivie, vol. 1 (London, 1729), 546–7; Jacob, *Compleat Chancery Practiser*, 2–3; Gilbert, *History and Practice of the High Court of Chancery*, 9–11.

58 Burroughs, *History of the Chancery*, 3, 11.

59 Ibid., 10–12.

there is recognition of the impact of royal authority in the development of the English courts, common law and constitution.[60] Moreover, in his narrative of the development of an equity jurisdiction Burroughs paid attention to continued changes in property relations caused by fluctuations in royal power, and related changes in feudal tenures, in order to explain the nature and expansion of Chancery business. Awareness of that historical development was crucial, Burroughs insisted, because it afforded an explanation for the changing responsibilities of the court's master of the rolls.[61] Burroughs confirmed the conventional belief that history provided proper justification for the authority exercised by English institutions and officials. But whereas his opponents Yorke and Jekyll adhered to the view that antiquity and continuity validated the master of the rolls' judicial functions, Burroughs offered a more complex view of changes in property and power that underlay judicial authority.[62]

According to Burroughs, new responsibilities for the chancellor and the master of the rolls arose as a result of the emergence of Chancery's equity jurisdiction. The jurisdictional expansion of the court was problematic, however, because it was caused by political and socio-economic instability. While the Chancery had begun to establish itself as an institution separate from the king's household in the reign of Edward III, Burroughs explained, the chancellor had no 'Court of Equity before the Time of *Henry* the IVth. in whose Days, by Reason of the Intestine Troubles, Feoffments to Uses did first begin, as some think, or else did grow common and familiar'.[63] Burroughs allowed that other feudal policies, and medieval statutes, had also contributed to Chancery development but he insisted that it was primarily this instability in fifteenth-century kingship, tied to resulting changes in property holding, that led to the growth of the Chancery as equity court. When wealthy Englishmen turned to uses and trusteeship in order to protect their property unexpected consequences ensued. The Chancery 'grew into Esteem and more Business by the intestine Broils that soon after follow'd between the Houses of *York* and *Lancaster*', Burroughs declared. 'The Partisans of each knew their Estates would certainly fall a Morsel to the prevailing House; the Unfortunate were sure to be call'd Rebels and Trayters; so many put their Land secretly into Use, to secure their Possessions against the Event of that doubtful Combat .' In these secret uses Englishmen 'convey'd their Lands to their Friends in Trust, to be return'd or re-convey'd at the End of the War'.

60 Ibid., 30–1. There is a strong admission of conquest and change, and a similar depiction of the chancellor as a Norman creation in another influential contemporary treatise, Arthur Duck, *Of the Use and Authority of the Civil Law in England*, appended to Claude Joseph de Ferriere, *The History of the Roman or Civil Law*, trans. J.B. (London, 1724), xv–xvii.

61 Burroughs *History of the Chancery*, 44, cf 71.

62 Yorke, *Discourse of Judicial Authority*, xxxiii–iv, cx, 18, 44, 59, 109.

63 Burroughs, *History of the Chancery*, 45.

Yet 'many of these Trustees would refuse to re-convey', 'Frauds and Breaches of Trust did ensue, and Suits for Relief', 'whereupon the Party wrong'd had his Relief by *Subpoena* in *Chancery*'.[64]

The expansion of Chancery business occurred, Burroughs maintained, because of this development of equitable protections for feeoffors and beneficiaries of uses. These protections also encouraged the continued growth of uses which, in time, furthered important changes in feudal property relations. Uses came to be employed as a kind of tax shelter, a way to avoid feudal dues owed to the king and great lords. This kind of evidence of the decay of feudal revenues and associated decline of feudal kingship led some other early eighteenth-century historians, like Thomas Madox, to conclude that a stronger English parliament, and English liberties, had begun to emerge as a consequence of these developments. Madox and others adhered to an analysis of the balance of property underlying constitutional change that had been advanced in the work of James Harrington, and subsequent 'neo-Harringtonian' theorists.[65] But the same evidence led Burroughs to trace instead the ways in which the growing socio-economic power of great lords fostered the expansion of conciliar and arbitrary power in new and unexpected ways.

It was here that that Burroughs located the origins of the judicial authority of the master of the rolls. In sixteenth-century England strong monarchical and clerical power was re-imposed, Burroughs averred. As the Tudor crown pushed legislation, like the Statute of Uses, in order to close the crown revenue loophole, the scope of Chancery jurisdiction increased even more:

> but now it began to swell out, there had been before several Acts of Parliament, giving special power to the Chancellor and others: Now they multiply'd, and a Profusion of Business was soon poured into the Court, by the broad-spreading Statutes of Uses (I take my Lord *Coke's* Expression) of Wills, Bankrupts, Charitable Uses, and others; also the sudden and vast Growth of Wealth, and personal Estates, and as a Consequence of that, Frauds and Corruption thickened and Follow'd in Abundance.[66]

To meet this challenge, Burroughs concluded, prescription and law were abandoned and a commission was given to the master of the rolls to hear causes at that time. This conclusion laid significant emphasis on the fact

64 Ibid., 53–4, and 49–51 on legislative factors. See also Roger Acherley, *The Jurisdiction of the Chancery as a Court of Equity Researched. And the Traditional Obscurity of its Commencement Cleared* (London, 1734), 12–17.

65 Smith, *Gothic Bequest*, 46 and 49 quoting Madox *Baronia Anglia*. On the complex history of uses, and the relevance of conflict between equity and law, see Baker, *Oxford History of the Laws of England: Volume* 6, ch. 35.

66 Burroughs, *History of the Chancery*, 107–8.

that an expansion of the Chancery's case load was originally due to the impact of royal absolutism met by fraud and corruption.

Like other eighteenth-century historians Burroughs regarded the founding of the Tudor dynasty, and the ensuing Reformation period, as a pivotal moment in England's history. And in this period he identified wealth, corruption and fraud as much as politics and power as the catalysts of historical change.[67] Burroughs' basic story of increasing wealth, and of conflict between the king and his great men as the cause of changes in law and institutions, was later developed by Adam Smith. Unlike Burroughs, Smith, of course, focused on the importance of commerce and the growth of towns in his account of the transition from feudalism in European economic history. But Smith, like Burroughs, was also interested in the unforeseen consequences of changing customs and economic development.

The debate between Burroughs and Yorke demonstrates that historians of law took part in the 'spread of feudal explanation', and the recourse to evidence for change as well as continuity, that were characteristic of eighteenth-century historiographical development.[68] Moreover, Burroughs' historical narrative and interpretation had a particular resonance in the aftermath of the South Sea crisis and Macclesfield's trial. When he emphasised the problem of fraud in order to defend Lord Chancellor King's programme of accountability, Burroughs tapped into that enlightened discourse about the moral implications of economic change; like Bolingbroke and others, he engaged with this moral-philosophical debate in historical terms. Burroughs' history sought to contrast the honesty and authority of the present chancellor with the avarice of a man like Macclesfield, the corruption of men like the former Chancery masters, and the desire for excessive power now apparent in the Master of the Rolls Joseph Jekyll.[69] His emphasis on the problem of breach of trust, which Chancery was supposed to remedy, was aimed to remind readers of recent protests over the betrayal of female beneficiaries under Macclesfield's chancellorship.

Finally, just as in Macclefield's trial, Burroughs' arguments against corruption and fraud led to a defence of common law justice. In an earlier age of good lawyers and good pleading, Burroughs recalled wistfully with a nod to Coke, there had been no need for equity.[70] Burroughs further underscored the benefits of common law certainty and stability against conscience and

67 Pocock, *Barbarism and Religion, Volume 2*, 170–1; O'Brien, *Narratives of Enlightenment*, 142–8; Smith, *Gothic Bequest*, 67; Okie, *Augustan Historical Writing*, 2; Johnson Kent-Wright, 'Historical Thought in the Era of Enlightenment', in Lloyd Kramer and Sarah Maza eds, *A Companion to Western Historical Thought* (Oxford, 2002), 133–4.

68 Smith, *Gothic Bequest*, 47–57; Knights, 'Tory Interpretation of History', 370.

69 Samuel Burroughs, *The Legal Judicature in Chancery Stated. With Remarks on a Late Book, Intitled, A Discourse of the Judicial Authority Belonging to the Master of the Rolls* (London, 1727), 277.

70 Burroughs, *History of the Chancery*, 48, see also 86.

natural justice in his final 'Reflections upon the Nature and Extent of the Discretionary Rules that govern in the Court'. Here he even had recourse to that familiar image of the pruning knife used by theorists like Thomas Wood, or Francis Bacon, to denote the proper balance of antiquity and adaptation, continuity and change, within a mixed common law.[71] His interlocutor, Philip Yorke, similarly concluded his *Discourse of Judicial Authority* with an emphasis on the values of stability, and adherence to precedent, as the foundations of justice and rights.[72] In the articulation of these ideas, and indeed in the very turn to history as a mode of argument and analysis, this part of the controversy over Chancery contributed to the evolution of eighteenth-century common law jurisprudence.

It is also clear that such institutional histories contributed to the 'generic evolution of history from political narrative to civil history' characteristic of enlightened historiography.[73] Legal historians like Samuel Burroughs and Geoffrey Gilbert began to expand on the idea that analysis of socioeconomic and sociocultural change was essential for a proper interpretation of events and institutions. This was implicit in Burroughs' focus on uses in order to explain that a decay of virtue, fuelled by growing wealth, underlay changes in the court of Chancery. And the idea was made explicit by Burroughs' co-author William Warburton, who argued elsewhere against histories that only catalogued the details of political affairs, or afforded scenes of revolution and battles. Rather, Warburton insisted, a useful history would be concerned with economic and cultural change:

> the History of the Arts of Peace and Commerce, in which we find the Amendments of Laws, the Refinements of Manners, the Advancement of Knowledge, the Improvements of publick Conveniences, and the Establishment of Liberty and Power; this is the Work of Use, and constant and universal Concernment.[74]

Warburton advocated this historiographical programme in his *Critical and Philosophical Enquiry into the Causes of Prodigies and Miracles as Related by Historians*, a work published in the same year as the *Legal Judicature*. If history would only refine its methods and reform its foundations, Warburton argued further, it might become like other enlightened sciences.[75] Warburton offered his own work as a first step in these efforts, echoing John Locke's well-known claim to lay the groundwork for further scientific research: 'And it is Honour enough for me to be employed as an Under-Labourer,'

71 Ibid., 113–15.

72 Yorke, *Discourse of the Judicial Authority*, 194, 196, 199.

73 O'Brien, 'History Market', 109.

74 William Warburton, A *Critical and Philosophical Enquiry into the Causes of Prodigies and Miracles as Related by Historians. With an Essay Towards Restoring a Method and Purity in History* (London, 1727), 45–6.

75 Ibid., 1–2, 99–100.

Warburton concluded, with similar false modesty, 'in clearing the Ground, and removing the Rubbish.'[76]

A crucial element of such contemporary ideas about improvement in historical writing, and its relation to scientific progress, lay in attitudes towards sources. Earlier scholars like Tyrrell, Petyt or Brady had already introduced claims about the irrefutable nature of documentary evidence in the Domesday book, or in borough charters, and they offered competing arguments about proper methods of source criticism.[77] Philip Yorke engaged in some very similar tactics, opening the second edition of his *Discourse* with a point-by-point refutation of Burroughs' interpretation of evidence found in the 'Records at the Tower or the Rolls Chapel' or in collected volumes like Thomas Rymer's *Foedera*. Yorke's catalogue of examples added up to a general complaint that Burroughs distorted the ancient records to suit his own ends.[78] In making this argument, just as in his defence of the persistence of legal practices and institutions since 'time immemorial', Yorke adhered to an older historiographical form. Yorke's text retained an antiquarian style as well as a disputatious tone, much like other English histories that relied upon the compilation of documents and examples. When they reproduced and catalogued vast amounts of research Yorke, Tyrrell and other historians actively took part in an erudite or antiquarian tradition that sought to collect and to catalogue the remains of the English past.

This tradition had grown in importance in England since the late sixteenth century but such erudition was also in transition in the eighteenth century. This transition took place especially because antiquarian research was becoming part of an expanding print culture. From the 1730s on, important collections of documents began to be published, thus making archival evidence increasingly available and likely to be incorporated into more general works. This meant that 'historical practice was very mixed', Karen O'Brien explains, 'with a number of narrative works ... incorporating massive primary documentation, and many more relying heavily and openly upon anthologies of source material such as the *Foedera* of Thomas Rymer *et al* (1704–35)'. Some eighteenth-century writers criticised this mixing, and emphasised a fissure between the elegant values of 'ancient' rhetoric and the vulgar tendency towards citation and unpolished compilation in 'modern' scholarship. Despite their loud complaints, O'Brien concludes, there was in fact no real 'polarization of antiquarianism and narrative history'.[79]

76 Ibid., 135; John Locke, *An Essay Concerning Human Understanding*, Peter Nidditch ed. (Oxford, 1975), 10; Porter, *Creation of the Modern World*, 60.

77 Smith, *Gothic Bequest*, 26–7; Rudolph, *Revolution by Degrees*, 75–9, 88–92, and above n. 27.

78 Yorke, *Discourse of Judicial Authority*, vi–ix, xxxvii, xxxix, xlvii–xlix, lvii–viii, lxxix.

79 O'Brien, 'History Market', 110; Devoney Looser, *British Women Writers and the Writing of History* (Baltimore, 2000), 13–15. Cf Mark Salber Phillips, 'Reconsiderations on History and Antiquarianism: Arnaldo Momigliano and the Historiography of

The authors of these mixed histories, like those authors of the varied practical legal literature, struggled with the new profusion of print and some, similarly, adopted elements of an enlightened encyclopedic tradition. The Anglican cleric Laurence Echard, for example, author of several political and ecclesiastical histories of England, described the challenges he faced in attempting historical research. In composing the second volume of a three-volume *History of England*, Echard explained, 'the Materials and Writings were so various and numerous, that I was two or three Years in Procuring, Collecting, and Perusing of them: And still I am not certain,' he added plaintively, 'whether I have got all that are material.' Echard outlined the purpose of his labours, and clearly echoed the promises made by the authors of eighteenth-century encyclopedias, dictionaries, libraries and legal abridgments when he affirmed that the aim of his history was to help young students, and readers more generally, by providing them with a 'single history' so that they might avoid the 'Trouble of reading over a Library'.[80] Like the authors of contemporary encyclopedic and abridgment works, Echard was concerned to digest, divide and organise his data in order to make it accessible to his reader. Indeed, Echard attested that his work was 'design'd so as to partake of the Advantages both of an *Original History* and an *Abridgement*; so as to preserve the Essentials and Beauties of the *Former*, and the Easiness and Conveniences of the *Latter*'.[81] To this end he turned to familiar methods like the marginal citation of sources, or the enumeration of important points, in order to guide his reader through the work.

An abridgment literature was, in fact, growing more prevalent and popular in history just as it was in other fields in the eighteenth century. Echard, compiler of an abridgment of Sir Walter Raleigh's *History of the World* in 1698, pointed to methodological and pedagogical justifications for abridgment. There were also market concerns that stimulated increasing production of an affordable historical abridgment literature.[82] Legal historians, like other historians, participated in these trends and openly turned to abridgment, compilation and classification. For example Samuel Burroughs, like Laurence Echard, noted the difficulty of digesting the necessary materials for his history of Chancery. 'The Materials I was to use lay scattered up and down,' he complained, 'and the Collection, such as it is, I have

Eighteenth-Century Britain', *Journal of the History of Ideas*, 57, 2 (April, 1996): 297–316. On ancients/moderns debate see Joseph M. Levine, *The Battle of the Books: History and Literature in the Augustan Age* (Ithaca, 1991), and Levine, *Humanism and History: Origins of Modern English Historiography* (Ithaca, 1987).

80 Laurence Echard, *The History of England, From the First Entrance of Julius Caesar and the Romans to the End of the Reign of King James the First*, vol. 2 (London, 1718), i–ii.

81 Ibid., vol. 1, i.

82 Woolf, *Reading History in Early Modern England*, 220–1, 245, 318; Hicks, *Neoclassical History*, 147; T.O. McLoughlin, 'Edmund Burke's Abridgment of English History', *Eighteenth-Century Ireland*, 5 (1990): 46–8.

sorted and connected as well as I could, and with all the Clearness and Consistence the Nature of it, and the Compass and Time I allow'd myself, would permit.'[83] Burroughs sorted, collected and connected when he wrote history. Moreover, Burroughs helped to 'index', 'methodize' and 'digest' vast stores of public records as a participant in the collaborative work of the 'Committee appointed to view the Cottonian Library'. In collection and collaboration Burroughs engaged in activities similar to those of eighteenth-century encyclopedists.[84] And in beginning to use these materials towards an expanded socio-economic analysis, Burroughs contributed to the work of historiographical transition.

Geoffrey Gilbert, the major English legal historian of the eighteenth century, also participated in these historiographical and cultural trends. However Gilbert went further than other historians, first in his commitment to producing a comprehensive history of law. While he employed the usual methods of compilation, enumeration, and topical or chronological organisation, Gilbert directed his efforts towards the creation of a total history of multiple legal institutions, forms of action and doctrines. This history was part of what Gilbert conceived of as a synthetic project on English law. Scholars have generally located Gilbert's project within the Institutional tradition, and have judged it, favourably, in comparison to Blackstone's later treatise on English law.[85] Yet it is equally important to understand Gilbert's texts within the contexts of eighteenth-century abridgment and encyclopedism, and to appreciate the ways in which he manipulated these genres. In its structure as well as its content Gilbert's project was an important part of the evolution of eighteenth-century common law jurisprudence.

Geoffrey Gilbert also went further than some of his contemporaries in exploring the impacts of economic development. His work, like Burroughs', attended to the history of feudalism and socio-economic change, but also afforded insights into the history of commerce and technological innovation. Such insights, interspersed throughout his texts, helped to lay the groundwork for historians' later interest in different forms of economic organisation underlying shifts in societal forms – an interest that found fruition in the stadial analyses of eighteenth-century Scottish historians.

As we know, Geoffrey Gilbert was not only a legal writer but he also had a judicial career. He served first in Ireland as puisne judge on the Kings Bench (1715) and as chief baron of the Exchequer (1715–1722), before

[83] Burroughs, *History of the Chancery*, 111.

[84] *Report from the Committee ... Cottonian Library*, 5–7; Yeo 'Encyclopedism and Enlightenment', 350, 354. Burroughs' activities were also similar to those of other scholar-clerics like William Wake and David Wilkins Blair, David C. Douglas, *English Scholars* (London, 1939), 275–84.

[85] Macnair, 'Gilbert and his Treatises', 258–9; Macnair, 'Gilbert', *ODNB*, emphasises the potential influence of Hale upon Gilbert, so as to depict Gilbert as a link, or stepping-stone, between Hale and Blackstone. And see chapter 2 pp. 61–2 above.

returning to England to serve as puisne judge (1722–25) and chief baron (1725–26) of the English Exchequer.[86] According to Michael Macnair, manuscript evidence indicates that Gilbert composed the majority of his legal texts before his appointment to the bench, in the first decade of the century. Yet Gilbert's judicial experience became relevant to the composition of his work because the judge returned to his scholarly project in 1720 and 1724–5. 'Shortly after 1720 he rewrote and updated the material on equity procedure and added new material on substantive equity doctrine,' Macnair explains, 'and in 1724–5 he produced an expanded and updated version of the text on the exchequer.'[87] It is likely that Gilbert returned to study the Exchequer in anticipation of his elevation to the post of chief baron on the English bench. Even more, his service in Ireland surely had an impact, leading Judge Gilbert to reflect on the rules of equity and the formation of the Exchequer at the same time that questions about the law of trusts, and about the impact of feudal tenures on the development of legal institutions, were being aired in Irish courtrooms, in the Irish and British parliaments, and in materials printed in London and Dublin.

Geoffrey Gilbert's work on equity and the court of Chancery was not published until 1756, and his research on the Exchequer was first published twelve years after his death, in 1738. But like Gilbert's other compositions these texts circulated in manuscript until, as well as after, they appeared in print.[88] This manuscript circulation is further evidence that Gilbert's project was typical of those encyclopedic, abridgment and commonplace traditions in which he, like other lawyers and legal writers, sought to collect and condense the whole of English legal knowledge. Toward this end Gilbert crafted different sections, or entries, which he envisioned as parts of a larger work. Gilbert also likely envisioned the overall project as a collaborative work, and looked to involve other legal scholars by circulating his own texts, and perhaps including others' work with his own. Multiple sections of Gilbert's manuscripts, like those on equity and Exchequer, were published posthumously as separate, stand-alone texts on a variety of topics including tenures, devises, uses and trusts and dower, Kings Bench, Exchequer, Chancery, Common Pleas, detinue and debt. Each one of these texts reveals

86 Foss, *Judges of England*, vol. 8, 31–3; Ball, *Judges in Ireland*, vol. 2, 191; Macnair, 'Gilbert and his Treatises', 254.

87 *ODNB*; Macnair, 'Gilbert and his Treatises', 267 n. 107.

88 Gilbert, *Historical View of the Court of Exchequer*; Gilbert, *Treatise on the Court of Exchequer*. The work on equity was first published as *Two Treatises on the Proceedings in Equity and the Jurisdiction of that Court* (Dublin, 1756) and appeared two years later in a London edition as *The History and Practice of the High Court of Chancery* (London, 1758). On the manuscript circulation of Gilbert's texts see Macnair, 'Gilbert and his Treatises', 258–9; Andrew Lyall, Introduction, *Irish Exchequer Reports*, Lyall ed. (London, 2009), lvii-viii; Simpson, 'Rise and Fall of Legal Treatise', 654–5; Holdsworth, *History of English Law*, vol. 12, 169–70.

Gilbert's tendency to mix different organisational structures and narrative styles. He frequently relied on typical abridgment and commonplace techniques, using heads or titles, sub-headings, enumeration, cross-reference and, occasionally, reverting to a simple digest of cases or examples. Equally important, however, Gilbert's texts often turned to a narrative and explanatory structure and style.

So for example *An Historical Account of the Original and Nature, as well as the Law of Devises and Revocations* (1739) opened with a lengthy historical narrative and expository analysis of the development of private property. Most of the text that followed this introduction then adhered to the logical structure of a topical abridgment, and was filled with exemplary materials and citations. This 'Method or Mould wherein the Treatise is cast', Gilbert's editor explained, was 'formed according to the most *Logical* or *Analytical* Plan, and the whole Doctrine ... distributed under Nine Heads, all which are particularly and methodically treated of ... wherein all the Cases found in our Books or Reports, or which fall within our Author's own Observation as necessary to illustrate or explain each respective Head, are introduced and applied'.[89] This kind of mixed structure and style is evident in those of Gilbert's texts that are more focused on the historical development of the law, as well as those that are not, and several of Gilbert's texts merge the exemplary and narrative sections quite closely.[90] In these works Judge Gilbert, like other eighteenth-century legal authors such as Henry Ballow, Thomas Wood, William Nelson or Matthew Bacon, conveyed the idea that English law was founded in exemplary tradition as much as in logical or natural principles. And in thus ascribing value and authority to prescription, Gilbert's work was congruent with the work of these other contributors to eighteenth-century common law jurisprudence.

Where Judge Gilbert differed most from his contemporaries was in his greater interest in writing works of history. This interest, and the value thus accorded to the study of history by Gilbert, was highlighted by that later editor in the preface to the treatise on the Exchequer cited above:

> It appears from Manuscripts now extant under his Lordship's own Hand, he had undertaken to write a general History of the Courts of *Justice*.... It were much to be wished, he had lived to complete the Execution of his Design; as the extensive Knowledge he has displayed, both of the antient History, and the modern

[89] Geoffrey Gilbert, *An Historical Account of the Original and Nature, as well as the Law of Devises and Revocations* (London, 1739), vi–vii (and note that this later editor added an alphabetical table to Gilbert's text). Another similar example is Geoffrey Gilbert, *The Law of Executions. To Which Are Added the History and Practice of the Court of King's Bench* (Dublin, 2nd edn., 1763).

[90] See for example Geoffrey Gilbert, *A Treatise of Tenures: In Two Parts* (London, 2nd edn., 1738), and Gilbert, *A Treatise of Dower*, appended to his *The Law of Uses and Trusts* (London, 1734), 353–437.

> Practice of the Law, with a Manner of writing uncommonly succinct and intelligible, give the strongest reasons to believe, his Work would have been of great Utility to those who may have Occasion to study the *English* Law on fundamental Principles.'[91]

Of course, this later editor was left to interpret the judge's intentions from evidence left in various 'Manuscripts now extant under his Lordships' own hand', since Gilbert did not leave his own prefatory claims for the methods and significance of his work. Gilbert did, however, give some indication of the intended scope of his historical project, and the interrelation between its parts, in a short essay on the early history of English legal institutions that was included among these manuscripts.[92] This essay was posthumously published as an introduction to *The History and Practice of the Court of Common Pleas* (1737), where it traced the history of law and constitution from the Saxon period to the thirteenth-century establishment of this court. The text also appeared in a later extended version which recounted developments leading to the establishment of the other central courts. Now entitled 'On the Constitution of England: Of the Division of the Courts', the essay was published at the conclusion of Gilbert's *Treatise on the Action of Debt* (1760).[93] It is apparent from the text of both versions that, first, Gilbert did envision writing a general history of English legal institutions and, second, that he believed useful knowledge would be gained if the reader appreciated the intersections and cross-references between the various elements of his work.

Judge Gilbert made it clear in this essay, and elsewhere, that he considered historical knowledge to be essential for comprehending both the general scope and fundamental principles of English law. 'To understand the Constitution of *England*,' he explained in introducing the Court of Common Pleas, 'we must consider it under a fourfold Period.' According to Gilbert this proper periodisation ranged from the earliest invasions of 'the first *Saxons*, before they were civilised, which was in Clans and Troops', to the period of unification 'into a firm State or Kingdom, under *Alfred*', and then moved through 'the great Alteration at the Conquest' in order to end with 'the present Scheme and Establishment of the law' dating from the reign of Edward I.[94] In this essay Gilbert began with the second period, offering a brief consideration of certain administrative forms, or preconditions, estab-

91 Gilbert, *Treatise on Exchequer*, iv.

92 Baker, *English Legal* Manuscripts, 40.

93 Geoffrey Gilbert, *The History and Practice of the Court of Common Pleas* (London, 1737), i–xviii; Gilbert, *Cases in Law and Equity … with Two Treatises, the One on the Action of Debt, the Other on the Constitution of England* (London, 1760), 449–68. See also Gilbert, *History and Practice of the High Court of Chancery* (London, 1758), ch. 1.

94 Gilbert, *History and Practice of the Court of Common Pleas*, i; Gilbert, *Cases in Law and Equity … On the Constitution*, 449.

lished during the era of Saxon unification. This beginning allowed Gilbert then to trace an evolution from the Saxon to the Norman period where, he argued, the essential origins of English law were to be found.[95] Gilbert's periodisation was likely drawn from the work of royal historiographer Thomas Madox. Madox, in his influential *History and Antiquities of the Exchequer of the Kings of England* (1711), had shown that English courts and jurisdictions gradually emerged during the period between the Norman Conquest and the reign of Edward II.[96] *The History and Antiquities of the Exchequer*, like Madox's other texts such as the history of boroughs, *Firma Burgi* (1722), were important sources that were frequently cited by Gilbert. These were generally popular works and, like Rymer's *Foedera*, considered authoritative in contemporary debates about institutions and personnel.[97] Gilbert may, in fact, have been inspired by Madox's work to attempt his broader history of English law since Madox characterised his own history of the Exchequer as a beginning 'apparatus' for such a future comprehensive legal history.[98]

Most of Gilbert's works emphasised Norman origins and Saxon preconditions. This was true even of his history of Chancery where he looked beyond early Saxon incivility to Roman legal and administrative practice.[99] Despite the frequent connections he drew between ancient English and Roman institutions and procedures in this work, Gilbert still traced the origins of the English Chancery to the emergence of Norman administration. He located its beginnings, just as Samuel Burroughs and others did, in the early formation of a royal secretariat.[100] Gilbert moved more decisively away from this usual periodisation, however, in his *Historical Account ... of Devises*.

95 Ibid. Cf Gilbert, *Treatise on Exchequer*, chs 1–3; Gilbert, *Law of Executions... History and Practice of the Court of King's Bench*, 307–8, 316.

96 Madox's *The History and Antiquities of the Exchequer of the Kings of England* (London, 1711) was subtitled: 'In Two Parts: From the *Norman Conquest* to the End of the Reign of K. *John*, and From the End of the Reign of K. *John* to the End of the Reign of K. *Edward* II.' Cf also Madox, *Formulare Anglicanum* (London, 1702) which was, like Rymer's influential text, a collection of documents, specifically charters and instruments from the Norman Conquest to the reign of Henry VIII. Douglas, *English Scholars*, 303; Catherine Strateman Sims, 'An Unpublished Fragment of Madox, "History of the Exchequer"', *Huntington Library Quarterly*, 23, 1 (November, 1959): 61–3.

97 Recall evidence of contemporary reference to Madox's work on the Exchequer during the impeachment trial of Lord Chancellor Macclesfield, and in Burroughs' and Yorke's histories of the Chancery. On his popularity more generally see Douglas, *English Scholars*, 307, 310; O'Brien, 'History Market', 110.

98 Madox, *History and Antiquities of the Exchequer*, iii.; Douglas, *English Scholars*, 312.

99 Gilbert, *History and Practice of Chancery*, for example 20–6, 29–37; cf Duck, *Use and Authority of the Civil Law in England*, i–xiv, esp xii.

100 Gilbert, *History and Practice of Chancery*, 1–2, 9–13; Duck, *Use and Authority of the Civil Law in England*, xvii. Contrast Roger Acherley who offers a description of the statutory origins of Chancery, and ties this to an insistence (similar to Robert Atkyns) that matters of property must be determined at common law. Acherley, *Jurisdiction of Chancery as a Court of Equity Researched*, 10–17.

There he opened with a description of the state of nature and turned to a labour theory of value in order to explain the very necessity for, and origins of, law. The text begins:

> Since all were by Nature in a State of Equality, independent on one another, they must have had the same Right to all things necessary and convenient for the Support of Life; but when, by their Labour and Industry, they took any thing out of the common Stock, it thereby became their own, and no one could dispossess them of it, without manifold Violence and Injustice; for they could not appropriate to themselves the Fruits of the Earth without Labour, which surely no body would pretend any right to, in this natural State of Equality. Hence we may infer, that every Man had a full Property in those things he had appropriated by his own Industry ...[101]

Once this natural 'full Property' was acknowledged 'reasonable men' developed methods for the sure transfer of property, Gilbert went on to explain, and these developments fostered exchange and a division of labour. Here Gilbert quickly moved from a Lockean account of the origins of property to a history of property transfer, and now he returned once again to an emphasis on Norman origins. Gilbert's brief account especially highlighted the differences between natural feelings of parental affection that should, rationally, lead men to establish property transfer by testament, and the historical reasons underlying feudal inheritance practices.[102]

Much like Adam Smith's economic history, introduced in book three of the *Wealth of Nations*, Gilbert emphasised the contrast between a natural order of economic growth and the distorted development that took place in Europe. Gilbert openly adopted elements of natural law philosophy in this introduction to his work on devises and revocation, and there is evidence that Gilbert was specifically influenced by some of the early attempts at conjectural history by men like Locke or Pufendorf. These conjectural or stadial histories of the universal progress of humankind, from savage to civilised, became a central part of eighteenth-century historiography.[103] And Gilbert made a significant contribution to this historiography because

101 Gilbert, *Historical Account of Devises*, 1–2. Gilbert's *The Law of Evidence* was another one of his texts clearly engaged with contemporary philosophical trends – especially Lockean empiricism – as well as with elements of civil law. See for example Gilbert, *The Law of Evidence* (2nd edn., London, 1760), 1–5, 7, 23, 58; Landsman, 'From Gilbert to Bentham: The Reconceptualization of Evidence Theory', 1151–60.

102 Gilbert, *Historical Account of Devises*, 5–6. Macnair, 'Gilbert and his Treatises', 267 n. 115, depicts Gilbert's Lockean account of property as one among other indications of the judge's Whiggism. Cf Kathleen Davis' account of Blackstone's similar articulation of 'natural' and 'civil' rights to property in his *Commentaries on the Laws of England*. Kathleen Davis, *Periodization and Sovereignty: How Ideas of Feudalism and Secularization Govern the Politics of Time* (Philadelphia, 2008), 63.

103 O'Brien, *Narratives of Enlightenment*, 132–61.

he conceived of a connection between those earliest, unrecorded periods of human development and the later emergence of feudal law. His work helped to shape that important transformation in the enlightened conceptualisation of feudalism, as it came to be seen as one among several stages of society traced in the philosophical histories of men like Smith, Robertson or Hume.[104] Both Hume and Smith cited Judge Gilbert's treatises, on tenures and on the Exchequer, in their own work, and a copy of Gilbert's *Treatise on the Court of Exchequer* can be found in the catalogue of Smith's library. It is likely that both men were also familiar with other texts written by Gilbert since his work circulated widely in manuscript as well as print.[105]

Common law history and Enlightenment

Geoffrey Gilbert's histories depicted certain transitions in English law, society and economy that would be familiar to his readers. Like Burroughs and others, Gilbert stressed the importance of royal initiative, and the salience of economic as well as political conflict, in the rise and demise of feudal law. For example, in discussing the evolution of English courts and of property law he too emphasised the significant development of uses, and he regarded the growth of wealth as well as human greed, as explanations for sociolegal change. Moreover in Gilbert's analysis English clerics played an active role in such change because they first turned to uses as a way to preserve, and expand, clerical property. The 'Invention of Uses', Gilbert explained, resulted from conflict between crown and clergy which was expressed in legislation like the Statute of Mortmain, as well as in the remedies afforded by a growing Chancery.[106] Gilbert's analysis considered legislative change, developments in legal process, and shifts in jurisdiction that were important to the history of English law. This analysis also, however, identified important tensions between secular and ecclesiastical

104 Smith, *Gothic Bequest*, 57, 71–3; Pocock, *Barbarism and Religion, Volume 2*, 12–21; O'Brien, *Narratives of Enlightenment*, 88–9, 112–13, 136–41.

105 Adam Smith, *An Inquiry into the Nature and Causes of the Wealth of Nations*, Edwin Cannan ed. (Chicago, 1976), bk 3, ch. 2; Smith, *Lectures on Jurisprudence*, R.L. Meek, D.D. Raphael and P.G. Stein eds, vol. 5, Glasgow Edition of the Works and Correspondence of Adam Smith (Indianapolis, 1982), chs Wednesday 9 March 1763 – Thursday 10 March 1763; David Hume, *The History of England From the Invasion of Julius Caesar to the Revolution in 1688*, vol. 2 (Indianapolis, 1983), ch. 13. Hiroshi Mizuta ed., *Adam Smith's Library: A Catalogue* (Oxford, 2000), 103. Note that in addition to Gilbert's text on the Exchequer, Smith owned other books by legal authors such as Fitzherbert, Finch, Coke, Hale, Hawkins, Jacob and Blackstone.

106 Gilbert, *Historical Account of Devises*, 9–12; Gilbert, *History and Practice of Chancery*, 17–20; Gilbert, *Two Treatises on Proceedings in Equity*, 28–32; Gilbert, *Law of Uses and Trusts*, 3–4. See William Blackstone's rehearsal of this argument, with citation of Gilbert's *Historical Account of Devises*, in his *Commentaries on the Laws of England*, vol. 1, bk 2, ch. 23.

authorities as the cause of ongoing political conflict, economic and social change, especially during the subsequent era of Tudor kingship.[107]

Gilbert further demonstrated this kind of interest in broader ideas about causation and periodisation when he narrated an early history of trade in his treatise on the Exchequer. There Gilbert carefully described the 'Invention of the Needle' first used for navigation by the Chinese and adopted by the English in the fourteenth century; he then used this key example of technological innovation in order to explain European economic growth, and warfare, as well as English legal change.[108] Here, as elsewhere, Gilbert's legal histories pointed towards the interest in civil theory and civil history usually associated with Enlightenment figures like Hume or Gibbon.[109] Gilbert perceived different stages in the development of human society, sought explanation for transitions from one stage to the next, and emphasised progression towards commercial wealth. While Gilbert's histories of English law certainly underscored the importance of political narrative, and largely conveyed detailed knowledge of English legal institutions and doctrines, they also betrayed that increasing preoccupation with the development of civil society. These same interests and methods were later articulated by Edmund Burke, who may well have been building upon Gilbert's work when he argued in a planned *Abridgment of English History* that 'the present system of our laws, like our language and our learning, is a very mixed and heterogeneous mass; in some respects our own; in more borrowed from the policy of foreign nations, and compounded, altered, and variously modified according to the various necessities, which the manners, the religion, and the commerce of the people have at different times imposed'.[110]

Geoffrey Gilbert's incipient narrative of civil history did not only affect the development of enlightened historiography. It was also important for

107 This kind of analysis of causation and periodisation is an important theme in Edward Gibbons' history, discussed by Pocock, 'Historiography and Enlightenment', 91–4, and O'Brien, *Narratives of Enlightenment*, 168–9, 195–8. There is of course a much bigger story regarding an enlightened history of religion and of the Christian church that I have not discussed here.

108 Gilbert, *Treatise on Exchequer*, 204–7, 216–19. Cf Kramnick, 'Augustan Politics and English Historiography', 44, on the appearance of similar kinds of arguments in Walpole's press about the development of trade and commons in the era of Edward III.

109 Karen O'Brien, 'History and the Novel in Eighteenth-Century Britain', *Huntington Library Quarterly*, 68, 1/2 (March, 2005): 401–2; Smith, *Gothic Bequest*, 73; Pocock, 'Historiography and Enlightenment', 94; Pocock, *Barbarism and Religion, Volume 2*, 12–13, 29–41; Pocock, 'Perceptions of Modernity in Early Modern Thinking', *Intellectual History Review*, 17, 1 (2007): 59.

110 O'Brien, *Narratives of Enlightenment*, 19, quoting Edmund Burke 'An Essay Towards an History of the Laws of England' in *An Abridgment of English History, from the Invasion of Julius Caesar to the End of the Reign of King John*. Burke's unfinished abridgment, like Gilbert's texts, remained in manuscript until after the author's death. McLoughlin, 'Burke's "Abridgment of English History"', 45.

eighteenth-century jurisprudence. His work conveyed the idea that the English legal tradition was a product of human and social evolution and, as such, was authoritative because it was adaptive and communal (ideas that we have come to associate with a 'Burkean' worldview). Moreover, Gilbert's legal treatises conveyed a belief in the value of prescriptive practice through their form as well as their content: Gilbert, like others, relied on collection and enumeration, as much as narrative and analysis, in order to produce reliable knowledge of English law. Yet even though Geoffrey Gilbert was a well-known author in the late eighteenth century, and a recognised influence on the development of enlightened historiography and jurisprudence, he has been forgotten – excised from a narrative of the Enlightenment especially as that narrative began to take shape in the early part of the nineteenth century.

Gilbert's disappearance can, in part, be attributed to the exclusion of common law jurisprudence from the definition of Enlightenment philosophy. That definition of Enlightenment philosophy (rationalist, French, individualist, revolutionary) was, as we have seen, predicated upon a history of philosophy formulated in the late eighteenth-century. The authors of this history focused exclusively on developments in the theory of knowledge, and celebrated the apparent novelty of their own rationalist and utilitarian views.[111] This philosophical history of philosophy reinforced Benthamite attacks on common law as incoherent, technical and arcane. And even when later critics, in turn, attacked these kinds of radical Benthamite and French rationalist views they continued to operate with that singular definition of Enlightenment philosophy from which common law jurisprudence was excluded.

The 'forgetting' of Gilbert can also, paradoxically, be attributed to seventeenth and eighteenth-century legal historians' own investigation of feudal law. This research had a real impact on historical periodisation, and shaped scholars' later claims about novelty and modernity. The association Gilbert encouraged between feudal law and the stadial narrative was especially important. The reification of 'feudal' and 'feudalism' emerged as legal historians' unintended legacy in the aftermath of Enlightenment. 'By 1800 the construct had been launched and the expression "feudal system" devised; by the mid-nineteenth century the word "feudalism" was in use,' Elizabeth Brown explains. 'The way was prepared for future scholars to study feudalism ... scientifically, and for others to employ the ism to refer, abusively, to those selected elements of the past that were to be overthrown, abolished, or inexorably superseded.'[112] A contrast between modern and feudal was added to those binaries of rational and irrational, universal and particularist, natural

[111] See above, chapter 1, pp. 10–13. And cf Pocock, 'Perceptions of Modernity', 61.

[112] Elizabeth A.R. Brown, 'The Tyranny of a Construct: Feudalism and Historians of Medieval Europe', *American Historical Review*, 73, 4 (October, 1974): 1065; Davis, *Periodization and Sovereignty*, 53–66.

law and common law. Common law was identified with feudalism and feudal law. And this only strengthened the belief that common law was no part of Enlightenment.

When scholars today tell a story about positivism, natural law and reform finally transforming the 'medievalism' and 'antiquarianism' of common law, they are building upon these early narratives.[113] These narratives have been surprisingly persistent, able to withstand multiple conceptual and methodological challenges. For example, it is almost forty years since Elizabeth Brown offered her critique of the misleading, even 'tyrannical', concept of feudalism. Brown crucially expressed her doubts not only about the applicability of this concept across time and space, but also about the false evaluations of progress ('fully feudal,' 'bastard feudalism') it encouraged. Related concerns have recently been articulated by historians who draw upon postcolonial analysis in order to problematise the 'demonization', 'romanticization' or simple 'dismissal' of both medieval and subaltern subjects within the modernising narrative.[114] Questions about the distortions imposed by a modernising narrative have also been raised by historians of religion who have successfully challenged conventional associations between Enlightenment, anticlericalism and secularisation.[115] The evidence presented in this book has similarly demonstrated that the conventional approach, which posits a stark contrast between common law traditionalism and Enlightenment modernity, can no longer be sustained. And it has made the case, finally, for a new narrative to replace the old story of common law's demise.

[113] Ibbetson, 'Natural Law and Common Law,' 6–7; Lemmings, *Professors of the Law*, 108–9, 140–1, 148, 305, 325–8.

[114] Brown, 'Tyranny of a Construct', 1074–7; see also Susan Reynolds, *Fiefs and Vassals: The Medieval Evidence Reinterpreted* (Oxford, 1994, reprint 2001). Carol Symes, 'When We Talk About Modernity', *American Historical Review*, 116, 3 (June, 2011): 716–19.

[115] See the works cited above in chapter 1, nn. 9–10.

Conclusion

The new history of English common law jurisprudence and culture introduced here emphasises development, relevance and vitality. Common law was fully engaged with multiple contemporary trends, and played a key role in the emergence of an enlightened society in eighteenth-century England. This is a fundamental revision of the long-held view that common law remained a bastion of tradition and technicality, its insularity and irrationality clearly antithetical to eighteenth-century enlightened culture and philosophy. This new history of common law also provides an important corrective to the old narrative of decline and fall, which posited that common law lost its intellectual and cultural preeminence in the eighteenth century as the previous period of Coke and Selden, custom and ancient constitution, gave way to a new era of rationalism, positivism and revolution. Once the premise of decline, and of a dichotomy between common law and Enlightenment are jettisoned, it becomes possible to recognise the ways in which common law approaches to evidentiary practices, to education and dissemination of knowledge, to commercial change and historical analysis were, in fact, in line with trends in enlightened science, encyclopedism, philosophy and historiography.

In demonstrating the dynamism of common law ideas and practices, especially in the early part of the eighteenth century, my intention, however, is not simply to replace that old narrative of decline and fall with a new story of rise and progress. Rather it is to recover the complexity of legal, intellectual and cultural change, and to foster an appreciation for the nature of continuity in action, and continuity as an approach. It is because common law flourished in multiple enlightened contexts that the belief in, and practice of, attributing value to prescription and precedent also evolved. This is a new history of common law, and a new historical understanding of common law jurisprudence. This is also a new history of Enlightenment which contributes to the ongoing revision of that term, and forces us to recognise the persistent influence of concepts of stability, custom and tradition (as much as universality, reason and nature) to eighteenth-century definitions of justice and knowledge.

Clearly the broad expansion of an eighteenth-century print culture was a critical factor in the history outlined here. By charting specific developments in legal education and legal publishing it was possible to demonstrate how English common law was fully implicated in the formation of an enlightened encyclopedic vision. Legal treatises, abridgments and dictionaries were large-scale commercial projects that took up the newly pressing challenges of collection and organisation. Much like the Enlightenment encyclopedias, these law books were concerned to achieve a systematic and coherent classification of knowledge. And these concerns were shared with another typical eighteenth-century production, the history book. Authors interested in profitability, and in the educative value of history, also employed collection and compilation as useful ways to convey historical knowledge. Increasing numbers of accessible, affordable and popular historical abridgments and digests (as well as numerous collections of archival materials) were published in this period. Authors of histories of common law and constitution certainly participated in these trends in the eighteenth-century book trade, yet the evidence of their contribution to historical knowledge goes farther than this. My study of the historical literature revealed that eighteenth-century legal histories had a considerable impact on the content and on the categories, or genres, of enlightened historiography. Historians of legal institutions, doctrines and constitutions began to offer the kind of socio-economic evidence and explanation that would later characterise the stadial analyses and histories of civil society written by men like Adam Smith or Adam Ferguson. This is a significant indication of the ways in which common law was fully implicated in the formation of enlightened historical writing.

Equally significant, common law's deep engagement with the growth of print was a crucial factor in the evolution of eighteenth-century jurisprudence. This engagement was effected through student commonplace techniques and practitioners' note-taking methods, as much as through the techniques of compilation and systematisation endorsed by the authors of printed law books. In the lengthy interaction between legal manuscript traditions and the new profusion of print, the bonds of a common law community were strengthened, and ideas about the nature and authority of common law were enhanced. The widespread recourse to collection and enumeration underscored lawyers' belief in the merits of inductive reasoning and prescriptive practice. Common lawyers typically formulated their arguments by means of citation and compilation of detailed examples, promoting adherence to formal rules and established remedies. This characteristic logic of early modern English common law continuously evolved in large part because of the expansion of this legal literature within these enlightened contexts.

English common law was also deeply involved in eighteenth-century commercial and financial change. Controversies that typified the new credit economy – such as disputes about the enforcement of contract, mortgage and trust – frequently stimulated debate about the jurisdiction and authority of common law. In the course of these disputes common law came to be appreciated as a necessary part of positive economic development. Its predictability and certainty were regarded as a secure basis for economic growth. Common law procedures and principles offered vital reassurance in the face of increasing concerns about fraud, unsecured credit and illicit gain. Such concerns were articulated as part of a wide-ranging public discussion about the profits and pitfalls of this new market-oriented culture. These concerns were also heightened as part of contemporary moral-philosophical debate over the dangerous tendency for commercialisation to lead to corruption. English jurists were interested in the philosophical investigation of economic change; they were influenced by new insights into the nature of human passion, and new arguments about its impact on the social order. Ideas about sentiment, desire and civility informed eighteenth-century legal disputes and legal theory.

Through this combination of philosophical and practical legal controversy over economic change, new definitions and defences of common law developed. Common law was powerfully identified with the positive moral values of honesty, sociability and credibility. Innovations in commercial law, including the growth of new financial instruments, were now, in turn, subject to a mounting insistence on the applicability (and desirability) of stable common law procedures and remedies. It is clear that the endorsement here of common law's jurisdiction was not a defence of stasis against change, or of tradition against modernity. Indeed, common law was understood to be peculiarly useful because it promoted the kind of security of property rights necessary for economic prosperity and commercial growth. Moreover, this kind of economic change, and enlightened philosophical debate, actually strengthened belief in the relevance of past practice to the authority of law.

Finally, gendered discourse and gendered assumptions played an important part in the development of common law jurisprudence, practice and culture. The new history of common law and Enlightenment introduced here has provided evidence of the kinds of gendered values that were central to public debate about the consequences of economic change. Many of the specific disputes over credit practices or over the transmission of property that came before the English courts were fuelled by contemporary attitudes towards women's and men's proper roles, rights and responsibilities. Such attitudes also informed contemporary debates over new developments in evidentiary practices, and intensified questions about the fairness of legal process in the emerging adversarial trial. Here common law interacted closely with enlightened intellectual and cultural trends in science as well as print, and became a site for sophisticated discussion regarding the substance of knowledge and of truth.

Attending to the history of gender is essential in order to uncover the multiple ways contemporaries understood, and disputed, the nature of legal authority. Gender history is also a key part of an approach, adopted here, that emphasises the relevance of legal practice as well as ideas. This approach opens up new sources for interpreting the development of common law jurisprudence and culture and, equally important, allows for closer ties to be forged between legal and intellectual historians. Courtroom arguments, commonplace books, library lists and letters, as much as formal legal treatises, provide evidence of the vitality of eighteenth-century common law. This evidence should no longer be ignored; the complex relationship between common law and enlightened ideas and practices must be studied further if we are finally to overcome the limitations, and distortions, of the conventional narrative. Indeed, once we better understand the evolution of common law arguments about stability, custom and collective wisdom in the eighteenth century, we will become able to recognise the ways in which prescription and precedent remained important values in the nineteenth century, and beyond.

Bibliography

Manuscript Sources

Arthur W. Diamond Law Library, Columbia University, New York
C 73 1700, Law Commonplace
M 73, Law Commonplace

Singleton Collection
36, Precedent Book; Legal Commonplace
37, Miscellaneous Notes and Definitions; Legal Commonplace 18th c
40, Hawkins Pleas of the Crown
41, Hale Pleas of the Crown
43, Doctrina Placitandi
69, Gilbert on Remainders; Commonplace Book

Beinecke Library, Yale University, New Haven
Osborn Manuscripts
52, box 2, Correspondence of Lord Hardwicke
52, box 9, Papers relating to the Court of Kings Bench

British Library, London
Additional Manuscripts
50117, Legal Commonplace Book of William Longueville

Hargrave
319, Roger North Law Commonplace

Stowe
750, Letters from Lawyers addressed to Thomas Parker, Earl of Macclesfield, with a few Draft Replies Interspersed
fol. 17, Letter from Solicitor General John Fortescue-Aland on Business of the Western Circuit, 20 March 1710/11
fol. 80, Letter from William Salkeld, Serjeant at Law on Appointment to Ireland, 31 October 1714
fol. 404, Draft, Lord Macclesfield to the Duke of Devonshire Defending himself from the Charge of Selling Offices in Chancery, 22 May 1722

Cambridge University Library, Cambridge
Dd14.19, Commonplace on Lords Jurisdiction
Ee.2.30, 9r-20v, Un Treatise Concernant le Ley (Richard Zouch?)

Cholmondeley (Houghton) Collection
65 29, fols 1–12, Papers from the Impeachment of the Earl of Macclesfield

Folger Shakespeare Library, Washington D.C.
C.c. 1, fols 20, 21, 39, Letters from Elizabeth Jekyll, Joseph Jekyll and John Somers to Jacob Tonson
G.c. 1, Lady Rebecca Atkins v. the Parish of Clapham, Surrey, in the Diocese of Winchester, Consistory Court 1691
M.a. 184, Commonplace 1804–1810
MS Add 585, Commonplace Book: Philosophy
MS Add 1025, Legal Document concerning a Case of Estate Fraud, ca. 1615
V.a. 121, Court of Chancery Miscellaneous Collection
V.a. 260, Miscellany 1613–ca. 1756
V.a. 426, Notes on Cases Adjudged in the King's Bench and Court of Common Pleas, and on Legal Terms compiled 1681–c. 1700
V.a. 487, Reports of Cases in the King's Bench ca. 1690–ca. 1712
V.a. 595, Remembrances for Order and Decency to be Kept in the Upper House of Parliament by the Lords When His Majestie is not There
V.b. 64, Osborne Practice of the Exchequer Court ca. 1625
V.b. 71, Osborne Practice of the Exchequer Court ca. 1650
V.b. 199, Commonplace book c. 1600
V.b. 266, Letter from Earl of Anglesey to Edward Southwell 1713 October 10
V.b. 268, Autograph Letter signed by Roger North, 1722 June 17
V.b. 298, Collection of Miscellaneous Legal and Historical Documents, ca. 1675–ca. 1700
W.b. 269, An Index to Certain Legal Text Books ca. 1725
W.a. 126, Miscellany of Reflections on Literature, Philosophy and Government ca. 1700–ca. 1725
X.d. 393, Historical Commonplace Book ca. 1625

Free Library, Philadelphia
Hampton L. Carson Collection
Carson Collection Letters, Form for the Sale or Transfer of Stock, D.S. August 27 1723
LC 14.33, Book of Legal Forms later 18th c
LC 14.34, Legal Commonplace 16th c
LC 14. 45, North on Pardons, etc.
LC 14.51, Manuscript Book of Law Terms 17th [&18th?] c
LC 14.54, Legal Commonplace
LC 14.65, Legal Notebook 16th / 17th c
LC 14.66, Herbert Jacob, Reports
LC 14.73, Legal Commonplace Later 17th c
LC 14.79, Legal Notebook Sir William Jones
LC 14.80, Crumwell Deth Commonplace
LC 14.81, Reports of Cases in the Court of Kings Bench
LC 14.86, John Strange, Opinions and Cases in Chancery; Commonplace Book
LC 14.91, Precedents of Declarations Later 18th c
LC 14.98, Legal Commonplace, Early 18th c (w/additions to 1754) Including Ecclesiastical Matters
LC 14.100, Commonplace Book of Horace Binney
LC 15 75.1, Legal Commonplace c. 1700

Harvard Law School Library, Cambridge MA
MSS HLS 1007, Exact Abridgment of Cases on Error ca. 1721
MSS HLS 1022, Dodderidge On the Study of the Laws ca. 1605
MSS HLS 1055, Precedents of Pleading ca. 1725–1775
MSS HLS 1144, Lawyer's Commonplace Book ca. 1670 (William Style)
MSS HLS 1166, Precedents of Pleading 1714–1749 (Matthew Skinner)
MSS HLS 1262, Lawyer's Commonplace ca. 1800
MSS HLS 1273, Commonplace after 1736
MSS HLS 4011, Abridgment of Exchequer Cases ca. 1740–1760
MSS HLS 4091, Lawyer's Commonplace Book ca. 1700
MSS HLS 6019, Lawyer's Commonplace Book ca. 1825
MSS HLS 6020, Lawyer's Commonplace Book ca. 1825

Hertfordshire Archives and Local Studies, Hertford
Panshanger Collection
D/EP F23–24, Family and General Correspondence of Sir William and Dame Sarah Cowper
D/EP F27, Miscellaneous Manuscripts and Verses
D/EP F54, General Correspondence to William, 1st Earl Cowper
D/EP F57, General Correspondence to William, 1st Earl Cowper
D/EP F58, Family Correspondence to William, 1st Earl Cowper
D/EP F69, Diary of William, 1st Earl Cowper c. 1705–1714
D/EP F81, Correspondence, Judith Cowper
D/EP F82, Commonplace Book c. 1690–1708
D/EP F84, Chancery Probate of Elizabeth Culling Will
D/EP F85, Correspondence to William, 1st Earl Cowper regarding Mary and William Culling
D/EP F92, Quarter Session Papers, William, 1st Earl Cowper as JP, 1687–c. 1700
D/EP F95, William, 1st Earl Cowper, Cases and Opinions to 1705
D/EP F96, Materials relating to the death of Sarah Stout and the Trial and Appeal
D/EP F97, William, 1st Earl Cowper, Cases and Opinions 1710–14, 1718–23
D/EP F98, William, 1st Earl Cowper, Notebook c. 1698–1700
D/EP F121, William, 1st Earl Cowper, Notes on Meeting of Lords Justices
D/EP F136, William, 1st Earl Cowper, Drafts, Notes and Miscellaneous Political Papers
D/EP F147, Official Papers, Lord Chancellor Cowper
D/EP F152–3, Official Papers Regarding Appointment, Recommendation etc., Lord Chancellor Cowper
D/EP F159, Records Relating to the Inns of Court
D/EP F212, Drafts and Copies of Bills and Answers in Chancery, Cowper v Cowper
D/EP F213, Miscellaneous Documents Relating to Cowper v Cowper
D/EP F214, William, 1st Earl, and Countess Cowper, Inventories of Personal Effects and Household Goods
D/EP F217, Accounts and Other Papers, Cowper v Cowper
D/EP F218, Miscellaneous Documents Relating to Cowper v Cowper
D/EP F219, Papers and Artifacts Relating to Spencer Cowper

William Blyth Gerish Collection
D/EGr 43, Article on Elizabeth Culling

Inner Temple, London (microfilm at Harvard Law Library)
Barrington
68, Eighteenth-Century Law Commonplace Book
60, Law Commonplace Book Containing Table to Scroggs etc.
63, Law Commonplace Book

Misc.
15, A Small Commonplace Book of Definitions and Legal Facts, Early Eighteenth Century
38, General Commonplace, Mainly Relating to Battles and Campaigns, Seventeenth and Eighteenth Centuries
63, Catalogue of the Library of Sir Martin Wright
76, A Law Commmonplace Book
125–30, Rolle's Abridgment Interleaved and Annotated by Baron Robert Price

Mitford
27, 28, 29, Legal Manuscripts, Commonplace Books

National Archives, London
C111/220, Chancery Master Brougham's Exhibits, Decree in the Exchequer in the Cause Atkyns v Took
Prob/11/429, Henry Stout, Will, 9 September 1695
Prob/11/454, Edward Atkyns Will, 9 August 1698
Prob/11/514, Robert Atkyns Will, 24 May 1709
Prob/11/561, Richard Atkyns Will, 24 May 1717
Prob/11/605, Herbert Jacob Will, 25 April 1724

National Library of Wales
Longueville, Deeds and Documents
1187, fols 1–70, Newsletters 11 February 1724 to 1 June 1725

Primary printed sources

An Abridgment of Mr. Locke's Essay Concerning Humane Understanding, 2nd edn (London, 1700)
Acherley, Roger, *The Britannic Constitution: Or, the Fundamental Form of Government in Great Britain* (London, 1727)
——, *The Jurisdiction of the Chancery as a Court of Equity Researched. And the Traditional Obscurity of its Commencement Cleared* (London, 1734)
An Account of the Full Tryal and Examination of Spencer Cooper Esq. at Harford Assizes on Wednesday the 19th of this instant July 1699. for the Murder of Mrs. Sarah Stout on the 13th of March Last, and of his Being Acquited, Before the Honorable Baron Hatsell (London, 1699)
Addison, Joseph, *The Freeholder, Or Political Essays* (London, 1716)
——, *A Poem to his Majesty, Presented to the Lord Keeper* (London, 1695)
——, *The Spectator*, vol. 4 (London, 1712)
—— and Richard Steele, *The Tatlers by Isaac Bickerstaff Esq.*, 2 vols (London, 1710)

BIBLIOGRAPHY

Arbitrium Redivivm: or the Law of Arbitration (London, 1694)
The Articles of Impeachment against the Lord Summers (London, 1701)
Atkyns, Richard, *The Kings Grant of Privilege for Sole Printing Common Law Books Defended* (London, 1669)
——, *The Original and Growth of Printing* (London?, 1660?)
Atkyns, Robert, *The Case of Sir Robert Atkyns … Upon his Appeal Against a Decree* (London, 1695)
——, *A Defence of the Late Lord Russel's Innocency … Together with an Argument in the Great Case Concerning Election of Members to Parliament* (London, 1689)
——, *A Discourse Concerning the Ecclesiastical Jurisdiction in the Realm of England: Occasioned by the Late Commission in Ecclesiastical Causes* (London, 1689)
——, *An Enquiry into the Jurisdiction of the Chancery in Causes of Equity* (London, 1695)
——, *Enquiry into the Power of Dispensing with Penal Statutes* (London, 1689)
——, *The Lord Russel's Innocency Further Defended* (London, 1689)
——, *Parliamentary and Political Tracts* (London, 1734)
——, *The Power, Jurisdiction and Priviledge of Parliament, and the Antiquity of the House of Commons Asserted* (London, 1689)
——, *A Treatise of the True and Ancient Jurisdiction of the House of Peers* (London, 1699)
The Attorney's Pocket Companion: Or a Guide to the Practisers of the Law, 2 vols (London, 1733)
Bacon, Francis, *Certain Miscellany Works of the Right Honourable Francis Lord Verulam, Viscount St Alban* (London, 1670)
——, *Elements of the Common Law of England, Branched into a Double Tract* (London, 1630)
——, *Law Tracts* (London, 1737)
Bacon, Matthew, *The Compleat Arbitrator, Or, The Law of Awards and Arbitraments* (London, 1731)
——, *A General Abridgment of Cases in Equity, Argued and Adjudged in the High Court of Chancery* (London, 1732; 2nd edn, 1734)
——, *A New Abridgment of the Law*, vols 1–3 (London, 1736–40)
Ballow, Henry, *A Treatise of Equity* (London, 1737)
——, *A Treatise of Equity, With the Addition of Marginal References and Notes by John Fonblanque, Esq.*, 2nd edn, vol. 1 (London, 1799)
Barbeyrac, Jean, *The Spirit of the Ecclesiasticks of all Sects and Ages, As to the Doctrines of Morality … Translated from the French by a Gentleman of Gray's Inn. With a Preface by the Author of the Independent Whig* (London, 1722)
Baron and Feme. A Treatise of Law and Equity, Concerning Husbands and Wives, 3rd edn (London, 1738)
Bassett, Thomas, *A Catalogue of the Common and Statute Law-Books of this Realm with Some Others Relating Thereunto, Alphabetically Digested under Proper Heads* (London, 1694)
——, *An Exact Catalogue of the Common and Statute Law Books* (London, 1684)
The Batchelor's Directory: Being a Treatise of the Excellence of Marriage, Of its Necessity and the Means to Live Happy in it (London, 1694)
Bayle, Pierre, *A General Dictionary Historical And Critical*, trans. Rev. John Peter Bernard, Thomas Birch, John Lockman, et al., vol. 2 (London, 1735)

Beckinham, Charles, *Lothario's Answer to Sarah the Quaker, in the Shades* (London, 1729)

——, *Sarah, the Quaker, to Lothario, Lately Deceased, on Meeting Him in the Shades* (London, 1728)

Bentham, Jeremy, *A Fragment on Government*, J.H. Burns and H.L.A. Hart eds, (Cambridge, 1988)

Bibliotheca Anatomica, Medica, Chirugica, &c. Containing a Description of the Several Parts of the Body, 3 vols (London, 1711–14)

Blackstone, William, *Commentaries on the Laws of England*, 4 vols (Chicago, 1979)

Blount, Thomas, *A Law Dictionary*, 3rd edn (London, 1717)

——, *The Resolution of the Judges upon Several Statutes of Bankrupts: As Also The Like Resolutions Upon 13 Eliz. and 27 Eliz. Touching Fraudulent Conveyances* (London, 1670)

Bohun, William, *Declarations and Pleadings in the Most Usual Actions Brought in the Central Courts of Kings Bench and Common Pleas at Westminster* (London, 1733)

Bolingbroke, Henry St John Viscount, *Political Writings*, David Armitage ed. (Cambridge, 1997)

Bond, Maurice F., ed., *The Manuscripts of the House of Lords, Volume 10, 1712–1714* (London, 1953)

Brown, William, *The Clerk's Tutor in Chancery; Giving True Directions by Authentick Precedents ... With Such Process, and Other Instruments as are Now in Use in that High and Honourable Court*, 2nd edn (London, 1688; 3rd edn 1705)

——, *Methodus Novissima Intrandi Placita Generalia: Or a New, Compleat and Exact Method...of Drawing and Entring Declarations, Pleas, Issues ... To Which is Added a Compleat Analysis of the Science of True and Correct Pleading* (London, 1699)

——, *Praxis Almae Curiae Cancellariae: A Collection of Precedents by Bill and Answer, Plea and Demurrer* (London, 1694; 2nd edn, 1705; 4th edn, 1725)

Browne, Daniel, *A Catalogue of the Libraries of the Honourable William Carr, of Lincoln's-Inn, ... And of the Reverend Mr. John Herbert* (London, 1721)

Bryson, W. Hamilton, ed., *Cases Concerning Equity and the Courts of Equity 1550–1660*, vol. 1 (London, 2000)

——, ed., *Equity Cases in the Court of Exchequer 1660 to 1714*, Medieval and Renaissance Texts and Studies, vol. 313 (Tempe, Arizona, 2007)

——, ed., *Samuel Dodd's Reports 1678–1713 and Miscellaneous Exchequer Cases 1671–1713* (Durham, 2000)

Burroughs, Samuel, *An Enquiry into the Customary-Estates and Tenant-Rights of those who hold Lands of Church and other Foundations* (London, 1731)

——, *The History of the Chancery; Relating to the Judicial Power of that Court and the Rights of the Masters* (London, 1726)

——, *The Legal Judicature in Chancery Stated. With Remarks on a Late Book, Intitled, A Discourse of the Judicial Authority Belonging to the Master of the Rolls* (London, 1727)

Carter, Samuel, *Legal Provisions for the Poor: or, a Treatise of the Common and Statute Laws Concerning the Poor either as to Relief, Settlement, or Punishment* (London, 1710)

——, *Lex Custumaria: or a Treatise of Copy-Hold Estates, in Respect of the Lord, Copy-Holder* (London, 1696)

——, *Lex Vadiorum, The Law of Mortgages* (London, 1706)

——, trans., *A Moral Treatise Upon Valour, Divided into Two Books: And Dedicated to Monsieur the Dauphin. Done into English by* Mr. *Carter, of the Inner-Temple* (London, 1695)

——, *Reports of Several Special Cases Argued and Resolved in the Court of Common Pleas* (London, 1688)

The Case of Mrs. Mary Stout, Widow (London, 1700)

The Case of Spencer Cowper Esq., John Marson, Ellis Stephens, and William Rogers Gentlemen (London, 1699)

A Catalogue of the Common and Statute Law Books of this Realm (London, 1714–31)

Cawdrey, Zachary, *A Preparation for Martyrdom, A Discourse About the Cause, the Temper, the Assistances and Rewards of a Martyr of Jesus Christ* (London, 1681)

Chambers, Ephraim, *Cyclopedia: or an Universal Dictionary of Arts and Sciences*, 2 vols (London, 1728)

Chapone, Sarah, *The Hardships of the English Laws in Relation to Wives. With an Explanation of the Original Curse of Subjection Passed upon the Woman, In an Humble Address to the Legislature* (London, 1735)

Charles Reynell, Esq., Administrator de Bonis non … appellant, John Atkins, Esq., late John Tracy, Administrator de Bonis non … respondent, The Respondent's Case (London, 1739)

The Clerk's Magazine or Law Repository (Dublin, 1749)

Cobbett, William, *Cobbett's Parliamentary History of England from the Norman Conquest in 1066 to the year 1803*, 12 vols (London, 1806–12; reprint, New York, 1966)

Coke, Edward, *The First Part of the Institutes of the Laws of England: Or, A Commentary Upon Littleton*, 4th edn (London, 1639)

——, *The Third Part of the Institutes of the Laws of England: Concerning High Treason and Other Pleas of the Crown, and Criminal Causes* (London, 1644)

Cole, Nathaniel, 'Prescription for Educating a Barrister', in David Lemmings, *Professors of the Law: Barristers and English Legal Culture in the Eighteenth Century* (Oxford, 2000), 240–3

A Collection of Heads and Titles proper for a Common Place-Book in Law and Equity, Interspers'd with Many Useful Words for the Benefit of References to the Titles, which Renders the Whole a Copious Index to the Law (London, 1733)

A Collection of the Parliamentary Debates in England from the Year MDCLVIII to the Present Time (London, 1739)

Collier, Jeremy, *Essays upon Several Moral Subjects: In Two Parts*, 3rd edn (London, 1698)

Cooksey, Richard, *Essay Upon the Life and Character of John Lord Somers, Baron of Evesham: Also Sketches of an Essay on the Life and Character of Philip Earl of Hardwicke. Proposed to be inserted in a Compendious History of Worcestershire* (London, 1791)

Cowell, John, *Institutiones Juris Anglicani* (Oxford, 1676)

Cowper, Mary, *Diary of Mary Countess Cowper, Lady of the Bedchamber to the Princess of Wales 1714–1720* (London, 1864)

Cowper, William, First Earl, *A Declaration of William Earl Cowper, Shewing that the Matters Contained in Some Hear-says, Relating to Him, in the Examination of Christopher Layer, are False and Groundless* (London, 1723)

——, *An Impartial History of Parties*, in John Lord Campbell, *The Lives of the Lord Chancellors and Keepers of the Great Seal of England*, vol. 4 (London, 1846), 421–9

——, *A Speech in the House of Lords, Upon the Third Reading of the Bill for Inflicting Pains and Penalties upon Francis, late Lord Bishop of Rochester* (London, 1723)

Cowper, William, 'An Account of Some Experiments Lately Made on Dogs, and of the Effects of Mr. John Colbatch's Styptick on Humane Bodies', *Philosophical Transactions*, 18 (1694), 42–4

—— and Hans Sloane, 'An Account of what Appeared on the Dissection of the Body of Mr.-Dove. By the Late Mr. William Cowper, Surgeon, F. R. S. In a Letter Communicated by Dr. Hans Sloane, R. S. Secr,' *Philosophical Transactions*, 27 (1710–1712), 512–14

——, *The Anatomy of Humane Bodies* (London, 1698)

——, 'A Letter from Mr. William Cowper, Giving an Account of a Very Large Diseased Kidney, Found on the Dissection of a Lady, with the Symptoms of the Disease before Her Death, and an Explanation of Their Phaenomena,' *Philosophical Transactions*, 19 (1695–1697), 301–9

——, *Myotomia Reformata, or, A New Administration of all the Muscles of Humane Bodies* (London, 1694)

Cox, Richard, *Hibernia Anglicana: Or, The History of Ireland from the Conquest thereof by the English to this Present Time*, 2 vols (London, 1689–90)

Crook, John, *Rebellion Rebuked, In an Answer to a Scandalous Pamphlet Entitled, The Quaker Converted to Christianity, &c.* (London, 1673)

Cumberland, Richard, A *Treatise of the Laws of Nature*, trans. John Maxwell (London, 1727)

D'Anvers, Knightley, *A General Abridgment of the Common Law, Alphabetically Digested Under Proper Titles: With Notes and References to the Whole*, 2 vols (London, 1705; 2nd edn, 1725)

Dawson, George, *Origo Legum: Or, a Treatise on the Origin of Laws, and their Obliging Power* (London, 1694)

Dennis, John, *Vice and Luxury Publick Mischiefs, Or Remarks on a Book Intituled the Fable of the Bees* (London, 1724)

A Dialogue between a Quaker and his Neighbor in Hertford, about the Murder of Mrs. Sarah Stout (London, 1699)

A Dissertation on the Law of Nature, the Law of Nations, and the Civil Law in General. Together with Some Observations on the Roman Civil Law in Particular. To Which is Added, by Way of Appendix, a Curious Catalogue of Books, Very Useful to the Students of these Several Laws (London, 1723; 2nd edn, 1726)

Dodderidge, John, *The Lawyers Light: Or Due Direction for the Study of the Law* (London, 1629)

Domat, Jean, *The Civil Law in Its Natural Order: Together with the Public Law. Written in French by Monsieur Domat … and translated into English by William Strahan LL.D*, 2 vols, (London, 1722)

——, *A Treatise on the First Principles of Law in General: Of their Nature and Design, and of the Interpretation of Them*, trans. Thomas Wood (London, 1705)

Duck, Arthur, *Of the Use and Authority of the Civil Law in England*, in Claude Joseph de Ferriere, *The History of the Roman or Civil Law*, trans. J.B. (London, 1724)

Dunscombe, Giles, *Tryals per Pais: Or, the Law of England Concerning Juries by Nisi Prius*, 3rd edn (London, 1695)

Echard, Laurence, *The Hainousness of Injustice Done Under the Pretence of Equity: In a Sermon Preach'd in the Cathedral Church of Lincoln* (London, 1698)

——, *The History of England, From the First Entrance of Julius Caesar and the Romans to the End of the Reign of King James the First*, 3 vols (London, 1718)
An Enquiry Into the Origin of Parliamentary Impeachments: With a History of the Most Remarkable … From the Beginning to Our Time (London, 1745?)
Euer, Samson, *Doctrina Placitandi, Or L'Art & Science De Bon Pleading* (London, 1677)
Father's Nown Child (London, 1694)
Fitzherbert, Anthony, *La Graunde Abridgment*, 3 vols (London, 1514–16?, 1577)
——, *La Nouvel Natura Brevium* (London, 1583)
——, *The New Natura Brevium of the Most Reverend Judge, Mr. Anthony Fitz-Herbert; Corrected and Revised* (London, 1704)
Francis, Richard, *Maxims of Equity, Collected From, and Proved by Cases, Out of the Books of the Best Authority, in the High Court of Chancery* (London, 1727)
Freeman, Richard, *Reports of Cases in Law and Equity: from 1670 to 1706* (London, 1742)
Fulbecke, William, *Direction or Preparative to the Study of the Law* (London, 1600)
Gardiner, Robert, *Ars Clericalis: The Art of Conveyancing Explain'd*, 2nd edn (London, 1692)
——, *Instructor Clericalis* (multiple parts and edns, London, 1693–1727)
——, *The Method of Pleading by Rule and President* (London, 1697)
Garth, Samuel, *The Dispensary: A Poem* (London, 1699)
Giannone, Pietro, *The Civil History of the Kingdom of Naples*, 2 vols, trans. Captain James Ogilvie (London, 1729)
Gilbert, Geoffrey, *An Abstract of the Essay of Human Understanding* (London, 1709)
——, *Cases in Law and Equity … with Two Treatises, the One on the Action of Debt, the Other on the Constitution of England* (London, 1760)
——, *An Historical Account of the Original and Nature, as well as the Law of Devises and Revocations* (London, 1739)
——, *An Historical View of the Court of Exchequer, and of the King's Revenues there Answered* (London, 1738)
——, *The History and Practice of the Court of Common Pleas* (London, 1737)
——, *The History and Practice of the High Court of Chancery … By the late Lord Chief Baron Gilbert. Printed from a Correct Manuscript Copy, Free from the Numerous Errors and Omissions of the Irish Edition* (London, 1758)
——, *The Law of Evidence*, 2nd edn (London, 1760)
——, *The Law of Executions. To Which Are Added the History and Practice of the Court of King's Bench*, 2nd edn (Dublin, 1763)
——, *The Law of Uses and Trusts … Together with a Treatise on Dower* (London, 1734)
——, *A Treatise of Tenures: In Two Parts*, 2nd edn (London, 1738)
——, *A Treatise on the Court of Exchequer* (London, 1758)
——, *Two Treatises on the Proceedings in Equity and the Jurisdiction of that Court* (Dublin, 1756)
Gordon, Thomas, *The Conspirators; Or, The Case of Catiline, As Collected from the Best Historians Impartially Examin'd*, 3rd edn (London, 1721)
——, *Francis, Lord Bacon, or the Case of Private and National Corruption and Bribery, Impartially Consider'd, Addressed to All South Sea Directors* (London, 1721)
——, *The Humourist, Being Essays Upon Several Subjects* (London, 1725)

——, *The Justice of Parliaments on Corrupt Ministers, in Impeachments and Bills of Attainder, Consider'd*, (London, 1725)

Grey, Zachary, *A Defense of Our Antient and Modern Historians; Against the Frivolous Cavils of a Late Pretender to Critical History* (London, 1725)

The Grounds and Rudiments of Law and Equity Alphabetically Digested: Containing a Collection of Rules or Maxims, with the Doctrine Upon Them, Illustrated by Various Cases Extracted from the Books and Records … (London, 1749)

Hale, Matthew, *The Analysis of the Law: Being a Scheme or Abstract of the Several Titles and Partitions of the Law of England Digested into Method* (London, 1713)

——, *The History of the Common Law of England*, Charles M. Gray ed. (Chicago, 1971)

——, 'Lord Hale's Preface to Rolle's Abridgment', in Francis Hargrave ed., *Collecteana Juridica: Consisting of Tracts Relative to the Law and Constitution of England*, vol. 1 (London, 1791; reprint, Littleton, CO, 1980), 263–282

——, *Pleas of the Crown in Two Parts: Or, A Methodical Summary of the Principal Matters Relating to that Subject* (London, 1716)

Hargrave, Francis, ed., *Collecteana Juridica: Consisting of Tracts Relative to the Law and Constitution of England*, 2 vols (London, 1791; reprint Littleton, CO, 1980)

——, 'Preface', in Hargrave ed., *The Jurisdiction of the Lords House, or Parliament … by Lord Chief Justice Hale* (London, 1796), i–ccxxx

Hatsell, John, *Precedents of Proceedings in the House of Commons … Vol. IV. Relating to Conference and Impeachment* (London, 1796)

Hawkins, William, *An Abridgment of the First Part of my Ld Coke's Institutes* (London, 1711; 5th edn, 1736)

——, *A Summary of the Crown Law, By Way of Abridgment of Serjeant Hawkins's Pleas of the Crown*, 2 vols (London, 1728)

——, *A Treatise of the Pleas of the Crown, Or a System of the Principal Matters Relating to that Subject, Digested Under their Proper Heads*, 2 vols (London, 1716–21)

The Hertford Letter: Containing Several Brief Observations on a Late Printed Trial, Concerning the Murder of Mrs. Sarah Stout (London, 1699)

An Historical Essay on the Jurisdiction of the Court of Chancery: And Incidently of the Other Courts (London, 1735)

The History and Proceedings of the House of Lords From the Restoration in 1660 to the Present Time, vol. 3 (London, 1742), House of Commons Parliamentary Papers: Eighteenth-Century Parliamentary Papers Collection 1688–1834, http://gateway.umi.bhowell.com/openurl?url_ver=Z39.88–2004&res_dat=xri:hcpp&rft_dat=xri:hcpp:rec:hp_lords-000011

Hobart, Henry, *The Reports of That Reverend and Learned Judge, the Right Honourable Sr Henry Hobart Knight and Baronet, Lord Chiefe Justice of His Majesties Court of Common Pleas* (London, 1650)

Hughes, William, *The Grand Abridgment of the Law Continued, Or a Collection of the Principal Cases and Points of the Common Law Continued in all the Reports Extant* (London, 1660)

——, *Hughes's Quaeries, Or, Choice Cases for Moots, Containing Several Points of Law not Resolved in the Books. Being very Useful for the Students of the Common Lawes* (London, 1675)

The Humble Representation made to the King's Majesty by the Lords Spiritual and Temporal in Parliament Assembled (Dublin, 1719)

Hutchinson, Francis, *A Defence of the Antient Historians: With Particular Application of it to the History of Ireland* (Dublin, 1733)

An Introduction to a Treatise Concerning the Legislative Power (London, 1708)

Jacob, Giles, *The Accomplished Conveyancer*, 3 vols (London, 1714–15)

——, *A Catalogue of all the Writs and Processes that Issue Out of the Several Courts at Westminster &c., With great Variety of Cases Relating to the Same. Together with a Full and Exact Account of their Nature and Use* (London, 1717)

——, *City Liberties: Or the Rights and Privileges of Freemen* (London, 1732)

——, *The Common Law Common-placed: Containing the Substance and Effect of all the Common Law Cases Dispersed in the Body of the Law, Collected as well from Abridgments as Reports, in a Perfect New Method* (London, 1726)

——, *The Compleat Attorney's Practice in English, in the Court of King's Bench and Common Pleas* (London, 1737)

——, *The Compleat Chancery Practiser: Or, The Whole Proceedings and Practice of the High Court of* Chancery *in a Perfect New Manner* (London, 1730)

——, *The Compleat Court Keeper; Or Land-Stewards Assistant* (London, 1713)

——, *The Compleat Parish Officer* (London, 1718)

——, *The Court Keeper's Companion* (London, 1717)

——, *Essays Relating to the Conduct of Life* (London, 1717)

——, *Every Man his Own Lawyer: Or a Summary of the Laws of England in a New and Instructive* Method (London, 1736)

——, *The Grand Precedent, Or the Conveyancer's Guide and Assistant* (London, 1716)

——, *An Historical Account of the Lives and Writings of Our Most Considerable English Poets, whether Epick, Lyrick, Elegiack, Epigrammatists, Etc.* (London, 1720)

——, *A Law Grammar: Or Rudiments of the Law, Compiled from the Grounds, Principles, Maxims, Terms, Words of Art, Rules and Moot Points of our Law, in a New Easy and Very Concise Method* (London, 1744)

——, *The Laws of Appeals and Murder* (London, 1719)

——, *The Laws of Liberty and Property, Or a Concise Treatise of All the Laws, Statutes and Ordinances Made for the Benefit and Protection of the Subjects of England* (London, 1734)

——, *Lex Constitutionis: Or, the Gentleman's Law* (London, 1719)

——, *Lex Mercatoria, Or the Merchant's Companion* (London, 1718)

—— (?), *Memoirs of the Life of the Right Honourable Joseph Addison Esq., Late One of his Majesty's Principal Secretaries of State. With a Particular Account of his Writings* (London, 1719)

——, *The Modern Justice: Containing the Business of a Justice of Peace in All its Parts* (London, 1716)

——, *A New Law-Dictionary* (London, 1729)

——, *The Poetical Register: Or the Lives and Characters of the English Dramatick Poets. With an Account of their Writings* (London, 1719)

—— ed.(?), *A Report of all the Cases Determined by Sir John Holt, Knt. From 1688 to 1710, During which Time he was Lord Chief Justice of England* (London, 1738)

——, *A Review of the Statutes Both Ancient and Modern* (London, 1715)

——, The *Statute-Law Common-plac'd: Or a Second General Table to the Statutes* (London, 1719)

——, *The Student's Companion: Or, the Reason of the Laws of England* (London, 1725; 2nd edn, 1734)

——, *A Treatise of Laws: Or, a General Introduction to the Common, Civil and Canon Law in Three Parts* (London, 1721)

Journal of the House of Lords, vols 15, 22, *British History Online*, http://www.british-history.ac.uk/source.aspx?pubid=36, http://www.british-history.ac.uk/source.aspx?pubid=1223

Keating, Geoffrey, *The General History of Ireland* (London, 1723)

Knapp, Coghill, *A Precaution to Young Gentlemen and Others who Mortgage Estates In a Letter from an O--dshire Gentleman, to a Certain P-----te* (London, 1741)

Lambarde, William, *Archaeion: Or a Discourse upon the High Courts of Justice in England* (London, 1635)

The Laws of England Delineated (London, 1729)

A Letter from a Member of the House of Commons in Ireland to a Gentleman of the Long Robe in England (London, 1720)

The Life of the Right Honourable Sir John Holt, Knight, Lord Chief Justice of the Court of King's-Bench; Containing Several Arguments Touching the Rights and Liberties of the People, Delivered by his Lordship ... And an Abstract of Lord Chief Justice Holt's Will... Also Points of Law Resolved by his Lordship (London, 1764)

Lilly, John, *Modern Entries, Being a Collection of Select Pleadings in the Courts of Kings Bench, Common Pleas and Exchequer*, 2 vols (London, 1723)

——, *The Practical Conveyancer: In Two Parts*, 2 vols, 2nd edn (London, 1732)

——, *The Practical Register: Or A General Abridgment of the Law*, 2 vols (London, 1719)

Locke, John, *An Essay Concerning Human Understanding*, Peter Nidditch ed. (Oxford, 1975)

——, *A New Method of A Common-Place Book*, in *The Posthumous Works of John Locke* (London, 1706)

'Lord Chief Justice Reeve to his Nephew', in Francis Hargrave ed., *Collecteana Juridica: Consisting of Tracts Relative to the Law and Constitution of England*, vol. 1 (London, 1791; reprint, Littleton, CO, 1980), 79–81

Lucas, Robert, *Cases in Law and Equity, Chiefly During the Time the Late Earl of Macclesfield Presided in the Court of Kings-Bench and Chancery* (London, 1736)

Luttrell, Narcissus, *A Brief Historical Relation of State Affairs from September 1678 to April 1714*, vol. 4 (Oxford, 1857; reprint Wilmington, DE, 1974)

Lyall, Andrew, *Irish Exchequer Reports: Reports of Cases in the Courts of Exchequer and Chancery in Ireland 1716–1734* (London, 2009)

Mackenzie, George, *Observations Upon the 18. act. 23. Parl. K. James VI. Against Dispositions Made in Defraud of Creditors, &c.*, 2nd edn (Edinburgh, 1698)

——, *Religio Stoici* (Edinburgh, 1663)

Madox, Thomas, *The History and Antiquities of the Exchequer of the Kings of England* (London, 1711)

Mandeville, Bernard, *The Fable of the Bees Or Private Vices, Publick Benefits*, with a commentary critical, historical, and explanatory by F.B. Kaye, 2 vols (Oxford, 1924; reprint Indianapolis, 1988)

——, *A Modest Defence of Publick Stews: Or, an Essay Upon Whoring, As it is Now Practis'd in these Kingdoms* (London, 1724)

——, *A Modest Defence of Publick Stews: Or, an Essay Upon Whoring, As it is Now Practis'd in these Kingdoms. Answer'd* (London, 1725)

The Manuscripts of the Earl of Buckinghamshire, The Earl of Lindsey, The Earl of

Onslow, Lord Emly, Theodore J. Hare Esq. and James Round Esq. M.P., Historical Manuscripts Commission, Fourteenth Report, Appendix Part 9 (London, 1895)
Meres, John, *The Equity of Parliaments, and Publick Faith Vindicated* (London, 1720)
Modern Cases in Law & Equity (London, 1730)
The Modern Conveyancer: Or Conveyancing Improved. Being a Choice Collection of Presidents on Most Occasions … Consisting of Settlements of Estates Upon Marriage, Bargains and Sales, Ecclesiastical Instruments, Mortgages, Leases, &c., 3rd edn (London, 1706)
——, *The Second part of the Modern Conveyancer, Or Conveyancing Improved, in Two Volumes. Being a Choice Collection of Presidents on Most Occasions…to Which are Added Opinions of Several Learned Council, Relating to Conveyancing and other Matters in Law*, 2 vols (London, 1704)
Modern Reports, Or Select Cases Adjudged in the Courts of King's-Bench, Chancery, Common-Pleas and Exchequer, Since the Restauration of His Majesty King Charles II, 2nd edn (London, 1700)
Molyneux, William, *The Case of Ireland being Bound by Acts of Parliament in England, Stated* (Dublin, 1698)
Musgrave, William, 'Part of a Letter from Dr. William Musgrave, Fellow of the College of Physicians and R.S. to Dr. Sloane, Concerning the Cause of Necessity of Breathing', *Philosophical Transactions*, 20 (1698), 178–81
Nelson, William, *An Abridgment of the Common Law: Being a Collection of the Principal Cases Argued and Adjudged in the Several Courts of Westminster Hall*, 3 vols (London, 1725–6)
——, The *Law of Evidence* (London, 1717)
——, *Lex Testamentaria, Or a Compendious System of all the Laws of England, as well Before the Statute of Henry VIII as Since, Concerning Last Wills and Testaments*, 2nd edn (London, 1724)
——, *The Office and Authority of a Justice of Peace: Collected Out of all the Books that have been Written on That Subject* (London, 1704)
——, *The Rights of the Clergy of Great Britain, As Established by the Canons, the Common Law, and the Statutes of the Realm* (London, 1709)
A New Commonplace Book being an Improvement on that Recommended by Mr Locke, 2nd edn (London, 1799)
North, Roger, *A Discourse on the Study of the Laws* (London, 1824)
——, *Notes of Me: The Autobiography of Roger North*, Peter Millard ed. (Toronto, 2000)
Philipps, John, *Georgii Regno Honores: Or a Short Account of the Peers and Peeresses of Great Britain and Ireland Created … By His Majesty King George* (London, 1724)
Phillips, William, *Studii Legalis Ratio, or Directions for the Study of the Law* (London, 1662; 3rd edn, 1675)
Proceedings in Parliament against William Earl of Portland, John Lord Sommers, Edward Earl of Orford and Charles Lord Halifax upon an Impeachment for High Crimes and Misdemeanors, in Sollom Emlyn ed., *A Complete Collection of State Trials and Proceedings for High Treason and other Crimes and Misdemeanors*, vol. 5, 2nd edn (London, 1730), 339–83
Proposals Humbly offer'd to the Parliament for Remedying the Great Charge and Delay of Suits at Law, and in Equity (London, 1707; 4th edn, 1724)
Pufendorf, Samuel, *De Jure Naturae et Gentium, Libri Octo*, trans. C.H. and W.A. Oldfather (Oxford, 1934)

Rastell, John, *Les Terms de la Ley* (London, 1685)

Reasons Humbly Offered to both Houses of Parliament, for Passing a Bill for Preventing Delays and Expences in Suits in Law and Equity (London, 1707)

Reflections or Hints Founded Upon Experience and Facts, Touching the Law, Lawyers … and Others Concerned in the Administration of Justice (London, 1759)

Regula Placitandi: A Collection of Special Rules for Pleading (London, 1691)

A *Reply to the Hertford Letter: Wherein the Case of Mrs. Stout's Death is More Particularly Considered, and Mr. Cowper Vindicated from the Slanderous Accusation of Being Accessory to the Same* (London, 1699)

A *Report from the Committee Appointed to View the Cottonian Library* (London, 1732)

The Report of the Lords Committee for Courts of Justice, upon the Petition of Alexander Burrowes Esq, Late High Sheriff of the County of Kildare … With an Appendix, Containing the injunction Made by the Chief Baron, and Other Barons of the Court of Exchequer (Dublin, 1719)

Reports of Cases Taken and Adjudged in the Court of Chancery in the Reign of King Charles I and to the 20th Year of King Charles II … To Which are Added Learned Arguments Relating to the Authority of the Said Court, its Dignity, Power and Jurisdiction (London, 1693)

Rolle, Henry, *Un Abridgment des Plusiers Cases et Resolutions del Common Ley: Alphabeticalment Digest Desouth Severall Titles* (London, 1668)

——, *Un Continuation des Reports de Henry Rolle Serjeant del' Ley, de Divers Cases en le Court del' Banke Le Roy, en le Temps del' Reign de Roy Jaques* (London, 1676)

The Rules of Practice Common-plac'd; With Remarks (London, 1740)

Saint-German, Christopher, *Two Dialogues in English, Between a Doctour of Divinity, and A Student in the Laws of England, of the Grounds of the said Laws, And of Conscience*, newly revised and re-printed (London, 1668)

Salkeld, William, *Reports of Cases Adjudged in the Court of King's Bench: With Some Special Cases in the Courts of Chancery, Common Pleas and Exchequer, From the First Year of K. William and Q. Mary to the Tenth Year of Q.* Anne, 3 vols, 3rd edn (London, 1731)

Salmon, Thomas ed., *A New Abridgement and Critical Review of the State Trials*, 2 vols (Dublin, 1737)

——, *State Trials and Proceedings upon High Treason and Other Crimes and Misdemeanors, From the Reign of King Richard II to the End of the Reign of King George I*, 9 vols (London, 1720–31)

A *Second Letter to a Gentleman of the Long Robe in Great Britain: Wherein some of the Late Illegal Proceedings of the Barons of the Exchequer in the Kingdom of Ireland are Plainly and Impartially Set Forth* (Dublin, 1720)

Selden, John, *Opera Omnia*, vol. 3, Thomas Wood ed. (London, 1726)

——, *Table Talk; Being the Discourse of John Selden Esq.*, 3rd edn (London, 1716)

Seymar, William, *Conjugium conjurgium: Or, Some Serious Considerations on Marriage* (London, 1694)

Shaftesbury, Anthony Ashley Cooper, Third Earl of, *Characteristics of Men, Manners, Opinions, Times*, Lawrence Klein ed. (Cambridge, 1999)

——, *The Life, Unpublished Letters and Philosophical Regimen of Anthony, Earl of Shaftesbury*, Benjamin Rand ed. (London, 1900; reprint, London, 1992)

Simpson, Joseph, *Reflections on the Natural and Acquired Endowments Requisite for the Study of the Law*, 4th edn (London, 1764)

Smart, Christopher, *The Student's Companion: Being a Collection of Historical Quota-*

tions from the Best Ancient *and* Modern *Authors on All Sorts of Subjects* (London, 1748)

Smith, Adam, *An Inquiry into the Nature and Causes of the Wealth of Nations*, Edwin Cannan ed. (Chicago, 1976)

Some Observations On the Trial of Spencer Cowper, J. Marson, E. Stephens, W. Rogers, That Were Tried at Hertford, About the Murder of Sarah Stout; Together With Other Things Relating Thereunto (London, 1701)

Somers, John, *A Discourse Concerning Generosity*, 2nd edn (London, 1695)

——, *A Vindication of the Proceedings of the Late Parliament of England* (London, 1690)

Stackhouse, Thomas, *An Abridgment of Bishop Burnet's History of His Own Times* (London, 1724)

Statham, Nicholas, *Abridgment* (Rouen, 1488?)

Stout, Mary, *The Testimony of the Hartford Quakers for the Man Christ Jesus, Vindicated … With a Brief and Serious Reply by Mary Stout* (London, 1676)

Style, William, *Regestum Practicale: Or the Practical Register, Consisting of Rules, Orders and Obligations Concerning the Common Laws and the Practice thereof* (London, 1657)

Toland, John, *Reasons Most Humbly Offer'd to the Honorable House of Commons why the Bill sent down to them from the Honorable House of Lords Entitul'd*, An Act for Better Securing the Dependency of the Kingdom of Ireland upon the Crown of Great Britain *shou'd not Pass into a Law* (London, 1720)

——, *The State Anatomy of Great Britain. Containing a Particular Account of its Several Interests and Parties, their Bent and Genius, and what Each of Them, with the Rest of Europe, May Hope or Fear, from the Reign and Family of King George*, 4th edn (London, 1717)

Townesend, George, *A Preparative to Pleading, Being a Work Intended for the Instruction and Help of Young Clerks of the Court of Common Pleas* (London, 1675)

Treatise of Feme Coverts or the Lady's Law, Containing all the Laws and Statutes Relating to Women under Several Heads (London, 1732)

A Treatise of Frauds, Covins, and Collusions. Wherein is Treated, of Fraudulent Conveyances to Defraud Creditors and Purchasers, by Fraudulent Mortgages, Marriage Agreements, Last Wills, … (London, 1710)

The Trial of Spencer Cowper, Esq., John Marson, Ellis Stevens, and William Rogers, gent., Upon an Indictment for the Murther of Mrs. Sarah Stout, a Quaker (London, 1699)

The Tryal of Thomas Earl of Macclesfield, in the House of Peers, for High Crimes and Misdemeanors, upon an Impeachment … Published by order of the House of Peers, (London, 1725)

Tyrrell, James, *Bibliotheca Politica: Or, An Enquiry into the Ancient Constitution of the English Government..in Fourteen Dialogues* (London, 1718; 2nd edn, 1727)

——, *The General History of England, Both Ecclesiastical and Civil*, 3 vols (London, 1704)

Vernon, Thomas, *Cases Argued and Adjudged in the High Court of Chancery*, 2 vols (Dublin, 1726)

A Vindication of the Lord Chancellor Bacon, from the Aspersion of Injustice Cast Upon Him by Mr. Wraynham (London, 1725)

Warburton, William, *A Critical and Philosophical Enquiry into the Causes of Prodigies and Miracles as Related by Historians. With an Essay Towards Restoring a Method and Purity in History* (London, 1727)

West, William, *Symboleography, Which May be Termed the Art, Description or Image of Instruments … Or the Paterne of Praesidents* (London, 1592)

Williams, Walter, *Proposals Humbly Offered to the Consideration of the King's most Excellent Majesty, and of the Lords and Commons in Parliament … in Order to Regulate Proceedings in Courts of Equity* (London, 1701)

Wilson, George, *Bribes no Perquisites, Or the Case of the Earl of Macclesfield, Being Impartial Observations Upon his Lordship's Tryal* (London, 1726)

——, *The Trial of the Earl of Macclesfield, Faithfully Abridg'd. With Remarks Thereon* 2nd edn (London, 1727)

Wingate, Edmund, *An Exact Abridgment of all the Statutes* (London, 1642)

——, *Maxims of Reason: Or the Reason of the Common Law of England* (London, 1658)

Wood, Thomas, *An Institute of the Laws of England; Or, the Laws of England in their Natural Order, According to Common* Use, 2nd edn (London, 1722)

——, *A New Institute of Imperial or Civil Law … Shewing in Some Principal Cases, amongst other Observations, how the Canon Law, the Laws of England, and the Laws and Customs of Other* Nations *Differ from it* (London, 1704)

——, *Some Thoughts Concerning the Study of Law, Particularly in the Two Universities* (London, 1708; 2nd edn, 1727)

Wright, Martin, *An Introduction to the Law of Tenures* (London, 1729)

Yorke, Philip, Earl of Hardwicke, *A Discourse of the Judicial Authority Belonging to the Office of Master of the Rolls in the High Court of Chancery* (London, 1727; 2nd edn, 1728)

The Young Lawyer's Recreation. Being a Choice Collection of Several Pleasant Cases, Passages and Customs in the Law (London, 1694)

Secondary Sources

Ackerknecht, Erwin H., 'Early History of Legal Medicine' in Chester R. Burns ed., *Legacies in Law and Medicine* (New York, 1977), 249–70

Adams, Beverly, 'The Body in the Water: Religious Conflict in Hertford 1660–1702' (Ph.D. diss., University of London, 2000)

——, '"The Durty Spirit at Hertford": A Falling Out of Friends,' *Journal of Ecclesiastical History*, 52, 4 (October, 2001), 647–74

Allan, David, *Commonplace Books and Reading in Georgian England* (Cambridge, 2010)

——, 'A Reader Writes: Negotiating the Wealth of Nations in an Eighteenth-Century English Commonplace Book', *Philological Quarterly*, 81, 2 (Spring, 2002), 207–33

Atiyah, P.S. and R.S. Summers, *Form and Substance in Anglo-American Law: A Comparative Study of Legal Reasoning, Legal Theory and Legal Institutions* (Oxford, 1987)

Aylmer, G.E., 'From Office-Holding to Civil Service: The Genesis of Modern Bureaucracy', *Transactions of the Royal Historical Society*, fifth series, 30 (1980), 91–108

——, 'The Meaning and Definition of Property in Seventeenth-Century England', *Past & Present*, 86 (February, 1980), 87–97

Baildon, W.P., ed., *Records of the Honorable Society of Lincoln's Inn. The Black Books*, vol. 3 (London, 1899)

Bailey, Joanne, 'Favoured or Oppressed? Married Women, Property and "Coverture" in England 1660–1800', *Continuity and Change*, 17, 3 (December, 2002), 351–71

Baker, J.H., *The Common Law Tradition: Lawyers, Books and the Law* (London, 2000)

——, 'English Law Books and Legal Publishing', in John Barnard, D.F. McKenzie and Maureen Bell eds, *The Cambridge History of the Book in Britain, Volume 4, 1557–1695* (Cambridge, 2008), 474–503

——, *English Legal Manuscripts in the United States of America Part II: 1558–1902* (London, 1990)

——, *An Introduction to English Legal History* (London, 2002)

——, *The Law's Two Bodies: Some Evidential Problems in English Legal History* (Oxford, 2001)

——, *The Legal Profession and the Common Law, Historical Essays* (London, 1986)

——, *Manual of Law French* (Amersham, 1979)

——, *The Oxford History of the Laws of England: Volume 6, 1483–1558* (Oxford, 2003)

——, '"United and Knit to the Imperial Crown": An English View of the Anglo-Hibernian Constitution', in D.S. Greer and N.M. Dawson eds, *Mysteries and Solutions in Irish Legal History* (Dublin, 2001), 73–95

Baker, Keith Michael and Peter Hanns Reill, eds, *What's Left of Enlightenment? A Postmodern Question* (Stanford, 2001)

Ball, F.E., *The Judges in Ireland*, 2 vols (London, 1926)

Ball, R.B., 'The Chancery Master', *Law Quarterly Review*, 77 (1961), 331–57

Banner, Stuart, *Anglo-American Securities Regulation: Cultural and Political Roots, 1690–1860* (Cambridge, 1998)

Beardsley, Monroe C., *Aesthetics from Classical Greece to the Present*, (Tuscaloosa, 1975)

Beattie, J.M., *Crime and the Courts in England 1660–1800* (Oxford, 1986)

——, 'London Crime and the Making of the "Bloody Code" 1689–1718', in Lee Davison et al. eds, *Stilling the Grumbling Hive: The Response to Social and Economic Problems in England 1689–1750* (New York, 1992), 49–76

——, *Policing and Punishment in London 1660–1750: Urban Crime and the Limits of Terror* (Oxford, 2001)

——, 'Scales of Justice: Defense Counsel and the English Criminal Trial in the Eighteenth and Nineteenth Centuries', *Law and History Review*, 9, 2 (Autumn, 1991), 221–67

Beck, Karen S., 'One Step at a Time: The Research Value of Law Student Notebooks', *Law Library Journal*, 91 (Winter, 1999), 29–138

Beiser, Frederick C., *The Sovereignty of Reason: The Defense of Rationality in the Early English Enlightenment* (Princeton, 1996)

Bennett, H.S., *English Books and Readers 1558–1603* (Cambridge, 1965)

Berg, Maxine and Elizabeth Eger, eds, *Luxury in the Eighteenth Century: Debates, Desires and Delectable Goods* (Basingstoke, 2003)

Berman, Harold J., 'The Impact of the Enlightenment on American Constitutional Law', *Yale Journal of Law and the Humanities*, 4, 2 (1992), 311–34

——, 'Medieval English Equity', in Berman, *Faith and Order: the Reconciliation of Law and Religion* (Atlanta, 1993), 55–82

——, 'The Origins of Historical Jurisprudence: Coke, Selden, Hale', *Yale Law Journal*, 103, 7 (May, 1994), 1651–1738

—— and Charles J. Reid Jr., 'The Transformation of English Legal Science: From Hale to Blackstone', *Emory Law Journal*, 45 (Spring, 1996), 437–522

Bevir, Mark, *The Logic of the History of Ideas* (Cambridge, 1999)

Bilder, Mary Sarah, 'The Lost Lawyers: Early American Legal Literates and Transatlantic Legal Culture', *Yale Journal of Law and the Humanities*, 11, 1 (Winter, 1999), 47–117

——, *The Transatlantic Constitution: Colonial Legal Culture and the Empire* (Cambridge, Mass., 2004)

Blair, Ann, 'An Early Modernist's Perspective', *Isis*, 95, 3 (September, 2004), 420–30

——, 'Annotating and Indexing Natural Philosophy', in Marina Frasca-Spada and Nick Jardine eds, *Books and the Sciences in History* (Cambridge, 2000), 69–89

——, 'Humanist Methods in Natural Philosophy: The Commonplace Book', *Journal of the History of Ideas*, 53, 4 (October- December, 1992), 541–51

——, 'Note Taking as an Art of Transmission', *Critical Inquiry*, 31 (Autumn, 2004), 85–107

——, 'Reading Strategies for Coping with Information Overload ca. 1550–1700', *Journal of the History of Ideas*, 64, 1 (January, 2003), 11–28

—— and Anthony Grafton, 'Reassessing Humanism and Science', *Journal of the History of Ideas*, 53, 4 (October-December, 1992), 535–40

Blake, R.B., 'Challenges for Cause, Stand-Asides, and Peremptory Challenges in the Nineteenth Century', *Osgoode Hall Law Journal*, 38 (Fall, 2000), 456–62

Bolland, W.C., 'A Mediaeval Lawyer's Commonplace Book', *The Law Quarterly Review*, 37 (July, 1921), 310–14

Bonfield, Lloyd, ed., *Marriage, Property and Succession* (Berlin, 1992)

——, *Marriage Settlements 1601–1740: The Adoption of the Strict Settlement* (Cambridge, 1983)

Brett, Annabel, 'What is Intellectual History Now?', in David Cannadine ed, *What is History Now?* (Basingstoke, 2002), 113–31

Brewer, John, and Susan Staves, eds, *Early Modern Conceptions of Property* (London, 1996)

——,*The Pleasures of the Imagination: English Culture in the Eighteenth Century* (New York, 1997)

——,*The Sinews of Power: War, Money and the English State 1688–1783* (New York, 1988)

Broman, Thomas H., 'The Medical Sciences', in Roy Porter ed., *The Cambridge History of Science, Volume 4: Eighteenth-Century Science* (Cambridge, 2003), 463–84

——, 'Periodical Literature', in Marina Frasca-Spada and Nick Jardine eds, *Books and the Sciences in History* (Cambridge, 2000), 225–38

Brooks, Christopher W. and Kevin Sharpe, 'Debate: History, English Law and the Renaissance', *Past & Present*, 72 (August, 1976), 133–42

——, 'Interpersonal Conflict and Social Tension: Civil Litigation in England 1640–1830', in A.L Beier, David Cannadine and James Rosenheim eds, *The First Modern Society: Essays in English History in Honour of Lawrence Stone* (Cambridge, 1989), 357–99

——, *Law, Politics and Society in Early Modern England* (Cambridge, 2008)

——, *Lawyers, Litigation and English Society since 1450* (London, 1998)

——, 'Litigation, Participation and Agency in Seventeenth and Eighteenth-Century England', in David Lemmings ed., *The British and their Laws in the Eighteenth Century* (Woodbridge, 2005), 155–81

Brophy, Alfred L., 'Book Review: The Law Book In Colonial America: A History of the Book in America: The Colonial Book in the Atlantic World', *Buffalo Law Review*, 51 (Fall, 2003), 1119–43

Brown, Elizabeth A.R., 'The Tyranny of a Construct: Feudalism and Historians of Medieval Europe', *American Historical Review*, 73, 4 (October, 1974), 1063–88

Bryson, W.H., *The Equity Side of the Exchequer: Its Jurisdiction, Administration, Procedures and Records* (Cambridge, 1975)

Bultmann, William A. and Phyllis W., 'The Roots of Anglican Humanitarianism: A Study of the Membership of the S.P.C.K. and the S.P.G., 1699–1720', *Historical Magazine of the Protestant Episcopal Church*, 33, 1 (1964), 3–48

Burgess, Glenn, *The Politics of the Ancient Constitution: An Introduction to English Political Thought 1603–1642* (University Park, PA, 1992)

Burrows, Andrew, 'We Do This at Common Law but That in Equity', *Oxford Journal of Legal Studies*, 22, 1 (March, 2002), 1–16

Burtt, Shelley, 'The Societies for the Reformation of Manners: Between John Locke and the Devil in Augustan England', in Roger D. Lund ed., *The Margins of Orthodoxy: Heterodox Writing and Cultural Response 1660–1750* (Cambridge, 1995), 149–69

——, *Virtue Transformed: Political Argument in England 1688–1740* (Cambridge, 1992)

Bussani, Mauro and Francesca Fiorentini, 'The Many Faces of Equity: A Comparative Survey of the European Civil Law Tradition', in Daniela Carpi ed., *The Concept of Equity: An Interdisciplinary Assessment*, Anglistische Forshungen 374 (Heidelberg, 2007), 101–35

Cairns, John W., 'Blackstone, An English Institutist: Legal Literature and the Rise of the Nation State', *Oxford Journal of Legal Studies*, 4, 3 (Winter, 1984), 318–60

——, 'Blackstone, the Ancient Constitution and the Feudal Law', *The Historical Journal*, 28, 3 (September, 1985), 711–17

——, 'Legal Theory', in Alexander Broadie ed., *The Cambridge Companion to the Scottish Enlightenment* (Cambridge, 2003), 222–42

Campbell, John Campbell, Baron, *The Lives of the Lord Chancellors and Keepers of the Great Seal of England*, vols 5–6 (London, 1868)

Campbell, R.H. and A.S. Skinner, eds, *The Origins and Nature of the Scottish Enlightenment* (Edinburgh, 1982)

Campbell, Tom D., ed., *Law and Enlightenment in Britain* (Aberdeen, 1990)

Canale, Damiano, Paolo Grossi and Hasso Hoffman, eds, *A History of the Philosophy of Law in the Civil Law World, 1600–1900*, vol. 9 of Enrico Pattaro ed., *A Treatise of Legal Philosophy and General Jurisprudence* (Dordrecht, 2009)

Cantor, Geoffrey, 'Quakers in the Royal Society, 1660–1750', *Notes and Records of the Royal Society of London*, 51, 2 (1997), 175–93

Capp, Bernard, 'Gender, Conscience and Casuistry: Women and Conflicting Obligations in Early Modern England', in Harald Braun and Edward Vallance eds, *Contexts of Conscience in Early Modern Europe, 1500–1700* (Basingstoke, 2004), 116–31

Carey, Daniel, 'Travel, Geography and the Problem of Belief: Locke as a Reader of

Travel Literature', in Julia Rudolph ed., *History and Nation* (Cranbury, NJ, 2006), 97–136

Carlos, Ann M., 'Bankruptcy and Creditors' Rights in Early Modern England', Working Paper, September 2009, http://www.econ.yale.edu/seminars/echist/eh09/carlos-091026.pdf;

——, Karen Maguire, and Larry Neal, 'Financial Acumen, Women Speculators, and the Royal African Company during the South Sea Bubble', *Accounting Business and Financial History*, 16, 2 (July, 2006), 219–43

—— and Larry Neal, 'The Micro-Foundations of the Early London Capital Market: Bank of England Shareholders during and after the South Sea Bubble, 1720–25', *Economic History Review*, 59, 3 (August, 2006), 498–538

—— and Larry Neal, 'Women Investors in Early Capital Markets 1720–1725', *Financial History Review*, 11, 2 (October, 2004), 197–224

Carruthers, Bruce G., *City of Capital: Politics and Markets in the English Financial Revolution* (Princeton, 1996)

——, 'Politics, Popery and Property: A Comment on North and Weingast', *The Journal of Economic History*, 50, 3 (September, 1990), 693–8

Carswell, John, *The South Sea Bubble* (Stanford, 1960)

The Catalogue of the Hampton L. Carson Collection: Illustrative of the Growth of the Common Law, 2 vols (Boston, 1962)

Cavallo, Gugliemo and Roger Chartier, eds, *A History of Reading in the West* (Amherst, 1999)

Champion, Justin, *Republican Learning: John Toland and the Crisis of Christian Culture 1696–1722* (Manchester, 2003)

Champion, W.A., 'Recourse to Law and the Meaning of the Great Litigation Decline, 1650–1750', in Christopher Brooks and Michael Lobban eds, *Communities and Courts in Britain 1150–1900*, (London, 1997), 179–98

Chartier, Roger, *The Cultural Origins of the French Revolution*, trans. Lydia G. Cochrane (Durham, 1991)

——, 'Intellectual History or Sociocultural History?', trans. Jane P. Kaplan, in Dominick LaCapra and Steven L. Kaplan eds, *Modern European Intellectual History, Reappraisals and New Perspectives*, (Ithaca, 1982), 13–46

——,*The Order of Books: Readers, Authors and Libraries in Europe Between the Fourteenth and the Eighteenth Centuries*, trans. Lydia G. Cochrane (Stanford, 1992)

Churches, Christine, 'Business at Law: Retrieving Commercial Disputes from Eighteenth-Century Chancery', *The Historical Journal*, 43, 4 (December, 2000), 937–54

——, 'Women and Property in Early Modern England: A Case Study', *Social History*, 23, 2 (May, 1998), 165–80

Clark, Peter, 'The Mother Gin Controversy in the Early Eighteenth Century', *Transactions of the Royal Historical Society*, Fifth Series, 38 (1988), 63–84

Cockburn, J.S., *A History of English Assizes, 1558–1714* (Cambridge, 1972)

Coleman, Charly, 'Resacralizing the World: the Fate of Secularization in Enlightenment Historiography', *The Journal of Modern History*, 82, 2 (June, 2010), 368–95

Conrad, Stephen A., 'James Wilson's "Assimilation of the Common-Law Mind"', *Northwestern University Law Review*, 84, (Fall, 1989), 186–219

Cook, Harold J., *The Decline of the Old Medical Regime in Stuart London* (Ithaca, 1986)

——, 'Good Advice and Little Medicine: The Professional Authority of Early Modern Physicians', *Journal of British Studies*, 33, 1 (January, 1994), 1–31

Cotterell, Roger, *The Politics of Jurisprudence: A Critical Introduction to Legal Philosophy* (Philadelphia, 1992)

Cowan, Brian, 'Reasonable Ecstasies: Shaftesbury and the Languages of Libertinism', *Journal of British Studies*, 37, 2 (April, 1998), 111–38

Cowley, John D., *A Bibliography of Abridgments, Digests, Dictionaries and Indexes of English Law to the Year 1800* (London, 1932)

Crawford, Catherine, 'Legalizing Medicine: Early Modern Legal Systems and the Growth of Medico-Legal Knowledge', in Michael Clark and Catherine Crawford eds, *Legal Medicine in History* (Cambridge, 1994), 89–116

Croft, Clyde, 'Lord Hardwicke's Use of Precedent in Equity', in Thomas G. Watkin ed., *Legal Record and Historical Reality: Proceedings of the Eighth British Legal History Conference* (London, 1989), 121–55

Cromartie, Alan, *The Constitutionalist Revolution: An Essay on the History of England 1450–1642* (Cambridge, 2006)

——, 'The Rule of Law', in John Morrill ed., *Revolution and Restoration* (London, 1992), 55–69

Cross, Rupert and J.W. Harris, *Precedent in English Law* (Oxford, 1991)

Dabhoiwala, Faramerz, 'Sex and the Societies for Moral Reform, 1688–1800', *Journal of British Studies*, 46, 2 (April, 2007), 290–319

Dacome, Lucia, 'Noting the Mind: Commonplace Books and the Pursuit of the Self in Eighteenth-Century Britain', *Journal of the History of Ideas*, 65, 4 (October, 2004) 603–25

——, 'Resurrecting by Numbers in Eighteenth-Century England', *Past & Present*, 193 (November, 2006), 73–110

Darnton, Robert, *The Business of Enlightenment: A Publishing History of the* Encyclopedie *1775–1800* (Cambridge, Mass., 1979)

——, *The Forbidden Best-Sellers of Pre-Revolutionary France* (New York, 1995)

——, 'In Search of the Enlightenment: Recent Attempts to Create a Social History of Ideas', *Journal of Modern History*, 43, 1 (March, 1971), 113–32

Darwall, Stephen, *British Moralists and the Internal 'Ought':1640–1740* (Cambridge, 1995)

Daston, Lorraine, 'Attention and the Values of Nature in the Enlightenment', in Lorraine Daston and Fernando Vidal eds, *The Moral Authority of Nature* (Chicago, 2004), 100–26

——, *Classical Probability in the Enlightenment* (Princeton, 1988)

—— and Peter Galison, 'The Image of Objectivity', *Representations*, 40 (Autumn, 1992), 81–128

——, 'Marvelous Facts and Miraculous Evidence in Early Modern Europe', and 'Historical Epistemology', in James Chandler, Arnold I. Davidson and Harry Harootunian eds, *Questions of Evidence: Proof, Practice and Persuasion Across the Disciplines* (Chicago, 1994), 243–74, 282–5

——, 'Probability and Evidence', in Daniel Garber and Michael Ayers eds, *The Cambridge History of Seventeenth-Century Philosophy*, vol. 2 (Cambridge, 1998), 1108–44

——, 'Taking Note(s)', *Isis*, 95, 3 (September, 2004), 443–8

—— and Katherine Park, *Wonders and the Order of Nature, 1150–1750* (Cambridge, Mass., 2001)

Davis, Kathleen, *Periodization and Sovereignty: How Ideas of Feudalism and Secularization Govern the Politics of Time* (Philadelphia, 2008)

Dawson, Hannah, *Locke, Language and Early Modern Philosophy* (Cambridge, 2007)

Dear, Peter, *Discipline and Experience: The Mathematical Way in the Scientific Revolution* (Chicago, 1995)

Dewhurst, Kenneth, *John Locke 1632–1704, Physician and Philosopher: A Medical Biography with an Edition of the Medical Notes in his Journals* (London, 1963)

——, 'Locke's Essay on Respiration', *Bulletin of the History of Medicine*, 34 (1960), 257–73

Dickson, P.G.M., *The Financial Revolution in England: A Study of the Development of Public Credit 1688–1756* (London, 1967)

Douglas, D.C., *English Scholars* (London, 1939)

Dwyer, Deirdre M., 'Expert Evidence in the English Civil Courts, 1550–1800', *The Journal of Legal History*, 28, 1 (April, 2007), 93–118

Earl, D.W., 'Procrustean Feudalism: An Interpretive Dilemma in English Historical Narration, 1700–1725,' *The Historical Journal*, 19, 1 (March, 1976), 33–51

Edmond, Gary, 'Whigs in Court: Historiographical Problems with Expert Evidence', *Yale Journal of Law and the Humanities*, 14, 1 (Winter, 2002), 123–75

Eggert, Kurt, 'Held up in Due Course: Codification and the Victory of Form over Intent in Negotiable Instrument Law', *Creighton Law Review*, 35 (February, 2002), 363–431

Erickson, Amy L., 'Coverture and Capitalism', *History Workshop Journal*, 59 (Spring, 2005), 1–16

——, 'Married Women's Occupations in Eighteenth-Century London', *Continuity and Change*, 23, 2 (2008), 267–307

——, 'Possession – and the Other One-Tenth of the Law: Assessing Women's Ownership and Economic Roles in Early Modern England', *Women's History Review*, 16, 3 (July, 2007), 369–85

——, *Women and Property in Early Modern England* (London, 1993)

Ernst, Daniel R., 'The Moribund Appeal of Death: Compensating Survivors and Controlling Jurors in Early Modern England', *The American Journal of Legal History*, 28, 2 (April, 1984), 164–88

Farr, James, 'Locke, Natural Law and New World Slavery', *Political Theory*, 36, 4 (August, 2008), 495–522

Fidler, Ann, '"Till You Understand Them in Their Principal Features": Observations on Form and Function in Nineteenth-Century American Law Books', *Proceedings of the Bibliographical Society of America*, 92, 4 (1998), 427–42

Findlen, Paula, 'The Two Cultures of Scholarship?', *Isis*, 96, 2 (June, 2005), 230–7

Finn, Margot, *The Character of Credit: Personal Debt in English Culture 1740–1914* (Cambridge, 2003)

Fisher, William W., 'Texts and Contexts: The Application to American Legal History of the Methodologies of Intellectual History', *Stanford Law Review*, 49, 5 (May, 1997), 1065–1110

Fissell, Mary and Roger Cooter, 'Exploring Natural Knowledge: Science and the Popular', in Roy Porter ed., *The Cambridge History of Science, Volume 4: Eighteenth-Century Science* (Cambridge, 2003), 129–58

——, *Vernacular Bodies: The Politics of Reproduction in Early Modern England* (Oxford, 2005)

Fitzpatrick, Martin, Peter Jones, Christa Knellwolf and Iain McCalman eds, *The Enlightenment World* (New York, 2004)

Flaherty, Martin S., 'The Empire Strikes Back: *Annesley v. Sherlock* and the Triumph of Imperial Parliamentary Supremacy', *Columbia Law Review*, 87 (1987), 593–622

Forbes, Duncan, *Hume's Philosophical Politics* (Cambridge, 1975)

——, 'Natural Law and the Scottish Enlightenment', in R.H. Campbell and A.S. Skinner eds, *The Origins and Nature of the Scottish Enlightenment* (Edinburgh, 1982), 186–204

Forbes, T.R., *Crowner's Quest, Transactions of the American Philosophical Society*, 68, 1 (1978), 1–52

——, *Surgeons at the Bailey, English Forensic Medicine to 1878* (New Haven, 1985)

Fortier, Mark, *The Culture of Equity in Early Modern England* (Aldershot, 2005)

——, 'Equity and Ideas: Coke, Ellesmere and James I', *Renaissance Quarterly*, 51, 4 (Winter, 1991), 1255–81

Foss, Edward, *The Judges of England*, vols 7–8 (London, 1864; reprint New York, 1966)

Frangsmyr, Tore, J.L. Heilbron and Robin E. Rider eds, *The Quantifying Spirit in the Eighteenth Century* (Berkeley, 1990)

Franklin, James, *The Science of Conjecture: Evidence and Probability before Pascal* (Baltimore, 2001)

Friedman, Lawrence M., 'Coming of Age: Law and Society Enters an Exclusive Club', *Annual Review of Law and Social Science*, 1 (December, 2005), 1–16

——, *Law and Society: An Introduction* (Englewood Cliffs, NJ, 1977)

Froide, Amy M., *Never Married: Singlewomen in Early Modern England* (Oxford, 2005)

Gallanis, T.P., 'The Rise of Modern Evidence Law', *Iowa Law Review*, 84 (March, 1999), 499–560

Gaskill, Malcolm, *Crime and Mentalities in Early Modern England* (Cambridge, 2000)

Getzler, Joshua, 'Chancery Reform and Law Reform', *Law and History Review*, 22, 3 (Fall, 2004), 601–8

Gill, Michael B., *The British Moralists on Human Nature and the Birth of Secular Ethics* (Cambridge, 2006)

Glaisyer, Natasha, 'Calculating Credibility: Print Culture, Trust and Economic Figures in Early Eighteenth-Century England', *Economic History Review*, 60, 4 (November, 2007), 685–711

——, *The Culture of Commerce in England 1660–1720* (Woodbridge, 2006)

Glassey, Lionel K.J., *Politics and the Appointment of Justices of the Peace, 1675–1720* (Oxford, 1979)

Golan, Tal, *Laws of Men and Laws of Nature: The History of Scientific Expert Testimony in England and America* (Cambridge, Mass., 2004)

Goldie, Mark, 'The English System of Liberty', in Mark Goldie and Robert Wolker eds, *The Cambridge History of Eighteenth-Century Political Thought* (Cambridge, 2006), 40–78

Goldsmith, M.M., 'Liberty, Luxury and the Pursuit of Happiness', in Anthony Pagden ed., *The Languages of Political Theory in Early Modern Europe* (Cambridge, 1987), 223–51

——, *Private Vices, Public Benefits: Bernard Mandeville's Social and Political Thought* (Cambridge, 1985)

Goldsworthy, Jeffrey, *The Sovereignty of Parliament: History and Philosophy* (Oxford, 1999)

Goodrich, Peter, 'Ars Bablativa: Ramism, Rhetoric, and the Genealogy of English

Jurisprudence', in Gregory Leyh ed., *Legal Hermeneutics: History, Theory and Practice* (Berkeley, 1992), 43–82

——, *Languages of Law: From Logics of Memory to Nomadic Masks* (London, 1990)

——, 'Lex Laetans: Three Theses on the Unbearable Lightness of Legal Critique', *Law & Literature*, 17, 3 (2006), 293–319

——, '"Poor Illiterate Reason": History, Nationalism and Common Law', *Social and Legal Studies*, 1 (1992), 7–28

Gordley, James, 'Enforcing Promises', *California Law Review*, 83, 2 (March, 1995), 547–614

——, 'The Moral Foundations of Private Law', *American Journal of Jurisprudence*, 47 (2002), 1–24

——, *The Philosophical Origins of Modern Contract Doctrine* (Oxford, 1991)

Gordon, Robert W., 'J. Willard Hurst and the Common Law Tradition in American Legal Historiography', *Law and Society Review*, 10, 1 (Autumn, 1975), 9–55

Gowing, Laura, *Common Bodies: Women, Touch and Power in Seventeenth-Century England* (New Haven, 2003)

Grundy, Isobel, 'Sarah Stone: Enlightenment Midwife', in Roy Porter ed., *Medicine in the Enlightenment* (Amsterdam, 1995), 128–44

Haack, Susan, 'On Logic in the Law: "Something but not All"', *Ratio Juris*, 20, 1 (March, 2007), 1–31

Haakonssen, Knud, ed., *Enlightenment and Religion: Rational Dissent in Eighteenth-Century Britain* (Cambridge, 1996)

——, 'German Natural Law', in Mark Goldie and Robert Wokler eds, *The Cambridge History of Eighteenth-Century Political Thought* (Cambridge, 2006), 251–90

——, 'The History of Eighteenth-Century Philosophy: History or Philosophy?', in Knud Haakonssen ed., *The Cambridge History of Eighteenth-Century Philosophy*, vol. 1 (Cambridge, 2006), 3–25.

——, 'The Idea of Early Modern Philosophy', in J.B. Schneewind ed., *Teaching New Histories of Philosophy* (Princeton, University Center for Human Values, 2004), 99–121

——, 'Natural Jurisprudence and the Theory of Justice', in Alexander Broadie ed., *The Cambridge Companion to the Scottish Enlightenment* (Cambridge, 2003), 205–21

——, *Natural Law and Moral Philosophy: From Grotius to the Scottish Enlightenment* (Cambridge, 1996)

——, *The Science of a Legislator: The Natural Jurisprudence of David Hume and Adam Smith* (Cambridge, 1981)

Habbakuk, H.J., 'Marriage Settlements in the Eighteenth Century', *Transactions of the Royal Historical Society*, Fourth Series, 32 (1950), 15–30

Halliday, Paul, *Habeas Corpus: From England to Empire* (Cambridge, Mass., 2010)

Halperin, Jean-Louis, 'French Legal Science in the 17th and 18th Centuries: To the Limits of the Theory of Law', in Damiano Canale, Paolo Grossi and Hasso Hoffman eds, *A History of the Philosophy of Law in the Civil Law World, 1600–1900*, vol. 9 of Enrico Pattaro ed., *A Treatise of Legal Philosophy and General Jurisprudence*, (Dordrecht, 2009), 43–67

Hamburger, Philip, 'The Conveyancing Purposes of the Statute of Frauds', *The American Journal of Legal History*, 27, 4 (October, 1983), 354–85

——, 'The Development of Law of Seditious Libel and the Control of the Press', *Stanford Law Review*, 37, 3 (February, 1985), 661–765

——, *Law and Judicial Duty* (Cambridge, Mass., 2008)

——, 'Revolution and Judicial Review: Chief Justice Holt's Opinion in *City of London v. Wood*', *Columbia Law Review*, 94, 7 (November, 1994), 2091–2153

Hamilton, Earl J., 'John Law of Lauriston: Banker, Gamester, Merchant, Chief?', *The American Economic Review*, 57, 2 (May, 1967), 273–82

Hand, Learned, 'Historical and Practical Considerations Regarding Expert Testimony', *Harvard Law Review*, 15, 1 (May, 1901), 40–58

Harkness, Deborah, 'Review: Entering the Labyrinth: Exploring Scientific Culture in Early Modern England', *Journal of British Studies*, 37, 4 (October, 1998), 446–50

Harley, David, 'The Scope of Legal Medicine in Lancashire and Cheshire, 1660–1760', in Michael Clark and Catherine Crawford eds, *Legal Medicine in History* (Cambridge, 1994), 45–63

Harris, Michael, 'Trials and Criminal Biographies: A Case Study in Distribution', in R. Myers and M. Harris eds, *Sale and Distribution of Books from 1700* (Oxford, 1982), 1–36

Harris, Ron, 'The Encounters of Economic History and Legal History', *Law and History Review*, 21, 2 (Summer, 2003), 297–346

——, 'Government and the Economy 1688–1850', in Roderick Floud and Paul Johnson eds, *The Cambridge Economic History of Britain since 1700, Volume 1, 1700–1850* (Cambridge, 2004), 204–37

——, *Industrializing English Law: Entrepreneurship and Business Organization 1720–1844* (Cambridge, 2000)

Harris, Tim, 'Problematising Popular Culture', in Tim Harris ed., *Popular Culture in England, 1500–1800* (New York, 1995), 1–27

——, *Revolution: The Great Crisis of the British Monarchy 1685–1720* (London, 2006)

Harrison, John, *The Library of Isaac Newton* (Cambridge, 1978)

—— and Peter Laslett, *The Library of John Locke* (Oxford, 1965)

Hayton, David W., 'Anglo-Irish Attitudes: Changing Perceptions of National Identity Among the Protestant Ascendancy in Ireland, ca. 1690–1750', *Studies in Eighteenth-Century Culture*, 17 (1987), 145–57

——, 'Moral Reform and Country Politics in the Late Seventeenth-Century House of Commons', *Past & Present*, 128 (August, 1990), 48–91

——, 'Patriots and Legislators: Irishmen and their Parliaments, c. 1689–c. 1740', in Julian Hoppit ed., *Parliaments, Nations and Identities in Britain and Ireland 1660–1850* (Manchester, 2003), 103–23

—— and Clyve Jones, 'Peers and Placemen: Lord Cowper's Notes on the Debate on the Place Clause in the Regency Bill, 31 January 1706,' *Parliamentary History*, 18, 1 (1999), 65–79

——, 'The Stanhope/Sunderland Ministry and the Repudiation of Irish Parliamentary Independence', *The English Historical Review*, 113, 452 (June, 1998), 610–36

Heaney, Howell J., 'A Signer of the Declaration of Independence Orders Books from London: Two Documents of George Read of Delaware in the Hampton L. Carson Collection of the Free Library of Philadelphia', *The American Journal of Legal History*, 2, 2 (April, 1958), 172–85

Helmholz, R.H., 'Natural Law and Human Rights in English Law: From Bracton to Blackstone', *Ave Maria Law Review*, 3, 1 (Spring, 2005), 1–22

Henry, John, 'Science and the Coming of Enlightenment', in Martin Fitzpatrick, Peter Jones, Christa Knellwolf and Iain McCalman eds, *The Enlightenment World* (New York, 2004), 10–27

Heward, Edmund, 'The Early History of the Court Funds Office', *The Journal of Legal History*, 4, 1 (1983), 46–53

Hicks, Philip, *Neoclassical History and English Culture: From Clarendon to Hume* (Basingstoke, 1996)

Himma, Kenneth Einar, 'Do Philosophy and Sociology Mix? A Non-Essentialist Socio-Legal Positivist Analysis of the Concept of Law', *Oxford Journal of Legal Studies*, 24, 4 (2004), 717–38

Hochstrasser, T.J., *Natural Law Theories in the Early Enlightenment* (Cambridge, 2000)

Hoeflich, Michael H., 'Law and Geometry: Legal Science from Leibniz to Langdell', *The American Journal of Legal History*, 30, 2 (April, 1986), 95–121

——, 'The Lawyer as Pragmatic Reader: The History of Legal Common-Placing', *Arkansas Law Review*, 55 (2002), 87–122

——, 'Legal History and the History of the Book: Variations on a Theme', *Kansas Law Review*, 46, 3 (April, 1998), 415–686

Holdsworth, W.S., *A History of English Law*, 12 vols (London, 1922–38)

Holmes, Clive, 'Women: Witnesses and Witches', *Past & Present*, 140 (August, 1993), 45–78

Hont, Istvan, 'The Early Enlightenment Debate on Commerce and Luxury', in Mark Goldie and Robert Wolker eds, *The Cambridge History of Eighteenth-Century Political Thought* (Cambridge, 2006), 379–418

—— and Michael Ignatieff, eds, *Wealth and Virtue: The Shaping of Political Economy in the Scottish Enlightenment* (Cambridge, 1983)

Hopfl, H.M., 'From Savage to Scotsman: Conjectural History in the Scottish Enlightenment', *Journal of British Studies*, 17, 2 (Spring, 1978), 19–40

Hoppit, Julian, 'Attitudes to Credit in Britain 1680–1790', *The Historical Journal*, 33, 2 (June, 1990), 305–22

——, 'The Myths of the South Sea Bubble', *Transactions of the Royal Historical Society*, Sixth Series, 12 (2002), 141–65

——, *Risk and Failure in English Business 1700–1800* (Cambridge, 1987)

Horle, Craig, *The Quakers and the English Legal System 1660–1688* (Philadelphia, 1988)

Horne, Thomas A., *The Social Thought of Bernard Mandeville: Virtue and Commerce in Early Eighteenth-Century England* (London, 1978)

Horsley, Lee Sonsteng, 'The Trial of John Tutchin, Author of the *Observator*', *The Yearbook of English Studies*, 3 (1973), 124–40

Horwitz, Henry, 'Chancery's "Younger Sister": The Court of Exchequer and its Equity Jurisdiction 1649–1841', *Historical Research*, 72, 178 (June, 1999), 160–82

——, 'Changes in the Law and Reform of the Legal Order: England (and Wales) 1689–1760', *Parliamentary History*, 21, 3 (October, 2002), 301–24

—— and Patrick Polden, 'Continuity or Change in the Court of Chancery in the Seventeenth and Eighteenth Centuries?', *Journal of British Studies*, 35, 1 (January, 1996), 24–57

——, *A Guide to Chancery Equity Records and Proceedings 1600–1800* (London, 1998)

—— and Lloyd Bonfield, 'The "Lower Branches" of the Legal Profession: A London Society of Attorneys and Solicitors of the 1730s and its "Moots"', *Cambridge Law Journal*, 49 (November, 1990), 461–90

Hulsebosch, Daniel, 'The Ancient Constitution and the Expanding Empire: Sir

Edward Coke's British Jurisprudence', *Law and History Review*, 21, 3 (Fall, 2003), 439–82

——, *Constituting Empire: New York and the Transformation of Constitutionalism in the Atlantic World, 1664–1830* (Chapel Hill, 2005)

Hundert, E.J., *The Enlightenment's Fable: Bernard Mandeville and the Discovery of Society* (Cambridge, 1994)

Hunnisett, R.F., ed., *Sussex Coroners' Inquests 1558–1603* (Kew, 1996)

——, *Sussex Coroners' Inquests 1603–1688* (Kew, 1998)

Hunt, Margaret R., *The Middling Sort: Commerce, Gender and the Family in England 1680–1780* (Berkeley, 1996)

——, 'Wives and Marital "Rights" in the Court of Exchequer in the Early Eighteenth Century', in Paul Griffiths and Mark C.R. Jenner eds, *Londonopolis: Essays in the Cultural and Social History of Early Modern London* (Manchester, 2000), 107–29

Hurl-Eamon, Jennine, 'Policing Male Heterosexuality: The Reformation of Manners Societies' Campaign Against the Brothels in Westminster, 1690–1720', *Journal of Social History*, 37, 4 (Summer, 2004), 1017–35

Ibbetson, David J., *Common Law and* Ius Commune (London, 2001)

——, *A Historical Introduction to the Law of Obligations* (Oxford, 1999)

——, 'Legal Printing and Legal Doctrine', *The Irish Jurist*, New Series, 35 (2000), 345–54

——, 'Natural Law and Common Law', *Edinburgh Law Review*, 5 (2001), 4–20

——, 'What is Legal History a History Of?', in Andrew Lewis and Michael Lobban eds, *Law and History* (Oxford, 2004), 33–40

Innes, Joanna, 'The King's Bench Prison in the Later Eighteenth Century: Law, Authority and Order in a London Debtor's Prison', in John Brewer and John Styles eds, *An Ungovernable People: The English and their Law in the Seventeenth and Eighteenth Centuries* (New Brunswick, 1980), 250–98

Israel, Jonathan, *Enlightenment Contested: Philosophy, Modernity and the Emancipation of Man 1670–1752* (Oxford, 2006)

——, *Radical Enlightenment: Philosophy and the Making of Modernity* (Oxford, 2001)

Jackson, H.J., *Marginalia: Readers Writing in Books* (New Haven, 2001)

Jackson, Mark, *New-Born Child Murder: Women, Illegitimacy and the Courts in Eighteenth-Century England* (Manchester, 1996)

Jacob, Margaret C., 'Newtonianism and the Origins of Enlightenment: A Reassessment', *Eighteenth-Century Studies*, 11, 1 (Autumn, 1977), 1–25

—— and Larry Stewart, *Practical Matter: Newton's Science in the Service of Industry and Empire 1687–1851* (Cambridge, Mass., 2004)

James, Susan, 'Reason, the Passions and the Good Life', in Daniel Garber and Michael Ayers eds, *The Cambridge History of Seventeenth-Century Philosophy*, vol. 2, (Cambridge, 1998), 1358–96

Johns, Adrian, 'History, Science, and the History of the Book: The Making of Natural Philosophy in Early Modern England', *Publishing History*, 30 (1991), 5–30

——, *The Nature of the Book: Print and Knowledge in the Making* (Chicago, 1998)

——, 'Print and Public Science', in Roy Porter ed., *The Cambridge History of Science, Volume 4: Eighteenth-Century Science* (Cambridge, 2003), 536–60

——, 'Science and the Book', in John Barnard, D.F. McKenzie and Maureen Bell eds, *The Cambridge History of the Book in Britain, Volume 4, 1557–1695* (Cambridge, 2002), 274–303

Jones, Carol A.G., *Expert Witnesses: Science, Medicine and the Practice of Law* (Oxford, 1994)

Jones, Clyve, 'The New Opposition in the House of Lords, 1720–3', *The Historical Journal*, 36, 2 (June, 1993), 309–29

——, '"Venice Preserv'd or a Plot Discover'd": The Political and Social Context of the Peerage Bill of 1719', in Clyve Jones ed., *A Pillar of the Constitution: The House of Lords in British Politics 1640–1784* (London, 1989), 79–112

Jones, Neil, 'Trusts in England after the Statute of Uses: A View from the 16th Century', in Richard Helmholz and Reinhard Zimmerman eds, *Itinera Fiduciae: Trust and Treuhand in Historical Perspective*, (Berlin, 1998), 173–205

——, 'Uses, Trusts and a Path to Privity', *Cambridge Law Journal*, 56, 1 (March, 1997), 175–200

——, 'The Use Upon a Use in Equity Revisited', *Cambrian Law Review*, 33 (2002), 67–80

Jones, W.J., 'The Foundations of English Bankruptcy: Statutes and Commissions in the Early Modern Period', *Transactions of the American Philosophical Society*, 69, 3 (1979), 1–63

Kargon, Robert, 'Expert Testimony in Historical Perspective', *Law and Human Behavior*, 10, 1/2 (1986), 15–27

Kassler, Jamie C., *The Honourable Roger North 1651–1734: On Life, Morality, Law and Tradition* (Farnham, 2009)

Kelley, Donald R., 'Between History and System', in Gianna Pomata and Nancy G. Siraisi eds, *Historia: Empiricism and Erudition in Early Modern Europe* (Cambridge, Mass., 2005), 211–38

——, 'History, English Law and the Renaissance', *Past & Present*, 65 (November, 1974), 24–51

——, 'History, English Law and the Renaissance: A Rejoinder', *Past & Present*, 72 (August, 1976), 143–6

——, *The Human Measure: Social Thought in the Western Legal Tradition* (Cambridge, Mass., 1990)

——, 'Law', in J.H. Burns ed., with the assistance of Mark Goldie, *The Cambridge History of Political Thought 1450–1700* (Cambridge, 1991), 66–94

——, '"Second Nature": The Idea of Custom in European Law, Society and Culture', in Donald R. Kelley, *The Writing of History and the Study of Law* (Aldershot, 1997), 131–72

Kelly, James, 'The Making of Law in Eighteenth-Century Ireland: The Significance and Import of Poynings' Law', in N.M. Dawson ed., *Reflections on Law and History* (Dublin, 2006), 259–77

Kelly, Patrick, 'Conquest *versus* Consent as the Basis of the English Title to Ireland in William Molyneux's *Case of Ireland … Stated* (1698)', in Ciaran Brady and Jane Ohlmeyer eds, *British Interventions in Early Modern Ireland* (Cambridge, 2005), 334–56

——, '"Industry and Virtue versus Luxury and Corruption": Berkeley, Walpole and the South Sea Crisis', *Eighteenth-Century Ireland*, 7 (1992), 57–74

——, 'Ireland and the Glorious Revolution: From Kingdom to Colony', in Robert Beddard ed., *The Revolutions of 1688* (Oxford, 1991), 163–90

Kenny, Colum, 'The Exclusion of Catholics from the Legal Profession in Ireland, 1537–1829', *Irish Historical Studies*, 25, 100 (November, 1987), 337–57

Kent-Wright, Johnson, 'Historical Thought in the Era of Enlightenment', in Lloyd

Kramer and Sarah Maza eds, *A Companion to Western Historical Thought* (Oxford, 2002), 123–42

Kenyon, J.P., *The History Men: The Historical Profession in England Since the Renaissance* (Pittsburgh, 1984)

Kidd, Colin, 'Gaelic Antiquity and National Identity in Enlightenment Ireland and Scotland', *The English Historical Review*, 109, 434 (November, 1994), 1197–1214

Kirk, Linda, 'The Matter of Enlightenment', *The Historical Journal*, 43, 4 (December, 2000), 1129–43

Klein Lawrence E. and Anthony J. La Vopa, eds, *Enthusiasm and Enlightenment in Europe, 1650–1850* (San Marino, 1998)

——, 'The Political Significance of "Politeness" in Early Eighteenth-Century Britain', in Gordon J. Schochet ed., *Politics, Politeness and Patriotism*, Proceedings of the Folger Institute Center for the History of British Political Thought, vol. 5 (Washington D.C., 1993), 73–108

___, *Shaftesbury and the Culture of Politeness: Moral Discourse and Cultural Politics in Early Eighteenth-Century England* (Cambridge, 1994)

——, 'Sociability, Solitude and Enthusiasm', *Huntington Library Quarterly*, 60, 1/2 (1997), 153–77

Klerman, Daniel, 'Jurisdictional Competition and the Evolution of the Common Law: A Hypothesis', *Australian Journal of Legal History*, 8 (2004), 1–19

Knafla, Louis A., 'Conscience in the English Common Law Tradition', *University of Toronto Law Journal*, 26, 1 (Winter, 1976), 1–16

Knights, Mark, 'The Tory Interpretation of History in the Rage of Parties', *Huntington Library Quarterly*, 68, 1–2, (March, 2005), 353–73

Konig, David, 'Legal Fictions and Rule(s) of Law', in Christopher L. Tomlins and Bruce Mann eds, *The Many Legalities of Early America* (Chapel Hill, 2001), 97–122

Korsten, F.J.M., *Roger North (1651–1734): Virtuoso and Essayist* (Amsterdam, 1981)

Kramnick, Isaac, 'Augustan Politics and English Historiography: The Debate on the English Past 1730–35', *History and Theory*, 6, 1 (1967), 33–56

Kugler, Anne, *Errant Plagiary: the Life and Writings of Lady Sarah Cowper 1644–1720* (Stanford, 2002)

Landsman, Stephan, 'From Gilbert to Bentham: The Reconceptualization of Evidence Theory', *Wayne Law Review*, 36 (1990), 1149–86

——, 'One Hundred Years of Medical Rectitude: Medical Witnesses at the Old Bailey 1717–1817', *Law and History Review*, 16, 3 (Autumn, 1998), 445–94

——, 'The Rise of the Contentious Spirit: Adversary Procedure in Eighteenth-Century England', *Cornell Law Review*, 75 (March, 1990), 497–608

——, 'Of Witches, Madmen and Product Liability: An Historical Survey of the Use of Expert Testimony', *Behavioral Sciences and the Law*, 13, 2 (Spring, 1995), 131–57

Langbein, John H., 'Chancellor Kent and the History of Legal Literature', *Columbia Law Review*, 93, 3 (April, 1993), 547–94

——, 'The Contractarian Basis of the Law of Trusts', *Yale Law Journal*, 105, 3 (December, 1995), 625–75

——, 'The Criminal Trial before the Lawyers', *University of Chicago Law Review*, 45, 2 (Winter, 1978), 263–316

——, 'Fact Finding in the English Court of Chancery: A Rebuttal', *Yale Law Journal*, 83, 8 (July, 1974), 1620–30

——, 'Historical Foundations of the Law of Evidence: A View from the Ryder Sources', *Columbia Law Review*, 96, 5 (June, 1996), 1168–1202

——, *The Origins of Adversary Criminal Trial* (Oxford, 2005)

——, 'Shaping the Eighteenth-Century Criminal Trial: A View from the Ryder Sources', *University of Chicago Law Review*, 50, 1 (Winter, 1983), 1–136

——, *Torture and the Law of Proof: Europe and England in the Ancien Regime* (Chicago, 1977; rev. edn, 2004)

Laurence, Anne, 'The Emergence of a Private Clientele for Banks in the Early Eighteenth Century: Hoare's Bank and Some Women Customers', *Economic History Review*, 61, 3 (2008), 565–86

——, 'Women Investors, "That Nasty South Sea Affair" and the Rage to Speculate in Early Eighteenth-Century England', *Accounting Business and Financial History*, 16, 2 (July, 2006), 245–64

Lemmings David, 'Blackstone and Law Reform by Education: Preparation for the Bar and Lawyerly Culture in Eighteenth-Century England', *Law and History Review*, 16, 2 (Summer, 1998), 211–55

——, ed., *The British and their Laws in the Eighteenth Century* (Woodbridge, 2005)

——, *Gentlemen and Barristers: The Inns of Court and the English Bar 1680–1730* (Oxford, 1990)

——, 'The Independence of the Judiciary in Eighteenth-Century England', in Peter Birks ed., *The Life of the Law: Proceedings of the Tenth British Legal History Conference* (London, 1993), 125–49

——, 'Lord Chancellor Cowper and the Whigs, 1714–16', *Parliamentary History*, 9, 1 (May, 1990), 163–74

—— and Claire Walker eds, *Moral Panics, the Media and the Law in Early Modern England* (Basingstoke, 2009), 139–56

——, *Professors of the Law: Barristers and English Legal Culture in the Eighteenth Century* (Oxford, 2000)

Levack, Brian P., 'English Law, Scots Law and the Union 1603–1707', in Alan Harding ed., *Law-making and Law-makers in British History* (London, 1980), 105–19

——, *The Formation of the British State: England, Scotland and the Union 1603–1707* (Oxford, 1987)

——, 'The Proposed Union of English Law and Scots Law in the Seventeenth Century', *Juridical Review*, 20, 2 (1975), 97–115

Levenbook, Barbara Baum, 'The Meaning of a Precedent', *Legal Theory*, 6 (2000), 185–240

Levine, David I., 'Calculating Fees of Special Masters', *Hastings Law Journal*, 37 (September, 1985), 141–200

Levine, Joseph M., 'Ancients and Moderns: Cross-Currents in Early Modern Intellectual Life', in Giles Mandlebrote and K.A. Manley eds, *The Cambridge History of Libraries in Britain and Ireland, Volume 2, 1640–1850* (Cambridge, 2006), 9–22

——, *The Battle of the Books: History and Literature in the Augustan Age* (Ithaca, 1991)

——, *Humanism and History: Origins of Modern English Historiography* (Ithaca, 1987)

Lieberman, David, 'Law/Custom/Tradition: Perspectives from the Common Law', in Mark Salber Phillips and Gordon Schochet eds, *Questions of Tradition* (Toronto, 2004), 233–57

——, 'Legislation in a Common Law Context', in Diethelm Klippel and Reiner

Schulze eds, *Common Law und Europaische Rechtsgeschichte, Zeitschrift fur Neuere Rechtsgeschichte*, 28, 1/2 (2006), 107–23

——, 'Mapping Criminal Law: Blackstone and the Categories of English Jurisprudence', in Norma Landau ed., *Law, Crime and English Society, 1660–1830* (Cambridge, 2002), 139–61

——, 'Property, Commerce and the Common Law: Attitudes to Legal Change in the Eighteenth Century', in John Brewer and Susan Staves eds, *Early Modern Conceptions of Property* (London, 1996), 144–60

——, *The Province of Legislation Determined: Legal Theory in Eighteenth-Century Britain* (Cambridge, 1989)

Lobban, Michael, 'The Ambition of Lord Kames's Equity', in Andrew Lewis and Michael Lobban eds, *Law and History* (Oxford, 2004), 97–121

——, 'Blackstone and the Science of Law', *The Historical Journal*, 30, 2 (June, 1987), 311–35

——, 'The Chancellor, the Chancery and the History of Law Reform', *Law and History Review*, 22, 3 (Autumn, 2004), 615–17

——, *The Common Law and English Jurisprudence 1760–1850* (Oxford, 1991)

——, 'Contractual Fraud in Law and Equity, c. 1750–c. 1850', *Oxford Journal of Legal Studies*, 17, 3 (Autumn, 1997), 441–76

——, 'Custom, Nature and Authority: the Roots of English Legal Positivism', in David Lemmings ed., *The British and their Laws in the Eighteenth Century* (Woodbridge, 2005), 27–58

——, 'The English Legal Treatise and English Law in the Eighteenth Century', in Serge Dauchy, Jos Monballyu and Alain Wijffels eds, *Auctoritates: Law Making and its Authors, Iuris Scripta Historica*, 13 (Brussels, 1997), 69–88

——, *A History of the Philosophy of Law in the Common Law World, 1600–1900*, vol. 8 of Enrico Pattaro ed., *A Treatise of Legal Philosophy and General Jurisprudence* (Dordrecht, 2007)

——, 'Introduction: The Tools and Tasks of the Legal Historian', in Andrew Lewis and Michael Lobban eds, *Law and History* (Oxford, 2004), 1–32

——, '"Old Wine in New Bottles": The Concept and Practice of Law Reform c. 1780–1830', in Arthur R. Burns and Joanna Innes eds, *Rethinking the Age of Reform, Britain 1780–1850* (Cambridge, 2003), 114–35

——, 'Preparing for Fusion: Reforming the Nineteenth-Century Court of Chancery, Part 1', *Law and History Review*, 22, 3 (Spring, 2004), 389–427

——, 'Preparing for Fusion: Reforming the Nineteenth-Century Court of Chancery, Part 2', *Law and History Review*, 22, 3 (Autumn, 2004), 565–99

Looser, Devoney, *British Women Writers and the Writing of History 1670–1820* (Baltimore, 2000)

Luig, K., 'The Institutes of National Law in the Seventeenth and Eighteenth Centuries', *Juridical Review*, 17 (1972), 193–226

Macaulay, T.B., *The History of England from the Accession of James II*, vol. 8 (New York, 1866)

Macnair, Michael, 'Common Law and Statutory Imitations of Equitable Relief under the Later Stuarts', in Christopher Brooks and Michael Lobban eds, *Communities and Courts in Britain 1150–1900* (London, 1997), 115–31

——, 'The Conceptual Basis of Trusts in the Later 17th and Early 18th Centuries', in Richard Helmholz and Reinhard Zimmerman eds, *Itinera Fiduciae: Trust and Treuhand in Historical Perspective* (Berlin, 1998), 207–36

——, *The Law of Proof in Early Modern Equity* (Berlin, 1999)

——, 'Lord King & Lord Talbot: An Eighteenth-Century Attempt to Reduce Delay in Chancery and its General Lessons', in C.H. van Rhee ed., *The Law's Delay: Essays on Undue Delay in Civil Litigation* (Antwerp, 2004), 252–68.

——, 'Sir Geoffrey Gilbert and his Treatises', *Legal History*, 15, 3 (1994), 252–68

Maitland, F.W., *Equity: Also the Forms of Action at Common Law: Two Courses of Lectures*, A.H. Chaytor and W.J. Whitaker eds (Cambridge, 1910)

——, *Why the History of English Law is not Written* (London, 1888)

Mandelbrote, Giles, 'Personal Owners of Books', in Giles Mandlebrote and K.A. Manley eds, *Cambridge History of Libraries in Britain and Ireland, Volume 2, 1640–1850* (Cambridge, 2006), 173–89

Mandelbrote, Scott, 'Professional Collections: Libraries for Scientists and Doctors', in Giles Mandelbrote and K.A. Manley eds, *Cambridge History of Libraries in Britain and Ireland, Volume 2, 1640–1850*, (Cambridge, 2006), 158–72

Mann, Bruce H., 'Afterword: The Death and Transfiguration of Early American Legal History', in Christopher L. Tomlins and Bruce H. Mann eds, *The Many Legalities of Early America* (Chapel Hill, 2001), 442–8

Marshall, John, *John Locke: Religion, Resistance, Responsibility* (Cambridge, 1994)

Maurer, Bill, 'The Cultural Power of Law? Conjunctive Readings', *Law and Society Review*, 38, 4 (December, 2004), 843–50

McConnell, Michael W., 'David C. Baum Memorial Lecture: Tradition and Constitutionalism Before the Constitution', *University of Illinois Law Review* (1998), 173–98

McDowell, Gary L., 'The Politics of Meaning: Law Dictionaries and the Liberal Tradition of Interpretation', *The American Journal of Legal History*, 44, 3 (July, 2000), 257–83

McDowell, Paula, *The Women of Grub Street: Press, Politics and Gender in the London Literary Marketplace 1678–1730* (Oxford, 1998)

McGowen, Randall, 'Law and Enlightenment', in Martin Fitzpatrick, Peter Jones, Christa Knellwolf and Iain McCalman eds, *The Enlightenment World* (New York, 2004), 502–15

McIntosh, Carey, 'Eighteenth-Century English Dictionaries and the Enlightenment', *The Yearbook of English Studies*, 28 (1998), 3–18

McLaverty, J., 'Pope and Giles Jacob's *Lives of the Poets*: The *Dunciad* as Alternative Literary History', *Modern Philology*, 83, 1 (August, 1985), 22–32

McLoughlin, T.O., 'Edmund Burke's Abridgment of English History', *Eighteenth-Century Ireland*, 5 (1990), 45–59

McMahon, Vanessa, 'Reading the Body: Dissection and the "Murder" of Sarah Stout, Hertfordshire, 1699', *Social History of Medicine*, 19, 1 (2006), 19–35

Melikan, R.A., 'Mr. Attorney General and the Politicians', *The Historical Journal*, 40, 1 (March, 1997), 41–69

Meyler, Bernadette, 'Toward a Common Law Originalism', *Stanford Law Review*, 59, 3 (December, 2006), 551–600

Meynell, G.G., 'John Locke's Method of Common-placing, as Seen in his Drafts and his Medical Notebooks, Bodleian MSS Locke D.9, f. 21 and f. 23', *Seventeenth Century*, 8 (1993), 245–67

Mitchell, Annie, 'Character of an Independent Whig – "Cato" and Bernard Mandeville', *History of European Ideas*, 29, 3 (September, 2003), 291–311

Mizuta, Hiroshi, ed., *Adam Smith's Library: A Catalogue* (Oxford, 2000)

Moglen, Eben, 'Taking the Fifth: Reconsidering the Origins of the Privilege Against Self-Incrimination', *Michigan Law Review*, 92 (March, 1994), 1086–1130

Moore, James, 'Natural Rights in the Scottish Enlightenment', in Mark Goldie and Robert Wolker eds, *The Cambridge History of Eighteenth-Century Philosophy* (Cambridge, 2006), 291–316

Mortensen, Preben, 'Shaftesbury and the Morality of Art Appreciation', *Journal of the History of Ideas*, 55, 4 (October, 1994), 631–50

Moss, Ann, *Printed Commonplace Books and the Structuring of Renaissance Thought* (Oxford, 1996)

Muldrew, Craig, 'Credit and the Courts: Debt Litigation in a Seventeenth-Century Urban Community', *Economic History Review*, New Series, 46, 1 (February, 1993), 23–38

——, *The Economy of Obligation: The Culture of Credit and Social Relations in Early Modern England* (New York, 1998)

——, 'Interpreting the Market: The Ethics of Credit and Community Relations in Early Modern England', *Social History*, 18, 2 (May, 1993), 163–83

Murphy, Anne L., *The Origins of English Financial Markets: Investment and Speculation before the South Sea Bubble* (Cambridge, 2009)

Murphy, Antoin, *John Law, Economic Theorist and Policy Maker* (Oxford, 1997)

Muthu, Sankar, *Enlightenment Against Empire* (Princeton, 2003)

Myers, Robin, Michael Harris and Giles Mandelbrote eds, *Owners, Annotators and the Signs of Reading* (London, 2005)

—— and Michael Harris, eds, *Property of a Gentleman: The Formation, Organization and Dispersal of the Private Library 1629–1920* (Winchester, 1991)

Neal, Larry, *The Rise of Financial Capitalism: International Capital Markets in the Age of Reason* (Cambridge, 1990)

Nelles, Paul A., 'Libraries, Books and Learning, from Bacon to the Enlightenment', in Giles Mandlebrote and K.A. Manley eds, *The Cambridge History of Libraries in Britain and Ireland, Volume 2, 1640–1850* (Cambridge, 2006), 23–35

Nonet, Philippe and Philip Selznick, *Law and Society in Transition: Toward Responsive Law* (New York, 2001)

North, Douglas C. and Barry R. Weingast, 'Constitutions and Commitment: The Evolution of Institutions Governing Public Choice in Seventeenth-Century England', *Journal of Economic History*, 49, 4 (December, 1989), 803–32

Norton David Fate and Manfred Kuehn, 'The Foundations of Morality', in Knud Haakonssen ed., *The Cambridge History of Eighteenth-Century Philosophy*, vol. 2 (Cambridge, 2006), 941–86

Nunn, Hillary M., *Staging Anatomies: Dissection and Spectacle in Early Stuart Tragedy* (Aldershot, 2005)

Oakley, Francis, *Natural Law, Law of Nature, Natural Rights* (New York, 2005)

O'Brien, Karen, 'History and the Novel in Eighteenth-Century Britain', *Huntington Library Quarterly*, 68, 1/2 (March, 2005), 397–413

——, 'The History Market in Eighteenth-Century England', in Isabel Rivers ed., *Books and their Readers in Eighteenth-Century England: New Essays* (London, 2001), 105–34

——, *Narratives of Enlightenment: Cosmopolitan History from Voltaire to Gibbon* (Cambridge 1997)

——, *Women and Enlightenment in Eighteenth-Century Britain* (Cambridge, 2009)

O'Day, Rosemary, *The Professions in Early Modern England 1450–1800: Servants of the Commonweal* (New York, 2000)

Okie, Laird, *Augustan Historical Writing: Histories of England in the English Enlightenment* (Lanham, MD, 1991)

Oldham, James, 'Eighteenth-Century Judges' Notes: How they Explain, Correct and Enhance the Reports', *The American Journal of Legal History*, 3, 1 (January, 1987), 9–42

——, 'From Blackstone to Bentham: Common Law versus Legislation in Eighteenth-Century Britain', *Michigan Law Review*, 89, 6 (May, 1991), 1637–60

——, *The Mansfield Manuscripts and the Growth of English Law in the Eighteenth Century*, 2 vols (Chapel Hill, 1992)

——, 'On Pleading the Belly: A History of the Jury of Matrons', *Criminal Justice History*, 6 (1985), 1–64

——, 'A Profusion of Chancery Reform', *Law and History Review*, 22, 3 (Autumn, 2004) 609–14

——, 'Truth-Telling in the Eighteenth-Century Courtroom', *Law and History Review*, 12, 1 (Spring, 1994), 95–121

Paget, John, *Paradoxes and Puzzles, Historical, Judicial and Literary* (Edinburgh, 1874)

Palmeri, Frank, 'Conjectural History and the Origins of Sociology', *Studies in Eighteenth-Century Culture*, 37 (2008), 1–21

Park, Katharine, *Secrets of Women: Gender, Generation and the Origins of Human Dissection* (New York, 2006)

——, 'Women, Gender and Utopia: *The Death of Nature* and the Historiography of Early Modern Science', *Isis*, 97, 3 (September, 2006), 487–95

Peck, Linda Levy, *Court Patronage and Corruption in Early Stuart England* (Boston, 1990)

Perinetti, Dario, 'Philosophical Reflection on History', in Knud Haakonssen ed., *The Cambridge History of Eighteenth-Century Philosophy*, vol. 2 (Cambridge, 2006), 1107–40

Philips, Mark Salber, 'Distance and Historical Representation', *History Workshop Journal*, 57 (2004), 123–41

——, 'Reconsiderations on History and Antiquarianism: Arnaldo Momigliano and the Historiography of Eighteenth-Century Britain,' *Journal of the History of Ideas*, 57, 2 (April, 1996), 297–316

——, *Society and Sentiment: Genres of Historical Writing in Britain 1740–1820* (Princeton, 2000)

Phillips, Nicola, *Women in Business 1700–1850* (Woodbridge, 2006)

Pincus, Steve, *1688: The First Modern Revolution* (New Haven, 2009)

Pocock, J.G.A., *The Ancient Constitution and the Feudal Law: A Study of English Historical Thought in the Seventeenth Century* (Cambridge, 1957; reissued with a retrospect 1987)

——, *Barbarism and Religion*, 5 vols (Cambridge, 1999–2011)

——, 'Clergy and Commerce: The Conservative Enlightenment in England', in R. Ajello ed., *L'Eta dei Lumi: Studi Storici sul Settecento Europeo in Onore de Franco Venturi*, vol. 1 (Naples, 1985), 524–62

——, 'The Concept of a Language, and the *Métier d'Historien*: Some Considerations on Practice', in Anthony Pagden ed., *The Languages of Political Theory in Early Modern Europe* (Cambridge, 1987), 19–38

——, 'Conservative Enlightenment and Democratic Revolutions: The American and French Cases in British Perspective', *Government and Opposition*, 24, 1 (January, 1989), 81–105

——, 'Enthusiasm: The Antiself of Enlightenment', *The Huntington Library Quarterly*, 60, 1/2 (1997), 7–28

——, 'Historiography and Enlightenment: A View of their History', *Modern Intellectual History*, 5, 1 (2008), 83–96

——, *The Machiavellian Moment, Florentine Political Thought and the Atlantic Republican Tradition* (Princeton, 1975)

——, 'Perceptions of Modernity in Early Modern Thinking', *Intellectual History Review*, 17, 1 (2007), 55–63

——, *Virtue, Commerce, and History: Essays on Political Thought and History, Chiefly in the Eighteenth Century* (Cambridge, 1985)

Pomata, Gianna, '*Praxis Historialis*: The Uses of *Historia* in Early Modern Medicine', in Gianna Pomata and Nancy G. Siraisi eds, *Historia: Empiricism and Erudition in Early Modern Europe* (Cambridge, Mass., 2005), 105–46

Poovey, Mary, *Genres of the Credit Economy: Mediating Value in Eighteenth and Nineteenth-Century Britain* (Chicago, 2008)

Porter, Roy, ed., *The Cambridge History of Science, Volume 4: Eighteenth-Century Science* (Cambridge, 2003)

——, *The Creation of the Modern World: The Untold Story of the British Enlightenment* (New York, 2000)

—— and Mikulas Teich, eds, *The Enlightenment in National Context* (Cambridge, 1981)

——, *Flesh in the Age of Reason: The Modern Foundations of Body and Soul* (New York, 2004)

—— and Mikulas Teich, eds, *The Scientific Revolution in National Context* (Cambridge, 1992)

Postema, Gerald, 'Classical Common Law Jurisprudence (Part I)', *Oxford University Commonwealth Law Journal*, 2, 2 (Winter, 2002), 155–80

——, 'Classical Common Law Jurisprudence (Part II)', *Oxford University Commonwealth Law Journal*, 3, 1 (Summer, 2003), 1–28

——, 'Some Roots of Our Notion of Precedent', in Laurence Goldstein ed., *Precedent in Law* (Oxford, 1987), 9–33

Prest, Wilfred, 'The Experience of Litigation in Eighteenth-Century England', in David Lemmings ed., *The British and their Laws in the Eighteenth Century* (Woodbridge, 2005), 133–54

——, *The Inns of Court under Elizabeth I and the Early Stuarts, 1590–1640* (Totowa, N.J., 1972)

——, 'Judicial Corruption in Early Modern England', *Past & Present*, 133 (November, 1991), 67–95

——, 'Law Books', in Michael F. Suarez S.J. and Michael Turner eds, *The Cambridge History of the Book in Britain, Volume 5, 1696–1830* (Cambridge, 2009), 791–806

——, 'Law, Lawyers and Rational Dissent', in Knud Haakonssen ed., *Enlightenment and Religion: Rational Dissent in Eighteenth-Century Britain* (Cambridge, 1996), 169–92

——, 'Law Reform and Legal Education in Interregnum England', *Bulletin of the Institute of Historical Research*, 75, 187 (February, 2002), 112–122

——, 'Law Reform in Eighteenth-Century England', in Peter Birks ed., *The Life of the Law: Proceedings of the Tenth British Legal History Conference* (London, 1993), 113–23

——, *William Blackstone: Law and Letters in the Eighteenth Century* (Oxford, 2008)

Price, Polly J., 'Natural Law and Birthright Citizenship in Calvin's Case', *Yale Journal of Law and the Humanities*, 9, 1 (1997), 73–145

Priest, Claire, 'Creating an American Property Law: Alienability and its Limits in American History', *Harvard Law Review*, 120, 2 (December, 2006), 385–459

Primer, Irwin, *Bernard Mandeville's 'A Modest Defence of the Public Stews': Prostitution and its Discontents in Early Georgian England* (New York, 2006)

Probert, Rebecca, *Marriage Law and Practice in the Long Eighteenth Century: A Reassessment* (Cambridge, 2009)

Quarrie, Paul, 'Introduction', in Sotheby's *The Library of the Earls of Macclesfield Removed from Shirburn Castle, Part One: Natural History* (London, 2004), 8–21

——, 'Introduction' in Sotheby's *The Library of the Earls of Macclesfield Removed from Shirburn Castle, Part Eight: Theology, Philosophy, Law and Economics* (London, 2008), 8–17

——,'The Scientific Library of the Earls of Macclesfield', *Notes and Records of the Royal Society*, 20 (2006), 5–24

Raven, James, 'The Book Trades', in Isabel Rivers ed., *Books and their Readers in Eighteenth-Century England: New Essays* (London, 2001), 1–34

Reay, Barry, 'The Social Origins of Early Quakerism', *Journal of Interdisciplinary History*, 11, 1 (Summer, 1980), 55–72

Reid, John Philip, *The Ancient Constitution and the Origins of Anglo-American Liberty* (Dekalb, 2005)

——, 'The Jurisprudence of Liberty: The Ancient Constitution in the Legal Historiography of the Seventeenth and Eighteenth Centuries', in Ellis Sandoz ed., *The Roots of Liberty: Magna Carta, Ancient Constitution, and the Anglo-American Tradition of Rule of Law* (Columbia, MO, 1993), 147–231

Reill, Peter Hanns, 'The Legacy of the Scientific Revolution', in Roy Porter ed., *The Cambridge History of Science, Volume 4: Eighteenth-Century Science* (Cambridge, 2003), 23–43

Risinger, D. Michael, with Michael J. Saks, 'Science and Nonscience in the Courts: Daubert Meets Handwriting Identification Expertise', *Iowa Law Review*, 82, 1 (October, 1996), 21–74

Rivers, Isabel, ed., *Books and their Readers in Eighteenth-Century England: New Essays* (London, 2001)

——, *Reason, Grace and Sentiment: A Study of the Language of Religion and Ethics in England, 1660–1780*, 2 vols (Cambridge, 1991, 2000)

Robbins, Caroline, *The Eighteenth-Century Commonwealthmen: Studies in the Transmission, Development and Circumstance of English Liberal Thought from the Restoration of Charles II until the War with the Thirteen Colonies* (Cambridge, Mass., 1959)

Robertson, John, *The Case for Enlightenment: Scotland and Naples, 1680–1760* (Cambridge, 2005)

Robinson, Robert B., 'The Two *Institutes* of Thomas Wood: A Study in Eighteenth Century Legal Scholarship', *The American Journal of Legal History*, 35, 4 (October, 1991), 432–58

Rogers, James Steven, *The Early History of the Law of Bills and Notes: A Study of the Origins of Anglo-American Commercial Law* (Cambridge, 1995)

Rogers, Pat, *Grub Street: Studies in a Subculture* (London, 1972)

Rose, Craig, 'Evangelical Philanthropy and Anglican Revival: The Charity Schools of Augustan London, 1608–1740', *The London Journal*, 16 (1991), 35–65

Rosenberg, Albert, 'The Sarah Stout Murder Case: An Early Example of the Doctor as an Expert Witness', *Journal of the History of Medicine and Allied Sciences*, 12 (1957), 61–70

Rosenthal, Laura J., *Infamous Commerce: Prostitution in Eighteenth-Century British Literature and Culture* (Ithaca, 2006)

Roseveare, Henry, *The Financial Revolution, 1660–1760* (London, 1991)

Ross, Richard J., 'The Commoning of the Common Law: The Renaissance Debate over Printing English Law, 1520–1640', *University of Pennsylvania Law Review*, 146, 2 (January, 1998), 323–461

——, 'The Legal Past of Early New England: Notes for the Study of Law, Legal Culture and Intellectual History', *The William and Mary Quarterly*, Third Series, 50, 1 (January, 1993), 28–41

——, 'The Memorial Culture of Early Modern English Lawyers: Memory as Keyword, Shelter and Identity, 1560–1640', *Yale Journal Of Law and the Humanities*, 10 (Summer, 1998), 229–326

Rudolph, Julia, 'Gender and the Development of Forensic Science: A Case Study', *The English Historical Review*, 123, 503 (August, 2008), 924–46

——, 'Rape and Resistance: Women and Consent in Seventeenth-Century English Legal and Political Thought', *Journal of British Studies*, 39, 2 (April, 2000), 157–84

——, *Revolution by Degrees: James Tyrrell and Whig Political Thought in the Late Seventeenth Century* (Basingstoke, 2002)

Sachse, William L., *Lord Somers, A Political Portrait* (Manchester, 1975)

Sakamoto, Tatsuya and Hideo Tanaka, eds, *The Rise of Political Economy in the Scottish Enlightenment* (London, 2003)

Saks, Michael J., 'Merlin and Solomon: Lessons from the Law's Formative Encounters with Forensic Identification Science,' *Hastings Law Journal*, 49, 4 (1998), 1069–1141

Sarat, Austin, et al., eds, *Crossing Boundaries: Traditions and Transformations in Law and Society Research* (Evanston, Ill., 1998)

Sawday, Jonathan, *The Body Emblazoned: Dissection and the Human Body in Renaissance Culture* (London, 1995)

Schauer, Frederick, 'Precedent', *Stanford Law Review*, 38 (February, 1987), 571–605

Schmidt, James, ed., *What is Enlightenment: Eighteenth-Century Answers and Twentieth-Century Questions* (Berkeley, 1996)

Schmitter, Amy M., '17th and 18th Century Theories of Emotions', in Edward N. Zalta ed., *The Stanford Encyclopedia of Philosophy (Fall 2008 Edition)* http://plato.stanford.edu/archives/fall2008/entries/emotions-17th18th/

Schneewind, J.B., *The Invention of Autonomy: A History of Modern Moral Philosophy* (Cambridge, 1998)

Schouls, Peter A., *Descartes and the Enlightenment* (Kingston, Ont., 1989)

Schwoerer, Lois G., *No Standing Armies! The Antiarmy Ideology in Seventeenth-Century England* (Baltimore, 1974)

Sedgwick, Romney, *The History of Parliament, The House of Commons 1715–1754*, 2 vols (London, 1970)

Sekora, John, *Luxury: The Concept in Western Thought, Eden to Smollett* (Baltimore, 1977)

Serjeantson, R.W., 'Testimony and Proof in Early Modern England', *Studies in the History and Philosophy of Science*, 30, 2 (June, 1999), 195–236

Shackleton, Robert, 'The *Encyclopedie* as an International Phenomenon', *Proceedings of the American Philosophical Society*, 114, 5 (October, 1970), 389–94

Shapin, Steven, 'Discipline and Bounding: The History and Sociology of Science as Seen through the Externalism-Internalism Debate', *History of Science*, 30 (1992), 333–69

——, 'The Image of the Man of Science', in Roy Porter ed., *The Cambridge History of Science, Volume 4: Eighteenth-Century Science* (Cambridge, 2003), 159–83

——, *A Social History of Truth: Civility and Science in Seventeenth-Century England* (Chicago, 1994)

Shapiro, Barbara J., *Beyond 'Reasonable Doubt' and 'Probable Cause': Historical Perspectives on the Anglo-American Law of Evidence* (Berkeley, 1991)

——, 'The Concept "Fact": Legal Origins and Cultural Diffusion', *Albion*, 26, 1 (Spring, 1994), 1–26

——, *A Culture of Fact: England 1550–1720* (Ithaca, 2000)

——, 'Law Reform in Seventeenth-Century England', *The American Journal of Legal History*, 19, 4 (October, 1975), 280–312

——, *Probability and Certainty in Seventeenth-Century England: A Study of the Relationships Between Natural Science, Religion, History, Law and Literature* (Princeton, 1983)

——, 'To A Moral Certainty: Theories of Knowledge and Anglo-American Juries 1600–1850', *Hastings Law Journal*, 38, 1 (1986), 153–93

Sheehan, Jonathan, 'Enlightenment, Religion and the Enigma of Secularization: A Review Essay', *American Historical Review*, 108, 4 (October, 2003), 1061–80

Sher, Richard B., *The Enlightenment and the Book: Scottish Authors and their Publishers in Eighteenth-Century Britain, Ireland and America* (Chicago, 2006)

Shetreet, Shimon, *Judges on Trial: A Study of the Appointment and Accountability of the English Judiciary* (Amsterdam, 1976)

Shoemaker, Robert, *Prosecution and Punishment: Petty Crime and the Law in London and Rural Middlesex c.1660–1720* (Cambridge, 1991)

——, 'Reforming Male Manners: Public Insult and the Decline of Violence in London, 1660–1740', in Tim Hitchcock and Michele Cohen eds, *English Masculinities, 1660–1800* (Harlow, 1999), 133–50

——,'Separate Spheres? Ideology and Practice in London Gender Relations, 1660–1740', in Muriel C. McClendon, Joseph P. Ward and Michael Macdonald eds, *Protestant Identities: Religion, Society and Self-fashioning in Post-Reformation England* (Stanford, 1999), 266–87

Simpson, A.W.B., ed., *Biographical Dictionary of the Common Law* (London, 1984)

——, 'The Common Law and Legal Theory', in A.W.B. Simpson ed., *Oxford Essays in Jurisprudence*, 2nd series (Oxford, 1973), 77–99

——, *A History of the Common Law of Contract: The Rise of the Action of Assumpsit* (Oxford 1975)

——, *An Introduction to the History of the Land Law* (Oxford, 1961)

——, *Leading Cases in the Common Law* (Oxford, 1995)

——,'The Rise and Fall of the Legal Treatise: Legal Principles and the Forms of Legal Literature', *University of Chicago Law Review*, 48, 3 (1981), 632–79

Sims, Catherine Strateman, 'An Unpublished Fragment of Madox' "History of the Exchequer"', *Huntington Library Quarterly*, 23, 1 (November, 1959), 61–94

Smith, Frederick Edwin, *Famous Trials of History* (New York, 1926)
Smith, R.J., *The Gothic Bequest: Medieval Institutions in British Thought, 1688–1863* (Cambridge, 1987)
Smith, Roger, *Trial by Medicine: Insanity and Responsibility in Victorian Trials* (Edinburgh, 1981)
Smyth, Jim, '"Like Amphibious Animals": Irish Protestants, Ancient Britons, 1691–1707', *The Historical Journal*, 36, 4 (December, 1993), 785–97
Snyder, Henry L., 'The Formulation of Foreign and Domestic Policy in the Reign of Queen Anne: Memoranda by Lord Chancellor Cowper of Conversations with Lord Treasurer Godolphin', *The Historical Journal*, 11, 1 (1968), 144–160
Sommerville, J.P., 'The Ancient Constitution Reassessed: The Common Law, The Court and the Languages of Politics in Early Modern England', in R. Malcolm Smuts ed., *The Stuart Court and Europe: Essays in Politics and Political Culture* (Cambridge, 1996), 39–64
Sotheby's, *The Library of the Earls of Macclesfield Removed from Shirburn Castle*, 12 vols (London, 2004–2008)
Soule, Charles C., *The Lawyer's Reference Manual of Law Books and Citations* (Boston, 1883)
Spring, Eileen, 'The Heiress-at-Law: English Real Property Law from the New Point of View', *Law and History Review*, 8, 2 (Fall, 1990), 273–96
——, *Law, Land and Family: Aristocratic Inheritance in England 1300–1800* (Chapel Hill, 1993)
St Clair, William, *The Reading Nation in the Romantic Period* (Cambridge, 2004)
Staves, Susan, 'Separate Maintenance Contracts', *Eighteenth Century Life*, 11, 2 (1987), 78–101
Stein, Peter, *Roman Law in European History* (Cambridge, 1999)
Stephan, Deborah, 'Laurence Echard – Whig Historian', *The Historical Journal*, 32, 4 (December, 1989), 843–66
Stewart, Larry R., *The Rise of Public Science: Rhetoric, Technology and Natural Philosophy in Newtonian Britain, 1660–1750* (Cambridge, 1992)
Stewart, M.A., ed., *English Philosophy in the Age of Locke* (Oxford, 2000)
Stolnitz, Jerome, 'On the Significance of Lord Shaftesbury in Modern Aesthetic Theory', *Philosophical Quarterly*, 11, 43 (April, 1961), 97–113
Strauss, David A., 'Common Law Constitutional Interpretation', *University of Chicago Law Review*, 63, 3 (Summer, 1996), 877–935
Stretton, Tim, 'Women, Property and Law', in Anita Pacheco ed., *A Companion to Early Modern Women's Writing* (Oxford, 2002), 40–57
Suarez, M.F., 'The Business of Literature: The Book Trade in England from Milton to Blake', in David Womersley ed., *A Companion to Literature from Milton to Blake*, (Cambridge, 2000), 131–50
Sugarman, David and Ronnie Warrington, 'Land Law, Citizenship and the Invention of "Englishness": The Strange World of the Equity of Redemption', in John Brewer and Susan Staves eds, *Early Modern Conceptions of Property* (London, 1996), 111–43
Sullivan, Robert, 'Rethinking Christianity in Enlightened Europe', *Eighteenth-Century Studies*, 34, 2 (Winter, 2001), 298–309
Symes, Carol, 'When We Talk About Modernity', *American Historical Review*, 116, 3 (June, 2011), 715–26

Tague, Ingrid, *Women of Quality: Accepting and Contesting Ideals of Femininity in England, 1690–1760* (Woodbridge, 2002)

Tamanaha, Brian Z., *A General Jurisprudence of Law and Society* (Oxford, 2001)

——, 'The Internal/External Distinction and the Notion of a "Practice" in Legal Theory and Sociolegal Studies', *Law and Society Review*, 30, 1 (1996), 163–204

Targett, Simon, 'Government and Ideology During the Age of Whig Supremacy: The Political Argument of Sir Robert Walpole's Newspaper Propagandists', *The Historical Journal*, 37, 2 (June, 1994), 289–317

Teeven, Kevin M., *A History of the Anglo-American Law of Contract* (Westport, CT, 1990)

Thomas, G.W., 'James I, Equity and Lord Keeper Williams', *The English Historical Review*, 91, 360 (July, 1976), 506–28.

Todd, Barbara J., '"To Be Some Body": Married Women and *The Hardship of the English Laws*', in Hilda Smith ed., *Women Writers and the Early Modern British Tradition* (Cambridge, 1998), 343–61

Topulos, Katherine, 'A Common Lawyer's Bookshelf Recreated: An Annotated Bibliography of a Collection of Sixteenth-Century English Law Books', *Law Library Journal*, 84 (Fall, 1992), 641–86

Townshend, Dabney, 'From Shaftesbury to Kant: The Development of the Concept of Aesthetic Experience', *Journal of the History of Ideas*, 48, 2 (April–June, 1987), 287–305

Trevor-Roper, Hugh, 'Pietro Giannone and Great Britain', *The Historical Journal*, 39, 3 (September, 1996), 657–75

Trumbach, Randolph, 'Sex, Gender and Sexual Identity in Modern Culture: Male Sodomy and Female Prostitution in Enlightenment London', *Journal of the History of Sexuality*, 2, 2 (October, 1991), 186–203

Tubbs, J.W., *The Common Law Mind: Medieval and Early Modern Conceptions* (Baltimore, 2000)

Tuck, Richard, 'Grotius and Selden', in J.H. Burns ed., with the assistance of Mark Goldie, *The Cambridge History of Political Thought 1450–1700* (Cambridge, 1991), 499–529

——, 'The "Modern" Theory of Natural Law', in Anthony Pagden ed., *The Languages of Political Theory in Early Modern Europe* (Cambridge, 1987), 99–119

Turner, David M., *Fashioning Adultery: Gender, Sex and Civility in England 1660–1740* (Cambridge, 2002)

——, '"Secret and Immodest Curiosities?" Sex, Marriage and Conscience in Early Modern England', in Harald Braun and Edward Vallance eds, *Contexts of Conscience in Early Modern Europe, 1500–1700* (Basingstoke, 2004), 132–50

Turner, R.W., *The Equity of Redemption: Its Nature, History and Connection with Equitable Estates Generally* (Cambridge, 1931)

van Kley, Dale, 'Christianity as Casualty and Chrysalis of Modernity: The Problem of Dechristianization in the French Revolution', *American Historical Review*, 108, 4 (October, 2003), 1081–1104

van Rhee, C.H., 'Trusts, Trust-Like Concepts and Ius Commune', *European Review of Private Law*, 2 (2000), 453–62

Velde, Francois R., 'John Law's System', *The American Economic Review*, 97, 2 (May, 2007), 278–9

Venn, John and J.A. Venn, comp., *Alumnae Cantabrigienses* (Cambridge, 1922–54)

Vernon, James, ed., *Re-reading the Constitution: New Narratives in the Political History of England's Long Nineteenth Century* (Cambridge, 1996)

Victory, Isolde, 'The Making of the 1720 Declaratory Act', in Gerard O'Brien ed., *Parliament, Politics and People: Essays in Eighteenth-Century Irish History* (Dublin, 1989), 9–29

Wahrman, Dror, 'Introduction, God and the Enlightenment', *American Historical Review*, 108, 4 (October, 2003), 1057–60

Walmsley, Jonathan, 'Locke's Natural Philosophy in Draft A of the *Essay*', *Journal of the History of Ideas*, 65, 1 (January, 2004), 15–37

Watson, Alan, *The Evolution of Western Private Law* (Baltimore, 2001)

——, *Roman Law and Comparative Law* (Athens, GA, 1991)

Wharam, Alan, *Murder in the Tower: And Other Tales from the State Trials* (Aldershot, 2001)

White, Jonathan, '"The Slow but Sure Poyson": The Representation of Gin and its Drinkers 1736–1751', *Journal of British Studies*, 42, 1 (January, 2003), 35–64

Whitman, James Q., *The Origins of Reasonable Doubt: Theological Roots of the Criminal Trial* (New Haven, 2008)

——, 'Why Did the Revolutionary Lawyers Confuse Custom and Reason?', *University of Chicago Law Review*, 58, 4 (Autumn, 1991), 1321–68

Willes, Margaret, *Reading Matters: Five Centuries of Discovering Books* (New Haven, 2008)

Williams, Abigail, *Poetry and the Creation of a Whig Literary Culture, 1681–1714* (Oxford, 2005)

Williams, Ian, '"He Credited More the Printed Booke": Common Lawyers' Receptivity to Print, 1550–1640', *Law and History Review*, 28, 1 (February, 2010), 39–70

Wokler, Robert, 'Anthropology and Conjectural History in the Enlightenment', in Christopher Fox and Roy Porter eds, *Inventing Human Science: Eighteenth-Century Domains* (Berkeley, 1995), 31–52

Wolff, Larry and Marco Cipolloni, eds, *The Anthropology of the Enlightenment* (Stanford, 2007)

Woolf, Daniel R., 'From Hystories to the Historical: Five Transitions in Thinking about the Past 1500–1700', *Huntington Library Quarterly*, 68, 1/2 (2005), 33–70

——, *Reading History in Early Modern England* (Cambridge, 2000)

Wright, Nancy E., Margaret Ferguson and A.R. Buck, eds, *Women, Property and the Letters of the Law in Early Modern England* (Toronto, 2004)

Wykes, David L., 'Friends, Parliament and the Toleration Act', *Journal of Ecclesiastical History*, 45, 1 (January, 1994), 42–63

——, 'Quaker Schoolmasters, Toleration and the Law, 1689–1714', *Journal of Religious History*, 21, 2 (June, 1997), 178–92

Yale, D.E.C., *Hale as A Legal Historian* (London, 1976)

——, ed. and introduction, *Lord Nottingham's Chancery Cases*, Selden Society vols 73, 79 (London, 1957–61)

——, ed. and introduction, *Manual of Chancery Practice, and Prolegomena of Chancery and Equity* (Cambridge, 1965)

Yeo, Richard, 'Classifying the Sciences', in Roy Porter ed., *The Cambridge History of Science, Volume 4: Eighteenth-Century Science* (Cambridge, 2003), 241–66

——, 'Encyclopaedic Knowledge', in Marina Frasca-Spada and Nick Jardine eds, *Books and the Sciences in History* (Cambridge, 2000), 207–24

——, *Encyclopaedic Visions: Scientific Dictionaries and Enlightenment Culture* (Cambridge, 2001)

——, 'Encyclopedism and Enlightenment', in Martin Fitzpatrick, Peter Jones, Christa Knellwolf and Iain McCalman eds., *The Enlightenment World* (London, 2004), 350–65

——, 'A Solution to the Multitude of Books: Ephraim Chambers's *Cyclopaedia* (1728) as "the Best Book in the Universe"', *Journal of the History of Ideas*, 64, 1 (January, 2003), 241–66

Young, Brian W., 'Newtonianism and the Enthusiasm of Enlightenment', *Studies in History and Philosophy of Science*, 35, 3 (September, 2004), 645–63

——, *Religion and Enlightenment in Eighteenth-Century England: Theological Debate from Locke to Burke* (Oxford, 1998)

——, 'Religious History and the Eighteenth-Century Historian', *The Historical Journal*, 43, 3 (September, 2000), 849–68

Index

STUDIES IN EARLY MODERN CULTURAL, POLITICAL AND SOCIAL HISTORY

I
Women of Quality
Accepting and Contesting Ideals of Femininity in England, 1690–1760
Ingrid H. Tague

II
Restoration Scotland, 1660–1690
Royalist Politics, Religion and Ideas
Clare Jackson

III
Britain, Hanover and the Protestant Interest, 1688–1756
Andrew C. Thompson

IV
Hanover and the British Empire, 1700–1837
Nick Harding

V
The Personal Rule of Charles II, 1681–85
Grant Tapsell

VI
Royalism, Print and Censorship in Revolutionary England
Jason McElligott

VII
The English Catholic Community, 1688–1745
Politics, Culture and Ideology
Gabriel Glickman

VIII
England and the 1641 Irish Rebellion
Joseph Cope

IX
Culture and Politics at the Court of Charles II, 1660–1685
Matthew Jenkinson

X
Commune, Country and Commonwealth:
The People of Cirencester, 1117–1643
David Rollison

XI
An Enlightenment Statesman in Whig Britain
Lord Shelburne in Context, 1737–1805
Edited by Nigel Aston and Clarissa Campbell Orr

XII

London's News Press and the Thirty Years War
Jayne E. E. Boys

XIII

God, Duty and Community in English Economic Life, 1660–1720
Brodie Waddell

XIV

Remaking English Society: Social Relations and Social Change in Early Modern England
Edited by Steve Hindle, Alexandra Shepard and John Walter

Printed and bound by CPI Group (UK) Ltd, Croydon, CR0 4YY

13/09/2026

14961003-0007